Essentials

of **Psychological Assessment** Series
Everything you need to know to administer, score, and interpret the major psychological tests.

I'd like to order the following *Essentials of Psychological Assessment:*

- ❑ WAIS®-IV Assessment (w/CD-ROM) / 978-0-471-73846-6 • $46.95
- ❑ WJ III™ Cognitive Abilities Assessment / 978-0-471-34466-7 • $36.95
- ❑ Cross-Battery Assessment, Second Edition (w/CD-ROM) / 978-0-471-75771-9 • $46.95
- ❑ Nonverbal Assessment / 978-0-471-38318-5 • $36.95
- ❑ PAI® Assessment / 978-0-471-08463-1 • $36.95
- ❑ CAS Assessment / 978-0-471-29015-5 • $36.95
- ❑ MMPI-2™ Assessment / 978-0-471-34533-6 • $36.95
- ❑ Myers-Briggs Type Indicator® Assessment, Second Edition 978-0-470-34390-6 • $36.95
- ❑ Rorschach® Assessment / 978-0-471-33146-9 • $36.95
- ❑ Millon™ Inventories Assessment, Third Edition / 978-0-470-16862-2 • $36.95
- ❑ TAT and Other Storytelling Assessments, Second Edition 978-0-470-28192-5 • $36.95
- ❑ MMPI-A™ Assessment / 978-0-471-39815-8 • $36.95
- ❑ NEPSY®-II Assessment / 978-0-470-43691-2 • $36.95
- ❑ Neuropsychological Assessment, Second Edition / 978-0-470-43747-6 • $36.95
- ❑ WJ III™ Tests of Achievement Assessment / 978-0-471-33059-2 • $36.95
- ❑ Evidence-Based Academic Interventions / 978-0-470-20632-4 • $36.95
- ❑ WRAML2 and TOMAL-2 Assessment / 978-0-470-17911-6 • $36.95
- ❑ WMS®-III Assessment / 978-0-471-38080-1 • $36.95
- ❑ Behavioral Assessment / 978-0-471-35367-6 • $36.95
- ❑ Forensic Psychological Assessment, Second Edition / 978-0-470-55168-4 • $36.95
- ❑ Bayley Scales of Infant Development II Assessment / 978-0-471-32651-9 • $36.95
- ❑ Career Interest Assessment / 978-0-471-35365-2 • $36.95
- ❑ WPPSI™-III Assessment / 978-0-471-28895-4 • $36.95
- ❑ 16PF® Assessment / 978-0-471-23424-1 • $36.95
- ❑ Assessment Report Writing / 978-0-471-39487-7 • $36.95
- ❑ Stanford-Binet Intelligence Scales (SB5) Assessment / 978-0-471-22404-0 • $36.95
- ❑ WISC®-IV Assessment, Second Edition (w/CD-ROM) 978-0-470-18915-3 • $46.95
- ❑ KABC-II Assessment / 978-0-471-66733-9 • $36.95
- ❑ WIAT®-III and KTEA-II Assessment (w/CD-ROM) / 978-0-470-55169-1 • $46.95
- ❑ Processing Assessment / 978-0-471-71925-0 • $36.95
- ❑ School Neuropsychological Assessment / 978-0-471-78372-5 • $36.95
- ❑ Cognitive Assessment with KAIT & Other Kaufman Measures / 978-0-471-38317-8 • $36.95
- ❑ Assessment with Brief Intelligence Tests / 978-0-471-26412-5 • $36.95
- ❑ Creativity Assessment / 978-0-470-13742-0 • $36.95
- ❑ WNV™ Assessment / 978-0-470-28467-4 • $36.95
- ❑ DAS-II® Assessment (w/CD-ROM) / 978-0-470-22520-2 • $46.95
- ❑ Executive Function Assessment / 978-0-470-42202-1 • $36.95
- ❑ Conners Behavior Assessments™ / 978-0-470-34633-4 • $36.95
- ❑ Temperament Assessment / 978-0-470-44447-4 • $36.95
- ❑ Response to Intervention / 978-0-470-56663-3 • $36.95

Please complete the order form on the back.
To order by phone, call toll free 1-877-762-2974
To order online: www.wiley.com/essentials
To order by mail: refer to order form on next page

Essentials

of **Psychological Assessment** Series

ORDER FORM

Please send this order form with your payment (credit card or check) to:
John Wiley & Sons, Attn: J. Knott, 111 River Street, Hoboken, NJ 07030-5774

QUANTITY	TITLE	ISBN	PRICE

Shipping Charges:	Surface	2-Day	1-Day
First item	$5.00	$10.50	$17.50
Each additional item	$3.00	$3.00	$4.00
For orders greater than 15 items, please contact Customer Care at 1-877-762-2974.			

ORDER AMOUNT _____
SHIPPING CHARGES _____
SALES TAX _____
TOTAL ENCLOSED _____

NAME_____

AFFILIATION_____

ADDRESS_____

CITY/STATE/ZIP _____

TELEPHONE _____

EMAIL_____

❏ Please add me to your e-mailing list

PAYMENT METHOD:

❏ Check/Money Order   ❏ Visa   ❏ Mastercard   ❏ AmEx

Card Number _____ Exp. Date _____

Cardholder Name *(Please print)* _____

Signature _____

Make checks payable to **John Wiley & Sons.** *Credit card orders invalid if not signed.*
All orders subject to credit approval. • Prices subject to change.

To order by phone, call toll free **1-877-762-2974**
To order online: www.wiley.com/essentials

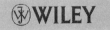 WILEY

Ess

Cor   nts

To Renew Books
Phone (925) 969-3100

Essentials of Psychological Assessment Series

Series Editors, Alan S. Kaufman and Nadeen L. Kaufman

Essentials of 16 PF® Assessment
by Heather E.-P. Cattell and James M. Schuerger
Essentials of Assessment Report Writing
by Elizabeth O. Lichtenberger, Nancy Mather, Nadeen L. Kaufman, and Alan S. Kaufman
Essentials of Assessment with Brief Intelligence Tests
by Susan R. Homack and Cecil R. Reynolds
Essentials of Bayley Scales of Infant Development–II Assessment
by Maureen M. Black and Kathleen Matula
Essentials of Behavioral Assessment
by Michael C. Ramsay, Cecil R. Reynolds, and R. W. Kamphaus
Essentials of Career Interest Assessment
by Jeffrey P. Prince and Lisa J. Heiser
Essentials of CAS Assessment
by Jack A. Naglieri
Essentials of Cognitive Assessment with KAIT and Other Kaufman Measures
by Elizabeth O. Lichtenberger, Debra Broadbooks, and Alan S. Kaufman
Essentials of Conners Behavior Assessments™
by Elizabeth P. Sparrow
Essentials of Creativity Assessment
by James C. Kaufman, Jonathan A. Plucker, and John Baer
Essentials of Cross-Battery Assessment, Second Edition
by Dawn P. Flanagan, Samuel O. Ortiz, and Vincent C. Alfonso
Essentials of DAS-II® Assessment
by Ron Dumont, John O. Willis, and Colin D. Elliot
Essentials of Evidence-Based Academic Interventions
by Barbara J. Wendling and Nancy Mather
Essentials of Forensic Psychological Assessment, Second Edition
by Marc J. Ackerman
Essentials of Individual Achievement Assessment
by Douglas K. Smith
Essentials of KABC-II Assessment
by Alan S. Kaufman, Elizabeth O. Lichtenberger, Elaine Fletcher-Janzen, and Nadeen L. Kaufman
Essentials of Millon™ Inventories Assessment, Third Edition
by Stephen Strack
Essentials of MMPI-A™ Assessment
by Robert P. Archer and Radhika Krishnamurthy
Essentials of MMPI-2™ Assessment
by David S. Nichols
Essentials of Myers-Briggs Type Indicator® Assessment, Second Edition
by Naomi Quenk
Essentials of NEPSY®-II Assessment
by Sally L. Kemp and Marit Korkman

Essentials of Neuropsychological Assessment, Second Edition
by Nancy Hebben and William Milberg
Essentials of Nonverbal Assessment
by Steve McCallum, Bruce Bracken, and John Wasserman
Essentials of PAI® Assessment
by Leslie C. Morey
Essentials of Processing Assessment
by Milton J. Dehn
Essentials of Response to Intervention
by Amanda M. VanDerHeyden and Matthew K. Burns
Essentials of Rorschach® Assessment
by Tara Rose, Nancy Kaser-Boyd, and Michael P. Maloney
Essentials of School Neuropsychological Assessment
by Daniel C. Miller
Essentials of Stanford-Binet Intelligence Scales (SB5) Assessment
by Gale H. Roid and R. Andrew Barram
Essentials of TAT and Other Storytelling Assessments, Second Edition
by Hedwig Teglasi
Essentials of Temperament Assessment
by Diana Joyce
Essentials of WAIS®-IV Assessment
by Elizabeth O. Lichtenberger and Alan S. Kaufman
Essentials of WIAT®-III and KTEA-II Assessment
by Elizabeth O. Lichtenberger and Kristina C. Breaux
Essentials of WISC-III® and WPPSI-R® Assessment
by Alan S. Kaufman and Elizabeth O. Lichtenberger
Essentials of WISC®-IV Assessment, Second Edition
by Dawn P. Flanagan and Alan S. Kaufman
Essentials of WJ III™ Cognitive Abilities Assessment
by Fredrick A. Schrank, Dawn P. Flanagan, Richard W. Woodcock, and Jennifer T. Mascolo
Essentials of WJ III™ Tests of Achievement Assessment
by Nancy Mather, Barbara J. Wendling, and Richard W. Woodcock
Essentials of WMS®-III Assessment
by Elizabeth O. Lichtenberger, Alan S. Kaufman, and Zona C. Lai
Essentials of WNV™ Assessment
by Kimberly A. Brunnert, Jack A. Naglieri, and Steven T. Hardy-Braz
Essentials of WPPSI™-III Assessment
by Elizabeth O. Lichtenberger and Alan S. Kaufman
Essentials of WRAML2 and TOMAL-2 Assessment
by Wayne Adams and Cecil R. Reynolds

Essentials

of Conners Behavior

Assessments

Elizabeth P. Sparrow

John Wiley & Sons, Inc.

Published by John Wiley & Sons, Inc., Hoboken, New Jersey.
Published simultaneously in Canada.

"Conners 3ʳᵈ edition" and *"Conners 3"* are trademarks of MultiHealth Systems, Inc. registered in the United States of America and/or other jurisdictions.

"Conners Comprehensive Behavior Rating Scales" and *"Conners CBRS"* are trademarks of MultiHealth Systems, Inc. registered in the United States of America and/or other jurisdictions.

"Conners Early Childhood" and *"Conners EC"* are trademarks of MultiHealth Systems, Inc. registered in the United States of America and/or other jurisdictions.

"Conners Line of Assessments" and *"Conners Behavior Assessments"* are trademarks of MultiHealth Systems, Inc. registered in the United States of America and/or other jurisdictions.

For general information on our other products and services please contact our Customer Care Department within the U.S. at (800) 762-2974, outside the United States at (317) 572-3993 or fax (317) 572-4002.

Wiley also publishes its books in a variety of electronic formats. Some content that appears in print may not be available in electronic books. For more information about Wiley products, visit our website at www.wiley.com.

Library of Congress Cataloging-in-Publication Data:

Sparrow, Elizabeth P.
Essentials of Conners behavior assessments/Elizabeth P. Sparrow.
    p. cm. — (Essentials of psychological assessment series)
Includes bibliographical references and index.
ISBN 978-0-470-34633-4 (pbk.)
  1. Psychological tests for children. 2. Behavioral assessment of children. 3. Behavioral assessment of teenagers. 4. Adolescents—Psychological testing. 5. Problem youth—Psychological testing. 6. Children with disabilities—Psychological testing. I. Title.
BF722.3.S67 2010
155.4028′7–dc22
                                                  2009041485

Printed in the United States of America

10 9 8 7 6 5 4 3 2 1

To my family, with appreciation for your time, support, and understanding.

To Jenni Pitkanen and Sara Rzepa, wonderful colleagues and contributors to this book and other projects.

To Penny Koepsel, who reviewed every chapter multiple times, and provided great questions and comments.

And finally, to the supportive and responsive staff of MHS who provided information, explanations, and corrections whenever needed, particularly Maggie Bailey, Charlene Colella, Penny Koepsel, Maria-Luisa Marocco, Danielle Politi, Gill Sitarenios, Hazel Wheldon, Josie Woodson, and many others.

Thank you all.

CONTENTS

Series Preface   xi

One   Overview   1

Two   Administration of the Conners Assessments   73

Three   Scoring the Conners Assessments   107

Four   Interpretation of the Conners Assessments   147

Five   Strengths and Weaknesses of the Conners Assessments   206

Six   Clinical Applications of the Conners Assessments   217

Seven   Illustrative Case Reports   269

Appendix A: Acronyms and Abbreviations Used in Conners Assessments   362

Appendix B: Calculating a Confidence Interval (CI) for Conners Assessments   364

Appendix C: Sample Tables for Reports   365

Appendix D: Calculating Conners CI Indicator Scores
from Full-Length Conners CBRS™ Form   372

References   386

Annotated Bibliography   388

About the Author   390

About the Contributors   391

Index   393

Series Preface

n the *Essentials of Psychological Assessment* series, we have attempted to provide the reader with books that will deliver key practical information in the most efficient and accessible style. The series features instruments in a variety of domains, such as cognition, personality, education, and neuropsychology. For the experienced clinician, books in the series will offer a concise yet thorough way to master utilization of the continuously evolving supply of new and revised instruments, as well as a convenient method for keeping up to date on the tried-and-true measures. The novice will find here a prioritized assembly of all the information and techniques that must be at one's fingertips to begin the complicated process of individual psychological diagnosis.

Wherever feasible, visual shortcuts to highlight key points are utilized alongside systematic, step-by-step guidelines. Chapters are focused and succinct. Topics are targeted for an easy understanding of the essentials of administration, scoring, interpretation, and clinical application. Theory and research are continually woven into the fabric of each book—but always to enhance clinical inference, never to sidetrack or overwhelm. We have long been advocates of "intelligent" testing—the notion that a profile of test scores is meaningless unless it is brought to life by the clinical observations and astute detective work of knowledgeable examiners. Test profiles must be used to make a difference in the child's or adult's life, or why bother to test? We want this series to help our readers become the best intelligent testers they can be.

This *Essentials* book describes the Conners 3rd edition (Conners 3^{TM}), Conners Comprehensive Behavior Rating Scales (Conners CBRS^{TM}), and Conners Early Childhood (Conners EC^{TM}), and how each can best be used to describe behavioral, emotional, social, and academic issues of children and adolescents (and developmental milestones for young children). The Conners EC^{TM} is normed for use with young children (2 to 6 years old), and the Conners 3^{TM} and Conners CBRS^{TM} are co-normed for use with school-aged children (6 to 18 years old); all three scales can be completed by parents or teachers, and a self-report form can be completed by 8- to 18-year-old youth. This book helps those who used the Conners' Rating Scales, Revised (CRS–R^{TM}) as they transition to these updated and improved assessment options. It also provides guidance for new examiners, suggesting structured techniques to organize and understand the scores that are produced by scoring these rating scales, so that valuable information is not lost in interpretation and application. This book, written by one of the world's experts on the Conners Scales, reviews not only the fundamentals of these Conners assessments, but adds sophistication and depth for meaningful and responsible use of these tools in the evaluation of children and adolescents.

Alan S. Kaufman, Ph.D., and Nadeen L. Kaufman, Ed.D., Series Editors
Yale University School of Medicine

One

Elizabeth P. Sparrow
Sara R. Rzepa
Jenni Pitkanen

F or decades the rating scales developed by Dr. C. Keith Conners have been
used worldwide for assessment of children with Attention-Deficit/Hyper-
activity Disorder (ADHD) and related issues. The Conners 3rd Edition
(Conners 3) continues this tradition of excellence for ADHD identification and
treatment monitoring. With the publication of the Conners Comprehensive
Behavior Rating Scales (Conners CBRS), this standard of clinical utility and
statistical foundations has been extended for assessment of a broad range of
issues that occur in school-aged youth.[1] Most recently, these same techniques
were applied for the development of a comprehensive rating scale for young
children—the Conners Early Childhood (Conners EC). Rapid Reference 1.1
provides a quick snapshot of the three assessments.

The main objective of this book is to offer a comprehensive and user-friendly
guide to the Conners 3, Conners CBRS, and Conners EC. This book was
developed for those who work with youth 2 through 18 years old in educational,
clinical, or research settings, including professionals in evaluation and treatment
roles. The subsequent chapters explain the core "essentials" of Conners rating
scale assessment and interpretation in a straightforward and understandable

---

1. The terms "youth" and "child/children" are used interchangeably throughout the book
   to include ages 6 through 18 years, rather than specifying "children and adolescents"
   every time. "Child/children" may also include young children who are 2 through 6 years
   old, as indicated by the context.

Rapid Reference 1.1

Snapshot of the Conners Assessments

	Conners 3rd Edition (Conners 3)	Conners Comprehensive Behavior Rating Scales (Conners CBRS)	Conners Early Childhood (Conners EC)
Author	C. Keith Conners, PhD		
Publication date	2008	2008	2009
Purpose	Focused assessment of ADHD and most commonly co-occurring problems and disorders in school-aged children	Comprehensive assessment tool for a wide range of behavioral, emotional, social, and academic concerns in school-aged children	Broad coverage of important behavioral, emotional, social, cognitive, and developmental issues in young children
Age Range	Parent & Teacher: 6–18 years Self-Report: 8–18 years	Parent & Teacher: 6–18 years Self-Report: 8–18 years	Parent & Teacher: 2–6 years Self-Report: n/a

	Conners 3[a] Conners 3 Short[a] Conners 3 ADHD Index[a] Conners 3 Global Index[b]	Conners CBRS[a] Conners Clinical Index[a]	Conners EC[b] Conners EC-BEH[b] Conners EC-BEH(S)[b] Conners ECGI[b] Conners EC-DM[b]
Available Forms			
Minimum Reading Levels[c]	Parent & Teacher: 5th grade Self-Report: 3rd grade	Parent & Teacher: 5th–6th grade Self-Report: 3rd–4th grade	Parent: 3rd–5th grade Teacher: 5th grade Self-Report: n/a
Rater Requirements	Must have known and had the opportunity to observe child for at least one month. Cognitive abilities and reading level must be adequate (see above). Must be motivated to assist in assessment.		
Examiner Requirements	Administration and scoring: Formal training in clinical psychology or psychometrics is not required Interpretation: Graduate-level courses in tests and measurement at a university (or other documented equivalent training)		
Publisher	Multi-Health Systems, Inc. 1-800-456-3003 in the United States; 1-800-268-6011 in Canada; 1-416-492-2627 International www.mhs.com		

[a] Available in forms for completion by parent, teacher, or youth.
[b] Available in forms for completion by parent or teacher.
[c] Approximate range listed here for quick reference; varies by form used. See relevant test manual for details.

manner, including not only key information from the test manuals, but also practical tips and high-level interpretation guidelines. Chapter 1 provides a historical context for understanding the Conners assessments as well as a quick overview of each rating scale. Chapter 2 reviews key assessment tips, such as choosing which rating scale is best for a specific child and deciding which form to use. Scoring is covered in Chapter 3. Chapter 4 explains a straightforward technique for interpreting the Conners assessments, with special sections for integrating results across more than one version of the rating scales. Chapter 5 offers a critical review of the strengths and weaknesses of the Conners assessments, and Chapter 6 explores clinical applications. Finally, Chapter 7 illustrates use of the Conners 3, Conners CBRS, and Conners EC through several case studies. Throughout the book, Rapid Reference, Caution, and Don't Forget boxes draw attention to critical points. Tables present information succinctly, and figures illustrate information in graphic form. Each chapter ends with a Test Yourself section to help review and check retention of important concepts. Information contained in this book should support responsible and competent use of the Conners 3, Conners CBRS, and Conners EC.

This chapter includes an overview of appropriate ways to use rating scales and a brief history of the Conners assessments. Each of the new rating scales is described, with an overview of key features, changes from the Conners' Rating Scales–Revised^{TM} (CRS–R^{TM}), and psychometric properties. See Rapid References 1.14, 1.18, and 1.23 for an overview of the content provided by each of the Conners assessments. Chapters 2, 3, and 4 in this book discuss the administration, scoring, and interpretation of each rating scale in more detail, including how to select which rating scale and form to use.

USE OF RATING SCALES

A rating scale is simply a group of items that are rated on a specified scale to describe an individual. For example, a food critic might use a rating scale of one to five stars to rate a chef on the appearance, speed, and taste of his food. In the world of educational and psychological measurement, some rating scales are not much more complicated than those used by a food critic. Some rating scales are just a group of items that can be rated, and interpretation is a matter of opinion. At the other end of the spectrum are rating scales that are derived solely from statistical analyses with little input as to the clinical utility of the factors for diagnosis or treatment, or rating scales that are based entirely on results of a single research project without consideration of generalizability. Ideally, a rating scale that is used in the assessment and monitoring of a child will have a blend of these features, combining clinical wisdom with research data and statistical expertise. See Rapid Reference 1.2 for important features of rating scales.

≡ Rapid Reference 1.2

Summary of Key Points to Consider in Rating Scale Selection

Ideally, a rating scale that is used in the assessment and monitoring of a child will have a blend of these features, combining clinical wisdom with research data and statistical expertise. Features to look for when selecting a rating scale include:

- Results that can be interpreted to answer your questions about a child and that can be explained to parents, teachers, and others who help the child.
- Item development and selection guided by clinicians with experience in relevant areas.
- Relevant research findings reflected in scale content and interpretation.
- Large and diverse standardization sample (i.e., considering different ages, genders, races/ethnicities, geographic regions, neighborhood types, and socioeconomic statuses), providing an appropriate comparison for each child assessed and helping to decide if any of these factors impact how results are interpreted (e.g., does age matter for this?).
- Data from relevant clinical groups, showing how results help distinguish between children with and without different diagnoses (i.e., specificity and sensitivity).
- Solid psychometrics, including reliability and validity, so you know how confident you can be that the rating scale is consistently measuring the targeted issues over different people and dates.
- Ease of use (administration, scoring, and interpretation).
- Results that help identify targets for treatment and then measure response to treatment.

Even when a rating scale has all of the features listed in Rapid Reference 1.2, it should not be used in isolation for assessment purposes. An assessment should be multimodal, based on information from multiple informants and multiple settings. A rating scale is only one mode of assessment; other modes might include interview, record review, observation, and direct assessment of knowledge, skills, and abilities. For example, you might review available records, interview the child and her parents, observe the child in the classroom and other settings, administer a rating scale, and administer tests of intellectual ability, academic achievement, and memory skills. This would be a multimodal evaluation. Assessments should not rely on information from a single source, but should include more than one informant. For children, informants can include parents, teachers, and service providers. Do not forget that the child is often a valuable source of information and that you are in fact an informant—your reactions to the child and your observations of him are very relevant. Finally, an assessment should combine information from multiple settings. Typical settings for children include home, school, and community. School does not just mean the academic classroom, but it also includes aspects of the child's functioning in other parts of the schoolday (e.g., the hallway between classes, the lunchroom, the bus-stop, the playground, special classes like art, music, and gym). The community setting might be after-school care, neighborhood park, religious centers, grocery stores, or community centers. For adolescents, there may be a work setting as well.

DON'T FORGET

The "Multi's" of Responsible Assessment

1. Multi-modal: Use more than one mode of assessment (e.g., interview, record review, observation, rating scale, individual testing).
2. Multi-informant: Gather data from more than one informant (e.g., child, parents, teachers, other professionals, yourself).
3. Multi-setting: Gather data from more than one setting, considering physical settings (e.g., home, school, community) and functional settings (e.g., social interactions, structured settings).

Once all the "multi" requirements are met (i.e., multimodal, multi-informant, and multiple settings), it is also important to gather sufficient depth and breadth of information to help with differential diagnosis decisions. These include deciding if the child's symptoms are due to one thing or another, or possibly a combination of more than one factor. In some cases, the decision is not a simple yes/no but whether additional evaluation might be helpful in answering questions and forming a plan to help the child. Again, no single instrument can serve in isolation for differential diagnosis decisions.

DON'T FORGET

Differential Diagnosis and Referrals

Gather sufficient breadth and depth of information to help you decide if the child's diagnosis is "either/or" (e.g., "Is it ADHD or something else?"), or if his diagnosis is "this and that" (e.g., "Does he have ADHD and comorbid CD?"). If you do not have expertise in an area that you think might be important for a child, get enough information to help you make a referral or to consult with a colleague.

When a rating scale has the features described above, and is used as part of a responsible assessment, it can contribute in a variety of ways, informing diagnosis, treatment planning/monitoring, research, and program evaluation. (See Chapter 6 for additional information on these applications of the Conners assessments.)

- Most people use rating scales primarily as diagnostic aids, as a rating scale can help you gather data from multiple settings and multiple raters. When referral questions are vague, information gathered by a rating scale can help focus initial efforts to begin assessment quickly and efficiently. Even when the referral is clear, results from a rating scale may identify additional issues to address or investigate through other modalities of assessment.
- Rating scales can be equally valuable in planning treatment. Results from raters in different settings can help you understand which settings are impacted by which issues and which settings do not seem to be affected. This information can help you discover potentially useful differences among raters/settings that could suggest interventions to try with a child in an RTI model (see also Rapid Reference 6.1). For example, if a child shows symptoms of anxiety and academic failure in a classroom with 25 students but is indistinguishable from peers in her reading group of 8 students, this might indicate the benefit of trying small group instruction for other subject areas while determining if the difference is content area, group size, or instructor characteristics (among other possible explanations). Results from rating scales can help identify target behaviors to address in treatment and can even help prioritize these targets. Rating scales can provide data to support treatment recommendations, showing why a particular suggestion is being made for the child in that setting.
- Once an intervention is begun, rating scales can help monitor changes in the child.[2] These might include improvement in the target behavior, lack of change, or deterioration in that area. Rating scales can indicate new areas that are emerging as concerns as old areas are addressed, or suggest a shift in relative importance of which target should be addressed first. Some rating scales can help track potential side effects of treatment—usually a consideration for pharmaceutical intervention. Results from a repeated rating scale can suggest considerations for change in a treatment

---

2. On the Conners assessments, the Reliable Change Indices (RCI) provide the absolute difference score needed to determine if there is a statistically significant change in scores between administrations. This provides utility when monitoring responses to intervention. See also Rapid Reference 6.2.

plan, whether adding services, decreasing intensity of services, shifting to maintenance levels, or discontinuing services.

- In research settings, rating scales offer a systematic way to identify children for inclusion in a research study or to identify children who might not be appropriate for that particular study. Data from rating scales are often used as a way to measure the outcome of a studied intervention or research manipulation.
- Finally, rating scales can be used programmatically. A rating scale can help screen a group of children to determine who might be candidates to participate in a special program (e.g., a reading enrichment program, a social skills group). Results from rating scales could be used to evaluate the effectiveness of such programs as might be needed when deciding whether to continue the program or to support continued funding for the program.

In summary, rating scales should reflect a combination of clinical, statistical, and research supports. When used for assessment purposes, they should be part of a complete evaluation that integrates data from multiple modalities, informants, and settings to obtain sufficient information for differential decisions or referrals. Rating scales can be used in a variety of ways, for individuals and groups of children. With this information in mind, let's take a look at the background for the Conners 3, Conners CBRS, and Conners EC.

HISTORY AND DEVELOPMENT OF THE CONNERS ASSESSMENTS

The Conners line of assessments has grown from a lifetime of clinical work and research (see Rapid Reference 1.3 for an overview of the timeline, and Rapid Reference 1.4 for a summary of published Conners rating scales). The earliest versions of rating scales by Dr. Conners were developed in the 1960s when he was training at Johns Hopkins Hospital. While studying the effects of stimulant medications on juvenile delinquents, Dr. Conners discovered that parents and teachers were effective observers of behavioral changes exhibited by this group of youth. He developed a list of items, grouped by problem area, that he could use to quantify changes parents and teachers observed. This list of items was shared with colleagues, who gathered further information about how parents and teachers rated children at different ages. Over time, sufficient data were collected to be a useful comparison when determining if a child's results were typical or atypical. Some felt the list of items was too long for use when monitoring a child's response to treatment, so Dr. Conners worked to create a shorter form. He selected the 10 best items for distinguishing children with hyperactivity from those without hyperactivity and called this the "Hyperactivity Index" (referencing the DSM-II diagnostic term in

≡ Rapid Reference 1.3

History of the Conners Assessments

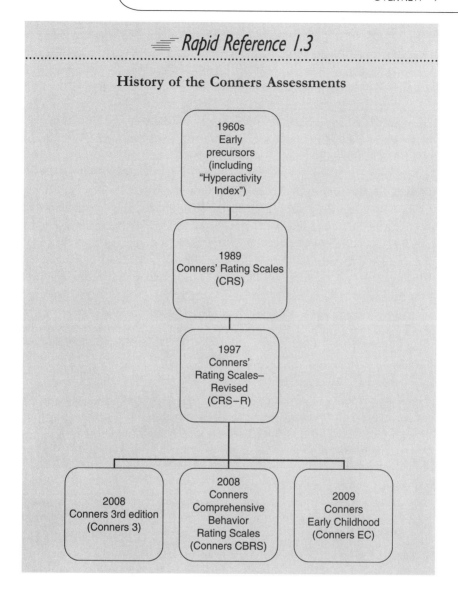

use at that time). It was not uncommon to see very faint copies of the Hyperactivity Index being used at that time, as the original typed list was photocopied many times and distributed. As copies reached the point where they could not be read, individual clinicians retyped the form, resulting in many variations in formatting and even wording as unintentional changes were made.

In the 1980s, Dr. Conners partnered with a small start-up company that was developing tests—Multi-Health Systems, Inc. (MHS). He worked with MHS to gather a more comprehensive normative sample, and in 1989, the first copyrighted version of the items was published as the Conners' Rating Scales (CRS). The CRS became very widely used across the globe and was translated into many languages. After many validation studies were conducted and published, the CRS was established as the gold standard for assessment of what is now called ADHD. Over the next 10 years, additional data were collected, items were reviewed, and statistical analyses were conducted. This led to revision of the CRS, and in 1997 the Conners' Rating Scales–Revised (CRS–R) was released for rating children ages 3 to 17.

The CRS–R reflected a larger, more diverse normative sample and improved psychometric properties. It expanded the rater options from parent and teacher by adding an adolescent self-report form (for use with youth ages 12 to 17). Items based on DSM-IV criteria for ADHD were added. In addition to continuing in-depth coverage of ADHD, the CRS–R included conduct problems, cognitive problems, family issues, emotional lability, and anger control. Items reflecting internalizing features were added, such as anxiety, psychosomatic symptoms, and perfectionism; coverage of these features was facilitated by the addition of the adolescent self-report form. The historic "Hyperactivity Index" (also known as the "Conners 10-item" or the "Abbreviated Symptoms Questionnaire [ASQ]") was updated and labelled the "Conners Global Index" to reflect its utility in identifying children with general pathology (not just hyperactivity). A statistically derived index was developed using the best items for distinguishing between children with ADHD and children in the general population; this was called the "ADHD Index." The physical forms for the CRS–R were improved, including simplified hand-scoring options and new feedback/progress forms. Both "long" and "short" forms were made available.

Changing the CRS–R

In 2003, the research and development team at MHS began gathering feedback from users of the CRS–R to update and revise the CRS–R into the Conners 3. Team members included Dr. Conners (the author of the Conners assessments), Dr. Sparrow (clinical consultant for the project), and MHS staff. During many conversations, we realized the need to develop a comprehensive rating scale that was built on the same principles as the CRS–R: guided by clinical experience and research, supported by solid psychometrics and statistical analyses, and useful to professionals who work with children and adolescents. As the rating scale grew longer and longer, it became clear that one rating scale could not responsibly

Rapid Reference 1.4

Published Conners Assessments Over the Years

	Parent (P)	Teacher (T)	Self-Report (SR)
Conners 3rd Edition (Conners, 2008)			
Full length	Conners 3	Conners 3–P	Conners 3–T	Conners 3–SR
Short	Conners 3 Short Conners 3(S)	Conners 3–P(S)	Conners 3–T(S)	Conners 3–SR(S)
Index/Auxiliary	Conners 3 Global Index Conners 3GI	Conners 3GI–P	Conners 3GI–T	—
	Conners 3 ADHD Index Conners 3AI	Conners 3AI–P	Conners 3AI–T	Conners 3AI–SR
Conners Comprehensive Behavior Rating Scales (Conners, 2008)			
Full length	Conners CBRS	Conners CBRS–P	Conners CBRS–T	Conners CBRS–SR
Index/Auxiliary	Conners Clinical Index Conners CI	Conners CI–P	Conners CI–T	Conners CI–SR

	Parent (P)	Teacher (T)	Self-Report (SR)
Conners Early Childhood (Conners, 2009)			
Full length	Conners EC	Conners EC–T	—
Behavior	Conners EC BEH	Conners EC BEH–T	—
Developmental Milestones	Conners EC DM	Conners EC DM–T	—
Short	Conners EC BEH(S)	Conners EC BEH–T(S)	—
Index/Auxiliary	Conners EC Global Index Conners ECGI	Conners ECGI–T	—
Conners' Rating Scales–Revised (Conners, 1997)			
Full length	Conners' Rating Scales–Revised: Long CRS–R:L	CPRS–R:L	CTRS–R:L	CASS:L[a]
Short	Conners' Rating Scales–Revised: Short CRS–R:S	CPRS–R:S	CTRS–R:S	CASS:S[a]

Index/Auxiliary	Conners' Global Index CGI	CGI-P	CGI-T	—
	Conners' ADHD/DSM-IV Scales CADS	CADS-P	CADS-T	CADS-A
Conners' Rating Scales (Conners, 1989, 1990)				
Full length	Conners' Rating Scales (CRS) Long Form	CPRS-93 item	CTRS-39 item	—
Short	Conners' Rating Scales (CRS) Short Form	CPRS-48 item	CTRS-28 item	—
Index/Auxiliary	Abbreviated Symptom Questionnaire (ASQ; Hyperactivity Index)	ASQ-P	ASQ-T	—

[a] CASS = Conners-Wells' Adolescent Self-Report Scales

serve as both a focused ADHD tool and a comprehensive survey. Thus, the Conners CBRS was added to the development plan to provide broad coverage of important clinical issues in children and adolescents, and the Conners 3 was streamlined to serve as a focused ADHD tool.

We reviewed the entire DSM-IV-TR and available research publications to determine which clinical constructs were most critical for inclusion on these two rating scales. Approaching this daunting task from many different angles, we agreed to select the initial constructs from a domain-based perspective as well as a DSM-based perspective. Domains and subcategories were generated from a review of clinic referrals and relevant research literature (see Rapid Reference 1.5 for a summary of these goals for content inclusion). We agreed to include information to help clinicians identify when the validity of results might be questionable. Items asking about impairment associated with symptoms were also added, given the importance of establishing impairment for educational identification and for DSM-based diagnosis. Finally, we set the goal of creating rating scales that would go beyond labeling a problem, continuing with identifying intervention goals and ways to monitor progress in treatment.

≡ Rapid Reference 1.5

Content Goals for Conners 3 and Conners CBRS

Domain	Subcategory	DSM-IV-TR Diagnostic Categories
Behavioral	• Aggressive/Oppositional behaviors • Hyperactive/Impulsive behaviors	• Attention and Disruptive Behavior Disorders (ADHD, ODD, CD)
Emotional	• Irritability, anxiety (worrying, separation fears, perfectionism) • General distress, symptoms of depression	• Anxiety Disorders (GAD, SAD, Social Phobia, OCD, Panic Attack, Specific Phobia, PTSD) • Mood Disorders (Major Depressive Episode, Manic Episode)
Social	• Social skills, social interests, social isolation	• Pervasive Developmental Disorders (Autistic Disorder, Asperger's Disorder)

Academic/ Cognitive	• Subject-specific difficulties • Inattention • Executive deficits	• Specific Learning Disorders
Other	• Predicting potential for violence • Risk factors for possible suicide attempt • Physical symptoms (medication side effects and/ or emotional correlates)	• Substance Use, Pica, Tics, Trichotillomania, Enuresis and Encopresis

Another topic of discussion was possible expansion of the self-report age-range. The CRS–R Adolescent Self-Report was limited to 12- to 17-year-olds based on opinions about the age at which a child could accurately and reliably describe his own symptoms. During the interval between publication of the CRS–R and this development project, research suggested that the CRS–R Adolescent Self-Report could be reliably used by children as young as 8 years old (Parker, Bond, Reker, & Wood, 2005). While some of the team members were skeptical, we agreed to collect self-report pilot data from children ages 8 and up, then revisit the issue. Pilot data confirmed the earlier publication; self-report data were reliable for children as young as 8 years old. These findings were supported by further analyses of self-report data from the full standardization sample. Thus, the Conners 3 and Conners CBRS both have self-report forms for use by children ages 8 through 18 years.

While planning the Conners 3 and Conners CBRS, one more critical issue emerged in discussion. Continuing to cover the same age range as the CRS–R (3 through 17 years old) significantly limited our choice of items; either items were so general that they did not capture important concerns, or items were inappropriate for part of the age-range. We and others commented that parents and teachers of young children tended to skip certain items when responding to the CRS–R (typically academic items), preventing some scales from being scored. Important questions to aid early identification and intervention efforts were not included as they did not apply to school-aged children. After some discussion, the team decided to create a separate scale for young children (the Conners EC) and to concentrate on school-aged youth with the Conners 3 and Conners CBRS.

Given our desire to create a developmentally appropriate rating scale for use with young children, the team did not limit the Conners EC to a downward

≡ Rapid Reference 1.6

Key Development Goals

Conners 3:
- Thorough and reliable ADHD assessment
- Added emphasis on associated features and commonly comorbid disorders
- New normative data and updated psychometric properties
- School-age focused age range
- Content alignment across Parent, Teacher, and Self-Report forms
- Simplification of DSM-IV-TR scale language
- Addition of new features (e.g., validity scales, executive functioning)
- Increased links to intervention

Conners CBRS:
- Comprehensive coverage of issues that arise in school-aged youth
- Strong statistical foundation and diagnostic utility
- Links to identification and diagnosis
- DSM-IV-TR symptoms for a number of diagnoses
- Links to intervention and treatment planning (e.g., IDEA 2004)
- Multiple ratings in multiple settings with easily integrated results

Conners EC:
- Comprehensive coverage of issues that occur in young children
- Developmentally sensitive items
- Strong statistical foundation and diagnostic utility
- Support early identification and intervention
- Multiple ratings in multiple settings with easily integrated results

extension of the Conners 3 and Conners CBRS. We again brainstormed, considered clinical cases, and reviewed relevant research and publications about young children. We agreed that it was critical to include items reflecting important research on early indicators of certain disorders. We considered whether to represent symptoms of DSM-IV-TR disorders, but we ultimately decided that the more important job for the Conners EC was to capture functional issues that are usually first observed in young children. As such, a set of developmental milestone items was added, requiring a departure from the traditional 0 to 3 Likert scale used in all previous versions of the Conners rating scales. All of this labor and deliberation delivered a robust tool with behavioral, emotional, social, and cognitive components, as well as norm-referenced markers for key developmental skills across a range of domains. See Rapid Reference 1.6 for a summary of the key development goals for the Conners 3, Conners CBRS, and Conners EC. See Rapid Reference 1.7 for an overview of changes made to the CRS–R and Rapid References 1.8 through 1.9 for a scale-by-scale comparison.

≡ Rapid Reference 1.7

Key Changes from the CRS–R to the Conners 3 and Conners CBRS

- Updated normative sample and normative groups.
  - Ensures that the norms reflect current levels of behaviors.
  - Separate norms for each age, by year (CRS–R norms were grouped by 3-year age bins)—this reflects findings that the scores were age sensitive, and that different areas changed at different ages. Using 1-year age groups provides more accurate and precise results.
  - Optional combined gender norms for boys and girls. As with the CRS–R, data were gender specific for many scales, with changes occurring at different ages for boys versus girls. Because some settings require combined-gender norms, combined-gender norms are provided for the Conners assessments (see Rapid Reference 1.24 for additional information).
- Expanded clinical samples. Data were collected about a much wider range of clinical diagnoses than for the CRS–R (see Rapid References 1.25 and 1.26). [a]
- Modified age range. Conners 3 and Conners CBRS norms begin at 6 years, 0 months and extend through 18 years, 11 months to capture the range of ages present in school-aged youth (CRS–R norms ranged from 3 years through 17 years, 11 months). Self-report forms can be completed by youth who are 8 to 18 years old.
  - Young children need different items to accurately capture important issues. Ages 2 to 6 years are now represented on the Conners EC. The Conners 3 and Conners CBRS begin at 6 years old, the age at which most children enter an academic setting in the first grade. [b]
  - Many youth turn 18 years old before they complete high school. The upward extension of the age range helps describe these students before they transition to instruments designed for use with adults, such as the Conners Adult ADHD Rating Scale[TM] (CAARS[TM]).
  - Based on data supporting the accuracy of self-report by children as young as 8 years old, norms are provided for the self-report forms when completed by 8- to 18-year-olds.

- Different approach to short forms. The CRS–R short forms included a subset of items from selected scales and the ADHD Index. The Conners 3 short form includes items from every Content scale; the ADHD Index can be added by use of the additional Conners 3AI form. The Conners CBRS does not have a short form for the content scales as this was counterintuitive for a comprehensive scale. (The Conners CI is a short form of sorts, as it gives information about five different diagnostic groups.)
- In-depth assessment of ADHD: Conners 3.
  - Detailed information about ADHD from clinical, research, and DSM perspectives is kept on the Conners 3.
  - Former CRS–R "Cognitive Problems/Inattention" scale is now two separate scales (Inattention, Learning Problems) to simplify interpretation.
  - Executive Functioning scale added to reflect an important associated issue for ADHD.
  - Features of disruptive behaviors retained on the Conners 3, and DSM-IV-TR symptoms of key comorbid diagnoses (CD, ODD) added.
  - The majority of CRS–R content about anxiety shifted to Conners CBRS, with Anxiety and Depression Screener items added to the Conners 3 to help indicate when further evaluation may be needed.
- Broad coverage of school-aged issues: Conners CBRS.
  - General information about behavioral, social, emotional, and academic issues shifted to the Conners CBRS and expanded.
  - Content from CRS–R Anxious/Shy, Emotional Problems, and Perfectionism now represented on Conners CBRS.
  - CRS–R "Psychosomatic" scale more accurately identified as "Physical Symptoms" on Conners CBRS.
  - DSM-IV-TR coverage expanded significantly beyond symptoms of ADHD (see Rapid Reference 1.18 for a complete listing of DSM-based scales).
- Simplified language. All items reflect the goal of reducing the required reading level for parent, teacher, and self-report forms. This includes rewording items about DSM-IV-TR symptoms so that they are more easily understood by nonprofessionals, thereby improving how accurately they can rate these items (CRS–R contained ADHD symptoms from the DSM-IV, verbatim). See Rapid Reference 1.1 for new reading levels.
- New elements.
  - Caution flags. The computerized reports for the Conners 3 and Conners CBRS flag items that suggest special attention when they are endorsed. This helps draw your attention to these individual items so they are not overlooked. These items are grouped into "Critical items" (Conners 3 and Conners CBRS), "Screener items" (Conners 3), and "Other Clinical Indicators" (Conners CBRS).
  - Validity scales. The Conners 3 and Conners CBRS each have three new Validity scales to help describe the rater's response style. The Positive Impression scale indicates when an overly positive response style is possible,

the Negative Impression scale an overly negative response style, and the Inconsistency Index inconsistent responding. These results can help you understand certain patterns in the data, including the possibility of invalid ratings (see Chapter 4 for additional guidance).

- Impairment items. These items help you assess the level of impairment in home, school, and social settings, as required for consideration of a DSM-IV-TR diagnosis and/or educational eligibility.

• Improved comparison across raters. The Conners 3 and Conners CBRS preserve similarities across parent, teacher, and self-report forms wherever appropriate to facilitate your comparison of results across multiple informants. A computerized Comparative Report is available for each of these rating scales that indicates statistically significant differences in ratings of a child.

• Improved comparison across time. Scores from a current administration of the Conners 3 or Conners CBRS can be compared statistically with results from past evaluations with these rating scales using the "Reliable Change Index" score reported in the Progress Report (see Chapter 4 for more information). This can be used to supplement clinical judgment of meaningful change.

• Cultural relevance. Items for the Conners 3 and Conners CBRS were reviewed by experts in multicultural issues of assessment to help select the items that were most culturally fair and applicable. Once items were selected, the Spanish translations of these rating scales were created through a careful process of forward and backward translations (i.e., the English words were translated into Spanish by one translator, the Spanish translations were translated into English by another translator, and the two versions were compared to make certain that nothing was "lost in translation," literally). See Rapid Reference 1.11 for additional information about Spanish translations of the Conners assessments.

• Inclusion of positively worded items. Items on past Conners rating scales were all phrased in the negative direction, describing problems. The new Conners line of assessments include positive items. See Rapid Reference 1.10 for discussion.

[a] The CRS–R Technical Manual (2001) mentions two clinical groups: ADHD and "emotional problems."
[b] Norms for the Conners EC overlap with those for the Conners 3 and Conners CBRS for one year at the 6-year-old age range. This reflects that some 6-year-old children are in pre-academic settings in which the Conners EC might more accurately assess their functioning. Other 6-year-old children are already in 1st grade, and items on the Conners 3 and/or Conners CBRS may be more appropriate. This overlap in normative data sets allows flexibility for assessors to choose the measure that is most relevant for a specific 6-year-old child.

≡ Rapid Reference 1.8

Comparison of CRS–R with Conners 3 and Conners CBRS

	CRS–R	Conners 3	Conners CBRS
Age range: – Parent and Teacher forms – Self-report forms	3–17 years [a] 12–17 years	6–18 years 8–18 years	6–18 years 8–18 years
Behavioral content	Oppositional (P & T) Conduct Problems (SR) Anger Control Problems (SR) Hyperactivity	Defiance/Aggression Hyperactivity/Impulsivity Critical items: Severe Conduct	Defiant/Aggressive Behaviors Hyperactivity/Impulsivity Critical items: Severe Conduct OCI: Bullying (victimization, perpetration)
Emotional content	Emotional Problems (SR) Anxious/Shy (P & T) Perfectionism (P & T)	Screener items: Anxiety	Emotional Distress Separation Fears Perfectionistic and Compulsive Behaviors (P & T) OCI: Panic Attack, PTSD, Specific Phobia, Trichotillomania

		Screener items: Depression	Critical items: Self Harm
Social content	Social Problems (P & T) Family Problems (SR)	Peer Relations (P & T) Family Relations (SR)	Social Problems (P & T)
Cognitive/Academic content	Cognitive Problems/Inattention	Learning Problems Inattention Executive Functioning (P & T)	Academic Difficulties
DSM-based scales	ADHD Inattentive ADHD Hyperactive-Impulsive	ADHD Inattentive ADHD Hyperactive-Impulsive Conduct Disorder Oppositional Defiant Disorder	ADHD Inattentive ADHD Hyperactive-Impulsive Conduct Disorder Oppositional Defiant Disorder Major Depressive Episode Manic Episode Generalized Anxiety Disorder Separation Anxiety Disorder Social Phobia Obsessive-Compulsive Disorder Autistic Disorder (P & T) Asperger's Disorder (P & T)

	CRS–R	Conners 3	Conners CBRS
Index scores	Conners ADHD Index	Conners 3 ADHD Index	Conners Clinical Index
	Conners Global Index (P & T)	Conners 3 Global Index (P & T)	
Other content	Psychosomatic (P)		Violence Potential Indicator
			Physical Symptoms
			OCI: Enuresis/Encopresis (P & T)
			OCI: Pervasive Developmental Disorder (SR)
			OCI: Pica (P & SR), Tics, Substance Use
		Validity scales	Validity scales
		Impairment items	Impairment items
		Additional Questions	Additional Questions

[a] Young children (2 – 6 years old) are now represented on the Conners Early Childhood (Conners EC).

Note: P = Parent form only, T = Teacher form only, SR = Self-report form only, OCI = Other Clinical Indicator(s), PTSD = Posttraumatic Stress Disorder, PI = Positive Impression, NI = Negative Impression, IncX = Inconsistency Index

≣ Rapid Reference 1.9

Transitions from the CRS–R to the Conners 3 and Conners CBRS Content Scales

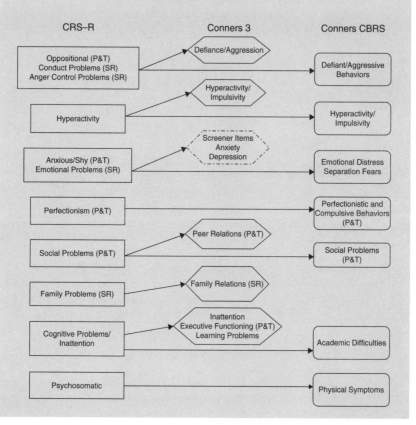

≣ Rapid Reference 1.10

Positive and Negative Wording

Many rating scales are written completely in the negative direction, listing only problems. This is certainly consistent with the idea that people complete rating scales to identify problems. When every item is written in the negative direction, however, it is easy for raters to fall into a "response bias" where they assign the same level of rating to almost every item; for example, "This child is fine" (rate everything a 0) or "Everything is wrong with this child" (rate everything a 3). This same response bias issue could occur if the rating scale was written entirely in the positive direction (i.e., listing intact skills and strengths).

One obvious solution is to create a rating scale that has both positively and negatively worded items. The interesting thing is that positively worded items (i.e., items that describe intact skills or strengths) don't perform as well statistically. The inclusion of positively worded items also complicates scoring, as ratings of these items must be converted during the scoring process.

The Conners assessments use a blended approach—primarily problem-focused items with a sprinkling of positively worded items. This gives the rater several chances to remember he is not just describing problems, but preserves the statistical strength of the rating scale.

Developmental Elements

The Conners 3 and Conners CBRS were published in 2008, with interpretive updates in 2009.[3] The Conners EC was published in 2009. The manuals for these three rating scales provide extensive coverage of the development process for these instruments. The general principles were consistent across all three rating scales and included the following elements:

- Item generation: The development team reviewed items from past versions of the Conners rating scales. We reflected on our experiences with the children, parents, and teachers in our clinical practices. We gathered input from many professionals through focus groups. We examined concepts from relevant research publications and various classification systems (including the DSM-IV-TR, ICD-10, and IDEA

3. These interpretive updates to the Conners 3 and Conners CBRS should be reviewed for complete details. In brief, three clarifications were provided for both rating scales. These included: (1) describing elevated results on the Validity scales as indicating "possibly positive," "possibly negative," and/or "inconsistent" response style rather than "possibly invalid" results; (2) relabelling the "borderline range" for T-score interpretation as "high average score (Slightly more concerns than are typically reported)"; and (3) relabelling the Aggression scale as "Defiance/Aggression" (Conners 3) and the Aggressive Behaviors scale as "Defiant/Aggressive Behaviors" (Conners CBRS). Two additional updates affected the Conners CBRS: (1) renaming the Violence Potential scale as "Violence Potential Indicator" and weighting relative contributions of items to the score; and (2) raising the minimum score for flagging the Specific Phobia Other Clinical Indicator item. These updates were issued to clarify these important aspects of interpretation so that professionals were more comfortable explaining results from the rating scales. Conners software scoring programs should be updated on a regular basis; see Chapter 3 for more information.

2004). We reviewed the content, strengths, and weaknesses of other instruments to ensure the new Conners assessments would make a unique contribution to the field. We considered the topics we thought were important to include. Based on all of these discussions, we generated many items for consideration, including multiple versions of some items. We considered how certain behaviors might be described by different observers, specifically parents, teachers, and children; this helped us create items that were appropriate for multiple types of raters in different settings.

- Expert review: A condensed list of items was sent to expert clinicians and researchers in relevant fields. Each was asked to review the items and send feedback, including topics included, coverage of the topics, wording of items, and additional considerations. The experts who reviewed each rating scale are listed in the relevant manuals. This step was included to help make sure the information on the rating scales was clinically meaningful and relevant and that no important topics or examples were omitted.

- Cultural relevance: A special type of expert review was conducted by professionals who specialize in multicultural issues of assessment. As items were being developed, they were reviewed not just by clinicians but by people with expertise in linguistic and cultural issues of translation. This helped create rating scales that could be translated into other languages for use with people from different cultures—particularly Spanish for use with the Hispanic population of the United States. The Spanish translations of the Conners 3 and Conners CBRS were developed simultaneously with the English versions. The Conners EC was translated into Spanish after data collection.

- Co-norming: Data for the Conners 3 and Conners CBRS were collected concurrently. Many of the children rated with the Conners 3 were also rated with the Conners CBRS. This means that the normative data for the Conners 3 and Conners CBRS describe a similar group of children, which facilitates comparison among scores from these two Conners assessments. This is useful when integrating results from co-administration of the Conners 3 and Conners CBRS forms or from multiple evaluations using different Conners assessments.

- Pilot data: Preliminary data were collected on the initial pool of items. These data were used to help select which items were the strongest when more than one item existed for a given concept. These data also helped identify which clinical concepts were statistically supported. The pilot data were used as the basis for discussions about which items were retained for the final data collection with the standardization samples. The preliminary structure for the Conners 3 and Conners CBRS was established with these data.

- Standardization: A large data collection project was undertaken. The general population sample was stratified by age and gender (i.e., equal numbers of boys and girls in each age group were represented), as well as by race/ethnicity (proportionate to the U.S. Census). Data were collected about children from different geographic regions, representing children with different backgrounds (including rural, suburban, and urban settings; safe and dangerous neighborhoods; low to high parental education and income levels).

- Clinical samples were also collected for relevant types of diagnoses for validation of constructs included on each rating scale (including both confirmation that the scales were capturing the targeted clinical group and that they were useful in distinguishing that group from the general population and from other clinical groups). See Rapid References 1.25 and 1.26 for a list of clinical groups sampled.

- The extensive data set was used to examine psychometrics of each rating scale. In cases where psychometrics were not solid, the constructs, scales, and items were re-examined to better understand the issue. For example, some items occurred at very low frequency in the general population, so there were not enough data to support keeping them on the scale; however, review of the clinical data indicated these items were very important for recognizing features of a certain diagnosis or identifying a child at risk for later difficulties. In cases like these, clinical judgment supported inclusion of the items for purposes of clinical utility. For the majority of the scales included in final versions of the Conners 3, Conners CBRS, and Conners EC, reliability and validity were good (see "Standardization and Psychometric Properties" in this chapter for an overview of reliability and validity; see relevant chapters in manuals for specific psychometrics).

- As the final structure of each rating scale was confirmed, we reviewed the clinical utility of each scale and how it might inform treatment efforts.

In summary, the Conners assessments have evolved over several generations of development to reach their current level of sophistication and utility. Each version shows refinements and improvements as well as updates corresponding with current needs of the educational, clinical, and research fields. Important considerations in the creation of the Conners 3, Conners CBRS, and Conners EC include depth and breadth of content, solid statistical basis, clinical utility for both identification and intervention, links to the DSM-IV-TR, and age-appropriate items/versions.

≡ Rapid Reference 1.11

Spanish Translations of the Conners Assessments

Parent and self-report forms were translated into Spanish for the initial release of the Conners assessments, as a large percentage of the U.S. population is primarily Spanish-speaking. Teacher forms for the Conners 3 and Conners CBRS were released in English only, as most U.S. schools require teachers to be literate in English. Conners EC Teacher forms were released in English and Spanish, as there is more linguistic variation among the teachers and caregivers of young children.

CONNERS 3rd EDITION (CONNERS 3)

The Conners 3 is a focused assessment tool for ADHD and associated issues in children ages 6 to 18 years. It includes items related to inattention, hyperactivity, and impulsivity, using relevant descriptions from clinical and research applications as well as the DSM-IV-TR symptoms of ADHD. Executive functioning, learning problems, and relationships are also included, as these are key areas often involved for youth with ADHD (see Rapid Reference 1.12 for additional information about executive functioning).

≡ Rapid Reference 1.12

Executive Functions

Executive functioning is a term used to describe the so-called "higher order" skills of the human brain. It seems that certain parts of the human brain (including the frontal lobes and white matter tracts) help coordinate all of the brain's functions, just like a Chief Executive Officer (CEO) coordinates the activities of a large corporation. Skills that are thought of as executive functions include: organization (both physical and mental), prioritization, integration of information, forming and implementing a problem-solving strategy (with back-up plans if the first way does not work), efficiency, self-regulation (of thoughts, actions, and emotions), and mental flexibility.

The human brain continues developing after birth, and the last areas to reach maturity are the frontal lobes and white matter tracts. These areas continue developing into early adulthood. Thus, as typically developing children grow older, we see increased ability to show self-control, be independent, and accept responsibility. This developmental path makes it difficult to recognize deficits in executive functioning at very young ages because most young children have limited skills in this area (e.g., it is typical for a 2-year-old child to have a temper tantrum). These deficits in executive functioning become more apparent as children grow older (e.g., it is unusual for a 13-year-old child to have a temper tantrum).

It is important to consider information about everyday functioning when evaluating executive functioning. Parents and teachers are often aware of these deficits because they see children in unstructured situations where executive functioning is required. The very nature of most formal, standardized evaluations makes it difficult to detect executive deficits, as the child is evaluated in a highly structured, reduced distraction setting with clearly stated rules and expectations.

Problems with executive functioning are described with terms like *executive deficits* or *executive dysfunction*. Although executive deficits are often seen with ADHD, they are not diagnostic and can also occur with Anxiety Disorders, Mood Disorders, Pervasive Developmental Disorders, and many other diagnoses. In fact, it is possible to see executive deficits in children who don't have a DSM-IV-TR diagnosis. Executive functioning is a broad concept, like attention, that is not limited to one diagnostic category.

The Disruptive Behavior Disorders, which often are comorbid with ADHD, are included on the Conners 3 with items representing DSM-IV-TR symptoms of CD and ODD as well as other content about defiance, aggression, and severe conduct problems. Parent, teacher, and self-report forms are available, in English or Spanish.[4] The Conners 3 has four different form lengths, summarized in Rapid Reference 1.13; the similarities and differences among these forms are discussed in Chapter 2. Each form can be completed in paper-and-pencil format or online. Scoring options include hand-scoring, online scoring, and computer scoring with the software package[5] (see Chapter 3). Typical time required to administer and score the Conners 3 forms is summarized in Rapid Reference 1.13. Computerized reports are available when using online or software scoring; see Chapter 3 for more information.

---

4. Additional translations may be available; check with the publisher if another language is needed. At the time this book was prepared, some Conners 3 forms were also available in French.

5. Note that the software package is stored on a portable USB drive rather than installed on a single computer's hard drive. See Chapter 3 for further discussion.

Overview of Conners 3 Options

	Conners 3 (Full-Length)	Conners 3(S) (Short Form)	Conners 3AI (ADHD Index Form)	Conners 3GI (Global Index Form)
Rater type (# items)	Parent (110) Teacher (115) Self-Report (99)	Parent (45) Teacher (41) Self-Report (41)	Parent (10) Teacher (10) Self-Report (10)	Parent (10) Teacher (10)
Language[a]	English (Parent, Teacher, and Self-Report forms) Spanish (Parent and Self-Report forms)			
Information	Content scales DSM-IV-TR Symptom scales Validity scales Index scales Screener items Critical items Impairment items Additional Questions	Content scales Validity scales Additional Questions	Conners 3AI	Conners 3GI

	Conners 3 (Full-Length)	Conners 3(S) (Short Form)	Conners 3AI (ADHD Index Form)	Conners 3GI (Global Index Form)
Administration[b]	Paper: 20–25 min. Online: 20–25 min.	Paper: 10 min. Online: 10 min.	Paper: 5 min. Online: 5 min.	Paper: 5 min. Online: 5 min.
Scoring[c]	Hand-score: 20 min. Online: 5 min. Software: 5 min.	Hand-score: 10 min. Online: 2–3 min. Software: 2–3 min.	Hand-score: 5 min. Online: 1 min. Software: 1 min.	Hand-score: 5 min. Online: 1 min. Software: 1 min.
Reports	Assessment (results from a single administration) Progress (change over time) Comparative (comparison of multiple ratings of a child at one point in time)			

[a] Additional translations may be available; check with the publisher if another language is needed. At the time this book was prepared, some Conners 3 forms were also available in French.

[b] Typical time to complete the form, not including instructions and review of completed form.

[c] Typical time to enter data or complete the QuikScore form (not including time to open scoring program or gather materials). Online scoring is immediate when online administration is used.

Structure of the Conners 3

The Conners 3 is composed of Content scales, DSM-IV-TR Symptom scales, Screener items, Critical items, Validity scales, the Conners 3 ADHD Index, the Conners 3 Global Index, Impairment items, and Additional Questions. See Rapid Reference 1.14 for an overview of the Conners 3 structure. Each of these components is briefly reviewed below; please see Chapter 3 Scoring and Chapter 4 Interpretation for additional information.

≡ Rapid Reference 1.14

Conners 3 Structure

Conners 3rd Edition (Conners 3)

Content Scales		
Parent (6-18yo)	**Teacher (6-18yo)**	**Self (8-18yo)**
Inattention	Inattention	Inattention
Hyperactivity/Impulsivity	Hyperactivity/ Impulsivity	Hyperactivity/Impulsivity
Learning Problems	Learning Problems /Executive Functioning	Learning Problems
Executive Functioning	- Learning Problems subscale - Executive Functioning subscale	—
Defiance/Aggression	Defiance/Aggression	Defiance/Aggression
Peer Relations	Peer Relations	Family Relations

DSM-IV-TR Symptom Scales	**Conners 3 ADHD Index (Conners 3AI)**	**Validity Scales**
ADHD Inattentive ADHD Hyperactive-Impulsive Conduct Disorder Oppositional Defiant Disorder	**Conners 3 Global Index (Conners 3GI; not on SR)** Restless-Impulsive subscale Emotional Lability subscale	Positive Impression (PI) Negative Impression (NI) Inconsistency Index (IncX)

Screener Items Anxiety Depression	**Severe Conduct Critical Items**	**Impairment Items**
		Additional Questions

- **Content Scales:** Each of these scales/subscales focuses on key content for ADHD and the Disruptive Behavior Disorders. Primary ADHD content is captured by the Inattention and Hyperactivity/Impulsivity scales. The Executive Functioning,[6] Learning Problems, and Peer/

---

6. Executive Functioning is a subscale of the Learning Problems/Executive Functioning scale on the Teacher form.

Family Relations[7] scales/subscales reflect issues that are often related to ADHD. Key behaviors that accompany the Disruptive Behavior Disorders are described on the Defiance/Aggression scale. There are differences among the different rater types on the Content scales, reflecting different ways behaviors are observed in different settings. Each of these scales is reported as a T-score (with optional percentile score), comparing ratings of the child with expectations based on age and gender (combined gender norms are also available; see Rapid Reference 1.24).

- **DSM-IV-TR Symptom Scales:** The Conners 3 includes DSM-IV-TR-based scales for three diagnoses: ADHD (by subtype), CD, and ODD. Each of these scales includes symptoms of the relevant diagnosis as listed in the DSM-IV-TR. Remember that symptoms alone are not adequate for diagnosis; other important criteria must also be met before a diagnosis can be assigned (see Caution: DSM-IV-TR Diagnosis in Chapter 6). Each of these scales is reported in two different ways: T-score and symptom count. The T-score describes whether the child is showing more severe/frequent demonstrations of the symptoms in comparison to age- and gender-matched peers (unless the combined gender option is selected). The symptom count score reflects how many of the DSM-IV-TR symptoms were endorsed at sufficient levels to be considered for a possible diagnosis of that particular disorder.

- **Screener Items:** There are two groups of Screener items on the Conners 3: Anxiety and Depression, with four items in each group. These items were selected from the larger set of anxiety and mood items on the Conners CBRS as the most likely to indicate possible anxiety or depression. When any of these Screener items are endorsed, it suggests the need for further investigation.

- **Critical Items:** The Conners 3 has a group of Severe Conduct Critical Items (see Rapid References 1.15 and 1.16). These items represent concerns about misconduct that should be investigated quickly when they are present, as they may require rapid intervention. The Severe Conduct Critical items include behaviors that may predict future violence or harm to others.

- **Validity Scales:** [8] These three scales help you identify potential biases in the rater's response style that could impact your interpretation of that

---

7. The Parent and Teacher forms both have a Peer Relations scale that describes the child's relationships with peers. The Self-Report form has a Family Relations scale that describes the child's relationships with her family.

8. The Conners 3 interpretative update issued in 2009 clarifies the interpretation of these Validity scales, as some clinicians were discarding all results when one or more of these scales was elevated. As described in the Interpretation chapter of the manual and of this book, an elevated Validity scale score may indicate many things, not just invalid ratings.

rater's results. They include the Positive Impression (PI) scale, Negative Impression (NI) scale, and Inconsistency Index (IncX). Elevated scores on these scales lead to careful examination of available information to determine what could lead to this response pattern, and may suggest caution during interpretation. In rare cases, extreme scores on validity scales may cause you to question the validity of the ratings.

- **Conners 3 ADHD Index (Conners 3AI):** This scale describes whether a child is more similar to children with a diagnosis of ADHD or to children in the general population, based on the rater's responses to these 10 items. The Conners 3AI is reported as a probability score, with higher scores indicating the child is more similar to children in the ADHD sample.

- **Conners 3 Global Index (Conners 3GI):** This index is the same 10 items as the original Conners Global Index (CGI; CRS–R). It is a good indicator of global concerns about a child's functioning. Research using these same 10 items from the CRS found good sensitivity to treatment effects. The Conners 3GI is reported as a *T*-score.

- **Impairment Items:** There is one item per setting, including academic, social, and home. Each item asks the rater to mark how much the child's symptoms impact his functioning in that setting. The raw scores are reviewed for these items.

- **Additional Questions:** These two items allow the rater to report additional information that may not be captured by the other items on the Conners 3. One item asks the rater to describe the child's strengths. The other item asks if there are any other concerns not described in their ratings. The text responses recorded here can add new information or clarify the rater's intentions with some of the ratings. These items are not scored.

≡ *Rapid Reference 1.15*

Sensitive Topics

There is considerable debate among professionals and laypeople regarding whether children should be asked about sensitive topics like suicide and sexual activity. We all know that children experience thoughts about such topics, and some children engage in behaviors related to these topics. Although the research literature shows that asking about sensitive topics does not increase the behaviors, and in fact may *decrease* thoughts about certain behaviors (for example, see Gould, Marrocco, et al., 2005 regarding suicide screening), some people continue to worry that asking questions may give children ideas. From a legal perspective, some argue that documenting the presence of risk factors could place an assessor at risk if he did not act quickly to intervene; I counter that failing to ask is a greater legal risk in the context of an evaluation. From an ethical perspective, it is critical to assess all factors that may be impacting a child's functioning, even if they are uncomfortable or risky to consider. The bottom line is that, if any behaviors related to these sensitive topics are present, it is important for assessors, parents, and teachers to be aware of them so appropriate investigation and intervention can be started.

A quick review of Rapid Reference 1.16 reveals that there are several critical concepts that are not included on the Conners self-report forms (i.e., suicide, thoughts of death/dying, caring about others, forced sex). During pilot data collection, the data collection team received feedback that many schools and parents were not comfortable with these items on a self-report form to be completed by 6- to 18-year-olds. This presented a difficult dilemma— should the items be retained at the risk of losing self-report for a portion of evaluations, or should the items be dropped from the self-report form? After much deliberation, the development team decided to keep the items on the parent and teacher forms, drop them on the self-report forms, and remind assessors that these are important concepts to include when interviewing a child. Two unique Critical items were included on the self-report form to serve as additional indicators of possible suicide risk (i.e., nobody cares, discouragement).

There are two Critical items that are reworded for self-report. The cruelty to animals item uses the word "mean" rather than "cruel." The fire-setting item is simply, "I like to set fires," which omits the concept of intention to cause damage. Both of these differences were implemented to reduce the overall reading level for the self-report form. It is important to realize these differences though, as they may impact a rater's willingness to endorse one of these items (i.e., a child may endorse the item which has milder wording even though the parent or teacher did not endorse the corresponding item).

One item is on the Conners 3 parent and teacher forms, but is not listed as a "Critical item." The "cold-hearted and cruel" item can certainly be considered when interpreting results from the Conners 3 even though it is not explicitly listed as a Critical item.

Finally, although the Conners EC does not list "Critical items," four of the Conners EC Other Clinical Indicators represent similar concepts (i.e., self-injury, stealing, cruelty to animals, fire-setting).

If you are faced with a parent or teacher who is uncomfortable with a topic included on the Conners assessments, it is important to clarify that not every item on the rating scale applies to every child, but that each item on the rating scale does happen for some children. You can also reassure the parent or teacher that the self-report form does not contain all of the items that are on the parent and teacher forms. Remind the rater that when one of these behaviors is present, it is extremely important for all helping the child to be aware so that they can respond appropriately.

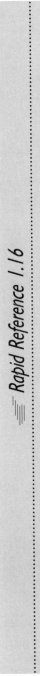

Rapid Reference 1.16

Comparison of Critical Items

Critical Item Concept	Conners 3			Conners CBRS			Conners EC
	Parent	Teacher	Self	Parent	Teacher	Self	
Hopelessness				✓	✓	✓	
Helplessness				✓	✓	✓	
Worthlessness				✓	✓	✓	
Nobody cares						✓	
Discouragement						✓	
Self-injury				✓	✓	✓	*
Suicide				✓	✓		
Thoughts of Death/Dying					✓		
Caring about others				✓	✓		
Breaking into property	✓	✓	✓	✓	✓	✓	

Critical Item Concept	Conners 3			Conners CBRS			Conners EC
	Parent	Teacher	Self	Parent	Teacher	Self	
Confrontational stealing	✓	✓	✓	✓	✓	✓	*
Forced sex	✓	✓		✓	✓		
Cruelty to animals	✓	✓	✓	✓	✓	✓	*
Cold-hearted and Cruel	(✓)	(✓)					
Fire-setting	✓	✓	✓	✓	✓	✓	*
Interest in Weapons				✓	✓		
Access to Weapons						✓	
Carries weapon				✓	✓	✓	
Uses weapon	✓	✓	✓	✓	✓	✓	
Gang membership			✓	✓	✓	✓	
Police activity		✓	✓	✓	✓		

* Concept represented in Conners EC Other Clinical Indicators; the Conners EC does not have "Critical items" per se.
(✓) = not listed as a Critical item in Conners 3 manual.

CONNERS COMPREHENSIVE BEHAVIOR RATING SCALES (CONNERS CBRS)

As indicated by the name, the Conners CBRS is a comprehensive tool to use in assessing a wide range of behavioral, emotional, social, and academic issues that are relevant in children ages 6 to 18 years. In addition to broad assessment of clinical issues that commonly arise in school-aged youth, the Conners CBRS includes less common but critical issues that require immediate intervention (e.g., self-harm, violence potential). The Conners CBRS results include information about general content areas as well as specific DSM-IV-TR diagnoses. Forms are available for completion by parents, teachers, and children, in English or Spanish.[9] In addition

≡ Rapid Reference 1.17

Overview of Conners CBRS Options

	Conners CBRS (Full-Length)	Conners CI (Clinical Index Form)
Rater type (# items)	Parent (203) Teacher (204) Self-Report (179)	Parent (24) Teacher (24) Self-Report (24)
Language[a]	English (Parent, Teacher, and Self-Report forms) French (Parent, Teacher, and Self-Report forms) Spanish (Parent and Self-Report forms)	
Information	Content scales DSM-IV-TR Symptom scales Validity scales Clinical Index Other Clinical Indicators Critical items Impairment items Additional Questions	Clinical Index

9. Additional translations may be available; check with the publisher if another language is needed.

	Conners CBRS (Full-Length)	Conners CI (Clinical Index Form)
Administration[b]	Paper: 20–25 min. Online: 20–25 min.	Paper: 10 min. Online: 10 min.
Scoring[c]	Hand-score: n/a Online: 10 min. Software: 10 min.	Hand-score: 10 min. Online: 2 min. Software: 2 min.
Reports	Assessment (results from a single administration) Progress (change over time) Comparative (comparison of multiple ratings of a child at one point in time)	

[a] Additional translations may be available; check with the publisher if another language is needed.
[b] Typical time to complete the form, not including instructions and review of completed form.
[c] Typical time to enter data or complete the QuikScore form (not including time to open scoring program or gather materials). Online scoring is immediate when online administration is used.

to the full Conners CBRS form, there is also a form that only contains the Conners Clinical Index (see Rapid Reference 1.17; see also Chapter 2 for more information about these two forms). Both forms can be completed in paper-and-pencil format or online. The Conners CBRS forms can be computer scored (either online or software[10]); the Conners CI form can also be hand-scored (see Chapter 3 for more information). Typical time required to administer and score the Conners CBRS forms is summarized in Rapid Reference 1.17. Computerized reports are available when using online or software scoring; see Chapter 3 for more information.

Structure of the Conners CBRS

The Conners CBRS is composed of Content scales, DSM-IV-TR Symptom scales, Other Clinical Indicators, Critical items, Validity scales, Clinical Index,

---

10. Note that the software package is stored on a portable USB drive rather than installed on a single computer's hard drive. See Chapter 3 for further discussion.

Impairment items, and Additional Questions. See Rapid Reference 1.18 for an overview of the Conners CBRS structure. Each of these components is briefly reviewed below; please see Chapter 3 Scoring and Chapter 4 Interpretation for additional information.

- **Content Scales**[11]: Each of these scales/subscales reflects a general content area that is important to assess in school-aged youth. These areas include behavioral issues (i.e., Defiant/Aggressive Behaviors, Violence Potential Indicator, Hyperactivity/Impulsivity), emotional issues (i.e., Emotional Distress, Separation Fears, Perfectionistic and Compulsive Behaviors), social issues (i.e., Social Problems), and academic issues (i.e.,

≡ Rapid Reference 1.18

Conners CBRS Structure

Conners Comprehensive Behavior Rating Scales (Conners CBRS)

Content Scales		
Parent (6-18yo)	**Teacher (6-18yo)**	**Self (8-18yo)**
Emotional Distress (Upsetting Thoughts, Worrying, Social Problems)	Emotional Distress (Upsetting Thoughts/Physical Symptoms, Social Anxiety, Separation Fears)	Emotional Distress
Defiant/Aggressive Behaviors	Defiant/Aggressive Behaviors	Defiant/Aggressive Behaviors
Academic Difficulties (Language, Math)	Academic Difficulties (Language, Math)	Academic Difficulties
Hyperactivity/Impulsivity	Hyperactivity	Hyperactivity/Impulsivity
(Social Problems subscale)	Social Problems	—
Separation Fears	(Separation Fears subscale)	Separation Fears
Perfectionistic and Compulsive Behaviors	Perfectionistic and Compulsive Behaviors	—
Violence Potential Indicator	Violence Potential Indicator	Violence Potential Indicator
Physical Symptoms	Physical Symptoms	Physical Symptoms

DSM-IV-TR Symptom Scales
ADHD Inattentive
ADHD Hyperactive-Impulsive
Conduct Disorder
Oppositional Defiant Disorder
Major Depressive Episode
Manic Episode
Generalized Anxiety Disorder
Separation Anxiety Disorder
Social Phobia
Obsessive-Compulsive Disorder
Autistic Disorder (not on Self)
Asperger's Disorder (not on Self)

Other Clinical Indicators
Bullying Perpetration
Bullying Victimization
Enuresis/Encopresis (not on Self)
Panic Attack
PDD (Self only)
Pica (not on Teacher)
Posttraumatic Stress Disorder
Specific Phobia
Substance Use
Tics
Trichotillomania

Critical Items
Severe Conduct
Self Harm

Validity Scales
Positive Impression (PI)
Negative Impression (NI)
Inconsistency Index (IncX)

Clinical Index (Conners CI)
Disruptive Behavior Disorder Indicator
Learning and Language Disorder Indicator
Mood Disorder Indicator
Anxiety Disorder Indicator
ADHD Indicator

Impairment Items

Additional Questions

---

11. Defiant/Aggressive Behaviors and Violence Potential Indicator are the updated scale names as per the Conners CBRS interpretative update issued in 2009. Note that, although the scale names changed, the item content did not change.

Academic Difficulties), as well as key Physical Symptoms. Some of the scales have subscale scores (e.g., Emotional Distress) on the Parent and Teacher forms. There are differences among the different rater types on the Content scales, reflecting different ways behaviors are observed in different settings. Each of these scales is reported as a *T*-score (with optional percentile score), comparing ratings of the child with expectations based on age and gender (combined gender norms are also available; see Rapid Reference 1.24).

- **DSM-IV-TR Symptom Scales:** The Conners CBRS has a number of DSM-IV-TR Symptom scales based on symptoms of the relevant diagnosis (see Rapid Reference 1.18 for a comprehensive list of these diagnoses; see Rapid References 1.19 and 1.20 for special information about how Pervasive Developmental Disorders and Mood Disorders are represented on the Conners CBRS). Remember that symptoms alone are not adequate for diagnosis; other important criteria must also be met before a diagnosis can be assigned (see Caution: DSM-IV-TR Diagnosis in Chapter 6). Each of these scales is reported in two different ways: *T*-score and symptom count. The *T*-score describes whether the child is showing more severe/frequent demonstrations of the symptoms in comparison to age- and gender-matched peers (unless the combined gender option is selected). The symptom count score reflects how many of the DSM-IV-TR symptoms were endorsed at

≡ Rapid Reference 1.19

Pervasive Developmental Disorders (PDD) on the Conners CBRS

The initial goal was to create parallel scales across all informant types (i.e., parent, teacher, and self-report). As the development team discussed DSM-IV-TR items for symptoms of Autistic Disorder and Asperger's Disorder (diagnoses in the PDD category), we shared concerns that children with these disorders might have difficulty recognizing and reporting these symptoms. We created many items to try to capture aspects of the experience that children with diagnoses in the PDD category would endorse. Pilot data from youth's self-ratings of the Conners CBRS did not support a solid DSM-IV-TR Autistic Disorder or Asperger's Disorder scale on the self-report form. There were three items that reflected aspects of PDD that were reliably rated by children with a diagnosis in the PDD category. These three items were retained and are listed as Other Clinical Indicators for PDD on the self-report form.

≡ Rapid Reference 1.20

Mood Disorders on the Conners CBRS

The diagnostic category of Mood Disorders in the DSM-IV-TR begins with descriptions of episodes, including Major Depressive Episode and Manic Episode. The episodes have criteria, including a list of observable symptoms. Mood episodes are not diagnoses; they are the building blocks used to establish diagnoses like Major Depressive Disorder and Bipolar Disorder. The actual Mood Disorder diagnoses require certain combinations of the mood episode building blocks in combination with other criteria (see Chapter 6, particularly Rapid Reference 6.9, and the DSM-IV-TR for more information). Consistent with the limitations of a rating scale, the Conners CBRS approaches these diagnoses from a symptomatic level, with the reminder that additional criteria must be met before a diagnosis can be assigned. Therefore, the Conners CBRS includes symptoms of Major Depressive Episode and Manic Episode. When either of these building blocks is present, further evaluation for possible mood disorder is recommended.

sufficient levels to be considered for a possible diagnosis of that particular disorder.

- **Other Clinical Indicators:** These topics are each covered by one or more items, rather than by entire scales. These are areas that are important to consider for school-aged children. When one of these items is endorsed at a certain level, the item is flagged for further consideration by the clinician.
- **Critical Items:** There are two groups of Critical items on the Conners CBRS: Severe Conduct and Self-Harm (see Rapid References 1.15 and 1.16). These items represent concerns that should be investigated quickly when they are present, as they may require rapid intervention. The Severe Conduct Critical items include behaviors that may predict future violence or harm to others. The Self-Harm Critical items include risk factors for possible suicide attempt and/or self-mutilation.
- **Validity Scales[12]:** These three scales help you identify potential biases in the rater's response style that could impact your

---

12. The Conners CBRS interpretative update issued in 2009 clarifies the interpretation of these Validity scales, as some clinicians were discarding all results when one or more of these scales was elevated. As described in the Interpretation chapter of the manual and of this book, an elevated Validity scale score may indicate many things, not just invalid ratings.

interpretation of that rater's results. They include the Positive Impression (PI) scale, Negative Impression (NI) scale, and Inconsistency Index (IncX). Elevated scores on these scales lead to careful examination of available information to determine what could lead to this response pattern, and may suggest caution during interpretation. In rare cases, extreme scores on validity scales may cause you to question the validity of the ratings.

- **Conners Clinical Index (Conners CI):** This scale describes whether a child is more similar to children with a clinical diagnosis or to children in the general population, based on the rater's responses to these 24 items. Five clinical groups were used to derive this index: Disruptive Behavior Disorders, Learning Disorders and Language Disorders, Mood Disorders, Anxiety Disorders, and ADHD. As illustrated in Rapid Reference 1.21, children with Pervasive Developmental Disorders (a.k.a., autism spectrum disorders) were not included in this analysis; as a result, this index is not applicable to consideration of that group of diagnoses.

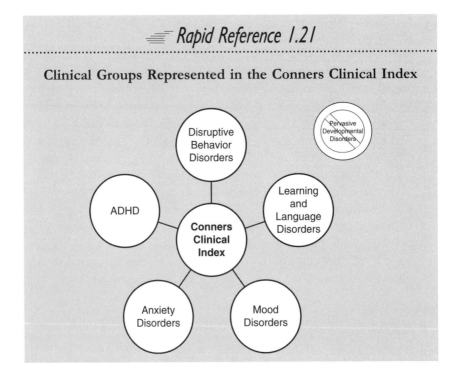

≡ Rapid Reference 1.21

Clinical Groups Represented in the Conners Clinical Index

Disruptive Behavior Disorders

Pervasive Developmental Disorders

ADHD

Conners Clinical Index

Learning and Language Disorders

Anxiety Disorders

Mood Disorders

The Conners CI is reported as a probability score, with higher scores indicating that the child is more similar to clinical populations. In addition, a T-score can be calculated for each of the five clinical categories in this index, suggesting which diagnostic group a child is most similar to on the basis of this quick index. (See Appendix D.)

- **Impairment Items:** There is one item per setting, including academic, social, and home. Each item asks the rater to mark how much the child's symptoms impact her functioning in that setting. The raw scores are reviewed for these items.

- **Additional Questions:** One of these two Additional Questions asks the rater to describe the child's strengths. The other item asks if there are any other concerns not described in their ratings. The text responses recorded here can add new information or clarify the rater's intentions with some of the ratings. These items are not scored.

CONNERS EARLY CHILDHOOD (CONNERS EC)

The Conners EC is a broadband assessment tool for important behavioral, emotional, social, cognitive, and developmental issues in young children, ages 2 to 6 years. It is divided into two main sections: Behavior scales and Developmental Milestone scales. The Behavior scales include key concepts of hyperactivity, defiance, aggressive behaviors, anxiety, mood/affect, social functioning, atypical behaviors, inattention, and physical symptoms. The Developmental Milestone scales have important markers for development in adaptive skills, communication, motor skills, play, and pre-academic arenas. As mentioned previously, the Conners EC does not include DSM-IV-TR Symptom scales; rather, the relevant areas are included conceptually. Parent and teacher/childcare provider forms are available in English and Spanish.[13] There are five different form lengths available for the Conners EC (see Rapid Reference 1.22; see also Chapter 2 for comparisons among these forms). All Conners EC forms can be completed in paper-and-pencil format or online. The Conners EC forms can be computer scored (either online or software[14]); the Conners ECGI form can also be hand-scored (see Chapter 3 for more information). Typical time required to administer

---

13. Additional translations may be available; check with the publisher if another language is needed.

14. Note that the software package is stored on a portable USB drive rather than installed on a single computer's hard drive. See Chapter 3 for further discussion.

≡ Rapid Reference 1.22

Overview of Conners EC Options

	Conners EC (Full-Length)	Conners EC BEH (Behavior Scales)	Conners EC BEH(S) (Behavior Short)	Conners ECGI (Global Index Form)	Conners EC DM (Developmental Milestone Scales)
Rater type (# items)	Parent (190) Teacher (186)	Parent (115) Teacher (116)	Parent (49) Teacher (48)	Parent (10) Teacher (10)	Parent (80) Teacher (74)
Language[a]	English (Parent and Teacher forms) Spanish (Parent and Teacher forms)				
Information	Behavior scales Validity scales Conners ECGI Other Clinical Indicators DM scales Impairment items Additional Questions	Behavior scales Validity scales Conners ECGI Other Clinical Indicators Impairment items Additional Questions	Behavior scales Validity scales Additional Questions	Conners ECGI	DM scales Impairment items Additional Questions

Administration[b]	Paper: 25 min. Online: 25 min.	Paper: 15 min. Online: 15 min.	Paper: 10 min. Online: 10 min.	Paper: 5 min. Online: 5 min.	Paper: 10 min. Online: 10 min.
Scoring[c]	Hand: n/a Online: 10 min. Software: 10 min.	Hand: n/a Online: 6 min. Software: 6 min.	Hand: n/a Online: 3 min. Software: 3 min.	Hand: 5 min. Online: 1 min. Software: 1 min.	Hand: n/a Online: 4 min. Software: 4 min.
Reports	Assessment (results from a single administration) Progress (change over time) Comparative (comparison of multiple ratings of a child at one point in time)				

[a] Additional translations may be available; check with the publisher if another language is needed. At the time this book was prepared, some Conners 3 forms were also available in French.

[b] Typical time to complete the form, not including instructions and review of completed form.

[c] Typical time to enter data or complete the QuikScore form (not including time to open scoring program or gather materials). Online scoring is immediate when online administration is used.

and score the Conners EC forms is summarized in Rapid Reference 1.22. Computerized reports are available when using online or software scoring; see Chapter 3 for more information.

Structure of the Conners EC

The Behavior scales section of the Conners EC is composed of Behavior scales, Other Clinical Indicators, Validity scales, and the Conners EC Global Index. The Developmental Milestone scales section of the Conners EC includes five scales, one for each area included (i.e., Adaptive Skills, Communication, Motor Skills, Play, and Pre-Academic/Cognitive). Some of the Developmental Milestone scales have subclusters of skills (e.g., Communication subclusters are Expressive and Receptive). The Conners EC also includes Impairment items and Additional Questions. See Rapid Reference 1.23 for an overview of the Conners EC structure. Each of these components is briefly reviewed below; please see Chapter 3 Scoring and Chapter 4 Interpretation for additional information.

- **Behavior Scales:** Each of these scales/subscales addresses general issues that arise in assessment of young children. These include behavioral issues (i.e., Defiant/Aggressive Behaviors, hyperactivity/impulsivity items on the Inattention/Hyperactivity scale), emotional issues (i.e., Anxiety, Mood, and Affect), social issues (i.e., Social Functioning), and cognitive issues (i.e., inattention items on the Inattention/Hyperactivity scale). There is a subscale for unusual behaviors (i.e., Atypical Behaviors), which includes red-flag items for early detection of possible autism spectrum disorders. There is also a Physical Symptoms scale. There are differences between the parent forms and the teacher/childcare provider forms on the Behavior scales, reflecting different ways behaviors are observed in various settings. Each of these scales is reported as a T-score (with optional percentile score), comparing ratings of the child with expectations based on age and gender (combined gender norms are also available; see Rapid Reference 1.24).
- **Other Clinical Indicators:** These items represent important issues that can arise during the early childhood period but that were not included on the Content scales (e.g., tics, fire-setting). When one of these items is endorsed at a certain level, the item is flagged for further consideration by the clinician. See also Rapid References 1.15 and 1.16.

≡ *Rapid Reference 1.23*

Conners EC Structure

Conners Early Childhood (Conners EC)

Behavior scales

Inattention/Hyperactivity

Defiant/Aggressive
Behaviors
  -Defiance/Temper
  -Aggression
Social Functioning/
Atypical Behaviors
  -Social Functioning
  -Atypical Behaviors
Anxiety

Mood and Affect

Physical Symptoms
  -Sleep Problems *(Parent)*

**Conners EC Global Index
  (Conners ECGI)**
Restless-Impulsive
Emotional Lability

**Other Clinical
Indicators**
Cruelty to animals
Fire setting
Perfectionism
Pica
PTSD
Self-Injury
Specific Phobia
Stealing
Tics
Trichotillomania

Validity Scales
Positive Impression
Negative Impression
Inconsistency Index

**Developmental Milestone
scales**

Adaptive Skills
  -Dressing
  -Eating/Drinking
  -Toileting
  -Hygiene
  -Helping
Communication
  -Expressive Language
  -Receptive Language
Motor Skills
  -Fine Motor
  -Gross Motor
Play

Pre-Academic/Cognitive

Impairment Items	Additional Questions

- **Validity Scales:** These three scales help you identify potential biases in the rater's response style that could impact your interpretation of that rater's results. They include the Positive Impression (PI) scale, Negative Impression (NI) scale, and Inconsistency Index (IncX). Elevated scores on these scales lead to careful examination of available information to determine what could lead to this response pattern, and may suggest caution during interpretation. In rare cases, extreme scores on Validity scales may cause you to question the validity of the ratings.

- **Conners EC Global Index (Conners ECGI):** This index is the original 10 items from the Conners Global Index (CGI on the CRS–R; Conners 3GI on the Conners 3). It is a good indicator of global concerns about a child's functioning. Research using these same 10 items from the CRS found good sensitivity to treatment effects. The Conners ECGI is reported as a *T*-score.

⩵ Rapid Reference 1.24

Age- and Gender-Based Norms?

There is an ongoing debate regarding whether normative data should be divided based on gender. Proponents of combined gender norms argue that boys and girls should be held to the same standard. Proponents of norms separated by gender state that some disorders present differently for boys than girls, and failure to recognize this results in over- and/or underdiagnosis for certain gender groups. The parallel of physical development is sometimes referenced, as nobody argues with the fact that boys and girls show growth spurts at different ages. The use of gender-based norms is an emotionally charged topic in many settings.

For some reason, the emotional tone disappears when discussing the use of age-based normative data. Most people in the assessment community agree that age should be a factor when deciding if a child's performance is typical or not. There are slight differences of opinion as to how precise age-based comparisons should be, in terms of whether normative data are used in large age bands (e.g., children 6 to 10 years old, 11 to 15 years old, 16 to 18 years old) or smaller age bands (e.g., one group per year, so 6-year-olds, 7-year-olds, and so on). It is less costly in time and money to collect normative data for larger age bands, as this approach requires fewer participants and less stringent standards (e.g., an age band for 6- to 10-year-old children might have a majority of 9-year-olds if that was a convenient age-group to capture, but it would not be as representative of the 6-year-old children). Collecting smaller age bands, while costly, allows more careful examination of developmental trends in the data and ultimately can produce a more exact description of a child's functioning relative to age-matched peers.

The development team for the Conners assessments agreed to review results from pilot data and make their recommendation for normative data based on these results. Data were collected from equal numbers of boys and girls in each age group (in 1-year age bands for the Conners 3 and Conners CBRS, and in 6-month age bands for the Conners EC). When these data were analyzed, there were statistically significant differences by gender, by age, and by gender and age considered together. In other words, boys and girls showed different patterns of behavior. Children showed different patterns of behavior at different ages. Finally, boys and girls showed changes in behavior by age, but boys changed at a different age than girls for some scales. When the data were grouped into 3-year age bands, some of these clinically important and statistically significant differences were obscured. These findings were confirmed when the complete standardization sample was analyzed.

Based on these findings, we recommend using age- and gender-based norms with the Conners 3, Conners CBRS, and Conners EC. This recommendation is made not from our personal biases, but from analyses of the large data set. Standard normative data for the Conners assessments are presented by gender in very precise age bands: 1-year groups (e.g., "6 years 0 months through 6 years 11 months 30 days" is a 1-year age band) for the Conners 3 and Conners

CBRS, and 6-month groups (e.g., "6 years 0 months through 6 years 5 months 30 days" is a 6-month age band) for the Conners EC.

For the Conners assessments, combined gender norms average out important differences between boys and girls, which could lead to underidentification or overidentification, depending on the direction of the gender difference for that particular scale. For those who have strong opinions or requirements, a set of combined gender norms is available.

- **Developmental Milestone Scales:** Each of these scales summarizes many aspects of a child's development in a given domain, based on independent mastery of key skills. The Adaptive Skills scale includes five subclusters: Dressing, Eating/Drinking, Toileting, Hygiene, and Helping. The Communications scale has two subclusters: Expressive Language and Receptive Language. The Motor Skills scale is divided into two subclusters: Fine Motor and Gross Motor. Each of the Developmental Milestone scales is reported as a T-score (with optional percentile score), comparing ratings of the child with expectations based on age and gender (combined gender norms are also available; see Rapid Reference 1.24). The subclusters are reviewed as groups of items rather than by a composite score.
- **Impairment Items:** There is one item per setting, including learning/ pre-academic, peer interactions, and home. Each item asks the rater to mark how much the child's symptoms impact his functioning in that setting. The raw scores are reviewed for these items.
- **Additional Questions:** These two items allow the rater to report additional information that may not be captured by the other items on the Conners EC. One item asks the rater to describe the child's strengths. The other item asks if there are any other concerns not described in their ratings. The text responses recorded here can add new information or clarify the rater's intentions with some of the ratings. These items are not scored.

STANDARDIZATION AND PSYCHOMETRIC PROPERTIES

Because the Conners 3, Conners CBRS, and Conners EC were developed during the same time period, there are similarities in their standardization process and statistical techniques used to establish psychometric properties. This section describes key aspects of standardization and psychometrics for these three rating scales. Please see the Conners 3rd Edition manual (Conners 2008a; Chapters 11,

12, and 13), the Conners Comprehensive Behavior Rating Scales manual (Conners 2008b; Chapters 11, 12, and 13), and the Conners Early Childhood manual (Conners 2009; Chapters 9, 10, and 11) for comprehensive sample descriptions and results from the studies summarized in this section. See Chapter 6 in this book for additional information on clinical studies used to examine discriminative validity.

Standardization Samples

Conners 3 and Conners CBRS

The Conners 3 and Conners CBRS were co-normed (i.e., 85 to 90 percent of the children in the standardization samples were rated with the Conners 3 *and* the Conners CBRS). Data collection for these assessments took place between March, 2006, and August, 2007. Data were collected by over 100 site coordinators in more than 25 states and provinces throughout the United States and Canada. Some of the rating scales described children with no history of a clinical diagnosis; these children were considered "general population data." In addition, some children with specific clinical diagnoses were involved in data collection; parent, teacher, and self-report forms about these children were considered "clinical data." A total of 6,825 (4,682 general population and 2,143 clinical) Conners 3 forms and 6,702 (4,626 general population, 2,076 clinical) Conners CBRS forms were completed.

A large set of data were selected from the general population cases to use as the normative sample, making sure that boys and girls were represented equally at each age and that race/ethnicity was distributed across the sample to match the U.S. Census. The normative sample is the group of children used for comparison when interpreting an individual child's results. Both the Conners 3 normative sample ($N = 3,400$; 1,200 parent, 1,200 teacher, and 1,000 self-report) and the Conners CBRS normative sample ($N = 3,400$; 1,200 parent, 1,200 teacher, and 1,000 self-report) included 50 boys and 50 girls from each age (1-year age bands from 6 to 18 years for the parent and teacher report, from 8 to 18 years for the self-report). The normative samples have a racial/ethnic distribution that closely matches that of the U.S. population (according to the 2000 U.S. Census figures). Demographic analyses revealed that both age and gender significantly affected the Conners 3 and Conners CBRS scale scores, while race/ethnicity had a negligible impact on scores (see Chapter 10 in both the Conners 3rd Edition manual [Conners 2008a] and Conners Comprehensive Behavior Rating Scales manual [Conners 2008b] for details). Because of these effects, separate gender- and age-based norms are provided (see Rapid Reference 1.24 for further discussion).

Ratings of youth with various clinical diagnoses were collected and stringent data collection procedures were employed in order to ensure the accuracy of the diagnoses.[15] In total, 2,143 Conners 3 (731 parent, 694 teacher, 718 self-report) and 2,076 Conners CBRS (704 parent, 672 teacher, and 700 self-report) ratings of youth with clinical diagnoses were collected (see Rapid Reference 1.25). The clinical samples did not have a 50/50 gender split. For example, there were more boys in the Pervasive Developmental Disorder groups, while there were more girls in the Anxiety Disorders group (see Chapter 10 in both the Conners 3rd Edition manual and Conners Comprehensive Behavior Rating Scales manual for details).

Conners EC

Data collection for the Conners EC took place between September, 2006, and October, 2008. Over 50 site coordinators throughout the United States and Canada collected 3,281 Conners EC assessments (2,567 general population and 714 clinical). The normative sample ($N = 1,600$; 800 parent and 800 teacher/childcare provider) was selected from the general population cases and includes 40 boys and 40 girls from each age group (6-month age bands from ages 2 to 6 years). These smaller age bands were chosen given the rapid rate of change during the early childhood period. The normative samples have a racial/ethnic distribution that closely matches that of the U.S. population (according to the 2000 U.S. Census figures). Results of demographic analyses revealed that both age and gender significantly affected the Conners EC scale scores, while race/ethnicity had a minimal impact on scores (see Chapter 8 in the Conners Early Childhood manual [Conners 2009] for details). Because of these effects, separate gender and age-based (in 6-month age bands) norms are provided (see also discussion in Rapid Reference 1.24).

Ratings of children with various clinical diagnoses were collected and stringent data collection procedures were employed in order to ensure the accuracy of the diagnoses.[16] In total, 714 Conners EC (340 parent and 374 teacher/childcare provider) ratings of children with clinical diagnoses were collected (see Rapid Reference 1.26). The clinical groups were not comprised of equal numbers of

---

15. In order for a case to be accepted for the clinical sample, information completed by the site coordinator had to meet certain criteria. These included: (1) only one primary diagnosis, (2) diagnosis was assigned by a qualified professional, (3) diagnosis was based on DSM-IV-TR or ICD-10 criteria, and (4) multiple methods of assessment were employed in the diagnosis (e.g., record review, rating scales, observation, and/or interviews).

16. Criteria for the Conners EC clinical cases matched requirements for the Conners 3 and Conners CBRS. See previous footnote.

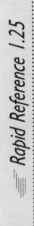

Rapid Reference 1.25

Conners 3 and Conners CBRS Clinical Samples

Clinical Group	Included Diagnoses	Conners 3			Conners CBRS		
		Parent (N)	Teacher (N)	Self (N)	Parent (N)	Teacher (N)	Self (N)
ADHD	ADHD Inattentive, ADHD Hyperactive-Impulsive, ADHD Combined	277	243	263	270	231	263
Disruptive Behavior Disorders	Conduct Disorder, Oppositional Defiant Disorder	60	58	69	51	50	59
Learning Disorders	Reading Disorder, Mathematics Disorder, Disorder of Written Expression	120	118	116	121	121	114
Anxiety Disorders	Generalized Anxiety Disorder, Separation Anxiety Disorder, Social Phobia, Obsessive-Compulsive Disorder	70	55	70	65	56	64

Major Depressive Disorder						
Major Depressive Disorder	42	43	43	41	41	42
Bipolar Disorder	35	34	35	34	32	34
Pervasive Developmental Disorders	32	47	31	35	48	32
Other (content of this group not specified in manual)	95	96	91	87	93	92
Total	731	694	718	704	672	700

Source: Information in this table was provided by the MHS Research and Development department.

 *Rapid Reference 1.26*

Conners EC Clinical Sample

Clinical Group	Included Diagnoses	Conners EC Parent (N)	Conners EC Teacher/ Childcare Provider (N)
ADHD	ADHD Inattentive, ADHD Hyperactive-Impulsive, ADHD Combined	57	71
Disruptive Behavior Disorders	Oppositional Defiant Disorder, Conduct Disorder	30	36
Delayed Cognitive Development	Mental Retardation	51	55
Delayed Communication Development	Expressive Language Disorder, Receptive Language Disorder, Mixed Receptive-Expressive Language Disorder	45	47
Delayed Social or Emotional Development	Disorders related to Anxiety and Depression	42	40
Delayed Adaptive Development	Autistic Disorder, Asperger's Disorder, Pervasive Developmental Disorder—Not Otherwise Specified	75	73
Other (content of this group not specified in manual)		40	52
Total		340	374

Source: Information in this table was provided by the MHS Research and Development department.

boys and girls. For example, the ADHD group had more boys than girls, consistent with gender ratios expected for this sample (see Appendix F in the Conners Early Childhood manual for more information).

Psychometric Properties

The psychometric properties (i.e., reliability and validity) of the Conners 3, Conners CBRS, and Conners EC were thoroughly assessed in a series of reliability and validity studies. A summary of results from these analyses is presented below; see the relevant test manual for detailed findings. See Rapid References 1.27 and 1.28 for tips to understand the statistics presented in this section.

Reliability

This section provides a summary of the results from the reliability analyses conducted on the Conners forms (see Rapid References 1.29 through 1.31 for an overview of these results, and see the relevant test manuals for detailed results). Reliability analyses included internal consistency, test-retest reliability, and inter-rater reliability.

The Conners forms were found to have high levels of **internal consistency.** The mean Cronbach's alpha for each rating scale, averaged across all scales and across all rater types, was:

- Conners 3 = .90
- Conners CBRS = .84
- Conners EC = .87

Test-retest reliability estimates were computed on a sample of participants who completed the Conners forms two times over a 2- to 4-week interval. Results indicated that all Conners forms have excellent temporal stability (all correlations significant, $p < .001$). The mean test-retest correlation for each rating scale, averaged across all scales and across all rater types, was:

- Conners 3 = .83
- Conners CBRS = .82
- Conners EC = .90

Results from the **inter-rater reliability** studies indicated that there was a great deal of consistency between multiple parents rating the same child and among multiple teachers rating the same child (all correlations significant,

≡ Rapid Reference 1.27

....

Psychometric Terms

Reliability Terms

Assessing the reliability of a rating scale means evaluating how consistently it measures what it was designed to measure. The reliability of an instrument is measured in a number of ways, including:

- **Internal Consistency:** how consistent the items on a scale are with each other in measuring the same concept. Often reported using Cronbach's alpha, which ranges from 0.0 to 1.0; higher numbers indicate higher internal consistency. Values from 0.70 to 0.79 are good, 0.80 to 0.89 very good, and 0.90 or higher excellent. This value typically increases as the number of items increases, so a larger scale is held to a higher standard.

- **Test-Retest Reliability:** the degree of similarity between two administrations of the same test to the same person. Usually tested with a short time between administrations (e.g., 2 to 4 weeks). Often reported with Pearson's r, ranging from −1.0 to 1.0; higher numbers indicate higher test-retest reliability. High test-retest reliability suggests greater confidence that changes in scores between two administrations are due to change in the child, rather than variation in the test. This value should be at least 0.60. Standards vary depending on the test-retest interval (i.e., time between two administrations) and construct (i.e., what is being tested). Relatively stable, trait-like constructs should have higher test-retest reliability, whereas dynamic, state-like constructs have lower test-retest reliability standards.

- **Inter-rater Reliability:** the degree of agreement between two parents' or two teachers' ratings of the same child. Often reported using Pearson's r, ranging from −1.0 to 1.0; higher numbers indicate higher inter-rater reliability. A value of 0.60 or higher is considered acceptable.

Validity Terms

Assessing the validity of a rating scale means evaluating how well it measures what it was designed to measure. The validity of an instrument is assessed in a number of ways, including:

- **Across-Informant Correlations:** the degree of similarity between two raters describing the same child when the raters are different types of raters (e.g., parent-to-teacher, parent-to-youth, teacher-to-youth). Often reported with Pearson's r, which ranges from −1.0 to 1.0; higher numbers indicate higher degree of similarity. Correlations should be moderate in size, as different raters provide different information (e.g., observed in different settings, at different times, in a different context)—if multiple raters provided the same information, there would be no reason to collect data from multiple informants in an assessment. Research shows that across-informant correlations for youth self-report versus parent- or teacher-report are often low.

- **Discriminative Validity:** the ability of a scale to differentiate between children from the general population versus a clinical group. Reported in terms of the following classification accuracy statistics; higher numbers indicate higher rates of accurate classification. Values ranging from 70 to 79 percent are good, 80 to 89 percent are very good, and 90 percent or higher are excellent. See also Rapid Reference 1.28.

  - **Overall Correct Classification Rate:** the percentage of children correctly classified on the basis of the scale score.

  - **Sensitivity:** the ability of a scale to detect clinical cases in a group, expressed as the percentage of children accurately classified as clinical (i.e., children who had a clinical diagnosis and who were classified as clinical on the basis of the scale score).

  - **Specificity:** the percentage of children accurately classified as being in the general population (i.e., children who did not have a clinical diagnosis and who were classified as belonging to the general population on the basis of the scale score).

- **Convergent Validity:** scores correlate with results from other tests of the same concept; reported with Pearson's r, which ranges from -1.0 to 1.0; larger correlations indicate scores are more convergent, or more similar. When two tests are scaled in opposite directions, large negative correlations indicate similarity (i.e., the Conners assessments are scaled such that high scores indicate big concerns; if compared with a test where high scores indicate very good functioning, a negative correlation would indicate agreement). There are many factors that impact this statistic, so it is difficult to give a general guideline. That being said, correlations of .20 to .34 (about 5 to 10 percent of the variance between the scores) suggests a mild relationship and therefore mild support for convergent validity, .35 to .49 (about 10 to 25 percent explained variance) suggests moderate support, and .50 and higher (more than 25 percent explained variance) suggests stronger support.

- **Divergent Validity:** scores do not correlate with results from other tests of different concepts; reported with Pearson's r, which ranges from -1.0 to 1.0; smaller correlations indicate scores are more divergent, or more dissimilar. As described above for convergent validity, either positive or negative correlations may indicate divergent validity depending on the direction of scaling. The important thing is that when a correlation is close to zero, it means very little agreement. Following the same caveats and rough guidelines from convergent validity above, correlations below .20 suggest weak relationship/correspondence, and therefore support for divergent validity.

Source: Information in this Rapid Reference was provided by Gill Sitarenios and Sara Rzepa (personal communication, July 6, 2009).

Rapid Reference 1.28

Understanding Discriminative Validity

		Group (according to site coordinator)	
		Clinical	General Population
Classification (according to score on Conners)	Clinical	Sensitivity Percentage of clinical cases identified as clinical by the score	Classification errors (if a general population case is classified as "clinical" by the score) Risk of calling a typical child "clinical"
	General Population	Classification errors (if a clinical case is classified as "general population" by the score) Risk of missing a clinical case	Specificity Percentage of general population cases correctly identified by the score

$p < .001$).[17] The mean inter-rater correlation for each rating scale, averaged across all scales and across parent and teacher ratings, was:

- Conners 3 = .78
- Conners CBRS = .73
- Conners EC = .74

Validity

This section provides a summary of the results from the validity analyses conducted on the Conners forms (see the relevant test manuals for detailed results). Validity analyses included across-informant correlations, discriminative validity, and convergent/divergent validity.

17. This statistic cannot be calculated for youth-youth, as only one person can complete the self-report form about a given child.

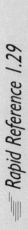

Rapid Reference 1.29

Summary of Conners 3 Reliability Coefficients

Reliability	Rater	Conners 3 Full-Length		Conners 3 Short		Conners 3AI	Conners 3GI	
		Mean	Range	Mean	Range	Value	Mean	Range
Internal Consistency (Cronbach's alpha)	Parent	.90	.83–.94	.89	.85–.92	.90	.85	.75–.90
	Teacher	.93	.77–.97	.91	.87–.94	.93	.87	.80–.91
	Self-Report	.86	.81–.92	.83	.77–.89	.80	—	—
Test-Retest (r)	Parent	.86	.72–.98	.86	.73–.97	.93	.87	.81–.91
	Teacher	.85	.78–.90	.78	.70–.83	.84	.79	.74–.82
	Self-Report	.77	.71–.83	.77	.74–.82	.88	—	—
Inter-Rater (r)	Parent-to-Parent	.82	.74–.94	.83	.79–.87	.85	.80	.78–.81
	Teacher-to-Teacher	.71	.52–.77	.77	.72–.83	.85	.76	.74–.80

Source: Information in this table was provided by the MHS Research and Development department.

Note: All rs significant, $p < .001$.

⟹ Rapid Reference 1.30

Summary of Conners CBRS Reliability Coefficients

Reliability	Rater	Conners CBRS		Conners Clinical Index	
		Mean	Range	Mean	Range
Internal Consistency (Cronbach's alpha)	Parent	.85	.73–.95	.79	.73–.85
	Teacher	.86	.69–.97	.76	.62–.83
	Self-Report	.86	.74–.96	.76	.73–.83
Test-Retest (r)	Parent	.85	.66–.96	.87	.83–.91
	Teacher	.86	.76–.96	.90	.83–.94
	Self-Report	.67	.56–.82	.82	.79–.85
Inter-Rater (r)	Parent to Parent	.74	.53–.89	.82	.55–.90
	Teacher to Teacher	.68	.50–.89	.79	.62–.88

Source: Information in this table was provided by the MHS Research and Development department.

Note: All rs significant, $p < .001$.

Because the different informants (i.e., Parent, Teacher, and Self-Report on the Conners 3 and Conners CBRS; Parent and Teacher/Childcare Provider on the Conners EC) all are rating similar constructs, similarity in scores across informants provides some support for the validity of the assessment. This similarity can be assessed with **across-informant correlations**. As expected, the across-informant correlations tended to be moderate in size (all correlations significant, $p < .001$; see Rapid Reference 1.32). The mean across-informant correlation for each rating scale, averaged across all scales and across all rater types, was:

- Conners 3 = .55
- Conners CBRS = .50
- Conners EC = .72

Rapid Reference 1.31

Summary of Conners EC Reliability Coefficients

Reliability	Rater	Conners EC Behavior (Full-Length)		Conners EC Developmental Milestones		Conners EC Behavior (Short)		Conners ECGI	
		Mean	Range	Mean	Range	Mean	Range	Mean	Range
Internal Consistency (Cronbach's alpha)	Parent	.86	.64–.94	.93	.89–.96	.79	.71–.87	.84	.75–.89
	Teacher/Childcare Provider	.89	.75–.96	.93	.91–.96	.84	.76–.94	.90	.86–.92
Test-Retest (r)	Parent	.87	.73–.92	.95	.93–.98	.83	.80–.88	.84	.78–.91
	Teacher/Childcare Provider	.93	.86–1.00	.94	.88–.97	.90	.80–.93	.92	.90–.95
Inter-Rater (r)	Parent to Parent	.72	.62–.85	.84	.77–.90	.65	.55–.73	.67	.62–.74

Source: Information in this table was provided by the MHS Research and Development department.

Note: All rs significant, $p < .001$. Inter-rater reliability data were not reported for the Conners EC Teacher/Childcare Provider form.

Rapid Reference 1.32

Summary of Across-Informant Correlations

| Form | Raters Being Compared | | | | | |
| | Parent-to-Teacher | | Parent-to-Child | | Teacher-to-Child | |
	Mean	Range	Mean	Range	Mean	Range
Conners 3 Full-Length	.60	.52–.67	.56	.49–.62	.48	.43–.56
Conners 3 Short	.59	.50–.66	.57	.50–.66	.49	.42–.57
Conners 3AI	Value = .61		Value = .57		Value = .51	
Conners 3GI	.56	.45–.61	—	—	—	—
Conners CBRS	.53	.29–.67	.51	.33–.61	.39	.20–.51
Conners CI	.58	.48–.63	.55	.50–.59	.48	.35–.54
Conners EC Behavior (Full-Length)	.72	.46–.87	—	—	—	—
Conners EC Developmental Milestones	.81	.77–.85	—	—	—	—
Conners EC Behavior (Short)	.66	.42–.79	—	—	—	—
Conners ECGI	.71	.62–.75	—	—	—	—

Source: Information in this table was provided by the MHS Research and Development department.

Note: All rs significant, $p < .001$.

Correlations of this magnitude indicate that, while there is some degree of consistency between ratings from different informants, there are also some differences in the information provided by different raters, underscoring the importance of obtaining ratings from multiple informants.

Data using the Conners assessments were collected for groups of children with clinical diagnoses. These clinical groups were compared to a general population group in order to provide evidence of the **discriminative validity** of the Conners assessments. See Rapid References 1.25 and 1.26 for a list of clinical groups in these analyses and for group sizes. Analyses of Covariance (ANCOVAs) were conducted to determine if there were significant differences in scores between the target clinical group and the general population, as well as between the target clinical group and the other clinical groups. The target clinical group was always the one most relevant to the scale (e.g., when examining the Learning Problems scale, the Learning Disorders group was the target clinical group). For every scale, scores for the target clinical group were significantly higher than scores for the general population group. Furthermore, in the vast majority of the analyses, scores for the target clinical group were significantly higher than scores for the other clinical groups. In other words, children in the target clinical group tended to have higher scores on the relevant Conners scale when compared with children in the general population sample or with children in a different clinical group.

Discriminant Function Analyses (DFAs) were conducted to determine if Conners scales could accurately predict group membership (i.e., whether a set of ratings came from the general population group or one of the clinical groups). The **overall correct classification rates, sensitivity** values, and **specificity** values for all scales were calculated (see relevant test manuals; see also summary of findings in Chapter 6). The Conners scale scores accurately classified most of the youth. The mean overall correct classification rate for each rating scale, averaged across all scales and across all rater types, was:

- Conners 3 = 75%
- Conners CBRS = 78%
- Conners EC = 86%

See Chapter 6 for more results from these analyses (ANCOVAs and DFAs); in brief, these results indicate that scales on the Conners assessments can help differentiate between clinical and general population cases *and* between the different clinical groups.

A group of parents, teachers, and youth[18] were asked to complete other measures of childhood psychopathology when they completed the Conners assessments (see Rapid Reference 1.33 for a list of these instruments and the

---

18. Self-report was only collected from 8- to 18-year-old children completing the Conners 3 and/or Conners CBRS.

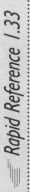

Rapid Reference 1.33

Instruments Used to Examine Convergent and Divergent Validity (and sample size for each comparison)

Comparison Measure	Conners 3	Conners CBRS	Conners EC
Achenbach System of Empirically-Based Assessment (ASEBA; Achenbach & Rescorla, 2001)	96	96	58
Behavior Assessment System for Children, Second Edition (BASC-2; Reynolds & Kamphaus, 2004)	365	365	88
Behavior Rating Inventory of Executive Function (BRIEF; Gioia, Isquith, Guy, & Kenworthy, 2000)	181	181	
Behavior Rating Inventory of Executive Function Preschool Version (BRIEF-P; Gioia, Espy, & Isquith, 2003)			186
Children's Depression Inventory (CDI; Kovacs, 2003)	—	480	
Multidimensional Anxiety Scale for Children (MASC; March, 1997)	—	248	
Vineland Adaptive Behavior Scales, Second Edition (Vineland-II; Sparrow, Cicchetti, & Balla, 2005)	—	—	98

Source: Information in this table was provided by the MHS Research and Development department.

Rapid Reference 1.34

Correlations Between Select Conners 3 Scales and Other Measures

Content Area	Conners 3 Scale	Other Measure	Parent	Teacher	Self-Report
Inattention and Executive Functioning	Inattention	ASEBA: Attention Problems	.92	.73	.96
	DSM-IV-TR ADHD Inattentive	BRIEF: Metacognition Index	.83	.97	—
	Executive Functioning	BRIEF: Metacognition Index	.81	.89	—
Hyperactivity and Impulsivity	Hyperactivity/Impulsivity	BASC-2 Adolescent: Hyperactivity	.77	.91	.62
	DSM-IV-TR ADHD Hyperactive-Impulsive	BRIEF: Inhibit	.78	.92	—
Defiance and Aggression	Defiance/Aggression	ASEBA: Aggressive Behavior	.93	.76	.69
	DSM-IV-TR Conduct Disorder	BASC-2 Adolescent: Conduct Problems	.78	.79	—
Social Problems	Peer Relations	ASEBA: Social Problems	.72	.84	—

Source: Information in this table was provided by the MHS Research and Development department.

Note: All rs significant, p < .05.

Correlations Between Select Conners CBRS Scales and Other Measures

Content Area	Conners CBRS Scale	Other Measure	Parent	Teacher	Self-Report
Emotional Distress, Depression, and Anxiety	Emotional Distress	BASC-2: Adolescent: Depression	.57	.67	.28
		BASC-2 Child: Anxiety	.67	.87	.66
		ASEBA: Anxious/Depressed	.85	.53	.78
	DSM-IV-TR Major Depressive Episode	BASC-2 Child: Depression	.61	.64	.59
		BASC-2: Adolescent: Depression	.62	.71	.38
		ASEBA: Anxious/Depressed	.83	.43	.71
		CDI: Total Score	.57	.48	.55
	DSM-IV-TR Generalized Anxiety Disorder	BASC-2 Child: Anxiety	.61	.62	.67
		ASEBA: Anxious/Depressed	.83	.51	.71
	DSM-IV-TR Social Phobia	MASC: Social Anxiety	.68	—	.62

Category	Construct	Measure			
Physical Symptoms	Physical Symptoms	BASC-2 Adolescent: Somatization	.78	.59	.59
		MASC: Physical Symptoms	.49	—	.57
Pervasive Developmental Disorders	DSM-IV-TR Autistic Disorder	BASC-2 Adolescent: Developmental Social Disorders	.69	.51	—
	DSM-IV-TR Asperger's Disorder	BASC-2 Adolescent: Developmental Social Disorders	.67	.54	—
Defiance and Aggression	Defiant/Aggressive Behaviors	ASEBA: Aggressive Behavior	.96	.72	.60
	DSM-IV-TR Conduct Disorder	BASC-2 Adolescent: Conduct Problems	.71	.80	—
		ASEBA: Aggressive Behavior	.93	.61	.55
	DSM-IV-TR Oppositional Defiant Disorder	BASC-2 Child: Anger Control	.61	.79	—
		ASEBA: Aggressive Behavior	.96	.73	.71

Content Area	Conners CBRS Scale	Other Measure	Parent	Teacher	Self-Report
Inattention and Hyperactivity	DSM-IV-TR ADHD Inattentive	ASEBA: Attention Problems	.91	.72	.79
		BRIEF: Metacognition Index	.80	.96	—
	DSM-IV-TR ADHD Hyperactive-Impulsive	BASC-2 Adolescent: Hyperactivity	.81	.78	.52
Social Problems	Social Problems	BASC-2 Child: Withdrawal	.68	.73	—
		ASEBA: Social Problems	.63	.69	—

Source: Information in this table was provided by the MHS Research and Development department.

Note: All *r*s significant, $p < .05$.

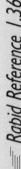 *Rapid Reference 1.36*

Correlations Between Select Conners EC Scales and Other Measures

Conners EC Scale		Other Measure	Parent	Teacher/ Childcare Provider
Behavior Scales	Inattention/ Hyperactivity	ASEBA: Attention Deficit/ Hyperactivity	.80	.92
		BRIEF-P: Global Executive Composite	.77	.81
	Defiant/Aggressive Behaviors	BASC-2-P: Aggression	.87	.91
		ASEBA: Oppositional Defiant	.91	.85
	Social Functioning/ Atypical Behaviors	BASC-2-P: Developmental Social Disorders	.71	.80
	Anxiety	ASEBA: Anxiety (DSM-Oriented)	.80	.59

Conners EC Scale	Other Measure	Parent	Teacher/ Childcare Provider
Behavior Scales (continued)	BASC-2-P: Depression	.87	.90
Mood and Affect	ASEBA: Affective	.69	.83
Physical Symptoms	ASEBA: Somatic Complaints	.60	.86
Developmental Milestone Scales Adaptive Skills	Vineland-II: Adaptive Behavior Composite[a]	-.37	-.68
Communication	Vineland-II: Communication[a]	-.51	-.73
Motor Skills	Vineland-II: Motor Skills[a]	-.43	-.55
Play/Curiosity	Vineland-II: Play/Leisure[a]	-.57	-.58
Pre-Academic/Cognitive	Vineland-II: Academic[a]	—	-.77

[a] Negative correlations with the Vineland-II scales are expected because higher scores on the Vineland-II indicate better functioning, in contrast to higher scores on the Conners EC, which indicate problematic functioning.

Source: Information in this table was provided by the MHS Research and Development department.

Note: All rs significant, $p < .05$.

number of raters who completed each pair of forms). Results from these other instruments were compared with results from the Conners assessments to examine **convergent validity** and **divergent validity**.

Overall, the correlations converged and diverged in a meaningful way. The correlations between scales that assess similar constructs tended to be moderate to strong in size, while the correlations between scales that did not assess similar constructs tended to be smaller in magnitude. See Rapid References 1.34 through 1.36 for examples of these findings.

COMPREHENSIVE REFERENCES

The Conners 3, Conners CBRS, and Conners EC each has a comprehensive manual published by Multi-Health Systems, Inc. (MHS). Each manual provides important information about the conceptual framework of each rating scale, as well as guidelines for administration, scoring, and interpretation of these scales. Suggestions for planning and monitoring intervention and applied case studies are provided in each manual. The manuals also contain very detailed information about statistical analyses and standardization samples. See Rapid Reference 1.1 for a summary of key information for these three rating scales. See Rapid References 1.13, 1.17, and 1.22 for details of each Conners assessment (also Rapid References 1.14, 1.18, and 1.23).

 TEST YOURSELF

1. **Which of the following Conners assessment tools include items about behavioral, emotional, social, and cognitive functioning?** *Mark all that apply.*
   (a) Conners 3
   (b) Conners CBRS
   (c) Conners EC

2. **Which of the following statements are *true* about responsible assessment?** *Mark all that apply.*
   (a) Responsible assessment should include multiple modalities.
   (b) Responsible assessment relies on information from more than one informant.
   (c) Responsible assessment can be conducted with a single, well-constructed rating scale such as the Conners assessments.
   (d) Responsible assessment includes data gathered from more than one setting.

3. **The Conners 3 and Conners CBRS have self-report forms that can be completed by children ages 8 to 18 years.**
   True or False?

4. Which of the following clinical groups is *not* represented in the Conners Clinical Index?

(a) Attention-Deficit and Disruptive Behavior Disorders

(b) Anxiety Disorders

(c) Learning and Language Disorders

(d) Mood Disorders

(e) Pervasive Developmental Disorders

5. Age and gender impact interpretation of scores for the Conners assessments, so it is recommended that age- and gender-specific norms be used.

True or False?

Answers: 1. a, b, c; 2. a, b, d; 3. True; 4. e; 5. True.

Two

ADMINISTRATION OF THE CONNERS ASSESSMENTS

Jenni Pitkanen
Elizabeth P. Sparrow

A
dministration of rating scales is somewhat less strict than administration of individual ability or achievement tests; however, there are a few key principles that must be followed for results to be interpretable. This chapter reviews *recommended* administration procedures and tips for the Conners assessments. All *required* administration procedures are highlighted in Caution and Don't Forget boxes. This chapter begins with practical administration issues, including who can administer these rating scales, who can complete them, testing materials, amount of time required, and testing environment. Next, differences in the various forms available for the Conners assessments are reviewed, with suggestions of when to use each version. Guidelines for interactions with the rater are discussed. Finally, information for modified administrations of the Conners assessments is provided.

PRACTICAL DETAILS: PERSON, MATERIALS, TIME, AND PLACE

Appropriate Administrators

Administration of the Conners assessments includes handing the selected form to the rater, explaining the instructions, answering questions about the instructions, collecting the form, and verifying completion of the form. Formal clinical training and background are not required for the person who physically administers these rating scales; however, she must be familiar with the administration guidelines described in this chapter and should have access to a trained clinician if difficult questions arise during form completion. The administration guidelines described in this chapter were developed to support valid ratings with minimal bias, as well as compliance with ethical and legal guidelines.

CAUTION

. . . .

Follow Standardized Administration Procedures

- Administration guidelines in this chapter should be followed closely.
- Modifications could create rater bias or otherwise invalidate results from the Conners assessments.

Appropriate Raters

Both the Conners 3 and the Conners CBRS have forms for parents, teachers, and youth. Parents and teachers can rate youth aged 6 to 18 years, and self-report ratings can be obtained from youth aged 8 to 18 years. The Conners EC has Parent and Teacher/Childcare Provider[1] forms that can be used to rate children ages 2 to 6 years. Parents are generally able to observe a child's behavior in both home and social settings, while teachers are an important source of information about the child's functioning at school or daycare. Self-reports provide the youth's own perceptions and feelings about her behavior across multiple contexts, including social settings where parents and teachers may not be able to observe him.

For all of the Conners assessments, the Parent form may be completed by parental figures, even if they are not biologic parents. This includes adoptive and foster parents. In some families, another person may serve the role of the parent (e.g., multigenerational homes in which a grandmother has primary responsibility for raising the child, even though she is not legally his guardian). Regardless of biologic relationship or legal status (i.e., legal guardian), the parent form can and should be rated by the people who are most familiar with a child's functioning in the home and community settings. Ideally, parent data are collected from more than one parent figure. If the child spends significant time in more than one home, gather information from at least one parent in each home setting. This provides you with useful information to understand what is happening in the home setting and can help identify contextual factors when different responses are obtained.

---

1. For simplicity and ease of reading, the Conners EC Teacher/Childcare Provider form will be referred to as a Teacher form throughout this book.

The Teacher form can be completed by any person who observes the child in a peer setting. The Conners EC normative data were collected from pre-academic preschool teachers as well as childcare providers in full-time daycare settings. The Conners 3 and Conners CBRS normative data used ratings completed by teachers in a traditional school setting, but these ratings were not limited to teachers of "academic" subjects such as math and reading. For many children, it is very informative to gather data from "non-academic" subject teachers, including art, music, and physical education, as the child may show different behaviors and interactions in different settings. In some instances, you may wish to collect data from other "teachers," including sports coaches and religious instructors. In addition to subject matter and class structure, you may want to consider gathering data from teachers who interact with the child at different times of day and with different groups of peers. As long as the person knows the child in an instructional context involving a group of peers, he will be able to provide meaningful information for your consideration. As discussed below, remember that a teacher cannot complete a Conners assessment in the first month of school, as he did not observe the child in the previous month (even if he was familiar with the child from other school years).

Obtaining parent, teacher, and self-report data will provide a comprehensive view of the child's functioning in multiple contexts and will help establish the pervasiveness of problems across different settings. Ratings from more than one parent can corroborate each other and help verify what is occurring in the home/family context. When parental responses substantially differ, inquiries regarding those differences can be very helpful in assessing the child. Collecting ratings from more than one teacher can help determine whether the child is consistently experiencing problems across different classroom settings. The child's behavior may vary across teachers due to issues such as the level of structure provided by the teacher or the child's interest and aptitude for the subject. For example, a student with math disability may show more behavioral issues in a math class compared with an English class.

DON'T FORGET

Multiple Informants

Collecting ratings from more than one parent and from multiple teachers helps determine the consistency of the youth's behaviors across different raters and settings.

Every rater must meet three key requirements:

1. **Length of acquaintance:** All of the Conners forms[2] inquire about behavior in the last month, so it is important that that rater has known the child for at least that time period. This requirement is especially pertinent to teacher ratings in the beginning of the school year. Teacher forms should be administered at least 1 to 2 months after the school year has begun in order to give the teacher an opportunity to observe the child.

2. **Reading level:** The rater should have a reading ability that meets or exceeds the minimum reading level requirements of the forms (see Rapid Reference 1.1). The reading levels are expressed in terms of grade levels. For example, because the estimated reading level of the Conners 3 Self-Report form is third grade, it is expected that the average third grader can comprehend items on the form.

3. **Motivation:** It is important that the rater is motivated to complete the rating scale thoroughly and accurately. Ratings by unmotivated or hurried respondents may provide an inaccurate description of the child and can have limited validity.

DON'T FORGET

No Time Frame Specified for Conners EC Developmental Milestones

The Conners EC Developmental Milestone scales do not specify "in the past month" as they are intended to capture overall development—even skills that were mastered prior to the past month. Regardless, it is still important that a rater is familiar with the child's functioning for at least a month.

Testing Methods and Materials

The Conners assessments can be administered in paper-and-pencil format or online. Your preferred method of scoring is a consideration when choosing administration format. Any version of the rating scales can be scored with the software or online options. If you need to hand-score a Conners form, you must

---

2. With the exception of the Developmental Milestones section of the Conners EC; however, it is still important that a teacher has observed the child for at least a month before rating him on the Conners EC.

CAUTION
Rater Requirements

• Raters must have the opportunity to observe a child at least 1 month before completing a Conners assessment. This is particularly relevant at the beginning of the school year, as teachers must have the chance to get to know and observe a student before completing the rating scale.

• Certain reading levels are required (see also "Modified Administration: Reading Aloud" in this chapter).

• The rater must be motivated to provide accurate information without rushing.

use a QuikScore™ form. See Rapid Reference 2.1 for an overview of administration options, including which scoring options are available for each administration method. See also Chapter 3 for further information on scoring issues. See Rapid Reference 2.2 for a list of what to remember when preparing to administer the Conners assessments.

DON'T FORGET
QuikScore Form Required for Hand-Scoring

Use a QuikScore form if you need to hand-score the Conners assessments. These are only available for the Conners 3 (all forms), Conners CI form, and Conners ECGI form.

For online administration, you can offer computer access on location or send the information to the rater by e-mail. Provide a notepad for the rater's comments and questions as she responds to the online items. See the test manual for details regarding computer requirements for online administration of the Conners assessments. In brief, Internet access and an updated Internet browser are required.

CAUTION
Supervise Use of Your Computer

If the rater is completing the online form in your office, you must supervise his use of your computer so that he does not access confidential information. It is possible to minimize the Internet browser and view your other files; also, the rater can use the "Back" button to return to the list of saved Conners assessments. If you are concerned that a rater might explore these options, generate an e-mail link for the rater or use paper-and-pencil administration.

Rapid Reference 2.1

Comparison of Administration Options

	Online[a]	QuikScore form	Response form
Materials	Computer with Internet access	QuikScore form, pen, clipboard or table	Response form, pen, clipboard or table
Availability	Can be used for all forms of the Conners assessments	Available for forms that can be hand-scored (i.e., all forms of Conners 3, Conners CI, and Conners ECGI)	Can be used for all forms of the Conners assessments
Scoring Options	Online[b]	Online Software (USB drive) Hand-scoring	Online Software (USB drive)
Cost[c]	Pay per use[d] (includes either online administration OR printing the assessment for paper-pencil administration)	Purchased in packs of 25 forms	Purchased in packs of 25 forms

Convenience	Most versatile; always have the correct form available; only purchase what you need. Can generate an e-mail link to send to rater; can also print the form for completion in paper-pencil format. Can access results from any computer with an Internet connection.	Very few materials required; do not need a computer, Internet connection, or printer. Scoring templates included in the QuikScore form	Very few materials required; do not need a computer, Internet connection, or printer to administer
Limitations	Must have Internet access	May end up with unused forms	May end up with unused forms

[a] Note that the Conners software packages (USB drives) are for scoring, not administration.

[b] Technically you could administer the Conners assessment online, then transfer rater responses into your software program or a QuikScore form, but the most logical choice is to use online scoring with online administration.

[c] Cost of administration, not including cost of scoring.

[d] Online subscription model is also available upon request, including unlimited uses of the Conners assessments for administration and scoring. Contact MHS for additional information.

≡ *Rapid Reference 2.2*

Preparing to Administer the Test

- Allocate sufficient time to complete the scale in one sitting.
- Provide a quiet, comfortable, distraction free setting.
- Gather required materials
  - Paper-and-pencil administration
    - Conners assessment form
    - Smooth writing surface (table or a clipboard)
    - Pencil or a pen
    - Extra paper for questions or comments
  - Online administration
    - Computer with an Internet connection
    - Extra paper for questions or comments

Testing Time

The administrator should allow time to explain instructions to the rater. Typical completion times for each form are provided in Rapid References 1.13, 1.17, and 1.22. It is important to note that completion times may vary from one rater to the next. Individual factors such as reading disabilities, limited literacy, or other issues can prolong administration time. There is no time limit for completing the assessment, although it is recommended that all the items be completed in one sitting. If too much time passes in between the administration of sections of a form, it may be necessary to ask the rater to complete the form again as it is important to collect data about the same time period for all the items. Unlike many achievement or intelligence measures, the Conners assessments do not employ separate age-based starting points or performance-based discontinue rules. In practical terms this means that all the test items should be completed each time the rating scale is administered.

DON'T FORGET

Time Limits for Completing Conners Assessments

There is no time limit for completing the Conners assessments, although each form should be completed in one sitting. Responding to the form over many days could limit interpretation of the results.

Testing Environment

Ideally, the Conners assessments are administered individually and at your location. The forms can be completed remotely (e.g., online or by mail). The forms can also be administered in a group setting (e.g., in a screening situation; see Modified Administration: Group Administration in this chapter). In each of these situations the testing environment should be quiet, comfortable, and with minimal distractions.

SELECTING THE RIGHT FORM

Choosing the Rating Scale: Conners 3, Conners CBRS, or Conners EC

It is important to choose a version of the Conners assessments that will provide the best information to answer referral questions, understand the child, and make appropriate recommendations. The child's age, his setting, the referral questions, and the purpose of the assessment can guide your choice of rating scale. See Rapid Reference 2.3 for a graphic representation of these decisions.

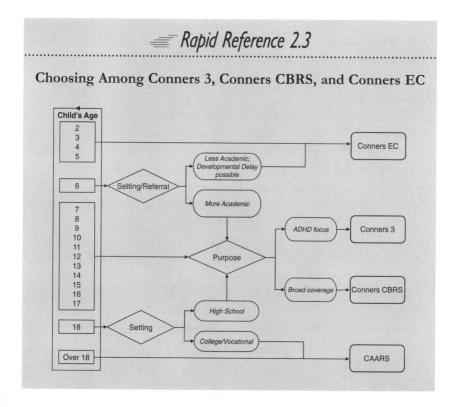

≡ Rapid Reference 2.3

Choosing Among Conners 3, Conners CBRS, and Conners EC

Age, Setting, and Referral Questions

The child's age is a concrete way to begin the decision among the Conners 3, Conners CBRS, and Conners EC. Young children (2 to 6 years old) can be rated with one of the Conners EC forms. The Conners 3 and/or Conners CBRS are appropriate for use with school-aged children (6 to 18 years old). Notice the overlap between the measures for 6-year-old children. The decision between measures for a 6-year-old child is based on factors such as setting and referral question(s). The Conners EC contains developmentally appropriate items for children in a preschool or daycare setting or for a child who is still being cared for at home. When referral questions suggest possible delays in development, or the child is not yet in a setting with academic demands, the Conners EC is more appropriate. The Conners 3 and the Conners CBRS are focused on the assessment of a school-aged youth and include items with academic content (e.g., reading, spelling, math). For a child who is already in an academic setting, such as first grade, or a child who has many skills that appear age-appropriate, the Conners 3 and/or Conners CBRS will likely provide more useful information.

Although adult assessment tools are not included in this book, note that a similar overlap occurs at 18 years old between the Conners 3 and the Conners Adult ADHD Rating Scale (CAARS). Setting is a primary consideration in this choice, as the CAARS items reflect a broader range of adult settings, including employment and relationships.

Purpose of Assessment

After considering age (and setting/referral issues for overlapping ages), the purpose of assessment is a critical factor in selecting among the Conners assessments. The Conners 3 is recommended for inclusion in the following test batteries:

- Initial evaluation when the referral question includes features of ADHD
- Re-evaluation following treatment for ADHD and related issues (to assess progress in targeted areas and monitor for emergence of other symptoms)
- Screening evaluation to determine if further consideration should be given to the possibility of ADHD, ODD, or CD
- Follow-up evaluation when the Conners CBRS indicates that more thorough assessment of ADHD and associated issues must be pursued (e.g., when the DSM-IV-TR Symptom Scale for ADHD is elevated)

The Conners CBRS is a useful tool to include in the following situations:

- Initial evaluation when the referral question is vague or reflects a broad range of issues

- Re-evaluation to help determine progress in treatment and to see if new issues have emerged
- Screening evaluation to determine areas of need for a student
- Follow-up evaluation when the Conners 3 suggests further investigation (e.g., when the Anxiety and/or Depression Screener items are elevated)

≡ Don't Forget

Age Range and Content

Conners EC: 2–6 years old, wide range of developmental issues
Conners 3: 6–18 years old, focus on ADHD and related issues
Conners CBRS: 6–18 years old, comprehensive coverage of behavioral, emotional, social, and academic issues

---

Selecting the Form

After deciding to use the Conners 3, Conners CBRS, or Conners EC, several factors impact choice of form, including: rater's primary language, available time, rater motivation, content, and purpose of the assessment. Forms differ by language, length, and content.

Language

When possible, choose a translation of the rating scale that will reduce language barriers for the rater. Parent and self-report forms of the Conners assessments are available in English and Spanish. Conners 3 and Conners CBRS Teacher forms are available in English; Conners EC Teacher/Childcare Provider forms are available in English and Spanish. If other languages are needed, it is worth contacting the publisher as additional translations may become available (see Rapid Reference 1.1).

Length

The full-length versions of the Conners assessments have the most in-depth coverage of content. There are times, however, when it is not reasonable to ask a rater to complete the full-length form. This is particularly true when a rater is asked to complete the form repeatedly, as is the case when monitoring response to treatment every month. There are also times when a rater may not be willing to spend more than 5 or 10 minutes on a form. When motivation is a concern, it may be better to complete a short version of the rating scale rather than obtain an incomplete full-length version. The rater's time and motivation can be important factors to consider when selecting a form to use.

DON'T FORGET

Selecting a Conners Assessment

Consider the child's age, setting, referral questions, and purpose of the assessment when selecting the most appropriate Conners assessment. The rater's primary language, available time, rater motivation, and content can guide your choice of forms.

Content

Each of the Conners assessment forms has slightly different content, which impacts the type of information available for interpretation after scoring. The full-length forms provide the most comprehensive information, and it is recommended that they be used in all initial evaluations and comprehensive re-evaluations. The short forms and the index forms are ideal for screening or for follow-up purposes (e.g., in intervention monitoring situations or focused re-evaluations). See Rapid References 2.4 through 2.6 for a summary of the depth and breadth of each form (i.e., the number of items per scale and the scales included on each form).

INTERACTING WITH THE RATER

The Conners manuals describe a standardized administration procedure that should be followed, particularly when administration is completed by an unlicensed individual. This procedure includes information that must be discussed before administration of the rating scale, instructions for completion of the rating scale, responding to questions about the rating scale, debriefing and thanking the rater, and recording observations/comments.

Before Administration

1. Before completing the assessment, make sure you have obtained *informed consent* from the child's parent or legal guardian.
2. Give a *general description* of the form using nonspecific language (e.g., "a rating scale about things that can happen in young children" [Conners EC]

(*continued on page 97*)

Rapid Reference 2.4

Conners 3 Content (including item count for each scale)

Age Range:	Parent 6–18 Years				Teacher 6–18 Years				Self-Report 8–18 Years		
Form:	Full	Short	ADHD Index	Global Index	Full	Short	ADHD Index	Global Index	Full	Short	ADHD Index
Conners 3 Content Scales											
Inattention	10	5	—	—	10	5	—	—	11	6	—
Hyperactivity/ Impulsivity	14	6	—	—	18	6	—	—	14	5	—
Learning Problems/ Executive Functioning[a]	—	—	—	—	16	6	—	—	—	—	—
Learning Problems	9	5	—	—	6	—	—	—	8	5	—
Executive Functioning	9	5	—	—	7	—	—	—	—	—	—
Defiance/ Aggression	14	5	—	—	18	5	—	—	15	6	—
Peer Relations	6	5	—	—	7	5	—	—	—	—	—
Family Relations	—	—	—	—	—	—	—	—	8	5	—

(continued)

| | Parent 6–18 Years | | | | Teacher 6–18 Years | | | | Self-Report 8–18 Years | | |
Age Range: Form:	Full	Short	ADHD Index	Global Index	Full	Short	ADHD Index	Global Index	Full	Short	ADHD Index
DSM-IV-TR Symptom Scales											
ADHD Inattentive[b]	10	—	—	—	10	—	—	—	11	—	—
ADHD Hyperactive-Impulsive[b]	11	—	—	—	11	—	—	—	11	—	—
Conduct Disorder	15	—	—	—	13	—	—	—	14	—	—
Oppositional Defiant Disorder	8	—	—	—	8	—	—	—	8	—	—
Screener Items											
Anxiety	4	—	—	—	4	—	—	—	4	—	—
Depression	4	—	—	—	4	—	—	—	4	—	—
Indices											
Conners 3 ADHD Index	10	—	10	—	10	—	10	—	10	—	10
Conners 3 Global Index	10	—	—	10	10	—	—	10	—	—	—
- Restless-Impulsive	7			7	6			6			
- Emotional Lability	3			3	4			4			

Category	Scale											
Critical Items	Severe Conduct	6	—	—	—	7	—	—	—	6	—	—
Validity Scales	Positive Impression	6	6	—	—	6	6	—	—	6	6	—
	Negative Impression	6	6	—	—	6	6	—	—	6	6	—
	Inconsistency Index	10pr	—	—	—	10pr	—	—	—	10pr	—	—
Impairment Items	Academic	—	—	—	—	—	—	—	—	—	—	—
	Social	—	—	—	—	—	—	—	—	—	—	—
	Home	—	—	—	—	—	—	—	—	—	—	—
Additional Questions	Other Concerns	—	—	—	—	—	—	—	—	—	—	—
	Strengths/Skills	—	—	—	—	—	—	—	—	—	—	—
	Total Number of Items[c]	110	45	10	10	115	41	10	10	99	41	10

Sources: Adapted from Conners 3rd edition manual (Multi-Health Systems, 2008) and Conners 3 Interpretive Update (Multi-Health Systems, 2009).

Note: "pr" indicates pairs of items.

[a] Some items are unique to the complete Learning Problems/Executive Functioning scale and do not appear on either subscale.

[b] The information from these two scales can be used when considering a possible diagnosis of ADHD, Combined type.

[c] The total number of items does not equal the sum of items across all scales, as some items are used on more than one scale.

Rapid Reference 2.5

Conners CBRS Content (including item count for each scale)

Form:	Conners CBRS-P	Conners CBRS-T	Conners CBRS-SR	Conners CI (P, T, SR)
Age Range:	6–18 years	6–18 years	8–18 years	6–18 years (P&T) 8–18 years (SR)
Conners CBRS Content Scales				
Emotional Distress[a]	37	34	38	—
- Upsetting Thoughts	6	—	—	—
- Worrying	9	—	—	—
- Social Problems	7	—	—	—
- Upsetting Thoughts/Physical Symptoms	—	14	—	—
- Social Anxiety	—	6	—	—
- Separation Fears	—	5	—	—
Defiant/Aggressive Behaviors	21	34	31	—
Academic Difficulties: Total	17	21	13	—
- Language	10	14	—	—
- Math	5	5	—	—

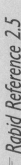

Conners CBRS Content Scales (continued)	Hyperactivity	—	8	—	—
	Hyperactivity/Impulsivity	11	—	11	—
	Social Problems	(7)[b]	11	—	—
	Separation Fears	6	(5)[b]	7	—
	Perfectionistic and Compulsive Behaviors	9	8	—	—
	Violence Potential Indicator	29	29	28	—
	Physical Symptoms	12	6	12	—
	ADHD Inattentive[c]	10	10	11	—
	ADHD Hyperactive-Impulsive[c]	11	11	11	—
	Conduct Disorder	15	13	14	—
	Oppositional Defiant Disorder	8	8	8	—
DSM-IV-TR Symptom Scales	Major Depressive Episode[d]	15	12	15	—
	Manic Episode[d]	10	9	9	—
	Generalized Anxiety Disorder	14	11	13	—
	Separation Anxiety Disorder	9	6	9	—
	Social Phobia	7	7	6	—

(continued)

Form:	Conners CBRS-P	Conners CBRS-T	Conners CBRS-SR	Conners CI (P, T, SR)
Age Range:	6–18 years	6–18 years	8–18 years	6–18 years (P&T) 8–18 years (SR)
DSM-IV-TR Symptom Scales (continued)				
Obsessive-Compulsive Disorder	6	6	6	—
Autistic Disorder	13	13	—	—
Asperger's Disorder	4	9	—	—
Indices				
Conners Clinical Index	24	24	24	24
- Disruptive Behavior Disorder Indicator	5	5	5	5
- Learning and Language Disorder Indicator	5	5	5	5
- Mood Disorder Indicator	5	5	5	5
- Anxiety Disorder Indicator	5	5	5	5
- ADHD Indicator	5	5	5	5
Critical Items				
Severe Conduct	11	11	8	—
Self-Harm	6	6	6	—
Other Clinical Indicators				
Bullying Perpetration	1	1	1	—
Bullying Victimization	1	1	1	—
Enuresis/Encopresis	1	1	—	—

Other Clinical Indicators (continued)	Panic Attack	3	3	3	—
	Pervasive Developmental Disorder	—	—	3	—
	Pica	1	1	1	—
	Posttraumatic Stress Disorder	1	1	2	—
	Specific Phobia	1	1	1	—
	Substance Use	4	4	4	—
	Tics	2	2	2	—
	Trichotillomania	1	1	1	—
Validity Scales	Positive Impression	6	6	6	—
	Negative Impression	6	6	6	—
	Inconsistency Index	10pr	10pr	10pr	—
Impairment Items	Academic	1	1	1	—
	Social	1	1	1	—
	Home	1	—	1	—

(continued)

Form:	Conners CBRS-P	Conners CBRS-T	Conners CBRS-SR	Conners CI (P, T, SR)
Age Range:	6–18 years	6–18 years	8–18 years	6–18 years (P&T) 8–18 years (SR)
Additional Questions	Other Concerns	—	—	—	—
	Strengths/Skills	—	—	—	—
Total Number of Items[e]	203	204	179	24

Sources: Adapted from Conners Comprehensive Behavior Rating Scales manual (Multi-Health Systems, 2008) and Conners CBRS Interpretive Update (Multi-Health Systems, 2009).

Note: "pr" indicates pairs of items.
[a] Some items are unique to the complete Emotional Distress scale and do not appear on any subscale.
[b] Subscale of Emotional Distress.
[c] The information from these two scales can be used when considering a possible diagnosis of ADHD, Combined type.
[d] The information from these two scales can be used when considering a possible Mixed Episode.
[e] The total number of items does not equal the sum of items across all scales, as some items are used on more than one scale.

Rapid Reference 2.6

Conners EC Content (including item count for each scale)

Age Range:		Parent 2–6 years old					Teacher 2–6 years old				
Form:*		Full	BEH	DM	BEH (S)	ECGI	Full	BEH	DM	BEH (S)	ECGI
Behavior Scales	Inattention/Hyperactivity	16	16	—	6	—	20	20	—	6	—
	Defiant/Aggressive Behaviors[a]	19	19	—	6	—	18	18	—	6	—
	- Defiance/Temper	11	11	—	—	—	7	7	—	—	—
	- Aggression	8	8	—	—	—	11	11	—	—	—
	Social Functioning/ Atypical Behaviors[b]	27	27	—	6	—	31	31	—	6	—
	- Social Functioning	13	13	—	—	—	16	16	—	—	—
	- Atypical Behaviors	13	13	—	—	—	11	11	—	—	—
	Anxiety	16	16	—	6	—	14	14	—	6	—
	Mood and Affect	11	11	—	6	—	10	10	—	6	—

(continued)

	Parent					Teacher				
Age Range:	2–6 years old					2–6 years old				
Form:*	Full	BEH	DM	BEH (S)	ECGI	Full	BEH	DM	BEH (S)	ECGI
Behavior Scales (continued)										
Physical Symptoms	11	11	—	6	—	8	8	—	6	—
- Sleep Problems	5	5	—	—	—	—	—	—	—	—
Developmental Milestone Scales										
Adaptive Skills	17	—	17	—	—	12	—	12	—	—
Communication	17	—	17	—	—	17	—	17	—	—
Motor Skills	17	—	17	—	—	17	—	17	—	—
Play	5	—	5	—	—	5	—	5	—	—
Pre-Academic/Cognitive	19	—	19	—	—	19	—	19	—	—
Index										
Conners EC Global Index	10	10	—	—	10	10	10	—	—	10
- Restless-Impulsive	7	7			7	6	6			6
- Emotional Lability	3	3			3	4	4			4

Category											
Other Clinical Indicators	Cruelty to Animals	—	—	—	—	—	—	—	—	—	—
	Fire setting	—	—	—	—	—	—	—	—	—	—
	Perfectionism	—	—	2	2	—	—	—	—	—	—
	Pica	—	—	—	—	—	—	—	—	—	—
	Posttraumatic Stress Disorder	—	—	—	—	—	—	—	—	—	—
	Self Injury	—	—	—	—	—	—	—	—	—	—
	Specific Phobia	—	—	—	—	—	—	—	—	—	—
	Stealing	—	—	—	—	—	—	—	—	—	—
	Tics	—	—	2	2	—	—	—	2	2	—
	Trichotillomania	—	—	—	—	—	—	—	—	—	—
Validity Scales	Positive Impression	—	6	6	6	—	6	—	6	6	—
	Negative Impression	—	6	6	6	—	6	—	6	6	—
	Inconsistency Index	—	—	10pr	10pr	—	—	—	10pr	10pr	—
Impairment Items	Learning/Pre—Academic	—	—	—	—	—	—	—	—	—	—
	Peer Interactions	—	—	—	—	—	—	—	—	—	—
	Home	—	—	—	—	—	—	—	—	—	—

(continued)

Age Range:		Parent					Teacher				
		2–6 years old					2–6 years old				
Form:*		Full	BEH	DM	BEH (S)	ECGI	Full	BEH	DM	BEH (S)	ECGI
Additional Questions	Other Concerns	—	—	—	—	—	—	—	—	—	—
	Strengths/Skills	—	—	—	—	—	—	—	—	—	—
Total Number of Items[c]		190	115	80	49	10	186	116	74	48	10

Source: Adapted from *Conners Early Childhood manual* (Multi-Health Systems, 2009).

Note: "pr" indicates pairs of items.

* Full = Full-length; BEH = Behavior; DM = Developmental Milestones; BEH(S) = Behavior (Short); ECGI = Conners Early Childhood Global Index.

[a] Some items are unique to the complete Defiant/Aggressive Behaviors scale and do not appear on either subscale.

[b] Some items are unique to the complete Social Functioning/Atypical Behaviors scale and do not appear on either subscale.

[c] The total number of items does not equal the sum of items across all scales, as some items are used on more than one scale.

or " . . . in school-aged children and adolescents" [Conners 3 or Conners CBRS]). The rater should not be told the specific purpose of the scale (e.g., to assess ADHD), as this may bias her responses.

3. Tell the rater the *reason* you are asking her to complete the rating scale and how the results will be used. For example, the rater can be told that her responses are combined with other information and will be used to help the child. In order to obtain honest and accurate responses, it is important to tell the rater that there are no right or wrong answers and that only the opinion of the person completing the form is sought. Remind the rater that she should not compare the child's behavior with other children. She does not need to consider whether a behavior occurred more or less than other children because the scoring procedure takes the youth's age into account.

4. Inform the rater about *confidentiality.* The rater needs to know whether the results will be shared with anyone. Being open about how the test results are shared is an ethical requirement. It is also an important aspect of positive interactions with the rater.

Giving Instructions

After explaining the purpose of the assessment, review *instructions* for how to complete the form. The general instructions below apply to paper-and-pencil administration and online administration. See Rapid Reference 2.7 for specific details that apply to online completion.

1. Tell the rater to complete all of the demographic information on the front page of the form.

2. Ask the rater to think about the past month and to mark how often a behavior was observed in the child being rated. The items can also be answered in terms of how well each item describes the child in the past month. If the child has displayed a certain behavior in the past, but not in the last month, the item should be rated as 0 ("Not true at all (Never, Seldom)") because the Conners assessments are intended to describe recent behavior. It may be helpful to highlight the phrase "in the past month" on the form.[3]

3. Review the available response options for each item (see Rapid Reference 2.8).

---

3. Note that a time period is not specified on the Conners EC Developmental Milestones form.

4. Emphasize that one response must be marked for every item. If the rater has not observed a particular behavior, she should give her best estimate. If an item is skipped, or more than one response is marked for an item, it may be difficult or impossible to score parts of the form.

5. If using a QuikScore form, ask the rater to avoid tearing the form open. Revealing the scoring key may invalidate the results. Remind her to cross out errors; do not erase or white out on QuikScore forms, as this complicates scoring.

6. Give the rater extra paper for any questions, explanations, or comments that she may have during completion of the form.

CAUTION

Rater Comments and Notes

When using the QuikScore form, remind the rater to use a separate notepad for any comments beyond his ratings. Extra marks may make it difficult to hand-score the form. Do not let the rater separate the perforated sheets. If he sees the internal scoring key, it may invalidate results.

≡ Rapid Reference 2.7

Special Instructions for Online Administration

In addition to the general instructions described above, here are some special instructions for online administration.

- Orient the rater to the general layout of each item. He should move the mouse over his response and click one time. The computer automatically moves forward to the next item. (Note: It is not possible to mark more than one response online.)

- He can click on the "Previous Item" button to return to an earlier item. He can click on the "Next Item" button to move forward. Do not use the "Back" button on the Internet browser.

- If he returns to a previous item, he can change his response by clicking on a different response. He can also click on "Clear Item" to erase his response.

- If he tries to move forward without choosing a response, he will get a reminder ("Are you sure you want to skip this item?"). Tell the rater he can still choose to skip the item, but you will get better information if he answers every item. If he has a question about an item, it will be helpful to record the item number before skipping it.

- Stop at the Additional Questions and review any questions or skipped items. Once he progresses through these two items, he cannot return to items he may have skipped (and you cannot review the items).

CAUTION

. . . .

Stopping Point for Online Administration in Your Office

When using online administration in your office, ask the rater to stop at the Additional Questions so you can review the items to make sure none were skipped. Supervise the rater during in-office administration to be certain he does not stray into confidential information stored on your computer.

≡ Rapid Reference 2.8

. . . .

Response Options for the Conners Assessments

	Conners 3, Conners CBRS, and Conners EC BEH: In the past month . . .	Conners EC DM: Does this child do this without help?
0	. . . this was **not true at all** about this child. It **never (or seldom)** happened.	**No**, he/she **never or rarely** does this without help.
1	. . . this was **just a little true** about this child. It happened **occasionally**.	He/she **sometimes** does this without help.
2	. . . this was **pretty much true** about this child. It happened **often (or quite a bit)**.	**Yes**, he/she **always** or **almost always** does this without any help.
3	. . . this was **very much true** about this child. It happened **very often (very frequently)**.	*n/a*

Source: Based on Conners assessment forms (Conners 3 and Conners CBRS Copyright © 2008, Conners EC Copyright © 2009, by Multi-Health Systems, Inc.).

Answering Questions

If the rater has questions while completing the Conners assessment, be careful to stay neutral in responding (see Rapid Reference 2.9 for suggested responses). Encourage him to base his response on his observations and opinions. You may read items aloud, using the same words (see also "Modified Administration:

≡ Rapid Reference 2.9

Suggested Responses to Rater Questions

- "I know that for some questions, it is difficult to know how to respond, but please try your best and choose one of the responses."
- "I am interested in *your* observations of this child, so pick the response that *you* think is best."
- "You can write any explanations or comments on this extra paper here."
- "I can read this aloud to you. If you're not sure what it means, we can circle it and talk about it after you finish answering the other items."

Reading Aloud" in this chapter). If the rater does not understand an item, ask him to mark the item and keep working on the others. At the completion of all other items, you may choose to paraphrase such items, but this should be noted in your interpretation and results. No matter how carefully you explain an item, by changing the text you are breaking standardization. The further you stray from standardized administration, the less appropriate it is to use normative data. Be especially cautious about providing examples or translating the rater's examples into a rating. This form is intended to be completed by the rater, not by the administrator. In general, avoid biasing the rater's response to any item. Even a simple clarification of one item can have an impact on responses to subsequent items. Make a note of all questions/comments during the form completion; this information may be relevant during interpretation.

CAUTION

Do Not Bias the Rater

Do not interpret items or give examples during administration of the Conners assessments. Doing so could prevent use of normative data for scoring and interpretation.

After Administration

After the rater has completed the form, review the form and make sure that the demographic information has been completed and that each item has a single response. Ensure that there are not multiple responses for an item. Ask the rater to clarify or correct any missing or unclear information (e.g., items with multiple erasures or changes in the response). If the rater cannot or will not respond to certain items, these items should be left blank.

Thank the rater for completing the form, and reassure her that her ratings will be used to help the child. Tell the rater when and how she will receive feedback on the results. In research settings, this debriefing process may need to be modified.

DON'T FORGET

Before the Rater Leaves . . .

Before the rater leaves, review the form to make sure all information is complete on all pages of the rating scale. Check that only one response is marked per item. Ask the rater to clarify any items where the response is unclear.

Observations and Comments

It is best to record any comments or observations from administration as soon as the form is completed. These might include the rater's questions or comments, as well as his physical appearance and behaviors. Such notes and observations can provide important qualitative context for interpretation. The content of the comments may add to available information beyond what is contained within the rating scale. Attach the rater's notes (if any) to the rating scale for consideration during interpretation.

DON'T FORGET

Keys to Positive Interactions

- Ensure that the rater is comfortable.
- Explain the purpose of the rating scale.
- Reassure the respondent that there are no right or wrong responses.
- Remind the rater that his/her results will be used in combination with other information.
- Assure confidentiality (or explain limits of confidentiality as appropriate).

MODIFIED ADMINISTRATION

Some cases will require modification of the standard administration procedure. Typical modifications include reading the rating scale aloud, remote administration of the rating scale, and administration in a group setting. Modified administration of the rating scales may have an impact on test results because the test norms are based on standardized administration of the scales. Notes (and specific item numbers where applicable) should be made about any modifications, including: items read aloud,[4] administrator recording responses, additional explanations provided, specific questions and responses, and administration setting. Having accurate notes is important for the appropriate interpretation of test results.

Reading Aloud

Some raters may require modified administration procedures due to visual impairment, limited literacy (see Rapid Reference 1.1 for minimum reading levels), or other individual needs. In such cases, it is acceptable to read the rating scale instructions and items aloud to the rater. Other aspects of the standardized administration procedure outlined in the test manuals should be followed as closely as possible. When reading the items aloud to the rater, it is important to keep in mind the following important considerations:

- Provide the rater with a copy of the form while you read aloud from another copy.
- If possible, the rater should record his own responses. Periodically check that he is on the same item that you are reading.
- If the rater has a physical disability that prevents him from recording responses, it is reasonable to record his responses verbatim.
- Avoid interpreting or explaining items; read them word-for-word as printed on the test form.
- Avoid the reinforcement or emphasis of any particular word or item.

Remote Administration

Although standardized administration of the Conners assessments is conducted in person, there are instances when this will not be practical. For assessors in school settings, parent data may be difficult to obtain in person. For assessors in clinics or hospitals, it may not be feasible to meet with teachers in person. In such

---

4. The publishers conducted a small study of Conners self-report data collected with standardized administration versus items read aloud to the youth (either by the assessor or by another person). There were no significant differences in results for the Conners 3 and negligible differences for the Conners CBRS. See the Standardization chapters in each test manual, "Administration Methods: Self-Report Dictation" for more information.

situations, the Conners assessments can be administered remotely. Options include mailing the form, sending the form via a reliable person, and generating an e-mail link for online completion. In some instances, it may be necessary to combine modifications (e.g., reading the rating scale aloud over the telephone). Regardless of the exact method, try to adhere to the principles of administration as described in the test manuals and summarized in this chapter. See Rapid Reference 2.10 for suggested information to include when sending the Conners assessments for off-site completion, whether in paper-pencil format or online format.

≡ Rapid Reference 2.10

Sample Messages for Remote Administration[a]

- Parent (e-mail for online administration after initial meeting):

  "Dear Ms. Jones, Thank you for meeting with me last week to discuss your concerns about Brian's behavior. At that time I mentioned that I would be sending you a link to an online rating scale. I realize you are extremely busy, but it is very important to have information about how he is doing at home. It is important that you answer every item so that I can score your answers. I need to have your responses no later than **Monday, March 15, 2010.** If you have any questions, please do not hesitate to contact me at 919-700-0000. Thank you for your information—it is very important as I try to understand how we can help Brian."

- Teacher (letter for paper-pencil administration with no previous contact):

  "Dear Ms. Mock, I am completing an evaluation of Darby Reed. I have spent time working with Darby to test her skills and performance levels. I have talked at great length with her mother to better understand concerns and skills seen at home. Teacher input is also a crucial part of this evaluation, and I value your contribution. It is important for me to include your observations in order to have a more complete picture of this child's school performance. Also, your perspective is unique, given that you see this child in a social context every day.

  I have enclosed one rating scale that assesses different aspects of performance, including behavior, cognition, and emotion. *As this is a standardized form, it is important that you complete all items, so that I can obtain scores.* Please return this form in the addressed, stamped envelope by **Monday, March 15, 2010**. If you include additional materials, additional postage may be needed.

  I appreciate how busy your days are, and recognize that I am asking you to do one more thing. Thank you for your contributions as a member of this child's diagnostic team. Please feel free to include additional comments beyond the items on this form. If you have any questions, please contact me directly at 919-700-0000.

- Youth (e-mail for online administration after initial meeting):

"Dear Brian, Thank you for meeting with me last week to talk about how things are going at school and home. You agreed that you would like to help your parents and teachers understand things about you. Please take a look at this online rating scale. Each item you answer gives me information about how we can make things better for you. I need your answers this week, so please finish this by **Monday, March 15, 2010.** If you have any questions, you can call me at (200) 900-0000. Thank you very much—this information will be very helpful."

[a]These sample messages are fairly generic. I often include specific details, particularly in cover letters for youth remote administration (e.g., "This information will help us figure out how to make school less frustrating for you.").

CAUTION
Modifying standardized procedure and using norms

- Modification of the standardized administration procedure may have an impact on the test results, as the normative data are based on standard administration.
- Attach notes to the test forms regarding any deviations from the standardized administration procedure and reasons the modifications were necessary.
- Report modifications when you report results from the rating scales.
- The potential impact of a modified administration should be considered when interpreting results.

Group Administration

The administration principles described in this chapter can be extended when administering the Conners assessments to more than one person simultaneously. Technically, when two parents are completing the forms at the same time (at home or in the waiting room), or more than one teacher is completing the form (e.g., after a team meeting), this is a group setting. The need for group administration also occurs when a Conners assessment is being used as a screening measure (e.g., a group of students completing self-reports to identify those who might benefit from participating in proactive and preventative anger management groups). Be particularly vigilant that raters do not bias each others' responses in group settings. It is important that each rater responds independently, describing her own observations of the child. If raters compare notes or ask for information from each other, this reduces the utility of gathering data from more than one informant. Ask raters to save their questions for the end of the group administration session, then discuss questions with each rater individually. As always, follow standard administration as closely as possible within this modification, and note the modification on all results from the group administration.

CAUTION

Common errors that limit use of results

- Seeking others' opinions when completing items
- Erasing or crossing-out responses
- Skipping items or entire pages
- Providing multiple responses
- Tearing the QuikScore form to reveal the scoring key

 TEST YOURSELF

1. **Which *one* of the following statements is *false* about administration options for the Conners assessments?**

   (a) Any form of the Conners assessments can be administered online, either on my computer or by an e-mail link.

   (b) Any form of the Conners assessments can be administered in paper-pencil format.

   (c) Any form of the Conners assessments can be administered via the software program, either on a desktop or laptop computer.

2. **What factors help you choose a form of the Conners assessments? *Mark all that apply.***

   (a) Child's age

   (b) Child's setting

   (c) Child's gender

   (d) None of the above

3. **What is the best way to handle a rater's questions about an item on one of the Conners forms?**

   (a) Explain any words that he does not understand in the item.

   (b) Give examples of behaviors that might help clarify what the item means.

   (c) Mark the item, and return to it after all other items are completed.

   (d) Encourage the rater to pick the first response that enters his head for the item.

4. **The Conners 3, Conners CBRS, and Conners EC all require that the rater has known the child for at least one month.**

   True or False?

5. **The Conners 3, Conners CBRS, Conners EC-BEH, and Conners EC-DM all ask the rater to describe the child's behavior over the past month.**

   True or False?

6. **Which of the following factors could potentially invalidate results from the Conners assessments?** *Mark all that apply.*

   (a) Skipped items

   (b) Multiple responses marked for a single item

   (c) Discussion of items with the administrator during administration

   (d) Discussion of items with another person during administration

   (e) None of the above could invalidate results

Answers: 1. c; 2. a, b; 3. c; 4. True; 5. False; 6. a, b, c, d.

Three

Elizabeth P. Sparrow

T he Conners assessments can all be scored by computer. Some forms have a hand-scoring option. This chapter provides an overview of both methods, with an emphasis on ways to avoid scoring errors. Please see the relevant test manual for a detailed explanation of scoring procedures. This chapter also reviews general scoring principles of the Conners assessments, including types of scores used.

OPTIONS

Scoring the Conners assessments does not require formal clinical training and background. Whoever scores the forms must be familiar with the scoring procedures outlined in this chapter and detailed in the test manuals. She must be trained and supervised by a qualified professional who regularly double-checks and supports scoring accuracy. Regardless of who scores the Conners assessments, a qualified professional must interpret results before they can be distributed (this includes distribution of the feedback handout, which can be generated with the computerized Assessment Report).[1] Scoring options may be limited by the choice of administration modality; see Rapid Reference 2.1.

---

1. The Feedback handout is available with the Assessment Report for all forms of the Conners assessments, except the stand-alone index forms (i.e., Conners 3AI, Conners 3GI, Conners CI, and Conners ECGI).

CAUTION

Qualified Professional Must Interpret

Scores and results from the Conners assessments must be interpreted by a qualified individual before they can be shared with parents, teachers, or other people who do not have sufficient background and training.

CAUTION

Always Get Consent Before Releasing Results

Remember to obtain consent from the youth's parent or guardian before you share results from the Conners assessments, including the feedback report.

Computerized Scoring: Online and Software Programs[2]

Computerized scoring options for the Conners 3, Conners CBRS, and Conners EC include online and software. The online scoring programs are available from any computer with Internet access (see test manuals for minimum system requirements). This makes it easy for multiple assessors to have access to scoring, even from multiple sites. When an online administration method is used (see Chapter 2), you can log onto your scoring program and generate a computerized report of results. If the rater completes a paper-and-pencil form, you can enter the rater's responses into the online scoring program and then receive the report. The online scoring program allows you to establish online files to organize and store your data.

The scoring software programs are stored on a portable USB drive and can be used on any computer with a USB port that meets other basic requirements (see test manuals). This makes it easy to share the scoring program at the same site without having to share the same computer (although only one user can use it at a time; the USB drive must be inserted into the computer for the program to work). For a single user, this also makes it easy to transport the program to multiple sites rather than having to take all forms to one site for scoring. When you are entering

---

2. See Chapter 5 for additional information about the computerized scoring options. Note that Macintosh users can access the online scoring program, but the USB drive software package is not compatible.

multiple forms about the same child, you can click on "load profile" to automatically enter the child's basic information for each form. Any of the paper-and-pencil forms can be entered into the software program for quick generation of the computerized report. If the online administration method is used, it does not make sense to use software scoring. The software program stores your data in an assessment file on your computer's hard drive. The data can be sorted and filtered in a variety of ways.

CAUTION

Entering Names for Computerized Scoring

Be thoughtful and consistent about how you enter the child's name, the rater's name, and your name in the computerized scoring programs. This is how the data will appear in your database for later searching/organization of records. The way you enter the child's name is how it will appear throughout the computerized report (e.g., if you enter "Reed, Darby" then the text in the report will read, "Based on Reed, Darby's ratings, . . . "). If your computerized scoring has shared access with other users, you should use the child ID rather than his name. You may wish to use initials for yourself and the person who enters data into the software scoring program.

Both the online and the software scoring options generate the same reports, with the same standard and optional features. There is no difference in the output choices (see "Report Options" below). You can cut and paste tables, text, and graphs from the computerized report to include in your written report of results.

CAUTION

Identifying Loose Report Pages

Be certain to staple together the pages of each computerized report immediately, or add the rater's name and date of rating to each page. Although every page is labeled at the top with the child's name as well as the Conners assessment and form type, the page header does not specify the rater's name. This can become confusing if pages are shuffled together, particularly when you have more than one teacher rating the same student. The only place the rater's name is listed is on the cover page of the report.

Hand-Scoring

Some forms of the Conners assessments are available in QuikScore™ format and can be scored by hand. This option is available for all Conners 3 forms (i.e., Conners 3 full-length, Conners 3[S], Conners 3AI, and Conners 3GI), the Conners CI form, and the Conners ECGI. Other forms of the Conners CBRS and Conners EC must be computer-scored given the complexity of calculations. Hand-scoring requires use of the QuikScore form, which has the necessary grids and tables embedded in the inner layers. For some forms (e.g., the 10-item Conners 3GI), hand-scoring is simple and convenient as it does not require a computer. The full-length Conners 3 is the most complex hand-scoring form available, but is feasible to hand-score for someone who has good attention to details to ensure accuracy.

CAUTION

Use Raw Scores for Calculations

When hand-scoring the Conners assessments, be sure to use *raw item scores* from the Scoring Grid when completing the inner scoring calculations. Do *not* copy the actual ratings from the response sheets—some items are reverse-scored, transposed, dichotomized, or otherwise converted for scoring purposes. See *"Converting to Raw Item Scores"* in this chapter for additional information.

The QuikScore forms can be used to calculate the basic scores for Conners assessments, including *T*-scores, DSM-IV-TR symptom counts, probability scores, and validity scale scores. Additional information may be obtained from the manual, including interpretative text, percentiles, standard error of measurement (*SEM*) for *T*-scores, common characteristics of high scorers, links to IDEA 2004,[3] and items grouped by scale (see Rapid References 3.6 through 3.8). It is also possible to calculate statistical values by hand to determine if the change in scores between two administrations of a Conners assessment is statistically significant ("Reliable Change Index," or "RCI" values are discussed further in each test manual; see also Rapid Reference 6.2). The QuikScore forms do not include some elements of computerized scoring, such as statistical

---

3. The full-length Conners 3 QuikScore forms include IDEA 2004 information. This information must be looked up for other QuikScore forms.

comparison of raters (computerized Comparative Report), consolidated tables of results and interpretive guidelines, rater's responses to items organized by scale for easy item-level analysis, feedback handout, and cut-and-paste report. See Appendix C for sample tables that you may reproduce and use in your written report of scores from the Conners assessments.

See Rapid Reference 3.1 for an overview of the differences among these three scoring methods (i.e., online, software, and hand-scoring). See Rapid Reference 3.2 for a quick overview of the various score types used on the Conners assessments. See Rapid References 3.6–3.8 for a comparison of the scoring

≣ Rapid Reference 3.1

Comparison of Scoring Options

	Online	Software	Hand-Score
Materials	Computer with Internet access	Computer with USB port, software program (on USB drive)[a]	QuikScore form, calculator, pencil, straight edge, and test manual
Applicability	Can be used for all forms of the Conners assessments		Limited to QuikScore forms[b]
Location	Can score any form at any computer location with Internet access	Can score any form at any computer location, as long as you have the USB drive	Can score QuikScore forms anywhere
Output	• T-scores • DSM-IV-TR symptom counts • Probability scores • Validity scale scores		On QuikScore form: • T-scores • DSM-IV-TR symptom counts • Probability scores • Validity scale scores
	• Interpretive text • Percentiles • SEM for T-scores		Can look-up: • Interpretive text • Percentiles • SEM for T-scores

(continued)

	Online	Software	Hand-Score
Output (continued)	• Common characteristics of high scorers and scale descriptions • Links to IDEA 2004 • Items grouped by scale (computerized report integrates with rater's responses) • Statistically significant change between two administrations • Consolidated tables of results and interpretive guidelines • Feedback handout (Assessment Reports) • Statistically significant differences between raters (Comparative Reports)		• Common characteristics of high scorers and scale descriptions • Links to IDEA 2004 • Items grouped by scale • Statistically significant change between two administrations *Not available:* • Consolidated tables of results and interpretive guidelines • Feedback handout • Statistically significant differences between raters
Reports	Computerized Assessment report, Progress report, or Comparative report generated for your review; tables, graphs, and text can be cut-and-pasted into your written report Feedback handout can be given to non-professionals		Can reference tables from manual and this book to create written report with scores from QuikScore form
Data storage	You create electronic files to organize and store data online; can save reports to your computer	All data stored in one location on your computer. Can export data to an Excel file. Can save reports to your computer.	You can create physical files for QuikScore forms

Usernames and Passwords	Can set-up as a single-user account or as a multi-user account (allows unlimited usernames with unique passwords)	Only one username and password can be established per USB drive	n/a
Cost[c]	Pay per use[d]	Purchase software with unlimited scoring/reports	No additional scoring cost
Convenience	Most versatile; good for use by multiple users at multiple sites. Online administration eliminates data entry time.	Good for use by multiple users at one site AND Good for use by one user at multiple sites[e]	Does not require a computer to score
Limitations	Once rater ends the session, cannot enter missing data	Data stored on one computer, not on portable USB drive	Not available for all forms; more time-consuming and error-prone than computer scoring

[a] Occasional internet access is required to download updates for the software program.
[b] QuikScore forms are available for Conners 3 (all forms), Conners CI, and Conners ECGI.
[c] Cost of scoring, not including cost of forms (either online administration or paper-and-pencil QuikScore form) or shipping costs.
[d] Online subscription model is also available upon request, including unlimited uses of the Conners assessments for administration and scoring. Contact MHS for additional information.
[e] Data are stored on the computer where they were entered and are only accessible for reporting when the USB drive is inserted into that computer.

information obtained from computerized versus hand-scoring. Chapter 1 provides information about relative time required for each scoring option (varies by form; see Rapid References 1.13, 1.17, and 1.22.

Report Options

Online and software report options include the Assessment Report, Progress Report, and Comparative Report. Each report can be saved as a .pdf file

≡ Rapid Reference 3.2

Types of Scores Used on Conners Assessments

Type of Score	Use on Conners Assessments		
	Conners 3	Conners CBRS	Conners EC
T-score and Percentile	Content scales/ subscales DSM-IV-TR scales Conners 3GI (Total and subscales) Conners 3AI[a]	Content scales/ subscales DSM-IV-TR symptom scales Conners CI Indicators[a]	Behavior scales/ subscales Developmental Milestone scales Conners ECGI (Total and subscales)
Symptom Count	DSM-IV-TR symptom scales	DSM-IV-TR symptom scales	n/a
Probability	Conners 3AI	Conners CI	n/a
Cut-off score	PI & NI scales	PI & NI scales	PI & NI scales
IncX	IncX	IncX	IncX
Trigger	Critical items	Other Clinical Indicators Critical items	Other Clinical Indicators
Qualitative	Screener items Impairment items Additional questions	Impairment items Additional questions	Developmental Milestone subclusters Impairment items Additional questions

[a] This T-score is a standard calculation for the Index forms; it can be calculated for the index on the full-length form also.

(the format used by Adobe Reader) or an .rtf file ("rich text format," easily read by word-processing programs) and can be customized to increase or decrease the amount of detail.

It is simple to select the relevant record(s) for reporting. The software and online scoring programs allow you to sort data by a number of fields (e.g., child's name, assessment type, date completed), in either direction (i.e., ascending or descending). The online scoring program assigns a "confirmation number" to each completed form; record this in the child's file to facilitate finding that record easily. When looking for a record in the software program, it is best to maximize the Saved Profiles window so you can see all available data fields.

Some of the computerized report information can be generated by hand for any form that is available in QuikScore format using the test manual. Sample tables for reporting results from hand-scored forms are provided in this book (see Chapter 4, "Report Results"; see also Appendix C). Aspects of the computerized report cannot be calculated by hand (see Rapid References 3.6 through 3.8).

CAUTION

Computerized Report Cannot Be Distributed

Never give the computerized report or hand-scoring results to an unqualified individual. The exception to this rule is the feedback handout (optional for some computerized reports), which may be given to parents, teachers, or other people after a qualified person with sufficient background and training has reviewed results and obtained appropriate consent.

The computerized Assessment Report includes results about a single administration of a Conners assessment presented in table, text, and graph formats. This can be generated each time you score a Conners form by computer. Information is presented in a way that makes it simple to follow the interpretation sequence described in Chapter 4, including assessment of validity, Content scale scores, Behavior scale scores, Developmental Milestone scale scores, DSM-IV-TR Symptom scale scores, Impairment items, Index scores, individual items (e.g., Screener items, Critical items, Other Clinical Indicators), and Additional Questions. An IDEA 2004 summary table can be added, as well as a list of items and ratings (grouped by scale). Most Conners assessment reports[4] have an optional feedback handout that can be used to summarize results using straightforward

---

4. The only Assessment reports without feedback handouts are the index forms (i.e., Conners 3AI, Conners 3GI, Conners CI, and Conners ECGI). The Progress and Comparative reports do not have feedback handouts.

language. This feedback handout is a nonclinical way of describing results, and can be helpful when identifying target areas for intervention. After obtaining appropriate consent from the child's parent/guardian, the feedback handout may be appropriate to share with parents, teachers, and other professionals including pediatricians, therapists, psychiatrists, educational advocates, and guardian ad litems.

The computerized Progress Report describes results from up to four administrations of a specific Conners form completed by the same rater (e.g., mother's ratings of the child over time using the Conners EC-P).[5] This helps you compare how the rater has described that child over time, highlighting areas of statistically significant change[6] that you may want to review for clinical significance. This is particularly helpful when assessing response to intervention (RTI). The Progress Report is appropriate when assessing whether a behavior has changed over time or after intervention. It is relevant whether comparing results over a short time period (e.g., every month, as might be relevant in a medication monitoring trial) or a long time period (e.g., at triennial evaluations). Data from this report can aid discussions regarding whether a particular treatment could be continued, modified, or possibly discontinued. Because multiple administrations are compared side-by-side, the Progress Report also helps you identify new areas of concern that may be emerging and require attention.

The computerized Comparative Report helps you compare results from up to five raters using the same Conners version (e.g., mother, father, step-mother, science teacher, and math teacher ratings on the Conners 3). This helps you compare how different raters describe the child in different settings. The report includes calculation of statistically significant differences in scores between pairs of raters, which can indicate areas you may want to examine for possible clinical significance.[7] This report can help you integrate data from multiple raters—an important component of interpretation (see Chapter 4). Because multiple raters are compared side-by-side, the Comparative Report helps you identify settings where the child shows her best (and worst) functioning.

---

5. Technically, these statistics are intended for use when comparing results from the same rater over time. Practically speaking, it is reasonable to use the Progress Report to compare results from the same *type* of rater over time, even if it is not the same person (e.g., first grade teacher, second grade teacher, and fourth grade teacher raters on the Conners 3-T). Be particularly aware of potential response style issues when using the Progress report in this manner.

6. Statistically significant change is based on the Reliable Change Index (RCI), the interpretation of which is discussed in Chapter 4. Statistically significant change can be evaluated when hand-scoring, using the RCI value tables provided in the relevant test manuals.

7. These calculations are not available for hand-scoring.

PRINCIPLES AND SCORES

Converting Rater Responses to Interpretable Data

Rater Responses
Almost every item on the Conners assessments is rated on a Likert scale ranging from 0 to 3. The two exceptions are the Conners EC Developmental Milestone items (which are rated on a Likert scale ranging from 0 to 2) and the two Additional Questions at the end of most forms (which are fill-in-the-blank text items). The text responses to the Additional Questions are not converted to scores but are reviewed for content. The ratings of all other items must be converted to item raw scores before any interpretation can take place.

CAUTION

Use Raw Scores—Not Ratings—for Item-level Interpretation

The rater's responses must be converted to item raw scores before they can be interpreted at the item level. The one exception to this rule is the Additional Questions, which are simply reviewed for content (not scored).

Converting to Raw Item Scores
Likert ratings on the Conners assessments are converted to raw item scores in one of four ways: (1) score = rating, (2) reverse-scoring, (3) categorical scoring, and (4) weighted scoring. Some items are used in more than one way for the final results; therefore, some items may be scored more than once.

For most of the items, the item raw score is the same as the rating. The rater's response to the item is simply transferred, keeping the same number. This is done for items where the phrasing describes a problem (i.e., a higher rating indicates a higher level of concern, as is the case for the item, "Acts as if driven by a motor."); no conversion is needed for these items.

Some items are written to describe intact functioning. For these items, a higher rating describes less concern about the behavior (e.g., "Interacts well with other children."). To be consistent with the overarching principle of the Conners assessments that higher scores indicate higher concerns, these positively worded items must be reversed for interpretation. For reverse-scored items, the score is the opposite of the rating (see Rapid Reference 3.3). All of the Conners EC Developmental Milestone scale items are reverse-scored, as well as a handful of other items on other Conners assessment scales.

Categorical scoring is used in instances where the full range of ratings was not meaningful—only whether the item falls in a certain category. For items on the Positive Impression and Negative Impression scales scoring is dichotomous, meaning there are just two categories of scores: 0 or 1. Statistical analyses were used for each of these items to determine which ratings should be scored as 0 and which ratings should be scored as 1. Items on the DSM-IV-TR symptom scales are categorized as "indicated," "may be indicated," or "not indicated" (see Rapid Reference 3.4). A combination of content and statistical analyses were used to determine which ratings translated into which categories for each DSM-IV-TR item. Finally, items on the Conners 3 ADHD Index (Conners 3AI) are each transposed into scores ranging from 0 to 2 (even though each item is rated from 0 to 3). The decision for which ratings transpose into which item raw scores was determined statistically for the Conners 3AI.

The last type of rating to raw item score conversion is weighted scoring. This only occurs on the Conners CBRS Violence Potential Indicator (VPI) scale. Given the range of severity of items included on this scale, scoring required a way to have some items count for more in the total scale score. Thus, the items were assigned relative weights. A rating of 3 on one of the VPI items is converted to a raw score of 1.5, 5, or 8, depending on the relative severity of the item. All of these conversions are completed by the computerized scoring program, as the Conners CBRS cannot be hand-scored. It is important to understand how these weighted scores are obtained, however, as differences in the relative weights of items may impact your interpretation when this scale is elevated. See Rapid Reference 3.3 for possible VPI item scores; see also Rapid Reference 4.13 for a listing of which items are in each weight category.

DON'T FORGET

High Scores = High Levels of Concern

On the Conners assessments, *higher scores indicate higher levels of concern*. (Note: a high *rating* may not have a high score; item responses must be converted to scores before they can be interpreted.)

Interpretable Scores

Next, these raw item scores are grouped, standardized, and/or compared to look-up tables for interpretation. A brief description of the types of interpretable scores that can be obtained on the Conners assessments is provided in this

≋ Rapid Reference 3.3

· ·

Ratings to Raw Item Scores

- Score = rating (e.g., a rating of 3 = score of 3): most items on the Conners assessments
- Reverse-scoring: items phrased to describe skills rather than problems

Rating ⇨ raw item score	
0 to 3 scale	**0 to 2 scale** **(Conners EC DM)**
0 ⇨ 3 1 ⇨ 2 2 ⇨ 1 3 ⇨ 0	0 ⇨ 2 1 ⇨ 1 2 ⇨ 0

- Categorical scoring: some item ratings are translated into categories; applicable to PI, NI, DSM-IV-TR symptom counts, and Conners 3AI items.
- Weighted scoring: some items are given more weight than others; applicable only to Conners CBRS VPI scale

VPI Weight Category (Level of Severity)	Weighted Scoring Rule Rating ⇨ raw item score
Mild	0 ⇨ 0 1 ⇨ 0.5 2 ⇨ 1.0 3 ⇨ 1.5
Moderate	0 ⇨ 0 1 ⇨ 1 2 ⇨ 3 3 ⇨ 5
Severe	0 ⇨ 0 1 ⇨ 4 2 ⇨ 6 3 ⇨ 8

Source: Adapted from *Conners CBRS Interpretive Update* (Multi-Health Systems, 2009).

section. Rapid Reference 3.2 lists where each of these score types is used on the Conners assessments. Rapid References 3.6 through 3.8 summarize each Conners assessment, listing score types available on the computerized report and hand-scoring form. See Chapter 4 for guidance in understanding and interpreting these scores.

- T-scores and percentiles: Item raw scores for a given scale are added together. This raw sum is compared to age- and gender-matched[8] normative data and converted to a T-score (with the option of also obtaining a percentile score). Note that the Conners assessments do not use T-scores greater than 90; raw scores that produce extremely high T-scores are reported as "T-score $\geq$ 90."
- Each T-score can be described using information from the interpretation guidelines and common characteristics of high scorers found in each test manual. It is reasonable for a technician to transcribe this information for use by a trained professional in interpretation. A technician can also calculate confidence intervals for T-scores (see Appendix B).

DON'T FORGET

Gender-Based Norms

Based on the normative data, the developers of the Conners assessments recommend using different normative comparisons for boys versus girls. The default scoring position for computerized scoring programs is gender-based norms. A combined-gender option is available for hand-scoring and computer-scoring the Conners assessments for those who have a strong rationale for using this option. See Rapid Reference 1.24 for additional information about gender-based norms.

- DSM-IV-TR symptom counts: The number of "indicated" and "may be indicated" items is counted to obtain the Total Symptom Count for that DSM-IV-TR symptom scale. The Total Symptom Count is compared to DSM-IV-TR symptom count requirements to help identify diagnoses that might require further consideration.

---

8. Unless combined gender norms are selected, in which case the raw sum is compared to age-matched norms only.

≡ *Rapid Reference 3.4*

....

Terms Used to Describe DSM-IV-TR Results on Conners 3 and Conners CBRS

- **DSM-IV-TR Symptom:** indicated, may be indicated, or not indicated. Each DSM-IV-TR item score is translated into one of these terms. The translation table was established by a combination of clinical wisdom and statistical findings, with the guiding principle that it is better to identify a child who may need additional evaluation than to miss a child who needs intervention.[a] The translation varies by item and by rater type in some instances. For example, the score "1" was common on the item "Loses temper" (Conners 3) when it was rated by parents and youth; this item score is "not indicated" as a symptom on parent and self-report forms. In contrast, it was unusual for a teacher to endorse this item at any level; an item score of "1" for this item on teacher report is marked "may be indicated." Some DSM-IV-TR symptoms are represented by more than one item on the Conners assessment; in these cases, the text of the DSM-IV-TR symptom was used to determine if both items were required or if one item would suffice for the symptom to be indicated.[b] See the Conners 3 and Conners CBRS manuals for a detailed listing of rules for each DSM-IV-TR item.

  - **"Indicated"** = counted toward the symptom count for each diagnosis (see below).

  - **"May be indicated"** = can also be included in the symptom count depending on your clinical judgment and preferences.[c]

  - **"Not indicated"** = not counted toward the symptom count.

- **DSM-IV-TR Total Symptom Count:** probably met or probably not met. The symptom count is compared to the cut-off score designated in the DSM-IV-TR (e.g., for Conduct Disorder, must have 3 or more of the symptoms present). Remember, the symptom count only describes one criterion of DSM-IV-TR diagnosis (see Chapter 6: DSM for additional information about diagnostic requirements).

  - **"Probably met"** = the symptom count is equal to or higher than the cut-off score.

  - **"Probably not met"** = the symptom count is lower than the cut-off score.

[a] Clinical recommendations were based on DSM-IV-TR text describing frequency and severity. Statistical recommendations were based on response frequencies in the general population sample. (If endorsed by less than 10 percent of the general population sample, "indicated"; by 10 to 20 percent, "may be indicated"; and by more than 20 percent, "not indicated.") In the few cases where these two approaches did not agree, consistency across raters was considered. In the rare event that this did not resolve the difference, the "may be indicated" category was used for that item score.

[b] For example, endorsement of either item "Is constantly moving" or "Acts as if driven by a motor" is sufficient for that DSM-IV-TR symptom of ADHD to be counted. In contrast, both items "Fails to complete schoolwork . . . " and "Does not follow through . . . " are required.

(continued)

[c] Depending on your setting and clinical experience, you may choose to treat these items in several different ways. The computerized scoring program automatically includes the "may be indicated" items in the symptom count. This is the safest default and results in identifying children who may need further consideration of a diagnosis. Another approach is to ignore the "may be indicated" items, using only the "indicated" items in the symptom count. This is a stricter rule and risks missing a child who may require intervention. Some experienced clinicians may choose to review each of the "may be indicated" items and make individual determinations for each item rather than applying a broader rule.

- Probability scores: Raw item scores are added together and the sum is compared to a look-up table to establish the probability score (automatic for computer scoring).
- Cut-off scores: Raw item scores for the relevant scale are added together, then the raw sum is compared to a reference table to determine what interpretation guidelines to follow (automatic for computer scoring).
- Inconsistency Index (IncX): This is scored using pairs of items on each rating scale. The raw item scores for each pair of items are compared, and the absolute difference is recorded. (The absolute difference is the difference between the two raw item scores, ignoring any minus sign.) The criteria differ slightly for the Conners 3 and Conners CBRS as opposed to the Conners EC, as described below:
  - Conners 3 and Conners CBRS: The absolute differences for all 10 pairs of items are added together. This sum is compared to a cut-off score. In addition, the number of absolute differences that are 2 or greater are counted, and this number is compared to a cut-off score. Both criteria must exceed the cut-off score for the IncX to be indicated (i.e., for the interpretation that it indicates a possible inconsistent response style).
  - Conners EC: For each absolute difference of 2 points, a count of 1 is added to the IncX raw score. For each absolute difference of 3 points, a count of 2 is added to the IncX raw score. The total IncX raw score is compared to a cut-off score.
- Triggers: Some raw item scores are flagged for additional attention if they meet or exceed a certain threshold that triggers concern. The score level that indicates concern was set through a combination of clinical experience and statistical findings (see Rapid Reference 3.5).
- Qualitative review: Some items are grouped together conceptually; then their raw item scores are reviewed using clinical judgment. The only

≡ Rapid Reference 3.5

Trigger Levels

The Critical items (Conners 3 and Conners CBRS) are flagged for scores higher than 0 (i.e., scored 1, 2, or 3).[a] Most of the Other Clinical Indicator items (Conners CBRS and Conners EC) are also flagged when scored higher than 0;[b] the only exceptions are:

• Specific Phobia (Conners CBRS and Conners EC): Requires score of 2 or 3 to be flagged. Data analyses showed that it is common for children in the general population to be afraid of something at least occasionally.

• Perfectionism (Conners EC only): Requires score of 2 or 3 to be flagged. Data analyses showed that it is common for young children in the general population to be perfectionistic on occasion.

• Pervasive Developmental Disorders (PDD; Conners CBRS Self-Report only). This group of items is flagged if:

At least one of these three items is rated a 3.

OR

At least two of these three items are rated a 2 or higher.

Source: This information was provided by the MHS Research and Development department.

[a] The Conners 3 and Conners CBRS Critical items were rated 0 by over 95 percent of the normative sample for parent and teacher ratings. Ratings of 1 for the Critical items were less rare for self-report, but 0 was still the predominant rating for these items. Current scoring conventions flag the Critical items when rated 1, 2, or 3, regardless of rater type.

[b] The Conners CBRS Other Clinical Indicator items are flagged on the basis of clinical considerations, with the exception of Specific Phobia and PDD items mentioned in the text above. The Conners EC Other Clinical Indicators were selected clinically and were rated "0" by over 95 percent of the normative sample. The exceptions to this are observed for the Specific Phobia item and the Perfectionism item; these were rated "1" by 20 percent of the normative sample, so they each require a rating of "2" or "3" to trigger a flag.

scoring aspect of this is grouping the items together. As a guideline, the Screener items are flagged if they are scored higher than 0 (1, 2, or 3).[9]

Reference Scores

Many of the Conners assessment scores can be reviewed from the perspective of IDEA 2004 eligibility and areas of need. Each test manual includes an IDEA 2004 table that links relevant scores from the Conners assessment with suggestions for commonly considered IDEA 2004 categories of need/service. This

---

9. Ratings of "1" are marked "Further investigation *may* be necessary"; ratings of "2" or "3" are marked "Further investigation *is* recommended."

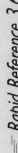

Rapid Reference 3.6

Comparison of Conners 3 Scores: Computerized versus Hand-Scoring

Conners 3	Scale	Computerized Scoring	Hand-Scoring
Validity Scales	Positive Impression	Raw score* Interpretive text*	On form: - Raw score* - Interpretive guideline* Look-up: - Interpretive text
	Negative Impression		
	Inconsistency Index		
Conners 3 Content Scales	Inattention	Color-coded T-score graph T-scores, SEMs, & percentiles (table) Interpretation Guideline* Common Characteristics of High Scorers	On form: T-score* (color-coded graph) Look-up: - percentiles & SEMs - Interpretation Guideline* - Common Characteristics of High Scorers
	Hyperactivity/Impulsivity		
	Learning Problems		
	Executive Functioning		
	Defiance/Aggression		
	Peer Relations		
	Family Relations		

DSM-IV-TR Symptom Scales	ADHD Inattentive	Overview of interpretation	On form: - T-score (color-coded graph) - Symptom count requirements and score - DSM-IV-TR tables
	ADHD Hyperactive-Impulsive	Color-coded T-score graph T-scores, SEMs, & percentiles (table)	
	ADHD Combined	Interpretation Guideline*	Look-up: - percentiles & SEMs - T-score Interpretation Guideline*
	Conduct Disorder	Symptom count requirements and score	
	Oppositional Defiant Disorder	DSM-IV-TR tables (symptoms and items)	
Impairment Items	Academic	Item content and ratings graph	On form: raw data
	Social	Interpretive text	Look-up: Interpretive text
	Home		
	Conners 3 ADHD Index	Probability score, graph, and interpretive text T-score (Conners 3AI form only)	On form: Probability score Look-up: - Interpretive text - T-score
Indices	Conners 3 Global Index - Restless-Impulsive - Emotional Lability	Total and subscale T-score graph T-scores, SEMs, & percentiles (table) Interpretation Guideline Common Characteristics of High Scorers	On form: - T-score (color-coded graph) - Subscale T-scores (Conners 3GI form only) Look-up: - Interpretive guideline and text* - Subscale T-scores (full-length form)

(continued)

Conners 3	Scale	Computerized Scoring	Hand-Scoring
Screener Items	Anxiety	Item content and ratings	On form:
	Depression	Guideline for follow-up	- Item content and scores
			- Guideline for follow-up
Critical Items	Severe Conduct	Item content and ratings	On form:
		Recommendation for follow-up	- Item content and scores
			- Recommendation for follow-up
Additional Questions	Other concerns Strengths/Skills	Rater's text response	On form: Rater's text response
Other		Summary of elevated scores	On form:
		Items & ratings grouped by scale/subscale to help item-level analysis	- Links to IDEA 2004 (full-length only)
		Links to IDEA 2004 (not Conners 3AI or Conners 3GI)	Look-up:
			- Items grouped by scale
		Feedback handout (not Conners 3AI or Conners 3GI)	- Links to IDEA 2004 (short form)

SEM = Standard Error of Measurement
* See Caution: Important Updates in this chapter.

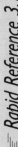

Rapid Reference 3.7

Comparison of Conners CBRS Scores: Computerized versus Hand-Scoring

Conners CBRS	Scale/Subscale	Computerized Scoring	Hand-Scoring[a]
Validity Scales	Positive Impression	Raw score*	n/a
	Negative Impression	Interpretive text*	
	Inconsistency Index		
Conners CBRS Content Scales and Subscales	Emotional Distress	Color-coded *T*-score graph	n/a
	- Upsetting Thoughts	*T*-scores, SEMs, & Percentiles (table)	
	- Worrying	Interpretation Guideline*	
	- Upsetting Thoughts/ Physical Symptoms	Common Characteristics of High Scorers	
	- Social Anxiety		
	Defiant/Aggressive Behaviors		
	Academic Difficulties		
	- Language		
	- Math		

(continued)

Conners CBRS	Scale/Subscale	Computerized Scoring	Hand-Scoring[a]
Conners CBRS Content Scales and Subscales (continued)	Hyperactivity		
	Hyperactivity/Impulsivity		
	Social Problems (P subscale)		
	Separation Fears (T subscale)		
	Perfectionistic and Compulsive Behaviors		
	Violence Potential Indicator		
	Physical Symptoms		
DSM-IV-TR Symptom Scales	ADHD Inattentive	Overview of interpretation Color-coded T-score graph T-scores, SEMs, & Percentiles (table) Interpretation Guideline* Symptom count requirements and score DSM-IV-TR tables (symptoms and items)	n/a
	ADHD Hyperactive-Impulsive		
	ADHD Combined		
	Conduct Disorder		

DSM-IV-TR Symptom Scales (continued)	Oppositional Defiant Disorder		
	Major Depressive Episode	Item content and ratings graph	n/a
	Manic Episode		
	Mixed Episode		
	Generalized Anxiety Disorder		
	Separation Anxiety Disorder		
	Social Phobia		
	Obsessive-Compulsive Disorder		
	Autistic Disorder		
	Asperger's Disorder	Interpretive text	
Impairment Items	Academic	Item content and ratings graph	n/a
	Social		
	Home	Interpretive text	
Index	Conners Clinical Index - Disruptive Behavior Disorder Indicator	Probability score, graph, and interpretive text	On form: - Probability score (color-coded graph)

(continued)

Conners CBRS	Scale/Subscale	Computerized Scoring	Hand-Scoring[a]
Index (continued)	- Learning and Language Disorder Indicator - Mood Disorder Indicator - Anxiety Disorder Indicator - ADHD Indicator	*Conners CI reports:[b]* Total and Indicator *T*-scores, SEMs, & Percentiles (graph and table) Interpretation Guideline* Indicator Description Items and ratings by subscale	- Subscale *T*-scores (color-coded graph) Look-up: - Interpretive guideline* and description - Items grouped by scale
Other Clinical Indicators	Bullying Perpetration	Item content and ratings Recommendation for follow-up	n/a
	Bullying Victimization		
	Enuresis/Encopresis		
	Panic Attack		
	Pervasive Developmental Disorder		
	Pica		
	Posttraumatic Stress Disorder		
	Specific Phobia		

Other Clinical Indicators (continued)	Substance Use		
	Tics		
	Trichotillomania		
Critical Items	Severe Conduct	Item content and ratings	n/a
	Self Harm	Recommendation for follow-up	
Additional Questions	Other concerns	Rater's text response	n/a
	Strengths/Skills		
Other		Summary of elevated scores	On form: n/a
		Items & ratings grouped by scale/subscale to help item-level analysis	Look-up:
		Links to IDEA 2004 (not Conners CI)	- Items grouped by scale
		Feedback handout (full-length only)	

* See Caution: Important Updates in this chapter

[a] The Conners CBRS cannot be hand-scored. This column is only applicable to the Conners CI form.

[b] The Conners CI Indicator information is not included in the full-length report, but it can be reviewed and calculated by hand using the manual. See also Appendix D in this book.

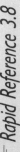

≡ Rapid Reference 3.8

Comparison of Conners EC Scores: Computerized versus Hand-Scoring

Conners EC	Scale	Computerized Scoring	Hand-Scoring[a]
Validity Scales	Positive Impression	Raw score	n/a
	Negative Impression	Interpretive text	
	Inconsistency Index		
Behavior Scales	Inattention/Hyperactivity	Color-coded T-score graph	n/a
	Defiant/Aggressive Behaviors	T-scores, SEMs, & percentiles (table)	
	- Defiance/Temper	Interpretation Guideline	
	- Aggression	Common Characteristics of High Scorers	
	Social Functioning/Atypical Behaviors		
	- Social Functioning		
	- Atypical Behaviors		
	Anxiety		
	Mood and Affect		
	Physical Symptoms		
	- Sleep Problems		

Index	Conners EC Global Index - Restless-Impulsive - Emotional Lability	Total and subscale T-score graph T-scores, SEMs, & percentiles (table) Interpretation Guideline Common Characteristics of High Scorers	On form: Total and subscale T-scores (color-coded graph) Look-up: Interpretive guideline and text
Developmental Milestone Scales	Adaptive Skills	Color-coded T-score graph T-scores, SEMs, & Percentiles (table) Interpretation Guideline Common Characteristics of High Scorers	n/a
	Communication		
	Motor Skills		
	Play		
	Pre-Academic/Cognitive		
Other Clinical Indicators	Cruelty to Animals	Item content and ratings Recommendation for follow-up	n/a
	Fire Setting		
	Perfectionism		
	Pica		
	Posttraumatic Stress Disorder		
	Self-Injury		
	Specific Phobia		
	Stealing		

(continued)

Conners EC	Scale	Computerized Scoring	Hand-Scoring[a]
Other Clinical Indicators (continued)	Tics		
	Trichotillomania		n/a
Impairment Items	Learning/Pre-Academic	Item content and ratings	
	Peer Interactions	Interpretive text	
	Home		
Additional Questions	Other Concerns	Rater's text response	n/a
	Strengths/Skills		
Other		Summary of elevated scores Overview graph of scores Items & ratings grouped by scale/ subscale/cluster to help item-level analysis Links to IDEA 2004 (not ECGI) Feedback handout (not ECGI)	On form: n/a Look-up: - Items grouped by scale Not Applicable: - Links to IDEA 2004

[a] Most forms of the Conners EC cannot be hand-scored. This column is only applicable to the Conners ECGI form.

information can be transferred to the score sheet by a technician for use by a qualified professional in interpretation.

Although not included in standard scoring procedures, the Conners EC has additional reference information that can be useful, especially when evaluating individual item data. It is appropriate for a technician to look up and record this information for subsequent interpretation by a qualified professional (see Rapid Reference 3.9).

- Base rates:[10] The frequency of each response option for each item and each rater was calculated using the normative sample and is reported in tables by age and gender. This helps establish whether a given rating is typical for a child of that age and gender, considering rater type. Consulting the base rates for items can help you determine how much concern is warranted for a given item rating (see Chapter 4 for interpretation tips).

CAUTION

Use Actual Ratings for Base Rate and Age of Attainment Interpretation

Although most of the references for the Conners assessments are provided for *raw item scores*, the Conners EC base rate tables and age of attainment tables are based on *actual ratings*. This is a critical point, particularly for reverse-scored items (including all Developmental Milestone items). Remember, when using Conners EC base rates or ages of attainment, compare the rater's *response* to the tables (*not* the raw item score).

- Age references: "Ages of Attainment" for each of the Conners EC Developmental Milestone items are provided in an appendix of the Conners EC manual. The rating of any DM item can be compared with these ages of attainment to get a sense of whether the child is on schedule or possibly delayed for that skill relative to the normative sample. Each item is described in terms of the "Developing" age and the "Mastery" age. See Chapter 4 for information to help understand these reference ages. The age of attainment tables are available for males, females, and combined gender; there are separate columns for parent versus teacher data. Be careful to reference the correct table.

---

10. Although these base rates are not printed in the manual, users of the Conners EC may call MHS Customer Service to request assistance in downloading the Conners EC base rates.

≡ Rapid Reference 3.9

Technician's Guide to Conners EC Base Rates and Ages of Attainment[a]

- Base Rates:[b]
    - Consult the correct table for the version of the Conners assessments you are scoring, attending to the rater type, child's age, and child's gender.
    - Compare the actual *rating* (i.e., the rater's response) for each item with the table.
    - For each Conners item, record the percentage of raters who used the same rating for that item. Alternatively, record the rating used by the majority of the raters (i.e., > 50 percent) for that item.
- Ages of Attainment:
    - Consult the correct Conners EC table according to the child's gender.
    - Review the correct columns in the table based on the rater type.
    - Compare the actual *rating* (i.e., the rater's response) for each Developmental Milestone item with the table.
    - For each item rated a 2, there is no need to record an age of attainment. Alternatively, you may record the Mastery age.
    - For items rated a 1, record the Mastery age.
    - For items rated a 0, record the Developing age.

[a] Technicians (i.e., people scoring the Conners assessments who are not considered "qualified users") should be guided by their supervisor as to what scores are recorded. These suggestions are intended to help quickly identify some options for consideration.
[b] Conners EC base rates must be obtained directly from MHS; call MHS Customer Service for assistance.

Reducing Scoring Errors

Scoring errors can occur for many reasons, including being tired, distracted, or unfamiliar with scoring procedures. Before anyone scores a Conners assessment, he should be familiar with the scoring procedures described in the test manuals and summarized in this chapter. This is particularly necessary when hand-scoring a QuikScore form. Although the QuikScore form has some instructions printed on the inner scoring grids, these are not sufficient until the full procedure printed in the test manual is mastered through repeated practice.

Computerized Scoring Tips

The computerized scoring options (both online and software programs) are fairly intuitive, requiring less reading and practice than hand-scoring to reach mastery. Because computerized scoring eliminates calculation errors, the biggest source of errors is data entry. There is an option for "data verification," which means you enter the rater's responses twice (a.k.a., "double entry"). If any item is entered differently the second time, the item is flagged for your review and correction. This significantly reduces the chance of data entry errors and errors in general from computerized scoring.

It is a good idea to regularly check for updates to your Conners scoring software. At the time of this printing, one set of updates had been provided to integrate changes from the Conners 3 and Conners CBRS interpretive updates (2009; see Caution: Important Updates in this chapter for a summary of these changes). The Conners scoring software has a "check for updates" feature in the Help menu that allows you to download updates to the software.

If you have difficulty with the online or software scoring programs for the Conners assessments, technical assistance is available from MHS.

DON'T FORGET

Check for Updates

Check for updates to the Conners assessments on a regular basis. Use the "check for updates" feature in the software program to find software updates. See the MHS website (www.mhs.com) or call MHS Customer Service (1-800-456-3003) for other updates. The online program is automatically updated.

Hand-Scoring Tips

Accurately hand-scoring the Conners assessments requires close attention to details and high vigilance. Follow these tips to avoid the most common types of errors for hand-scoring:

- Use the correct look-up table. If you use more than one Conners assessment, be certain you are using the correct manual (i.e., Conners 3, Conners CBRS, Conners EC).[11] Check the rater type (i.e., parent, teacher, self-report) and form (e.g., full-length, short). Be sure you are using the correct look-up table for the child's age and gender. You may want to use tabs to help you quickly find frequently used tables and highlight key words to make sure you are on the right page.

---

11. Remember that the hand-scoring forms are color-coded to match the Conners manuals. All Conners 3 manuals, response booklets, and QuikScore forms are red; all Conners CBRS materials are green; and all Conners EC materials are yellow.

- Use the correct QuikScore Profile form. As long as you leave one edge of the QuikScore form intact, you will be assured of having the correct set of scoring grids for that rating scale, form, and rater type. Remember that there are different Profiles for boys and girls and different columns for each age group. Make certain you are using the correct Profile and column in the Profile. One suggestion is to circle the child's gender at the top of the Profile sheet and his age at the top of the scoring column. This helps keep you on track, particularly when you are scoring more than one child's forms in a given scoring session.
- Use the correct column or row. A ruler or index card may help you visually track down columns and across rows as you look-up scores or transfer scores across the scoring grid. Some clinicians choose to highlight every fifth column or row of frequently used tables in their manuals to help them stay on the correct path.
- Use a calculator or spreadsheet to add raw item scores. You may have noticed that bank tellers use a calculator every time you make a deposit, even when the sum is a simple one. Apply this same standard of caution to hand-scoring a child's testing results. This is particularly important when you are tired or if you tend to make calculation errors.
- Include all relevant items in each sum. It is particularly easy to miss an item score from the top row or bottom row of the scoring grid. Be certain to include these raw item scores in the sum for the column.
- Double-check your sums. Each test manual has a table with the maximum raw scores for each scale (see the Scoring chapter in each test manual). Compare your sums with the relevant table to make sure they are all within the possible range. If a sum falls outside the range, recalculate the score for that scale.

If you have copies from early printings of the Conners 3 full-length or Conner 3(S) QuikScore forms, you will need to adjust a few things to be compliant with the Conners 3 Interpretive Update issued in 2009. The main issue that impacts hand-scoring is scoring the Conners 3 Validity scales. Old copies of the QuikScore forms have the outdated terminology of "probably valid," "possibly invalid," and "probably invalid," as well as the outdated cut-off scores. Use Rapid Reference 3.10 to score these scales. The Conners 3AI, Conners 3GI, Conners CI (on the Conners CBRS), and Conners ECGI QuikScore forms are not impacted by the interpretive updates.

≡ Rapid Reference 3.10

Interpretive Updates for the Conners 3 and Conners CBRS Validity Scales

Validity Scale	Parent Raw Scores	Teacher Raw Scores	Self-Report Raw Scores	Interpretive Guideline
PI	0–4	0–4	0–3	Overly positive response style not indicated.
	5–6	5–6	4–6	Possible positive response style. Scores may present a more favorable impression than is warranted.
NI	0–4	0–4	0–4	Overly negative response style not indicated.
	5–6	5–6	5–6	Possible negative response style. Scores may present a less favorable impression than is warranted.
Conners 3 IncX	0–6 *or* ≥2 absolute differences equal to 2 or 3	0–5 *or* ≥2 absolute differences equal to 2 or 3	0–8 *or* ≥2 absolute differences equal to 2 or 3	Inconsistent response style not indicated.
	≥7 *and* ≥2 absolute differences equal to 2 or 3	≥6 *and* ≥2 absolute differences equal to 2 or 3	≥9 *and* ≥2 absolute differences equal to 2 or 3	Possible inconsistent response style. Responses to similar items showed high levels of inconsistency. Scores may not accurately reflect the individual due to a

(continued)

Validity Scale	Parent Raw Scores	Teacher Raw Scores	Self-Report Raw Scores	Interpretive Guideline
Conners 3 IncX (continued)				careless or unusual response to some items.
Conners CBRS IncX	0–5 or <2 absolute differences equal to 2 or 3	0–4 or <2 absolute differences equal to 2 or 3	0–8 or <2 absolute differences equal to 2 or 3	Inconsistent response style not indicated.
	≥6 and ≥2 absolute differences equal to 2 or 3	≥5 and ≥2 absolute differences equal to 2 or 3	≥9 and ≥2 absolute differences equal to 2 or 3	Possible inconsistent response style. Responses to similar items showed high levels of inconsistency. Scores may not accurately reflect the individual due to a careless or unusual response to some items.

Sources: Adapted from *Conners 3 Interpretive Update* (Multi-Health Systems, 2009) and *Conners CBRS Interpretive Update* (Multi-Health Systems, 2009).

CAUTION

Important Updates

If your Conners 3 or Conners CBRS manual is from the first printing in 2008, be sure you have a copy of the relevant Interpretive Update issued in 2009.[a] This contains information on important updates that impact scoring and interpretation. These changes should be noted in your manual and on any remaining forms. Keep your Conners software updated to include these features. Key updates include:

1. Validity scale interpretation (cut-off scores, interpretive guidelines).
2. *T*-score Interpretation (extreme scores, new "high average" range, interpretive cautions).
3. Renamed scale to better reflect content (updated characteristics of high scorers).
   - Conners 3 Aggression scale → Defiance/Aggression scale
   - Conners CBRS Aggressive Behaviors scale → Defiant/Aggressive Behaviors scale
4. Conners CBRS Violence Potential scale renamed Violence Potential Indicator scale.
   - Renamed scale to urge caution in interpretation (indicator that child may behave violently in the future, not necessarily that he is now or ever has been violent)
   - Weighted raw item scores to reflect relative contributions of mild, moderate, and severe items
5. Adjusted trigger point for Conners CBRS Other Clinical Indicator: Specific Phobia item (now requires rating of 2 or 3 to be flagged).

Sources: Adapted from *Conners 3 Interpretive Update* (Multi-Health Systems, 2009) and *Conners CBRS Interpretive Update* (Multi-Health Systems, 2009).

[a] The Interpretive Updates can be downloaded from the MHS website, www.mhs.com.

Difficult Scoring Decisions

Regardless of whether you hand-score or computer-score the Conners assessments, you will be faced with difficult scoring decisions at times. Many of these can be prevented through careful administration as described in Chapter 2 (especially the reminder to make sure each item has one and only one response before the rater leaves). No matter how careful your administrator is, there will be times when difficult scoring decisions arise. The most important thing is to be consistent in how you handle these situations and document your decisions.

DON'T FORGET
....
Document Difficult Scoring Decisions

When difficult scoring decisions arise, document how you resolved the issues.

Common issues that arise from incomplete administration include:

- Rater left an item blank, no response
- Rater marked more than one response for an item
- Rater wrote a text response rather than rating an item
- Rater added her own response option beyond those printed on the form (e.g., "1.5" or "100")

In all of these instances, if it is the same day and you still have access to the rater, ask her to clarify her response to the item or to provide a response. Remind her that there can only be one response per item, and that it must be from the provided response options. Offer to make notes of any qualifications she may want to attach to the item rating.

If you do not realize the problem until the next day, technically you should treat the item as "missing," using the techniques described in this chapter (i.e., "Handling Missing Data"). It is tempting to extrapolate from other data to "estimate" the rater's response, but this violates standard method. The Conners assessment should be completed by the rater in one session based on his observations of the child over the past month. If you fill in data that you obtained during an interview, you have changed the person completing the form, the time the information was obtained, the mode of obtaining the information, and probably the time period being described.

CAUTION

Blank Items on Conners Assessments

If a rater leaves an item blank on the rating scale, the item must be treated as missing data—even if you think you know what his response would have been. The exception to this rule is if the rater can be reached on the same day to provide his response for the item. Be sure to make a note of this exception to standardized administration.

This being said, there will be instances in which the rater's response makes it very clear what his intentions were (e.g., rater writes in "all the time—never stops" by an item, suggesting that he might have intended a rating of "3"; rater adds and circles the response option of "100," suggesting that the item occurs at least at the level of a "3"). In strict data collection settings (e.g., research studies), the item must be entered as missing (unless other options are provided in the study protocol). In clinical settings, a qualified professional may choose to use clinical judgment as to how to score such items.

Likewise, some raters will circle two adjoining ratings, or show indecision through multiple corrections on an item such that you cannot resolve which rating was the final response. In research and other data collection settings, these items must be treated as missing data. In clinical settings, a qualified professional may choose to follow the convention to use the lower rating (which reduces the chance of inflating the score, but risks underestimating the true level of the behavior). Alternately, a qualified professional may choose to use the higher rating (which reduces the chance of missing a true concern, but risks inflating the score).

Usually, even when some responses are missing or questionable, you can still score the form. As described below, most of the scales can be prorated to accommodate one or two missing items. Even if one scale score cannot be calculated, the other scales can still be calculated, which is better than nothing. In extreme cases (e.g., the rater skips entire pages in the response booklet), you may not be able to obtain any standardized scores on the rating scale; however, you can still review content at the item level that may provide additional information for you to consider.

DON'T FORGET
Scoring with Missing Data

In most instances the form can still be scored even if a few items are missing. Even if one of the scores cannot be obtained, scores on the other scales will be informative.

Handling Missing Data

When a rater's response is missing for one or more items, this is considered "missing data" (a.k.a., "data omissions"). Statistically speaking, a scale becomes unstable when many items are missing. The solid reliability and validity of the Conners assessments are threatened with each additional missing item. For these reasons, each test manual provides a table that indicates how many missing items are acceptable for each scale score. If the number of missing items is at or less than that number, you may proceed with scoring. If there are more missing items than the allowable number, you should not score that particular part of the rating scale.[12] Note that the computerized scoring programs (online and software) include all necessary information to evaluate whether it is safe to proceed with calculating a score. The computerized program will advise you when too many items are missing and it is risky to score the rating scale.

CAUTION

Excessive Omissions

The number of missing items must not exceed the limits set for each form and each scale. To report scores when there are excessive omissions is irresponsible and unethical, unless it is clearly stated that standardized scoring procedures were violated and the rationale for doing so.

If the number of omitted items is acceptable, you may choose to prorate the raw score for that particular scale (with the exception of the DSM-IV-TR symptom counts; see Rapid Reference 3.12). This is standard procedure for computerized scoring when there are missing data. The score tables will indicate in these instances that a score is based on prorated data. When hand-scoring, you must look-up the number of items on the scale (item counts by scale are listed in an appendix at the end of each test manual, "Items by Scale"). The number of items on the scale for the Inconsistency Index is based on the number of pairs (i.e., 10); likewise, the number of items on the scale with responses refers to the number of complete pairs for the Inconsistency Index. The item count is needed to calculate the prorated score (see Rapid Reference 3.11).

Missing or questionable responses for the DSM-IV-TR symptom count are treated in a different way.[13] These cannot be prorated, as they are compared with an absolute number of symptoms established by the DSM-IV-TR. See Rapid Reference 3.12 for a summary of how to handle missing data for the DSM-IV-TR symptom count if you are hand-scoring. The computerized scoring programs (online and software) will employ this procedure automatically.

---

12. There is one exception to this rule. If the raw sum for a scale with missing items converts to a T-score that is 90 or higher, it is acceptable to proceed with scoring the scale and reporting the T-score. This exception is allowable because any additional data would only raise the T-score for the scale, and T-scores greater than 90 are reported as 90 for the Conners assessments.

13. Note that DSM-IV-TR symptom scale *T-scores* can be calculated with the prorating formula. This special procedure only applies for the DSM-IV-TR *symptom count.*

≡ Rapid Reference 3.11

....

Prorating a Scale Score[a,b]

$$\text{Prorated score} = \frac{(\text{Obtained raw score for scale}) \times (\text{Total \# of items on scale})}{\text{Total \# of items on scale with responses}}$$

Source: This formula is described in the Scoring chapters of the *Conners 3rd edition manual* (Multi-Health Systems, 2008), *Conners Comprehensive Behavior Rating Scales manual* (Multi-Health Systems, 2008), and *Conners Early Childhood manual* (Multi-Health Systems, 2009). Information about the Inconsistency Index is adapted from the same manuals.

[a] This formula cannot be used for the DSM-IV-TR symptom counts.
[b] For the Inconsistency Index, use the number of *pairs* where the formula states "number of items".

≡ Rapid Reference 3.12

....

Calculating DSM-IV-TR Symptom Count with Missing Data

1. Obtain the symptom count for that DSM-IV-TR symptom scale using the available items.
2. Count the number of missing items for that DSM-IV-TR symptom scale.
3. Look up the minimum symptom count requirement for "probably met" (in the relevant test manual).
4. Compare these numbers as follows:

DSM-IV-TR Symptom Count Guideline			Outcome
If . . .	Symptom Count (based on available items) $\geq$	Minimum symptom count requirement for "probably met"	Then "probably met"
If . . .	Symptom Count (based on available items) + Number of missing items $<$	Minimum symptom count requirement for "probably met"	Then "probably *not* met"
Otherwise . . .			"cannot be determined"

Sources: This table is based on information from *Conners 3rd edition manual* (Multi-Health Systems, 2008) and *Conners Comprehensive Behavior Rating Scales manual* (Multi-Health Systems, 2008).

🐾 TEST YOURSELF 🐾

....

1. **Which one of the following statements is *false* about scoring options for the Conners assessments?**

   (a) Any form of the Conners assessments can be scored online.
   (b) Any form of the Conners assessments can be scored by hand.
   (c) Any form of the Conners assessments can be scored via the software program, either on a desktop or laptop computer.

2. **The default for computerized scoring of the Conners assessments is to use age- and gender-specific norms, but you can select combined gender norms if necessary.**

   True or False?

3. **When are the Critical items and Other Clinical Indicator items flagged for review?**

   (a) When they are rated higher than a 0
   (b) When they are rated a 0
   (c) It varies by item and rater type

4. **What happens when you have missing items on a Conners assessment? *Mark all that apply.***

   (a) The entire assessment is invalidated and cannot be scored.
   (b) Any scale including those items cannot be scored, but the rest of the assessment can be scored.
   (c) It depends on how many items are missing; it may still be possible to calculate some scores.
   (d) Any scale including those items can be prorated.
   (e) You can fill in the missing item if you have the information available from another source, such as interview or questionnaire.

5. **On the Conners assessments, higher scores always indicate higher levels of concern.**

   True or False?

6. **Which of the following are requirements for someone to score the Conners assessments? *Mark all that apply.***

   (a) The person must be familiar with the scoring procedures.
   (b) If the person is not a qualified professional, he must be supervised by a qualified professional who routinely checks for scoring accuracy.
   (c) The person must be a qualified professional with a background in assessment and measurement.
   (d) The person must attend a workshop about scoring the Conners assessments.

7. **Which one of the following statements is *true* about distributing the computerized report of Conners assessment results?**

   (a) The computerized report can only be viewed by a qualified professional.
   (b) The computerized report can be given to parents/guardians.
   (c) The computerized report can be shared with parents, teachers, and other professionals (after obtaining written permission from the parent/guardian).

Answers: 1. b; 2. True; 3. c; 4. c; 5. True; 6. a, b; 7. a

Four

INTERPRETATION OF
THE CONNERS ASSESSMENTS

Elizabeth P. Sparrow

D espite the complex scores produced for all three Conners assessments, interpretation is a straightforward process. This chapter begins with a review of step-by-step interpretation guidelines that can be used to systematically review the scores and integrate them into a meaningful whole. Specific elements of each Conners assessment are examined, with relevant details for interpretation of each score. The chapter ends with suggestions for integrating results across multiple Conners assessments. The goal of this chapter is to guide examiners through interpretation of the Conners assessments in a way that demystifies the process and helps produce a meaningful summary of results to support diagnostic decisions and guide intervention planning.

INTERPRETATION ELEMENTS

There are just a few basic steps involved in interpreting any of the Conners assessments. The step-by-step interpretation guidelines for each rating scale are summarized in Rapid Reference 4.1. Although there are slight variations in the Conners EC interpretation sequence when compared to the Conners 3 and Conners CBRS, the elements are the same.[1] Relevant test-specific details are described in this section. For abbreviated forms of the Conners assessments,

---

1. Because the Conners EC has two main sections (i.e., Behavior scales and Developmental Milestone scales), it is simpler to conduct item-level analysis while reviewing each section's scale scores, then move to the overall profile analysis. The sequence of interpretation is not as critical as the content. Regardless of which sequence you use, be sure to carefully consider all Conners assessment scores and describe them in a meaningful way.

≡ *Rapid Reference 4.1*

Summary of Interpretation Guidelines for Conners Assessments

Step	Conners 3	Conners CBRS	Conners EC
1.	Assess validity. a. Consider common threats to validity. b. Describe response style. (cut-offs) i Positive Impression ii Negative Impression iii Inconsistency Index	Assess validity. a. Consider common threats to validity. b. Describe response style. (cut-offs) i Positive Impression ii Negative Impression iii Inconsistency Index	Assess validity. a. Consider common threats to validity. b. Describe response style. (cut-offs) i Positive Impression ii Negative Impression iii Inconsistency Index
2.	Interpret scale scores. a. Content scales (T-scores) b. DSM-IV-TR scores (T-scores and symptom counts)	Interpret scale scores. a. Content scales (T-scores) b. DSM-IV-TR scores (T-scores and symptom counts)	Interpret Behavior scales. a. Behavior scale T-scores, subscale T-scores, and items b. Conners ECGI (T-scores) c. Other Clinical Indicators (trigger)
3.	Examine the overall profile, including: - Profiles of T-scores - Impairment items (raw) - Conners 3AI (probability) - Conners 3GI (T-scores)	Examine the overall profile, including: - Profiles of T-scores - Impairment items (raw) - Conners CI (probability)	Interpret Developmental Milestone scales. a. Developmental Milestone scale T-scores b. Clusters (raw) c. Individual items (base rates, ages of attainment)

4.	Consider item-level responses: - Items on elevated scales (raw) - Items with high ratings (raw) - Screener items (item guidelines) - Severe Conduct Critical items (trigger) - Additional Questions (text) Integrate results: a. Within a single rater's Conners 3 b. Across multiple raters on Conners 3 c. With other sources of information	Consider item-level responses: - Items on elevated scales (raw) - Items with high ratings (raw) - Other Clinical Indicators (trigger) - Critical items (trigger) - Additional Questions (text) Integrate results: a. Within a single rater's Conners CBRS b. Across multiple raters on Conners CBRS c. With other sources of information	Examine the overall profile, including: - Profiles of T-scores - Impairment items (raw) - Additional Questions (text) Integrate results: a. Within a single rater's Conners EC b. Across multiple raters on Conners EC c. With other sources of information
5.	Integrate results: a. Within a single rater's Conners 3 b. Across multiple raters on Conners 3 c. With other sources of information	Integrate results: a. Within a single rater's Conners CBRS b. Across multiple raters on Conners CBRS c. With other sources of information	Integrate results: a. Within a single rater's Conners EC b. Across multiple raters on Conners EC c. With other sources of information
6.	Report results.	Report results.	Report results.

Source: Based on information from Conners 3rd edition manual (Multi-Health Systems, 2008), Conners Comprehensive Behavior Rating Scales manual (Multi-Health Systems, 2008), and Conners Early Childhood manual (Multi-Health Systems, 2009).

apply the relevant interpretation elements described in this chapter (see Rapid References 2.4 through 2.6 for a listing of which elements occur on which forms). Chapter 3 provides information about the scores used for each element of the Conners (see especially Rapid References 3.6 through 3.8).

DON'T FORGET

High Scores = High Levels of Concern

On the Conners assessments, *higher scores indicate higher levels of concern.* When interpreting item-level data, remember that a high *rating* may not have a high score (e.g., positively worded items are reverse-scored); item responses must be converted to scores before they can be interpreted.

Validity of Ratings

The first step for interpreting results from the Conners assessments results is to consider factors that might impact validity of the ratings. Validity of ratings should not be confused with psychometric validity (i.e., validity of the test, as discussed in Chapter 1). This interpretation step involves examining issues that might cause you to be cautious about how you use a certain rater's results. This should be done when interpreting the results from *any* psychological instrument.

Usually validity is not a yes/no decision (i.e., "valid" versus "invalid") but a relative level of confidence that the scores reflect the child's functioning in a given setting. If you doubt the validity of a rater's results, you will be more cautious in interpreting the scores and give less weight to the test results when integrating them with other sources of information.

DON'T FORGET

Validity of ratings

This is not an absolute "valid" versus "invalid" decision. Your validity statement describes your level of confidence that the rater responses accurately describe the child's functioning.

Common Threats to Validity

- Response bias (e.g., the rater conveys an overly positive or overly negative impression, a parent tells the child how to respond, the rater responds in a way that she thinks will help to secure a certain outcome)

- Random responding (e.g., the rater makes patterns such as zig-zags on the response sheet)
- Impulsive or careless responding (e.g., the rater gives little thought to her responses)
- Comprehension errors (e.g., the rater misunderstands items due to a language impairment or limited skills in the language of the assessment)
- Missing items (see Chapter 3 for additional information)
- Inappropriate use of normative data (e.g., the child's demographics do not match the normative sample because the child is outside of the age range, or the child is a recent immigrant from a foreign country, given that the norms are based on North American data)
- Human error (e.g., the assessor made data entry errors when computer-scoring or calculation errors when hand-scoring)

Conners Validity Scales[2]

In addition to subjective consideration of validity of a rater's report, the Conners assessments offer Validity scales to help you describe response style:

- **Positive Impression (PI):** The raw score on this scale is categorized as "Overly positive response style not indicated" or "Possible positive response style." The label "Possible positive response style" (i.e., high score) indicates that the rater described the child in very positive terms. This can indicate a positive bias, which could jeopardize validity of the ratings overall. Raters who describe a child in overly positive terms may underrepresent the severity or frequency of problems. An elevated Positive Impression score suggests caution in interpretation of other scores on the Conners, given the possibility that the rater may minimize concerns. It is possible for the Positive Impression scale to fall in the "Possible positive response style" category even when ratings are valid. Some children may show extremely good behavior in certain settings or with certain people. Some raters have an optimistic view of children. At times, a rater may be erroneously basing his ratings on comparisons with other children (e.g., siblings, classmates) who have worse behavior than the child being rated. Some raters may rate

---

2. The terms used in this section reflect current Conners terminology, as reflected in the interpretive updates for the Conners 3 and Conners CBRS (2009) and the Conners EC manual (2009). Old copies of the QuikScore forms may still have the outdated terminology of "probably valid," "possibly invalid," and "probably invalid," as well as the outdated cut-off scores. You should use the updated terms and reference tables when reporting results from the Conners validity scales (see Rapid Reference 3.10).

behaviors after taking into account certain excuses or circumstances. These are among the reasons it is important to review the instructions before a rater completes the rating scale. In some cases, a rater may deny problems to avoid possible stigma of a child labeled with a diagnosis or receiving special services. Some raters may be poor observers due to their own characteristics (e.g., lack of awareness, attention/memory deficits). Overall, if the Positive Impression scale falls in the "Possible positive response style" range, this should be considered throughout interpretation of that rater's results.

- **Negative Impression (NI):** As with the Positive Impression scale, the Negative Impression raw score is categorized as "Overly negative response style not indicated" or "Possible negative response style." If the scale is marked "Possible negative response style" (i.e., high score), this suggests that the rater described the child in very negative terms. This can indicate a negative bias, which in extreme cases could invalidate the results. In most cases, the rest of the scores can still be reviewed, using some caution. Raters who describe a child in overly negative terms may overrepresent the severity or frequency of problems. An elevated Negative Impression score suggests caution in interpretation of other scores on the Conners, given the possibility that the rater may exaggerate concerns. It is possible for the Negative Impression scale to fall in the "Possible negative response style" category even when ratings are valid. Some children may show more problematic behavior in certain settings or with certain people. Some raters have unrealistic expectations of children. In some cases, a rater may emphasize problems to try to obtain a certain diagnosis or access to funding/services. Overall, if the Negative Impression scale falls in the "Possible negative response style" range, this should be considered throughout interpretation of that rater's results.

- **Inconsistency Index (IncX):** The third validity scale assesses whether the rater was consistent in responding to items throughout the Conners assessments. As described in Chapter 3, raw item scores on the IncX are evaluated in two ways before the scale is categorized as "Inconsistent response style not indicated" or "Possible inconsistent response style." This classification is based on the rater's responses to pairs of items that are typically rated similarly. When a rater's Inconsistency Index is elevated, this indicates that the rater was not as consistent as expected. This may suggest invalid results, as inconsistent responding could indicate poor attention to the Conners items. It is possible to obtain an elevated Inconsistency Index even when the ratings are accurate; for example, the child's behavior might be inconsistent (rather than the rater's ratings). As with the PI and NI scales, it is important to carefully review the rater's responses in the context of other available information to help determine how to proceed with interpretation.

Scale Scores

After considering validity of the ratings, the next step is to review scores on the main scales and subscales. These scores include the Content scales (Conners 3 and Conners CBRS), DSM-IV-TR symptom scales (Conners 3 and Conners CBRS), Behavior scales (Conners EC), and Developmental Milestone scales (Conners EC). Some of these scales have subscale scores. The relative elevations of subscale scores can help the assessor understand the scale score. It is appropriate to interpret elevated subscale T-scores even if the overall scale is not elevated.

Standardized Scores

The raw score for each Conners scale is converted into a T-score,[3] with the option of a percentile score. These standardized scores describe the child's score in the context of what is typical for her age and gender (see Rapid Reference 1.24 for discussion of why age and gender matter). T-scores allow comparison of information across different ages (e.g., comparing a child's initial evaluation results with re-evaluation results), across different raters (e.g., parent versus teacher versus self-report), and across different scales (e.g., to determine a child's relative strengths and weaknesses).

It is difficult to say when a T-score is "too high," as this decision may change depending on the examiner's setting and other contextual information. Statistically speaking, a T-score has a mean of 50, with a standard deviation (SD) of 10 points. Some clinicians use a statistical guideline that "typical" is in the range of the mean $+/-$ 1 standard deviation (i.e., 50 $+/-$ 10, or 40 to 60). About 66 percent of a normally distributed sample falls within that T-score range of 40 to 60. Other clinicians set stricter standards, such as 1.5 or even 2 standard deviations above the mean (i.e., T-scores above 65 or 70, respectively). An

---

3. Although it is mathematically possible to have a T-score greater than 90, any T-score that is that elevated indicates extreme atypicality and concern (whether the T-score is 90 or 120). In order to reduce the chance of erroneous interpretation, the Conners assessments cap T-scores at 90; any T-score that is 90 or higher is simply reported as "T-score $\geq$ 90." See the Conners 3 and Conners CBRS Interpretive Updates (2009) and Conners EC manual (2009) for additional information.

≡ Rapid Reference 4.2

Understanding *T*-Scores and Percentiles

T-Score	Percentile	Guideline
70–90 [a]	98+	Very Elevated Score (Many more concerns than are typically reported)
65–69	93–97	Elevated Score (More concerns than are typically reported)
60–64	84–92	High Average Score (Slightly more concerns than are typically reported)
40–59	16–83	Average Score (Typical levels of concern)
<40	<16	Low Score (Fewer concerns than are typically reported)

Sources: This descriptive system is reported in the *Conners 3 Interpretive Update* (Multi-Health Systems, 2009), *Conners CBRS Interpretive Update* (Multi-Health Systems, 2009), and *Conners Early Childhood manual* (Multi-Health Systems, 2009).

[a] The Conners assessments report any *T*-score greater than 90 as "90." See Rapid Reference 4.2 for explanation.

examiner's decision impacts the number of cases identified as needing services. Setting a liberal standard may result in labeling children who are within the normal range (i.e., using a lower cut-off score may lead to overidentification); in contrast, setting a conservative standard may result in missing children who need intervention (i.e., using a higher cut-off score may lead to underidentification). The Conners assessment manuals and computerized reports offer suggestions for interpreting *T*-scores and percentiles (see Rapid Reference 4.2).

In reality, a one-point difference is not meaningful clinically; therefore, a rigid adherence to a strict cut-off is not recommended. Most clinicians use a general rule-of-thumb with some flexibility based on the context. For example, if an examiner decides to require 1.5 SD above the mean (i.e., *T*-score $\geq$ 65) for identification of a child's needs, a child's score of 64 should still be examined.

Content Scales and Behavior Scales

T-scores from the Conners 3 Content scales, the Conners CBRS Content scales, and the Conners EC Behavior scales can be interpreted using the *T*-score guidelines described above. Rapid References 4.3 and 4.4 summarize the Conners

DON'T FORGET

....

Clinical Training and Judgment Required

Clinical training and judgment are required for responsible interpretation of any test score. Score classification guidelines are approximations and should never be applied automatically. A difference of a few points can change classification but may not be clinically meaningful. Be cautious when applying scale labels, scale descriptions, and interpretive guidelines; confirm their appropriateness for an individual child by examining item-level data for the child as well as other sources of information to explain the context for the ratings. A qualified professional must be involved in interpreting Conners assessment results and providing feedback on the results.

≡ Rapid Reference 4.3

....

Conners 3 Content Scales and Common Characteristics of High Scorers

Scale	Common Characteristics of High Scorers
Inattention	May have poor concentration/attention or difficulty keeping his/her mind on work. May make careless mistakes. May be easily distracted. May give up easily or be easily bored. May avoid schoolwork. May have difficulty starting and/or finishing tasks.
Hyperactivity/ Impulsivity	High activity levels. May be restless and/or impulsive. May have difficulty being quiet. May interrupt others or talk too much. May be easily excited.
Learning Problems/ Executive Functioning (T)	Academic struggles. May have difficulty learning and/ or remembering concepts. May need extra instructions. May have executive deficits.
Learning Problems (P & SR)	Academic struggles (reading, spelling, and/or math). May have difficulty learning and/or remembering concepts. May need extra explanations or help.
Executive Functioning (P)	May have difficulty starting or finishing projects. May complete projects at the last minute. May have poor planning, prioritizing, or organizational skills.

(continued)

Scale	Common Characteristics of High Scorers
Defiance/Aggression	May be argumentative. May defy requests from adults. May have poor control of anger and may lose temper. May be physically and/or verbally aggressive. May show violent or destructive tendencies. May bully others. May be manipulative or cruel. May break rules and/or have legal issues.
Peer Relations (P & T)	May have difficulty with friendships, poor social skills, and limited social connections. May appear to be unaccepted by the group.
Family Relations (SR)	May feel that parents do not love or notice him/her. May feel unjustly criticized and/or punished at home.

Sources: Adapted from Conners 3rd edition manual (Multi-Health Systems, 2008) and Conners 3 Interpretive Update (Multi-Health Systems, 2009).

P = Parent, T = Teacher, SR = Self-Report.

3 and Conners CBRS Content scales. Rapid Reference 4.5 describes the Conners EC Behavior scales. Keep in mind that these "common characteristics of high scorers" summarize typical descriptors of children with elevated scores. It is possible to have an elevated score on one of these scales without having all of the described features. This is particularly true for scales with combined names (e.g., Conners CBRS Defiant/Aggressive Behaviors; some children are defiant without being aggressive, and vice versa). Be certain to review relative contributions of the items on each scale to better understand how the score became elevated (see "Don't Forget: Clinical Training and Judgment Required"; see also Item-Level Responses: Items to Review for more guidance).

DSM-IV-TR Symptom Scales[4]

The DSM-IV-TR symptom scales correspond to symptoms of each DSM-IV-TR diagnosis (or episode, in the case of the Mood Disorders as discussed in Chapter 1). The Conners 3 and Conners CBRS manuals provide tables showing the correspondence between specific Conners items and DSM-IV-TR symptoms for these disorders. An elevated **T-score** on the DSM-IV-TR symptom scales can be described as, "This child shows greater symptoms of the DSM-IV-TR diagnosis

---

4. DSM-IV-TR symptom scales are only available on the Conners 3 and Conners CBRS; these are not relevant for the Conners EC.

≡ *Rapid Reference 4.4*

Conners CBRS Content Scales and Common Characteristics of High Scorers

Scale	Common Characteristics of High Scorers
Emotional Distress	Worries a lot (including possible social and/or separation anxieties). May feel nervous. May have low self-confidence. May show signs of depression. May have physical complaints (aches, pains, difficulty sleeping). May have repetitive thoughts or actions. May seem socially isolated. May have rumination.
Upsetting Thoughts (P)[a]	Has upsetting thoughts. May get stuck on ideas or rituals. May show signs of depression, including suicidal ideation.
Worrying (P)[a]	Worries a lot, including anticipatory and social worries. May experience inappropriate guilt.
Upsetting Thoughts & Physical Symptoms (T)[b]	Has upsetting thoughts and/or ruminations. May complain about physical symptoms. May show signs of depression.
Social Anxiety (T)[b]	Worries about social and performance situations. Worries about what others think.
Defiant/Aggressive Behaviors	May be argumentative. May defy requests from adults. May have poor control of anger and may lose temper. May be physically and/or verbally aggressive. May show violence, bullying, and destructive tendencies. May seem uncaring. May have legal problems.
Academic Difficulties	Problems with learning, understanding, or remembering academic material. Struggles with reading, writing, spelling, and/or arithmetic. Poor academic performance. May have difficulty keeping up in school. May struggle with communication skills.
Academic Difficulties: Language (P & T)	Problems with reading, writing, spelling, and/or communication skills.

(continued)

Scale	Common Characteristics of High Scorers
Academic Difficulties: Math (P & T)	Problems with math.
Hyperactivity/ Impulsivity[c]	High activity levels, may be restless, may have difficulty being quiet. May have problems with impulse control. May interrupt others or have difficulty waiting for his/her turn.
Separation Fears (P & T)[b]	Fears being separated from parents/caregivers.
Social Problems (P & T)[a]	Socially awkward, may be shy. May have difficulty with friendships, poor social connections, limited conversational skills. May have poor social reciprocity. May seem socially isolated.
Perfectionistic and Compulsive Behaviors (P & T)	Rigid, inflexible, perfectionistic. May become "stuck" on a behavior or idea. May be overly concerned with cleanliness. May set unrealistic goals.
Violence Potential Indicator	At risk for being violent.[d]
Physical Symptoms	May have issues with sleeping, eating, appetite, or weight issues.

Sources: Adapted from Conners *Comprehensive Behavior Rating Scales manual* (Multi-Health Systems, 2008) and Conners *CBRS Interpretive Update* (Multi-Health Systems, 2009). P = Parent, T = Teacher, SR = Self-Report.

[a] Subscale of Emotional Distress on Conners CBRS–T.
[b] Subscale of Emotional Distress on Conners CBRS–P.
[c] Hyperactivity on Conners CBRS–T.
[d] See "Caution: Retrospective versus Prospective Research: VPI" in this chapter.

[fill in diagnosis here] than expected for his age, although a diagnosis cannot be assigned without additional information."

In addition to the *T*-scores and percentiles described previously, the DSM-IV-TR symptom scales are also reported as **symptom counts**. This is a raw score of the number of symptomatic criteria endorsed by a rater at levels sufficient to warrant consideration for diagnosis. Each symptom count is classified as "probably met" or "probably not met" (see Chapter 3 for additional information about how this classification is reached, including the determination of which

≡ Rapid Reference 4.5

Conners EC Behavior Scales and Common Characteristics of High Scorers

Conners EC Behavior Scale	Common Characteristics of High Scorers	
	Conners EC or Conners EC BEH	Conners EC BEH(S)
Inattention/Hyperactivity	Difficulty with control of attention and/or behavior. May have poor concentration or be easily distracted. May lose interest quickly or have difficulty finishing things. May have high activity levels and difficulty staying seated. May be easily excited. May be impulsive and/or fidgety.	Difficulty with control of attention and/or behavior. May have poor concentration and/or be easily distracted. May have high activity levels and/or impulsivity. May be easily excited.
Defiant/Aggressive Behaviors	May be argumentative, defiant, destructive, or dishonest. May have problems with controlling temper. May have problems with physical and/or verbal aggression.	May be argumentative, defiant, destructive, or dishonest. May have problems with controlling temper. May have problems with physical and/or verbal aggression.
Defiance/Temper	Difficult. May be argumentative, defiant, or manipulative. May be moody or have poor anger control.	—
Aggression	Aggressive. May fight or bully. May be rude, destructive, or dishonest.	—
Social Functioning/Atypical Behavior	Poor social skills and/or odd and unusual. May have difficulty with friendships; socially awkward. May appear disinterested in social interactions. May have difficulty with emotions. May have unusual interests, behaviors, and/or language patterns. May show repetitive or rigid behavior.	May be odd and unusual. May have difficulty with friendships. May appear disinterested in social interactions. May have difficulty with social cues.

(continued)

Conners EC Behavior Scale	Common Characteristics of High Scorers	
	Conners EC or Conners EC BEH	Conners EC BEH(S)
Social Functioning	Poor social skills. May have difficulty with body language, social cues, or emotions. May seem rude or unfriendly. May have no friends; may be unliked, unaccepted, or ignored by peers.	—
Atypical Behaviors	Odd and unusual. May have unusual interests and/or language. May have repetitive body movements or play. May be rigid or inflexible. May appear uninterested in social interactions. May have limited emotional expression. May engage in unusual behaviors (e.g., self-harm, pica, tics).	—
Anxiety	Anxious, including emotional or physical symptoms. May be fearful or have difficulty controlling worries. May be clingy or easily frightened. Feelings may be easily hurt. Physical symptoms may include feeling sick and aches/pains; may have sleep difficulties or seem tired.	Anxious, including emotional or physical symptoms. May be fearful. May be clingy or easily frightened. Physical symptoms may include feeling sick and/or sleep difficulties.
Mood and Affect	Shows symptoms of depression. Mood problems may include irritability, sadness, negativity, and anhedonia. May be tearful. May display sad or morbid themes in play.	Shows symptoms of depression. Mood problems may include irritability, sadness, negativity, and anhedonia. May be tearful.
Physical Symptoms	Physical symptoms that may have medical/emotional roots. May complain of aches/pains or feeling sick. May have eating issues. May seem tired and/or have sleep difficulties.	Physical symptoms that may have medical/emotional roots. May complain of aches/pains. May seem tired and/or have sleep difficulties.
Sleep problems (P)	May have sleep difficulties or nightmares.	—

Source: Adapted from Conners Early Childhood manual (Multi-Health Systems, 2009).

Note. P = This subscale is on the parent form only.

CAUTION
....

Retrospective versus Prospective Research: VPI

The features identified by retrospective research are not always the same as those identified by prospective research. Features identified by retrospective research may not be predictive of future behavior.

Retrospective research: Look back into the history of people who are in a group now to identify common features. These features may or may not be predictive.

Prospective research: Look at a group of people now who share common features, and follow them over time to see if those features predict anything.

Consider this example: As I reflect on shared features, I realize that all the talkative children in my class took the bus to school this morning (*retrospective* research). Does this mean that all students who ride the bus are talkative? Tomorrow, I will make a list of all children in my class who rode the bus, and watch them to see if they are all talkative (*prospective* research). I will find out if the common features suggested by the retrospective research are possibly predictive of future behavior.

The Conners CBRS Violence Potential Indicator (VPI) scale is based on items identified by *retrospective* research. Without *prospective* research on school violence and violence prevention, nobody can make definitive predictions regarding which students may become violent in the future. Some of the items on the VPI that reflect current violent and aggressive behaviors are weighted more heavily in the scoring process, and should be investigated immediately (see Rapid Reference 4.13; see also Caution "Interpreting Item-Level Data" in this chapter). Other items on the VPI reflect possibly benign items that are indirectly related to the potential for violence. See the Conners CBRS Interpretive Update (2009) for further information.

An elevated VPI score on the Conners CBRS is only a suggestion that a child *may* be at risk for behaving violently in the future. It does not necessarily mean that the child *has* been violent in the past, or that he *will* be violent in the future. Be particularly cautious when interpreting an elevated score on the VPI.

symptoms are "indicated"). When a symptom count is "probably met," this can be described as, "This child shows many symptoms of the DSM-IV-TR diagnosis [fill in diagnosis here], although a diagnosis cannot be assigned without additional information." A high symptom count alone is not sufficient support for a diagnosis. Clinical judgment is required to establish whether a symptom is present at pathologic levels. Additional criteria such as course, age of onset, pervasiveness, level of impairment, and differential diagnosis must be met. In some cases, results from the Conners assessments may *not* indicate a high symptom count even when clinical judgment suggests the diagnosis is present. It is critical to remember that results from the Conners assessments are part of the clinical picture for a child but cannot determine diagnosis. No single measure provides sufficient evidence to support or reject a clinical diagnosis; diagnosis is a clinical art that requires relevant training and experience. A complete review of DSM-IV-TR principles is beyond the scope of this book; the reader is referred to the DSM-IV-TR (APA, 2000) for additional guidance.

DON'T FORGET

No single measure provides sufficient evidence to support or reject a clinical diagnosis.

When interpreting results from the DSM-IV-TR symptom counts, some elements can be combined to add content. If the symptom count for the DSM-IV-TR ADHD Hyperactive/Impulsive scale is "probably met," *and* the symptom count for the DSM-IV-TR ADHD Inattentive scale is "probably met," add the diagnosis of ADHD Combined Type to your list of possibilities. Similarly, if the symptom count for the DSM-IV-TR Major Depressive Episode scale is "probably met," and the symptom count for the DSM-IV-TR Manic Episode scale is "probably met," consider the possibility of a Mixed Episode. See the DSM-IV-TR for guidance as to what constitutes a Mixed Episode and how this might impact diagnostic decisions.[5]

In certain circumstances, the *T*-scores for the DSM-IV-TR symptom scales and the symptom counts are discrepant. This does not necessarily invalidate the results or indicate scoring errors as these two scores are calculated from different metrics. As discussed in Rapid Reference 4.6, the DSM-IV-TR *T*-scores are *relative* indicators of the DSM-IV-TR symptoms; in other words, these scores describe a child's level of certain symptomatic behaviors relative to his age- and gender-matched peers. In contrast, the DSM-IV-TR symptom counts are *absolute* indicators of DSM-IV-TR symptoms; that is, these scores describe whether certain symptoms of a diagnosis are considered present or absent for a child, regardless of age or gender. The *T*-scores are generally more sensitive to developmental atypicality for a given age or gender, which is important even when a child may not be demonstrating the full symptom count as required by the DSM-IV-TR. See Rapid Reference 4.6 for a brief summary of these two types of

---

5. In brief, the presence of a Mixed Episode can impact the choice of Bipolar I versus Bipolar II, but there are many historic and contextual elements that must be considered in this determination.

≡ Rapid Reference 4.6

....

DSM-IV-TR Symptom Scales: *T*-scores and Symptom Counts

DSM-IV-TR *T*-score	DSM-IV-TR Symptom Count
Relative: compared to peers; how much of it is there	Absolute: compared to rules from DSM-IV-TR; is each symptom indicated or not (yes/no); are symptom criteria met or not (present/absent)
Describes a child's level of these behaviors relative to age- and gender-matched peers; developmentally sensitive comparison helps determine if something is atypical for child's age and gender	Describes whether symptoms of the diagnoses are present or absent
Considers age and gender	Ignores age and gender
Sensitive to developmental atypicality	Corresponds to part of DSM-IV-TR diagnostic criteria
Elevated score indicates the child shows greater symptoms of the disorder than is typical for his age and gender (i.e., higher frequency, more symptoms, or both)	Symptom count "probably met" indicates enough symptoms of the diagnosis were endorsed at high enough levels that the diagnosis might be a consideration

DSM-IV-TR scores. See also the table printed in each assessment manual for suggestions when integrating DSM-IV-TR *T*-scores and symptom counts.[6]

Developmental Milestone (DM) Scales

Each of the Conners EC Developmental Milestone scales is reported as a *T*-score. These scales include developmental markers that are grouped conceptually to facilitate interpretation and intervention planning. An average or lower *T*-score indicates a report that the child is demonstrating typical levels of independence and skill acquisition in that area. An elevated *T*-score indicates

---

6. There is a table in the Interpretation chapter of the Conners 3 and Conners CBRS manuals titled "Interpretation Guidelines for DSM-IV-TR Scores . . . " for guidelines to help you interpret the relationship between these two metrics.

an area that warrants closer examination for possible developmental delay, based on the rater's descriptions. See Rapid Reference 4.7 for a brief description of each DM scale.

Three of the Developmental Milestone scales are grouped into **conceptual clusters** to help with interpretation:

1. Adaptive Skills: Dressing, Eating/Drinking, Toileting, Hygiene, Helping.
2. Communication: Expressive, Receptive.
3. Motor Skills: Fine, Gross.

Although there are not summary *T*-scores for these clusters, it is helpful to review items in these conceptual groupings to help identify patterns of strength/weakness within a given domain of functioning. It is possible for a child to have difficulties in a Developmental Milestone cluster even when the scale *T*-score is not elevated, especially if other clusters in that scale are developing without concern, and vice versa.

≡ Rapid Reference 4.7

Conners EC Developmental Milestone Scales and Content

Conners EC Developmental Milestone Scale	Content
Adaptive Skills	Adaptive functioning skills, including dressing, eating/drinking, toileting, personal hygiene, and helping.
Communication	Expressive and receptive language, including verbal, facial, and gestural communication.
Motor Skills	Fine and gross motor skills.
Play	Imaginative and pretend play.
Pre-Academic/Cognitive	Knowledge of pre-academic concepts (e.g., shapes, colors, letters, numbers, body parts), pre-reading skills (e.g., rhyming, name recognition), and early memory/reasoning skills.

Source: Adapted from *Conners Early Childhood manual* (Multi-Health Systems, 2009).

Use **item-level analysis** to better understand the DM scales and clusters. As suggested in the general interpretation guidelines, examine items contributing to elevated DM scale *T*-scores. Keep in mind that the DM items are rated on a different scale than the other Conners items. A rating of "2" (i.e., the child always, or almost always, performs this skill independently) suggests mastery of the skill and thus does not warrant any concern. Ratings of "1" (i.e., the child sometimes performs this skill independently) and "0" (i.e., the child never, or rarely, performs this skill independently) cannot be understood out of context; it is necessary to consider the child's chronologic age relative to typical acquisition of the skill to interpret these ratings.

CAUTION

Clinical Judgment and Competence

Clinical judgment is required when using Conners EC reference data like base rates and ages of attainment. Be careful to practice within your range of competence and seek supervision as needed.

The Conners EC provides two types of reference data to evaluate single DM item ratings: base rates and ages of attainment.[7] The base rates (a.k.a., "item response frequencies") for a specific item can provide a reference for whether an individual's rating is typical or atypical for the child's age and gender. When the majority of age- and gender-matched children are rated higher than the child on a Developmental Milestone item, it suggests possible concern. The larger the gap between the child's rating and the majority rating, the more concern (e.g., a rating of 1 when most children are rated 2 is less concerning than a 0 to 2 difference). Also, more concern is warranted when the percentage of children rated at the same level is extremely low (e.g., 2 percent base rate for the given rating indicates more concern than a 30 percent base rate).

DON'T FORGET

Compare Actual Ratings with Base Rates and Ages of Attainment

Conners EC Base Rates and Age of Attainment values are based on the item *rating* rather than the raw item score. This is an exception to the general guideline to use item *scores* when interpreting item-level data. See Chapter 3 for more information.

---

7. Conners EC base rates can be obtained through the MHS Customer Service department. Age of attainment tables are provided in an appendix of the Conners EC manual.

≡ Rapid Reference 4.8

"Developing" and "Mastered" Age References

These age references are available for each item on the Conners EC Developmental Milestone scales.

- The "Developing" age is the youngest age at which most of the normative sample was rated a 1 or 2 (i.e., the majority of these children were at least developing the skill). This is the age by which a child should *sometimes* be able to perform the specific skill without help.
- The "Mastered" age is the youngest age at which most of the normative sample was rated a 2 (i.e., the majority of these children had mastered the skill). This is the age by which a child should be able to *consistently* perform the specific skill without help.

Age of Attainment values (*"Developing"* or *"Mastered"*) help establish if a given skill is consistent with age- and gender-based expectations (see Rapid Reference 4.8). When a child is older than these reference ages, it suggests possible concern (with increasing concern as the gap between the child's chronologic age and the age of attainment increases). There is not an absolute rule for how much of an age discrepancy is interpretable when using age of attainment data. This decision must be made based on your practice, experience, and assessment goals. Issues to consider include the child's age; 6 months represents a 25 percent delay for a 2-year-old child but less than a 10 percent delay for a 6-year-old child. At the same time, skills emerge and change rapidly for younger children, so a skill that was not observed one week may suddenly be mastered a month later. In general, it is reasonable to use a 1-year discrepancy between the reference age and the child's chronologic age when determining when to express concern about an individual skill.

Another consideration in interpreting any developmental milestone data is the child's opportunities to learn and practice skills. If a child has been cared for in an informal setting or by family members, she may not have been exposed to certain skill sets or demands; it is possible that she has good *abilities* but inadequate *opportunities* thus far. For example, a caregiver might anticipate the child's needs rather than requiring her to use expressive language. This context suggests different interpretation than a child who has been in a formal pre-school setting with consistent skill demonstration and expectations but still does not demonstrate the skills.

Remember that low ratings on the Developmental Milestone items can indicate issues with actual skill attainment, consistency of demonstration, and/or independent demonstration in that setting. Situational factors such as expectations and demands can impact a child's opportunities to demonstrate a skill. See Chapter 3 for information about looking up Conners EC reference data, including which age of attainment to use. See Rapid Reference 4.9 for suggested text to use when interpreting base rates and ages of attainment for Developmental Milestone items.

Whether comparing item-level DM data with Conners EC references (i.e., base rates and ages of attainment) or with other sources of information (e.g., developmental milestone checklists, experts in child development), the important part of item-level analysis is to identify skills or groups of skills that may warrant closer evaluation or intervention. These items can also guide interpretation of the DM scale *T*-scores.

≡ *Rapid Reference 4.9*

Interpreting Base Rates[a] and Ages of Attainment for the Developmental Milestones

Base Rates

Item Rating	Majority Rated	Suggested Text
0	2	It is unusual that this child is not demonstrating this skill yet, as most boys/girls his/her age have mastered the skill.
	1	It is unusual that this child is not demonstrating this skill yet, as most boys/girls his/her age show evidence that they are developing the skill.
	0	*No need to comment; this is a typical rating for the child's age and gender.*
1	2	It is unusual that this child is not consistently and independently demonstrating this skill, as most boys/girls his/her age have mastered the skill.
	1, 0	*No need to comment; this is a typical rating for the child's age and gender.*
2	n/a	*No need to compare with base rates; a rating of "2" indicates no concerns as the child is consistently demonstrating the skill in this setting.*

[a]Base rates may be obtained by contacting MHS Customer Service.

(continued)

Ages of Attainment

Item Rating	Reference Age	Comparison	Suggested Text
0	Developing	Ref > CA	Most boys/girls show evidence of this skill by this age, but this child is not demonstrating the skill in this setting.
		Ref ≤ CA	This child is not showing evidence of this skill in this setting, but this is common for boys/girls at this age.

Ages of Attainment

Item Rating	Reference Age	Comparison	Suggested Text
1	Mastery	Ref > CA	Most boys/girls consistently demonstrate this skill by this age, but this child's skill demonstration is not consistently independent yet.
		Ref ≤ CA	This child is not consistently and independently demonstrating this skill in this setting, but this is common at this age.
2	n/a	n/a	*No need to compare with ages of attainment; a rating of "2" indicates no concerns as the child is consistently demonstrating the skill in this setting.*

Note: Ref = Reference Age, CA = chronologic age, "Ref > CA" indicates child is younger than reference age, "Ref ≤ CA" indicates child is close to or older than reference age.

DON'T FORGET

....

Understanding Low DM Ratings

Low ratings on the Developmental Milestone items can indicate issues with actual skill attainment, consistency of demonstration, and/or independent demonstration in that setting. Situational factors such as expectations and demands can impact a child's opportunities to demonstrate a skill.

Overall Profile

In this interpretation step, the examiner focuses on global descriptions of the child. These include the profile of *T*-scores, the Impairment items, and the Index scores.

Profile of **T-scores**

The first global indicator is the profile of *T*-scores. Reviewing the relative elevations of *T*-scores helps the examiner describe the child and/or rater in broad terms.

- When a few *T*-scores are elevated, this summarizes the rater's primary areas of concern. This is particularly helpful in cases where the referral question was vague. In contrast with *T*-scores that fall in the average or below average ranges, this type of profile can help describe a child's relative strengths and weaknesses, suggesting targets for treatment and tools to help reach treatment goals.
- When all of the *T*-scores are elevated, this indicates that the rater has many concerns about the child. In some cases, a child is truly struggling in every area assessed; in other cases, a few serious concerns have caused the rater to indicate high levels of concern about everything (i.e., a "negative halo effect").
- When all of the *T*-scores are in the average range, this suggests that the rater either has no concerns or that his concerns are typical for children of that age and gender. This can be very helpful feedback to guide realistic expectations for parents, teachers, or others who refer a child for evaluation.
- When all of the *T*-scores are below average, the rater has described the child as having fewer problems than most children that age and gender. This is statistically unusual and warrants a closer look at other aspects of the child's functioning. This pattern can indicate denial of a child's problems.

Impairment items

The Impairment items provide another global description of the child. Each Conners assessment has Impairment items asking the rater to describe how the child's problems impact his functioning in multiple settings. The parent forms ask about academic, social, and domestic domains; teacher forms are limited to academic and social functioning.

- When all of the Impairment items are elevated, this indicates that the child is being impacted in multiple settings. Some form of intervention is usually required in these cases.

- When one or two of the Impairment items is elevated, this suggests the setting that should be targeted in intervention plans. It can be helpful to discuss the setting in which no impairment is noted, as these exceptions might help identify useful accommodations for the other settings.
- When no Impairment items are elevated, this suggests that the child's problems (if any were described on the rating scale) are not currently impacting his functioning in these domains. For young children, this does not prevent consideration of diagnosis or intervention. For school-aged children, the DSM-IV-TR and most school settings require evidence of impairment before diagnosis can be assigned or intervention can be initiated.

Index scores

Each Conners assessment has at least one Index score. These index scores were statistically derived, meaning the items were selected based on numeric data rather than clinical experience.

The Conners 3 and Conners CBRS each have a differential index (Conners 3 ADHD Index and Conners Clinical Index, respectively) that helps describe whether a child is more similar to children in a diagnostic group or children with no clinical diagnosis. The ratings for the Conners 3 ADHD Index and the Conners Clinical Index are reported as a probability score ranging from 0 percent to 99 percent (see Rapid Reference 4.10).[8] This probability score indicates the percentage of time that an Index score occurred in children with a clinical diagnosis versus children with no clinical diagnosis. For example, a probability score of 35 percent indicates that the raw Index score occurred 35 out of 100 times for children in that diagnostic group (as compared to children with no clinical diagnosis).

The **Conners 3 ADHD Index** (Conners 3AI) is composed of 10 items selected as the best group of items to distinguish between children with ADHD and children with no clinical diagnosis. This is an important distinction; the Conners 3AI does not compare a child with ADHD with children from other diagnostic groups. The comparison is with children in the general population who have never been diagnosed. Conners 3AI probability scores range from 11 percent (parent), 19 percent (teacher), and 26 percent (self-report) to 99 percent (all raters).

---

8. The actual range for each Index probability score is restricted based on data; this describes the total possible range. Specific ranges for each Index are reported in the following paragraphs.

≡ *Rapid Reference 4.10*

Probability Score Guidelines (Conners 3 ADHD Index, Conners CBRS Clinical Index)[a]

Probability %	Guideline
<20%	Very low; responses are very similar to those for the general population; a clinical classification is highly unlikely.
20–39%	Low; responses are similar to those for the general population; a clinical classification is unlikely.
40–49%	Borderline; responses are slightly more similar to the general population than to the clinical groups.
50%	Equal Probability; this score is equally likely to occur for youth from the general population and youth in clinical groups.
51–60%	Borderline; responses are slightly more similar to the clinical groups than to the general population.
61–79%	High; responses are similar to those for the clinical groups; a clinical classification is likely.
>80%	Very high; responses are very similar to those for the clinical groups; a clinical classification is very likely.

Sources: Adapted from *Conners 3rd Edition manual* (Multi-Health Systems, 2008) and *Conners Comprehensive Behavior Rating Scales manual* (Multi-Health Systems, 2008).

[a]See Caution: Interpreting Probability Scores in this chapter.

CAUTION

Interpreting Probability Scores

The probability scores used to report the Conners 3 ADHD Index and the Conners CBRS Clinical Index describe how often a score occurred in children with a clinical diagnosis as opposed to youth in the general population. A high probability score indicates that the child's score is similar to scores for children in the relevant clinical group. A low probability score indicates that the child's score is similar to scores for children in the general population group.

The probability score does *not* tell you how likely it is that a child has a diagnosis.

A high Conners 3AI indicates that the child is more similar to children with ADHD than children in the general population; this can provide support for consideration of an ADHD diagnosis. When the Conners 3AI is low, the child is more similar to children in the general population than to most children with ADHD. A low Conners 3AI does not provide sufficient evidence to reject a diagnosis of ADHD; it simply indicates that the child's Conners 3 scores are not typical of children with ADHD.

In addition to the probability score, the examiner can also obtain a *T*-score for the Conners 3AI. This is a standard calculation on the Conners 3AI form. Please see the Conners 3 manual for information about calculating the Conners 3AI *T*-score from the Conners 3 full-length form. Because the probability score and the *T*-score are based on different metrics, these two results may be discrepant in some cases. Rapid Reference 4.11 provides guidelines for interpreting these scores.

DON'T FORGET

Conners 3 ADHD Index

The Conners 3 ADHD Index (Conners 3AI) was developed using a group of children with ADHD and a group of children with no clinical diagnosis. It does not differentiate ADHD from other clinical diagnoses.

The **Conners Clinical Index** (Conners CI) is a small group of items selected as the best group of items to distinguish between children with a *clinical diagnosis* and children with no clinical diagnosis. Diagnoses included in this analysis were disruptive behavior disorders (ODD, CD), Learning Disorders, Language Disorders, Mood Disorders, Anxiety Disorders, and ADHD. Each of these areas is represented by five items on the Conners CI. The overall Conners CI score is based on the highest clinical area score. The clinical sample used to establish the Conners CI did *not* include youth with diagnoses in the autism spectrum (e.g., Autistic Disorder, Asperger's Disorder, Pervasive Developmental Disorder Not Otherwise Specified or PDD-NOS). This aspect of development is important to remember for interpretation, as the Conners CI is unlikely to be elevated for youth who present with primary features of the autism spectrum (see Rapid Reference 1.21). Conners CI probability scores range from 1 percent to 98 percent on the parent form, 1 percent to 94 percent on the teacher form, and 5 percent to 99 percent on the self-report form.

A high Conners CI indicates that the child is more similar to children with a clinical diagnosis than to children in the general population; this provides support

≡ Rapid Reference 4.11

Conners 3 ADHD Index: T-scores and Probability Scores

	Conners 3AI Probability Score	Conners 3AI T-score	Interpretation Guidelines
Both scores elevated	≥ 61%	Elevated	• Ratings of the youth are very similar to those of youth with ADHD. • More of the key features of ADHD are present than expected for this age and gender.
Probability score borderline, T-score elevated	51–60%	Elevated	• Ratings of the youth are somewhat similar to those of youth with ADHD. • More of the key features of ADHD are present than expected for this age and gender.
Only T-score elevated	≤ 50%	Elevated	• Ratings of the youth are not similar to those of youth with ADHD, but the key features of ADHD are occurring in excess of what is typical for that youth's age and gender. • The assessor may wish to consider alternate explanations for why the T-score could be elevated (e.g., another issue besides ADHD may be producing these types of concerns in that particular setting).

(continued)

	Conners 3AI Probability Score	Conners 3AI T-score	Interpretation Guidelines
Only probability score elevated	≥ 61%	Not elevated	• Ratings of the youth are very similar to those of youth with ADHD, but key features of ADHD are at (or below) developmental expectations for that age and gender. • Although ratings of the youth are like those of youth with ADHD, the current presentation is not atypical for this age and gender. The assessor should give careful consideration as to whether the symptoms are present in excess of developmental expectations.
Probability score borderline, T-score average/low	51–60%	Not elevated	• Ratings of the youth are somewhat similar to those of youth with ADHD, but any key features of ADHD that are present are at (or below) developmental expectations for that age and gender.
Both scores average/low	< 50%	Not elevated	• Ratings of the youth are more similar to those made by the general population than to ratings of youth with ADHD. • Any key features of ADHD that are present are at or below developmental expectations for that age and gender.

Source: Adapted from *Conners 3rd edition manual* (Multi-Health Systems, 2008).

for consideration of a clinical diagnosis. When the Conners CI is low, the child is more similar to children in the general population than to most children with a clinical diagnosis. A low Conners CI does not provide sufficient evidence to reject a diagnosis; it simply indicates that the child's Conners CBRS scores are not typical of children with one of the clinical diagnoses included in this analysis.

T-scores can be calculated for each of the five clinical areas included in the Conners CI: Disruptive Behavior, Learning & Language, Mood, Anxiety, and ADHD. When one or more of these indicators is elevated, this supports further consideration of a clinical diagnosis in one of these categories. The relative elevation of a Conners CI Indicator can indicate which clinical group is most similar to the child's presentation. While this is not diagnostic, it can help determine which area might warrant further investigation or intervention. These five Conners CI Indicators are standard calculations on the Conners CI form. Please see Appendix D for information about how to calculate the Conners CI Indicator *T*-scores from the full-length Conners CBRS form.

DON'T FORGET

Index Scores Do Not Determine Diagnoses

The Conners 3 ADHD Index, Conners Clinical Index, and Conners Clinical Index Indicators are not absolute proof of an individual child's diagnostic status, nor of the best diagnosis for a child. These scores are based on group data and may not be accurate in individual cases. Each score indicates whether a child's scores are more similar to children in certain clinical samples or children from the general population. The Conners Clinical Index does not include *all* clinical groups—only the ones specified in the five Indicators.

The Conners 3 and Conners EC each have a Global Index (**Conners 3 Global Index** and **Conners EC Global Index**, respectively). The Global Index is reported as a *T*-score that follows the same general principles described in the previous "Standardized Scores" section. The 10 items on the Global Index are the same items as used on the Conners' Rating Scales–Revised (CRS–R) as the "Conners Global Index." Research has found that this scale is a good indicator of overall psycho-pathology. A high score on the Global Index is usually associated with broad issues in general functioning; this score may not be elevated if a problem is circumscribed and not pervasive. This index is usually sensitive to treatment effects.

The Global Index has two subscale *T*-scores: Restless-Impulsive and Emotional Lability. When the Total score is elevated, one or both of the subscale

≡ *Rapid Reference 4.12*

Common Characteristics of High Scorers on the Conners Global Index (Conners 3GI or Conners ECGI)

Conners Global Index Scale/Subscale	Common Characteristics of High Scorers
Restless–Impulsive	May be easily distracted. May be restless, fidgety, or impulsive. May have trouble finishing things. May distract others.
Emotional Lability	Moody and emotional; may cry, lose temper, or become frustrated easily.
Total	Moody and emotional; restless, impulsive, inattentive.

Sources: Adapted from *Conners 3rd edition manual* (Multi-Health Systems, 2008) and *Conners Early Childhood manual* (Multi-Health Systems, 2009).

scores is usually elevated as well. The relative elevations of the subscales can aid in the interpretation of the Total score. It is also appropriate to interpret elevations of either subscale, even if the Total score is not elevated. Typical interpretations of elevated Global Index scores are provided in Rapid Reference 4.12.

Item-Level Responses

This step moves from the "big picture" of scale scores to the details of individual items. This interpretation step requires significant clinical judgment as it is risky to make item-level decisions or recommendations. Composite scores, such as *T*-scores obtained on main scales, are more reliable as they are based on a compilation of many responses in comparison to age- and gender-based normative data. With these cautions in mind, there are situations in which it is helpful to consider item-level contributions to the overall profile.

Items to Review

- **Items on elevated scales:** When a *T*-score is elevated, the examiner should review item scores contributing to the total score. In some instances, a scale is elevated because a few items were endorsed at very high levels. Other times, a scale is elevated because many items were endorsed at mild or moderate levels. Some items on the scale may be nonproblematic for a given child even when the scale score is elevated. Some scales can be reviewed by conceptual clusters, even when they don't have subscale scores. These include the Conners CBRS Violence Potential Indicator (VPI) scale (which can be reviewed by severity[9]; see Rapid Reference 4.13; see also Caution: Retrospective versus Prospective Research: VPI in this chapter), Conners EC Inattention/Hyperactivity scale (Inattention versus Hyperactivity/Impulsivity; see Rapid Reference 4.14), and Conners EC Anxiety scale (physical versus emotional expression of anxiety; see Rapid Reference 4.15). Knowledge of what led to the scale elevation improves the examiner's understanding of the score, resulting in a more meaningful interpretation.

- **Items with high scores:** Although an entire interpretation should not be built around a single elevated item, that item's content may be relevant in developing treatment plans. Examiners should look over item-level *scores* for the rating scale (which take into account reverse-scored items; see Chapter 3) and note which items have high scores.
- **Grouped items:** Some of the Conners assessments have groups of clinically meaningful items that should be reviewed. These include Screener items (Conners 3), Other Clinical Indicators (Conners CBRS and Conners EC), and Critical items (Conners 3 and Conners CBRS). The computerized report flags items in these clusters that may need further investigation. These grouped items are discussed in more detail below.
- **Text responses:** All of the Conners assessments provide two Additional Questions that ask the rater to describe any additional concerns and the child's strengths/skills. Text responses to these items as well as any other comments provided by the rater are important to consider when interpreting results from the Conners assessments.

Types of Review

Item-level data can be reviewed quantitatively and qualitatively. Base rates were used to determine some of the flags described below. Base rates are available for

---

9. The scale name and weighting categories reflect information from the Conners CBRS Interpretive Update (2009).

≡ Rapid Reference 4.13

Severity of Violence Potential Indicator (VPI) Items[a]

Level of Severity[b]	Item Content
Mild	Trouble controlling anger Feels rejected Loses temper Argues with adults Poor school performance Feels disrespected Annoys others Gets into trouble Is lonely
Moderate	Picked on or bullied Disregard for others' rights Drinks alcohol Lost interest/pleasure Gets even Starts fights Seeks danger/risks/thrills Angry/resentful Uses drugs Cruel to animals Bullies/threatens/scares others Damages/destroys others' property Gets high with household materials Shows interest in weapons Knows where to get a weapon Gets into trouble at school
Severe	Made plans to hurt others Carries a weapon Uses a weapon Gang membership Violent/aggressive Physically hurts others Trouble with police

Source: Based on scoring guidelines from Conners CBRS Interpretive Update (Multi-Health Systems, 2009).

[a] See Caution regarding interpreting elevated scores on the VPI.
[b] Level of severity is based on Transposing Rules from Conners CBRS interpretive update (2009).

≡ Rapid Reference 4.14

Content of the Conners EC Inattention/Hyperactivity Scale

Content	Parent Item
Hyperactivity and/or Impulsivity	Acts as if driven by a motor
	Acts before thinking
	Excitable, impulsive
	Fidgeting
	Gets overstimulated or "wound-up" in exciting situations
	Has difficulty staying in seat
	Is always "on the go"
	Jumps from one activity to another
	Restless or overactive
	Runs or climbs when supposed to walk or sit
Inattention	Does not pay attention
	Fails to finish things he/she starts
	Has a short attention span
	Has difficulty focusing on just one thing
	Inattentive, easily distracted
	Loses interest quickly

Source: Adapted from Items by Scale listing for Inattention/Hyperactivity in Appendix of the Conners Early Childhood manual (Multi-Health Systems, 2009).

all Conners EC assessment items (see Chapter 3); these offer a way to evaluate whether the rater's response to a single item is typical or atypical for a young child's age and gender. The Conners EC Developmental Milestone items have special quantitative information—the ages of attainment (discussed in

≡ Rapid Reference 4.15

Content of the Conners EC Anxiety Scale

Content	Parent Item
Physical	Complains about aches and pains
	Has nightmares or night terrors
	Has trouble falling asleep when alone
	Has trouble falling asleep
	Wakes up during the night, then has trouble falling back to sleep
Emotional	Anticipates the worst
	Appears "on edge," nervous, or jumpy
	Cries often and easily
	Feelings are easily hurt
	Has trouble controlling his/her worries
	Is afraid of one or more specific objects or situations (for example, animals, insects, blood, doctors, water, storms, heights, or places)
	Is afraid to be alone
	Is anxious
	Is overly clingy or attached to parent(s)
	Is timid, easily frightened
	Worries
	Complains about aches and pains

Source: Adapted from Items by Scale listing for Anxiety in Appendix of the *Conners Early Childhood manual* (Multi-Health Systems, 2009).

Chapter 3). Qualitative review involves reviewing the item content and the rater's response.

Grouped Items

Screener items on the Conners 3 cover key concepts pertaining to anxiety and depression. The four Anxiety Screener items relate to generalized worrying, and the four Depression Screener items represent symptoms of depression in children. These items are flagged on the computerized report when the rater marks that they are present at any level. Clinical judgment is required to determine how vigorously to pursue these suggestions of possible anxiety and/or depression. The Conners 3 manual suggests considering the extremity of any single Screener item as well as the combination of multiple Screener item endorsements when deciding whether further investigation is warranted. Presence of these symptoms is not sufficient to justify a diagnosis of an Anxiety Disorder or Mood Disorder; however, these Screener items could suggest the need for additional evaluation to consider the possibility of these issues. Even when symptoms of anxiety and/or depression are not present at a diagnostic level, they can impact a child's functioning and response to treatment, so it is important to consider these Screener items when formulating a summary of the Conners 3 results.

Other Clinical Indicators on the Conners CBRS and Conners EC refer to important issues not otherwise covered on the rating scale. These items were included on the final scale due to the importance of recognizing these issues when they occur, even though they were not represented by full scales. These items are flagged on the computerized report when they are endorsed at unusual levels (see Chapter 3, particularly Rapid Reference 3.5).[10] Clinical judgment is required to determine how vigorously to pursue these indicators. Endorsement of these indicators does not necessarily warrant treatment but indicates areas to address during clinical evaluation. Even when such symptoms are not present at a diagnostic level, they can impact a child's functioning and response to treatment, so it is important to consider these Other Clinical Indicators when formulating a summary of the Conners assessment results.

The Conners 3 and Conners CBRS include **Severe Conduct Critical items**. These items represent severe misconduct that warrants immediate investigation, such as cruelty to animals and fire-setting. Research has indicated that such behaviors may predict future violence or harm to others. The Conners CBRS also has **Self-Harm Critical items**. These items represent self-injurious behaviors,

---

10. Be certain you are using updated computer scoring software, as the scoring guidelines for the Conners CBRS Other Clinical Indicator: Social Phobia were updated in 2009.

including behaviors that research has indicated are associated with increased risk of self-harm, such as suicide. For the Self-Harm and Severe Conduct Critical items, it is important to remember that group data do not always predict the behaviors of an individual. See Rapid References 1.15 and 1.16.

The computerized report flags these items when they are endorsed at unusual levels when compared with base rates from the normative sample.[11] If any of these items are flagged for a child (particularly if more than one item in a group is flagged), it is important to discuss the item with the rater as soon as possible to better understand the reason for the rating and determine what steps need to be taken in terms of further investigation and/or immediate intervention.

DON'T FORGET

Group Data and Individual Findings

Group data do not always predict the behaviors of an individual. In some cases, elevations on the Critical items may not warrant immediate intervention; however, they always warrant further investigation.

CAUTION

Interpreting Item-Level Data

Use the item scores and flags (not the actual ratings) from the computerized report when interpreting item-level data. For many Conners items, the score is the same as the rating; exceptions are described below. See Chapter 3 for additional information about how these items are scored.

- Some items on the Conners describe positive functioning, so they are reverse-scored (e.g., "Is good at planning ahead"). On a reverse-scored item, a rating of 3 indicates no concerns as it is scored a 0.
- All of the Developmental Milestone items are reverse-scored. Each is rated from 0 to 2 (i.e., 3 is not an option); a rating of 2 indicates no concerns as it is scored a 0.
- The PI and NI item ratings are dichotomized (i.e., the full rating range of 0 to 3 is condensed to possible scores of 0 or 1).
- DSM-IV-TR item ratings are categorized before calculating the symptom count. Each item is classified as "indicated," "may be indicated," or "not indicated."
- The Conners 3AI item ratings are each transposed into scores ranging from 0 to 2.

---

11. See Rapid Reference 3.5 for discussion of what constitutes "unusual" levels.

- Items on the Conners CBRS Violence Potential Indicator (VPI) scale are weighted, meaning that a rating of 1 on one item could be scored higher (i.e., carry more weight) than a rating of 3 on another item. Possible VPI item scores range from 0 to 8.
- The Critical items and most of the Other Clinical Indicators are flagged for any response greater than 0, but some of these items require a higher response to be flagged (i.e., to indicate significant concern; see Rapid Reference 3.5). Refer to flags printed in the computerized report (or to look-up values in the manuals and interpretive updates) to be certain about your interpretation; do not rely on your memory for interpreting these items.

Integrate Results

When the examiner has completed the previous steps, she has reviewed each score from the Conners assessments in isolation and has begun some rudimentary comparisons among scores. The next step is to integrate these scores and form impressions of what they mean as a whole, embedded in context.

Single Rater

Begin by integrating results within a single rater's Conners form. Although each score describes one type of information, there are groups of scores that may correspond. Compare the scores using Rapid Reference 4.16, which groups scales into larger domains (i.e., behavioral, emotional, social, academic, and other domains). Reviewing combinations of scores can help support or reject hypotheses about a child.

When reviewing Conners CBRS results, a rater may have discrepancies between the T-scores for the DSM-IV-TR symptom scales and the Conners CI Indicators (e.g., the Conners CI ADHD subscore may be elevated although the Conners CBRS DSM-IV-TR ADHD T-score is not, or vice versa). This is possible because these two types of scores are based on different item sets. In these cases, the DSM-IV-TR T-score is the more stable indicator.

DON'T FORGET

If there are discrepancies between the DSM-IV-TR T-score and the corresponding Conners CI Indicator T-score, rely on the DSM-IV-TR T-score.

Multiple Raters

Next, compare results across multiple raters for the same type of Conners assessment (e.g., Conners 3-P and Conners 3-T[S]; not Conners 3-P and Conners

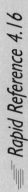

=== *Rapid Reference 4.16*

Overlapping Content Among Conners Assessments

	Conners 3	Conners CBRS	Conners EC
Behavioral Content	Defiance/Aggression Hyperactivity/Impulsivity Critical items: Severe Conduct	Defiant/Aggressive Behaviors Hyperactivity/Impulsivity Critical items: Severe Conduct OCI: Bullying (Perpetration, Victimization)	Defiant/Aggressive Behaviors Inattention/Hyperactivity OCI: Cruelty to animals, Fire setting, Stealing
Emotional Content	Screener items: Anxiety Screener items: Depression	Emotional Distress Separation Fears Perfectionistic and Compulsive Behaviors OCI: Panic Attack, PTSD, Specific Phobia, Trichotillomania Critical items: Self Harm	Anxiety OCI: Perfectionism OCI: PTSD, Specific Phobia, Trichotillomania Mood and Affect OCI: Self-Injury
Social Content	Peer/Family Relations	Social Problems	Social Functioning/Atypical Behaviors

Cognitive/Academic Content	Executive Functioning Learning Problems Inattention	Academic Difficulties	Pre-Academic/Cognitive Inattention/Hyperactivity
Developmental Milestones			Adaptive Skills Communication Motor Skills Play Pre-Academic/Cognitive
DSM-IV-TR Symptom Scales	ADHD Hyperactive-Impulsive ADHD Inattentive Conduct Disorder Oppositional Defiant Disorder	ADHD Hyperactive-Impulsive ADHD Inattentive Conduct Disorder Oppositional Defiant Disorder Major Depressive Episode Manic Episode Generalized Anxiety Disorder Separation Anxiety Disorder Social Phobia Obsessive-Compulsive Disorder Autistic Disorder Asperger's Disorder	

(continued)

	Conners 3	Conners CBRS	Conners EC
Other Content		Violence Potential Indicator Physical Symptoms OCI: Enuresis/Encopresis OCI: Pervasive Developmental Disorder OCI: Pica, Tics, Substance Use	Physical Symptoms Social Functioning/Atypical Behaviors OCI: Pica, Tics
Index Scores	Conners 3AI Conners 3GI Impairment items Additional Questions	Conners CI Impairment items Additional Questions	Conners ECGI Impairment items Additional Questions
Validity Scales	PI, NI, and IncX	PI, NI, and IncX	PI, NI, and IncX

Note: OCI = Other Clinical Indicator(s), PTSD = Posttraumatic Stress Disorder, AI = ADHD Index, GI = Global Index, CI = Clinical Index, ECGI = Early Childhood Global Index, PI = Positive Impression, NI = Negative Impression, IncX = Inconsistency Index

CBRS-P). Within a single evaluation,[12] this step involves integration of parents (mother, father, step-parent, etc.), teachers (multiple subjects/settings), and/or self-report (available for children 8 years old and older). Remember, use of standardized scores like T-scores allows the examiner to compare scores across these different scales even though raters may have responded to different items. The T-scores take into account the rater type (i.e., parent, teacher, self-report) and how that impacts overall ratings, as well as the child's age and gender. Keep in mind that some items vary between parent, teacher, and self-report forms; when you notice a discrepancy in scores it is a good idea to review your item-level analyses to better understand why the scores are discrepant among different types of raters.

DON'T FORGET
....

Standardized scores allow the examiner to compare scores from different raters and from different form lengths.

Examiner characteristics may guide which technique is most efficient for comparison of results across multiple raters. Some examiners find it useful to put scores into a comparison table that can also be used in the final report of results; different colors could be used to highlight high and low scores for ease of comparison. See Appendix C for an example of this type table. Other examiners may prefer a graphic comparison, such as that obtained by plotting the raters' results on a single graph. Remember that tables, graphs, and text can be cut-and-pasted from the computerized reports. Examiners with strong verbal skills may choose to review their notes from the previous steps and create an integrated report for each of those sections. Regardless of which technique is chosen, it is important to focus on comparing patterns of results rather than overfocusing on exact scores. This is particularly true if a rater has elevations on the Validity scales. Think about how the raters are similar or different in the profile peaks and valleys.

- In many cases, results from multiple raters are highly similar. It is not difficult to integrate these results.
- At times, results from multiple raters may seem discrepant, but closer analysis may reveal that the raters are actually describing similar concerns

---

12. The next section, "Other Data," provides some information about comparison of ratings with the same Conners tool over multiple dates; see also Chapter 6, "Change Over Time." See "Integrating Results from the Conners Assessments[0]" in this chapter for information about integrating information across multiple evaluations with different Conners tools.

and similar strengths about a child. It can be useful to review the scales that tend to correspond to help determine whether the raters are describing fundamentally different concepts or whether there are slight differences in where they rated concerns, producing slightly different profiles of results.

• There are instances when different raters describe different levels of concern or even concern versus no concern. These differences are important to consider and understand, as examples of when a child shows better functioning can help when developing a treatment plan. Discrepancies can be related to many variables, including:

  ▪ Response style: Consider whether a rater's response style could account for the discrepancy.

  ▪ Personality factors: Some children are more sensitive to personality factors than others. A child's preference for (or against) a particular parent or teacher can impact ratings. Likewise, a rater's feelings about a child can bias his responses.

  ▪ Environmental features: Different children are affected differently by environmental features such as level of structure, noise, or expectations. Some children respond better than others to demands from adults and/ or peers.

  ▪ Content: Many children show different behavior when engaged in preferred activities than when asked to perform a difficult or disliked task. A child's interest in a given subject or activity can impact her behavior in that setting.

Other Data

Results from the Conners assessments should also be integrated with information from other aspects of an evaluation. In some cases, the evaluator might have data from more than one type of Conners assessment, such as when both the Conners 3 and the Conners CBRS were administered. Available data could also include other rating scales, observation, interview, record review, questionnaires, and cognitive evaluation. See Rapid Reference 4.17 for suggestions about information to obtain in interview and record review. Review of results from cognitive evaluation can help establish appropriate developmental expectations for a child, which may adjust interpretation of the Conners assessments. For example, if a child is found to be functioning in an intellectually deficient range, it might be helpful to consider the child's Conners assessment results relative to a younger peer group. Interactions with raters beyond their Conners ratings can inform interpretation of possible response bias and accuracy. Observation of the child in his natural environment, including settings where his functioning is described as good versus problematic, gives the examiner unique data for consideration in forming clinical opinions. Interviews conducted after reviewing Conners results can seek focused information to test hypotheses the examiner formed during this interpretation process.

This step also involves integrating current Conners results with information from past evaluations. It is important to reflect on how the child's presentation has changed over time and whether he has made interim progress relative to the most recent evaluation as well as earlier evaluations. This historical data is necessary to support some diagnoses in terms of age of onset, persistence, and course. It is also useful in assessing the effectiveness of intervention plans and determining if any changes are needed in treatment.

When repeating the administration of a Conners assessment, you can calculate whether the amount of change between administrations is **statistically significant**. The test manuals describe the use of the Reliable Change Index (RCI); this can be calculated by hand or generated through the computerized Progress Report. When the RCI value indicates that the difference in scores between two administrations is statistically significant, the difference must be examined for **clinical significance**. The test manuals describe a guideline that, when a score moves from one classification category to another (e.g., Very Elevated to Elevated), it may be considered meaningful. Really, any change that results in functional improvement is clinically significant. This decision requires clinical judgment. See Rapid Reference 6.2 for further discussion of describing change over time with the Conners assessments.

Data obtained from other rating scales, review of records, questionnaires, and other sources can provide necessary context for interpreting results from the Conners assessments. Please see "Integrating Results from the Conners Assessments" in this chapter for tips regarding combining results from various Conners assessments.

Report Results

The final step for interpretation of any Conners assessment is to report results in a meaningful way. This interpretation sequence produces specific information about the child that can be shared with parents, teachers, and other relevant personnel in a feedback session or IEP meeting. When results are reported, it is important to include these relevant details:

- These scores were obtained by combining the rater's responses to many different items about the child. The rater was asked to describe his

≡ Rapid Reference 4.17

Important information for background history

Background history can be obtained from:

- Interview or questionnaires with
  - Parent
  - Student
  - Teacher
- Records, such as
  - Report cards
  - Teacher comments
  - Pediatrician records

Content should include:

- Pregnancy, delivery, developmental milestones
- Family history
  - Mental health issues/diagnosis
  - Behavioral/legal issues, substance use
  - Medical conditions (e.g., thyroid problems, sleep disorders)
- Student's history
  - Medical
    ○ Hearing/vision
    ○ Thyroid issues, sleep problems, etc.
    ○ Neurologic impairment (seizure disorder, head injury, near drowning, HIV, tumor)
    ○ Medications
    ○ Other diagnoses that have been considered
  - Academic
    ○ Grades: patterns by content? teacher type? time of day? (fatigue)
    ○ Lose points for missing assignments? bombing tests?
  - Social
    ○ Peer relations
    ○ Social skills
    ○ Pragmatics
  - Emotional
    ○ History of abuse, neglect, trauma
    ○ Coping
    ○ Frustration tolerance
    ○ Lability

Presenting symptoms: critical for diagnostic decisions, including:
- Age of onset: When were problems first noted, and by whom?
- Course of symptoms:
  - Normal development until X, then problems noted?
  - Symptoms changed at some point, when X happened?
- Duration and persistence of symptoms: How long have symptoms been present? Any interruptions in symptoms?
- Frequency: How often are symptoms observed?
- Intensity/severity: How intense are the symptoms, or how severe are they?
- Impairment: Are the symptoms associated with impairment in the child's functioning? Do they impact functioning in more than one domain (school, home, social)—can be obtained by considering results from parent, teacher, and self-report forms.

observations of the child over the past month. He did not know the final categories that were used to summarize the results.

- Standardized scores (like *T*-scores and percentiles) help compare this child with other children who are the same age and gender. This is important because some of these behaviors change as children get older. Some of these behaviors occur at different levels in boys and girls, or develop at different rates in boys and girls.
- High scores show that the rater has high levels of concern in that area. Low scores show average or no concern in that area. (Include some indication of what is considered high or low for the purposes of the current evaluation.)
- Labels for each area of the results describe the typical meaning of that group of scores for most children. Sometimes a child gets a high score in an area for a different reason. The examiner is interested in your questions about the scores, as you might have information to help her use the results to help the child. A score should not be ignored just because the label does not seem to fit a child.

The examiner can choose to summarize results in a table or graph within the written report (see Appendix C for sample tables that can be reproduced in your written report). Users of the Conners assessments are granted permission to reproduce text from the Common Characteristics of High Scorers tables within their written reports. Computerized scoring options include several different report types; see Chapter 3 for additional information on these.

Some computerized reports have an optional feedback form that can be printed and handed to any layperson who is authorized to receive results from the evaluation. This feedback form summarizes results in a way that is meaningful to people who do not have the training or background to understand all of the scores.

INTEGRATING RESULTS FROM THE CONNERS ASSESSMENTS

There will be times when an evaluation requires integration of results from different Conners assessments. As mentioned previously, an examiner might wish to integrate results from the Conners 3 and Conners CBRS within the same evaluation, or to consider how current results relate to past evaluation data using different versions of the Conners assessments (e.g., CRS–R to Conners 3 or Conners CBRS; Conners EC to Conners 3 or Conners CBRS). The following sections provide hints to streamline integration of various Conners assessments, assuming use of the full-length version for each scale. When interpreting other forms, disregard elements that may not be present on those forms.

Integrating the Conners 3 and Conners CBRS

Because these two instruments can both be used with school-aged youth, there are times when they will be used concurrently (see also "Purpose of Assessment" in Chapter 2). It is also possible that the Conners CBRS might be used in an initial evaluation and the Conners 3 used in a follow-up evaluation (or vice versa). Regardless of the reason, there are several overlapping content areas that can (and should) be integrated between these two measures. Although some of the scale names are very similar, there are differences in content that should be considered, particularly when trying to understand discrepant scores.

Refer to Rapid Reference 4.16 for a quick overview of overlapping content areas for the Conners 3 and Conners CBRS. In general, both rating scales cover behavioral and social issues. The Conners CBRS is more comprehensive, particularly for emotional issues. The Conners 3 has more coverage of cognitive/academic issues and more in-depth coverage of ADHD-related issues.

Compare the following scales/items when examining a child's behavior using both the Conners 3 and the Conners CBRS:

- Defiance/Aggression (Conners 3) versus Defiant/Aggressive Behaviors (Conners CBRS): There is some overlap in items for these scales, but most of the items are unique. Both scales cover similar topics, including verbal/physical aggression, violence, destruction, anger control, possible emotional detachment, and possible legal issues. The Conners CBRS scale includes somewhat more extreme behaviors (e.g., planning and organizing aggressive acts against others).

- Other Clinical Indicators—Bullying (Conners CBRS): The perpetration item corresponds to an item on the Conners 3 (included in scores for the Defiance/Aggression and DSM-IV-TR CD scales). The victimization item is unique to the Conners CBRS.
- Severe Conduct Critical Items: The Conners 3 contains a subset of 6 items from the Conners CBRS Severe Conduct items, including breaking and entering, forced sexual activity, pyromania, cruelty to animals, confrontational stealing, and weapon use. The additional 5 items on the Conners CBRS expand the list to include gang membership, carrying a weapon, interest in weapons, legal problems, and emotional detachment. See also Rapid Reference 1.16.
- DSM-IV-TR Conduct Disorder and DSM-IV-TR Oppositional Defiant Disorder: These items are the same for the Conners 3 and Conners CBRS.
- Hyperactivity/Impulsivity: The Conners CBRS has a subset of these items from the Conners 3. This is consistent with the principle that the Conners 3 explores ADHD and related issues in greater depth, while the Conners CBRS is a broader survey. The Conners 3 adds a unique item extending the concept of verbal impulsivity ("Blurts out the first thing that comes to mind") and three unique items that reflect general descriptions of children who are hyperactive or impulsive, including fidgeting, excitable/impulsive, and overstimulated.
- DSM-IV-TR ADHD, Hyperactive-Impulsive: These items are the same for the Conners 3 and Conners CBRS.

There is less overlap for emotional content on the Conners 3 and Conners CBRS. The Conners CBRS has a number of scales considering anxiety, mood, affect, and related issues such as self-harm, as well as information about a number of DSM-IV-TR diagnoses pertaining to these concepts. The Conners 3 has Screener items:

- Anxiety Screener items (Conners 3): These four items are a subset of items from the Conners CBRS. Two are from the Emotional Distress scale and two are from the DSM-IV-TR GAD scale.
- Depression Screener items (Conners 3): The four Depression Screener items are a subset of items from the Emotional Distress scale on the Conners CBRS.

There are overlaps in social concepts on the Conners 3 and Conners CBRS, but not overlapping items. The Peer Relations scale (Conners 3) and Social Problems scale/subscale (Conners CBRS) both include issues with friendships, social skills, and peer rejection. The Conners 3 focuses more on impact of these issues on relationships with peers (e.g., "Has no friends"), while the Conners CBRS includes more content on the emotional correlates of social problems and related issues like depression (e.g., "Seems lonely"). The Conners 3 content has some items that may be endorsed about children in the autism spectrum. The Conners 3 Self-Report includes unique content on the Family Relations scale that is not paralleled on the Conners CBRS Self-Report.

In terms of cognitive and academic content, there are some areas of overlap between the Conners 3 and Conners CBRS:

- Learning Problems (Conners 3) and Academic Difficulties (Conners CBRS): There is very little overlap between these two scales—only two items (i.e., "Needs extra explanation..." and "Spelling is poor"). The Conners 3 includes more general consequences of learning problems, whereas the Conners CBRS lists symptoms often associated with learning disabilities, including language and math issues. The Conners CBRS includes two general items about academic performance—"Performs poorly at school" and "Takes a long time to complete classwork or homework."
- Executive Functioning (Conners 3): This scale is unique to the Conners 3, as a key related area for ADHD. Only one of these items occurs on the Conners CBRS—"Has trouble organizing tasks or activities" (a DSM-IV-TR item for ADHD Inattentive type).
- Inattention (Conners 3): Most of these items are unique to the Conners 3, given the focus of this rating scale. Three of the items are DSM-IV-TR symptoms of ADHD Inattentive type and thus occur on the Conners CBRS as well.
- DSM-IV-TR ADHD, Inattentive: These items are the same for the Conners 3 and Conners CBRS.

As would be expected from a broadband measure (in comparison to a focused ADHD measure), the Conners CBRS contains some additional material not paralleled in the Conners 3. Many items from the Violence Potential Indicator scale can be reviewed in conjunction with behavioral scales, although some are appropriate to consider when interpreting emotional scales (e.g., "Has lost interest or pleasure in activities"). The Physical Symptoms scale is unique to the Conners CBRS, as are the Other Clinical Indicators covering a range of topics.

Both rating scales have an index score comparing the child to general population versus a clinical population. The Conners 3 has the Conners 3 ADHD Index, in which the clinical population is children with ADHD. The Conners CBRS uses a broader clinical sample for comparison, including but not limited to ADHD. The historic Conners Global Index is not calculated for the Conners CBRS—just the Conners 3. Both rating scales have essentially the same items on the PI and NI[13,14] scales but different pairs of items on the IncX. The Impairment items and Additional Questions are the same.

Integrating the Conners EC and Conners CBRS

Another common comparison is required when a child's initial evaluation is completed during the early childhood period using the Conners EC, then a subsequent evaluation is completed during the school-aged years with the Conners CBRS. It is conceivable that both of these rating scales could be used in the same evaluation for a child who was 6 years old, but this is unlikely as the examiner typically will select the rating scale that is more consistent with the child's functioning and the referral questions (see "Age, Setting, and Referral Questions" in Chapter 2 for additional guidance about how to select which scale to use). In either case, there are overlapping content areas to integrate when comparing results from the two rating scales.

Consult Rapid Reference 4.16 for a summary of similarities and differences for the Conners EC and Conners CBRS. In general, both rating scales cover a wide range of content, including behavioral, emotional, and social domains. The Conners EC includes pre-academic and cognitive skills in contrast with academic difficulties on the Conners CBRS (consistent with expectations for the different age ranges). The Conners EC has unique content in the Developmental Milestone scales. The Conners CBRS includes symptoms of DSM-IV-TR diagnoses that are not on the Conners EC (see Chapter 1 for further discussion of this difference in content).

---

13. With the exception of a single item on the Self-Report versions of the NI scales: "I can't do things right" (Conners 3) versus "I like getting gifts" (Conners CBRS).

14. There is also a slight variation in wording for an item on the NI scales: "Is hard to motivate (even with rewards like candy or money)" (Conners 3 Parent & Teacher, Conners CBRS Parent) versus "Is hard to motivate (even with highly desirable rewards)" (Conners CBRS Teacher). It is unlikely that this will impact a rater's response or your interpretation of the scale.

Behavioral elements of the Conners EC and Conners CBRS can be integrated with the following tips:

- Defiant/Aggressive Behaviors: The core concepts of these scales are very similar, including physical/verbal aggression, destructive behaviors, and argumentative tendencies. Most of the items are different, reflecting examples of these constructs that are relevant to the different developmental stages.
- Other Clinical Indicators—Bullying (Conners CBRS): There are no items labeled as "Bullying" on the Conners EC, but there are items on the Aggression subscale about bullying perpetration, including "Picks on other children" and "Threatens people." The Conners EC also contains an item relevant to bullying victimization—"Is picked on by other children" (Social Functioning/Atypical Behaviors scale).
- Severe Conduct Critical Items: The Conners CBRS covers a broader range of these behaviors, including more sophisticated examples than expected for a young child. Three of the Conners EC Other Clinical Indicators are relevant to consider here: "Is cruel to animals," "Sets fires or plays with matches," and "Steals." See also Rapid Reference 1.16.
- DSM-IV-TR Conduct Disorder and Oppositional Defiant Disorder: The DSM-IV-TR symptom scales are unique to the Conners CBRS, although some of the concepts are reflected in the Conners EC content described above.
- Inattention/Hyperactivity (Conners EC) and Hyperactivity/Impulsivity (Conners CBRS): Pay close attention to the difference in scale names for this comparison. Statistical analyses did not support subscales for the Inattention/Hyperactivity scale on the Conners EC, so these concepts are combined into one scale. For your convenience, the items on this scale are divided by concept in Rapid Reference 4.14. When considering Conners EC items pertaining to hyperactivity/impulsivity, many of the concepts carry through into the Conners CBRS with developmentally appropriate changes. Few items are repeated verbatim.
- DSM-IV-TR ADHD, Hyperactive-Impulsive: This scale is unique to the Conners CBRS, but many of the concepts are relevant to consider alongside the Conners EC hyperactivity/impulsivity items described above.

The Conners EC and Conners CBRS have a great deal of overlap for emotional content also. Both rating scales address anxiety, mood/affect, and other related issues. Think about these comparisons:

- Anxiety (Conners EC), Separation Fears (Conners CBRS), and Emotional Distress (Conners CBRS): The Conners EC Anxiety scale contains two types of items: emotional expressions of anxiety and physical expressions of anxiety. These items are grouped in Rapid Reference 4.15 to aid interpretation.
  - The Conners CBRS includes many of the concepts for emotional expressions of anxiety, expanded with more specific examples that tend to develop over time. For example, the Conners EC item, "Worries," is a more general description as suited for that age group; the Conners CBRS has multiple items describing different types of worries. Some content on the Conners EC Anxiety scale mirrors content of Conners CBRS DSM-IV-TR symptom scales, including Separation Anxiety and Generalized Anxiety Disorder.
  - The Conners CBRS also includes the physical aspects of worrying, although some of these are described in the Physical Symptoms scale (with the exception of the Teacher form, which includes some physical symptoms in the Emotional Distress scale).
- Other Clinical Indicator—Perfectionism (Conners EC) and Perfectionistic and Compulsive Behaviors (Conners CBRS): The Conners EC has a single item, "Is a perfectionist," that matches the expanded content for this topic area on the Conners CBRS. Some of the Atypical Behaviors subscale content on the Conners EC has slight overlap with the compulsive behaviors on the Conners CBRS, including items about repetitive play, movements, and sounds, as well as preferring a routine.
- Other Clinical Indicators: The PTSD, Specific Phobia, and Trichotillomania items are the same on the Conners EC and Conners CBRS. The Panic Attack item is unique to the Conners CBRS.
- DSM-IV-TR Generalized Anxiety Disorder, Separation Anxiety Disorder, Social Phobia, and Obsessive-Compulsive Disorder: The DSM-IV-TR scales are not part of the Conners EC, but there are items on the Conners EC that pertain to these diagnoses, as described above.
- Other Clinical Indicator—Self-Injury (Conners EC) and Critical Items—Self-Harm (Conners CBRS): The Self-Injury item on the Conners EC is repeated on the Conners CBRS. The Conners CBRS has additional items reflecting research on predictors for possible suicide risk. These can be considered in conjunction with the Conners EC Mood and Affect items described below.
- Mood and Affect (Conners EC) and Emotional Distress (Conners CBRS): The Mood and Affect items on the Conners EC are based on

research with young children who are depressed. Some of the content on the Conners CBRS Emotional Distress scale is comparable, though not restricted to any one of the subscales.

• DSM-IV-TR Major Depressive Episode and Manic Episode: The DSM-IV-TR scales are not included in the Conners EC; the Mood and Affect scale includes items relevant to these mood episodes.

The Conners EC and Conners CBRS have some overlaps for social functioning. The Conners EC Social Functioning subscale includes more items, reflecting broad issues with social functioning as well as specific behaviors often observed with autism spectrum disorders. The Conners CBRS Social Problems scale/subscale has fewer items and reflects generic issues rather than those seen with one group of diagnoses.

Inattention is the primary overlapping area for cognitive skills on the Conners EC and Conners CBRS. The items pertaining to inattention on the Inattention/Hyperactivity scale (Conners EC; see Rapid Reference 4.14) are conceptually similar to the symptoms of DSM-IV-TR ADHD, Inattentive type as represented on the Conners CBRS scale. The Pre-Academic/Cognitive scale (Conners EC Developmental Milestones) includes markers for general cognitive development that are not reflected on the Conners CBRS. Given different developmental expectations, it is not surprising that there are differences in academic content on the Conners EC and Conners CBRS. The Pre-Academic/Cognitive scale (Conners EC Developmental Milestones) includes early indicators that a child may be at risk for later struggles with reading and/or math, as well markers for general pre-academic skill acquisition. These early indicators of reading and math problems may emerge into symptoms of learning disabilities as academic demands intensify, as described by the Academic Difficulties scale on the Conners CBRS.

The Developmental Milestone scales on the Conners EC are unique, although certainly delays in these areas may be associated with concerns in school-aged children as captured by the Conners CBRS. For example, a child with elevated scores on the Conners EC Communication Skills and Play scales might show elevated scores on the Conners CBRS Social Problems scale in a follow-up evaluation, given the importance of communication and play in developing friendships. Possible connections between the Developmental Milestone scales and Conners CBRS results should be examined and hypotheses developed on a case-by-case basis when these two rating scales are being integrated.

There are other areas of overlap between the Conners EC and Conners CBRS, including:

- Physical Symptoms: The majority of these items are the same across the Conners EC and Conners CBRS, reflecting concerns about aches/pains, sleeping, and eating. The Conners CBRS includes two items referencing appetite/weight; these are not on the Conners EC (which makes sense, given that young children are notorious for variable appetites, and meaningful weight changes can be difficult to capture in this time of rapid growth). The Conners EC has a unique item about nightmares and night terrors.
- Other Clinical Indicators: The Pica and Tics items are the same on the Conners EC and Conners CBRS. The Substance Use and Enuresis/Encopresis items are unique to the Conners CBRS.
- Violence Potential Indicator (Conners CBRS): This scale is unique to the Conners CBRS, although some of the concepts are reflected in Conners EC items. Overlapping content includes temper, defiance, aggression, fighting, social rejection, anhedonia, destructive tendencies, and cruelty to animals (including Conners EC items from Defiant/Aggressive Behaviors, Mood and Affect, Social Functioning, and Other Clinical Indicators).
- Social Functioning/Atypical Behaviors (Conners EC), DSM-IV-TR Autistic Disorder (Conners CBRS), DSM-IV-TR Asperger's Disorder (Conners CBRS), and Other Clinical Indicator—PDD (Conners CBRS Self-Report): There is a good bit of overlap among these scales, reflecting the importance of recognizing early signs of Pervasive Developmental Disorders in young children. Remember that the Social Functioning/Atypical Behaviors scale on the Conners EC can be elevated for many reasons, not necessarily indicating presence of a diagnosis like Autistic Disorder. If this scale is elevated in early evaluation with the Conners EC, *and* the Conners CBRS DSM-IV-TR Autistic Disorder or Asperger's Disorder scale is elevated in a subsequent evaluation, this diagnostic area should be carefully considered.

The Conners EC Global Index (Conners ECGI) and Conners CBRS Clinical Index (Conners CI) are not comparable. Both rating scales have essentially the same items on the PI and NI scales, but different pairs of items on the IncX. The Impairment items and Additional Questions are the same.

Integrating the Conners EC and Conners 3

There will be times when a child is given the Conners EC during an initial evaluation and, upon return, it appears that ADHD is a primary concern (warranting use of the Conners 3). It is also possible that a 6-year-old child could be given both the Conners EC and the Conners 3 in the same evaluation, although this is less likely (see "Age, Setting, and Referral Questions" in Chapter 2 for further discussion). In either situation, the examiner will need to integrate findings from the Conners EC with those from the Conners 3.

Rapid Reference 4.16 compares and contrasts the Conners EC and Conners 3. In brief, both rating scales include behavioral, social, and cognitive concerns. The Conners EC covers more emotional and physical symptoms than the Conners 3 and adds unique content with the Developmental Milestone scales.

There is a fair degree of similarity in behavioral content for the Conners EC and Conners 3, including:

- Defiant/Aggressive Behaviors (Conners EC) and Defiance/Aggression (Conners 3): The content of these scales is similar, although most of the items are worded differently. Both rating scales include issues related to verbal and physical aggression, such as fighting, threatening, arguing, swearing, anger, defiance, and destructive tendencies. Manipulation and dishonesty are represented on both rating scales. The Conners EC reflects some related issues that are not part of the Conners 3 scale, including rudeness, bossiness, stubbornness, moodiness, sulking, and whining. The Conners 3 includes aspects of aggression that tend to develop later, including using a weapon, seeking revenge, and intentional stealing.
- Other Clinical Indicators—Cruelty to animals, fire-setting, and stealing (Conners EC) and Severe Conduct Critical Items (Conners 3): Both rating scales include items about cruelty to animals, fire-setting, and stealing. The Conners 3 adds a generalized item about cruelty (i.e., "Is cold-hearted and cruel"). The Conners 3 requires intentionality for endorsement of the fire-setting item (as opposed to the Conners EC item, which references playing with fire). The Conners EC has a very generic stealing item, while the Conners 3 item requires confrontational stealing to be endorsed. Note that the Conners 3 has another stealing item on the Defiance/Aggression scale that is not flagged as a Critical item (i.e., "Steals secretly..."). The Conners 3 includes a few additional concepts less likely to occur in young children, such as breaking and entering, forced sexual activity, and weapon use (see Rapid Reference 1.16).

- DSM-IV-TR Conduct Disorder and DSM-IV-TR Oppositional Defiant Disorder: The DSM-IV-TR symptom scales are unique to the Conners 3, although some of the concepts are reflected in the Conners EC content described above.
- Inattention/Hyperactivity (Conners EC) and Hyperactivity/Impulsivity (Conners 3): Be careful when comparing these two scores, as the Conners EC Inattention/Hyperactivity scale includes inattention (see Rapid Reference 4.14 for conceptual grouping of these items). Many of these items on the two rating scales are conceptually similar, with a handful of identical items. The Conners 3 adds the concepts of verbal impulsivity, difficulty waiting, noisiness, and interrupting; these topics are not reflected on the Conners EC given the difficulty of separating such behavior from typical behaviors in young children.
- DSM-IV-TR ADHD, Hyperactive-Impulsive: This scale is unique to the Conners 3, but many of the concepts are relevant to consider alongside the Conners EC hyperactivity/impulsivity items described above.

The Conners 3 has minimal coverage of emotional issues, but it does correspond with aspects of the Conners EC:

- Anxiety (Conners EC) and Anxiety Screener items (Conners 3): Two of the four Anxiety Screener items on the Conners 3 are identical to items on the Conners EC Anxiety scale. Both rating scales have at least one "worrying" item. The fourth Anxiety Screener item ("Becomes irritable when anxious") has no direct parallel on the Conners EC Anxiety scale, but it is similar to an item on the Conners EC Mood and Affect scale ("Is irritated easily"). In general, the Conners EC has a broader range of anxiety-related issues than the Conners 3, including physical symptoms, separation issues, and other emotional aspects of anxiety.
- Other Clinical Indicators (Conners EC): Perfectionism, PTSD, Specific Phobia, and Trichotillomania are not represented on the Conners 3.
- Mood and Affect (Conners EC) and Depression Screener items (Conners 3): The Conners 3 includes four screening items for depression, while the Conners EC has a full scale that reflects results of research on depression in young children. Anhedonia, sadness, and low self-worth are similar concepts. The Conners 3 includes an item on tiredness and low energy. As would be expected when comparing a set of screener items to a full scale, the Conners EC scale covers a broader range of concepts related to depression.

- Other Clinical Indicator—Self Injury (Conners EC): This unique content is not represented on the Conners 3.

In terms of social content, the Conners 3 Peer Relations and the Conners EC Social Functioning subscale both include items about friendships, social inclusion/rejection, and general relationships. The Conners EC scale includes unique content about social skills (including atypical social skills such as seen in the autism spectrum). The Family Relations scale on the Conners 3 Self-Report has no equivalent on the Conners EC, as self-report data are not collected from young children.

Both rating scales include some cognitive content, although much of it does not overlap. The inattention items from the Conners EC Inattention/Hyperactivity scale (see Rapid Reference 4.14) correspond to the concepts on the Conners 3 Inattention scale, as well as aspects of the Conners 3 DSM-IV-TR ADHD Inattentive scale. The Learning Problems scale of the Conners 3 and the Pre-Academic/Cognitive scale (Conners EC Developmental Milestones) both reflect some general issues with learning and remembering. The Conners EC scale lists many issues that may predict later problems with academic work, and the Conners 3 includes a few basic items about problems with reading, spelling, and math. Although there are not direct parallels between these two scales, they should correspond for most children. The Executive Functioning scale on the Conners 3 is not represented on the Conners EC.

Although the Developmental Milestone scales on the Conners EC are not part of the Conners 3, elevated scores on these scales may be associated with elevated scales on the Conners 3. These milestone items describe the basic building blocks of development and, when they are delayed or missing, one might expect problems as the child ages. For example, a child whose Conners EC includes an elevated Communication scale might later show an elevation on the Conners 3 Defiance/Aggression scale as he expresses frustration physically rather than verbally. This might be true especially if the Conners EC Defiant/Aggressive Behaviors scale was not elevated in the initial evaluation. Relationships among the Conners EC Developmental Milestone scales and subsequent Conners 3 scores should be considered for each individual, based on other aspects of available data.

The Conners EC has several other content areas that are unique and are not represented on the Conners 3. These include:

- Physical Symptoms scale
- Other Clinical Indicators—Pica and Tics
- Atypical Behaviors subscale

In terms of indices, the Conners 3 has a unique Conners 3 ADHD Index, with no parallel on the Conners EC. The historic Conners Global Index is on the Conners EC and Conners 3, with the same 10 items; the slight difference in names (ECGI versus C3GI) reflects the different normative samples used to calculate T-scores. Both rating scales have essentially the same items on the PI and NI scales, but different pairs of items on the IncX. The Impairment items and Additional Questions are the same.

Integrating the Conners Rating Scales–Revised (CRS–R) and Conners 3

When evaluating a child who was initially tested prior to 2008, results from the CRS–R may need to be integrated with those from the Conners 3. See Rapid References 1.8 and 1.9 for an overview of overlapping content between the CRS–R and the Conners 3. The Conners 3 manual has a section in Chapter 1: Introduction describing key changes from the CRS–R to the Conners 3 and a useful set of tables comparing these two versions for each rater (parent, teacher, and self-report). This information should be adequate for the single time this transition must be described for a given child.

Integrating the Conners Rating Scales–Revised (CRS–R) and Conners CBRS

There may be times when an examiner is comparing results from an evaluation prior to 2008 using the CRS–R with current administration of the Conners CBRS. As in the previous section, this transition will only occur once per child. See Rapid References 1.8 and 1.9 for an overview of overlapping content between the CRS–R and the Conners CBRS. Note the shift from using the term "psychosomatic" to "physical symptoms"; the intention of this label change was to accurately describe the items as reflecting physical issues such as eating, sleeping, and aches/pains without assuming emotional underpinnings as this scale can also be elevated for medical reasons (e.g., side effects of medications, medical conditions).

🐟 TEST YOURSELF 🐟

1. **What is the correct interpretation for the Validity scales?**
   (a) They indicate whether the Conners assessment has good validity.
   (b) They indicate whether the rater has valid observations of the child.

(c) They indicate whether aspects of the rater's response style might indicate caution in interpreting scores from the assessment.

(d) They determine whether the assessment results are valid or invalid.

2. **Which *two* of the following statements are *true* about the DSM-IV-TR Symptom scale scores?**

(a) The DSM-IV-TR *T*-score is relative, describing how the child's level of symptoms compares with other children the same age and gender.

(b) The DSM-IV-TR symptom count score is relative, describing how the child's level of symptoms compares with other children the same age and gender.

(c) The DSM-IV-TR *T*-score is sensitive to developmental atypicality.

(d) The DSM-IV-TR *T*-score and the DSM-IV-TR symptom count score correspond with each other (e.g., if one is elevated, so is the other).

3. **Which of the following situations means you should assign a DSM-IV-TR diagnosis? *Mark all that apply.***

(a) DSM-IV-TR symptom scale *T*-score is elevated

(b) DSM-IV-TR symptom scale *T*-score is *not* elevated

(c) DSM-IV-TR symptom count is "probably met"

(d) DSM-IV-TR symptom count is "probably not met"

(e) No combination of the above is sufficient for diagnosis; you must obtain additional information beyond the Conners assessments to assign a DSM-IV-TR diagnosis.

4. **When a DSM-IV-TR Symptom scale *T*-score is *not* elevated, you cannot assign that DSM-IV-TR diagnosis.**

True or False?

5. **Which of the following statements are *true* about probability scores and the Conners 3AI? *Mark all that apply.***

(a) A low probability score indicates that the child is probably normal.

(b) A low probability score indicates that the child probably has ADHD.

(c) A low probability score indicates that the child's score is similar to scores from children in the general population sample.

(d) A low probability score indicates that the child's score is similar to scores from children in the ADHD sample.

6. **An elevated VPI score on the Conners CBRS: *Mark all that apply.***

(a) Warrants immediate hospitalization

(b) Means that the student has been violent in the past

(c) Means that the student will be violent in the future

(d) Suggests that the student may be at risk for behaving violently in the future

7. **Which of the following are requirements for someone to interpret the Conners assessments? *Mark all that apply.***

   (a) The person must be familiar with interpretation guidelines outlined in the manual and/or this chapter.

   (b) If the person is not a qualified professional, he must be supervised by a qualified professional who routinely checks for interpretation accuracy.

   (c) The person must be a qualified professional with a background in assessment and measurement.

   (d) The person must attend a workshop about interpreting the Conners assessments.

8. **Interpreting the Conners assessments is a science, and requires no clinical judgment.**

   True or False?

Answers: 1. c; 2. a, c; 3. e; 4. False; 5. c; 6. d; 7. a, c; 8. False

Five

STRENGTHS AND WEAKNESSES OF THE CONNERS ASSESSMENTS

Elizabeth P. Sparrow

There is no psychological assessment tool that is perfect for every use; every test or measure that is available has strengths and weaknesses. Within the genre of rating scales, there are limitations as to what can be reliably assessed in this modality. This is why any rating scale should be used within the context of a comprehensive evaluation, or the results must clearly state any cautions about interpretation and application. The Conners assessments, like all psychological assessment tools and like all rating scales, have strengths and weaknesses. This chapter describes strengths and weaknesses in the areas of test development and content, standardization, reliability and validity, administration and scoring, and interpretation (Rapid References 5.1 through 5.5).

At the time this chapter was being prepared, the Conners 3 and Conners CBRS had been in use for about a year and the Conners EC had just been released. Early feedback about interpreting the Conners 3 and Conners CBRS results led to interpretive updates for each of these assessments, which were reviewed as this chapter was being written. These updates put several changes into effect that seem to have relieved these interpretation concerns. It is possible that, over time, additional strengths or weaknesses of the Conners assessments will become apparent as more people use these tools in assessment of children. For example, it may be determined that these rating scales are relevant when describing features of children with certain neurologic conditions, or another clinical group that was not evaluated in the development of the assessments. Additional research may identify specific scales on the Conners assessments that are sensitive to treatment effects as these tools are used in pre- and post-intervention studies. Clinicians may find that these rating scales are more effective with some populations than with others. Regardless of what may be discovered, this chapter summarizes strengths and weaknesses of the Conners assessments as they are currently known, based on the 50-year history of rating scales authored by Dr. Conners, the solid psychometric properties of the current rating scales, and results from pilot and normative studies with these assessments.

OVERVIEW OF STRENGTHS AND WEAKNESSES

The Conners assessments begin from a position of strength, as they reflect half a century of clinical and measurement experience combined with recent research findings on a solid statistical base. Overall, the test development and content and standardization are excellent. The scales are well conceptualized, covering key issues for assessment of young children and school-aged children. The addition of validity scales to help describe possible rater bias in responding helps users feel more confident about interpreting results. The size and stratification of the normative samples are impressive. Psychometric properties are solid for all forms of all Conners assessments. Administration is simple, although some may feel overwhelmed by the many forms available.[1] Computerized scoring is simple; hand-scoring can be time-consuming for the full-length Conners 3, requiring close attention to details. While some users of the CRS–R bemoan the change in age range (splitting the young children from the school-aged children), most clinicians appreciate having items that are more developmentally sensitive and relevant. The manuals outline a straightforward interpretation sequence that simplifies understanding how these scores relate to each other and reduces confusion. The manuals also provide some guidance as to how Conners assessment results can guide intervention, including planning, monitoring, and revising treatment. In fact, the manuals are very user-friendly and quite comprehensive.[2]

---

1. See Rapid Reference 2.3 for a simple decision tree that may help you select the most appropriate Conners assessment for a given child. See "Selecting the Right Form" in Chapter 2, especially "Length" and "Content" for discussion of issues to consider in choosing a form to use.

2. Having a single manual for each Conners assessment is seen as a boon by most, as they appreciate having all of this information in one place. A few wish the old model of a concise User's Guide with a lengthy companion Technical Manual had been retained, given the weight of a single manual. The Quick Reference card for each Conners assessment, which summarizes the interpretation and intervention planning sequences, offers a lightweight solution for most users.

No major weaknesses are apparent at this time. Early concerns about the Conners 3 and Conners CBRS reflected risk for misinterpretation of scales based on their labels or interpretive text; these concerns have been resolved through the interpretative updates. Minor concerns are primarily subjective rather than substantive, such as rewording DSM-IV-TR symptoms. High intercorrelations between some scales are not an issue, as these pairings represent overlap in items and symptoms between Content scales and corresponding DSM-IV-TR symptom scales (e.g., Conners 3-P Hyperactivity/Impulsivity and DSM-IV-TR Hyperactive-Impulsive). It was important to include both types of scales as they structure information in a different way (i.e., construct versus diagnostic criteria). Some occurrences reflect conceptual overlap between statistic-based scales and theoretical scales (e.g., Conners 3-T Executive Functioning and Inattention). On the Conners EC there are high intercorrelations among Developmental Milestone scales. Finally, the clinical samples might have been better stratified and described, but this is outweighed by appreciation for the breadth of clinical groups studied and the depth of reported analyses. Overall, the Conners 3, Conners CBRS, and Conners EC are valuable tools for use in assessing children, with far more strengths than weaknesses.

☰ Rapid Reference 5.1

Test Development and Content

Strengths	Weaknesses
Item development and selection had strong rationale, supporting clinical wisdom and research concepts with statistical analyses. Key clinical concepts represented on each Conners assessment correspond to stated purpose (e.g., Conners 3 covers ADHD and closely related diagnostic issues; Conners CBRS provides comprehensive coverage of behavioral, emotional, and social functioning; Conners EC covers key issues in early development including behavioral, emotional, and social functioning)	Some items identical on C3 and CBRS; could be repetitive for a rater asked to complete both forms

Built on multiple theoretical frameworks; examiners can choose to interpret results using DSM-IV-TR, IDEA 2004, or domain-based perspectives	Some items are compound, combining more than one concept (e.g., Conners 3 "Demands must be met immediately—easily frustrated."), or have contingencies that create a double-bind (e.g., Conners CBRS "Can pronounce words but has difficulty understanding what they mean")
Simplified DSM-IV-TR language that is easier for raters to understand	Purists may object to changing the DSM language, although this seems preferable to having raters unable to read or understand these items
Assess wide range of ages, with 1-year overlap between measures to give greater flexibility based on child's functioning and setting. Separate assessment for young children allows developmentally appropriate content and items. • Conners EC: 2–6 years • Conners 3 and Conners CBRS: 6–18 years (8–18 years for self-report)	Cannot use one form over full range of childhood (CRS–R covered 3–17yo); transition required at 6yo
New Validity scales help identify when a rater's endorsements may indicate extreme bias in his responses	Those who do not attend to the interpretive cautions for the Validity scales may inappropriately discard data, even when it could be interpreted
Reduced reading levels to very low levels (3rd grade for self-report, 5th grade for parent and teacher report)	
Use of extensive item analysis procedures to retain the strongest items and to eliminate items with poor psychometric properties	
Consultation with multicultural assessment experts during development to eliminate biased items (gender, race, culture) and to provide a cultural rather than a literal translation	

(continued)

Strengths	Weaknesses
C3 and CBRS conormed, which facilitates interpretation of results when co-administered	
Materials are well-organized and clearly referenced, with comprehensive, easy-to-read manuals and Quick Reference cards	
Portable; can be added to a battery as needed with lightweight paper form or e-mail and Internet administration/scoring options	
Parallel structure across rater types (including scales and items) helps with interpretation	

Rapid Reference 5.2

Standardization

Strengths	Weaknesses
Large standardization sample well stratified by age, gender, and race/ethnicity[a]	No major weaknesses
Large normative sample	
Relevant clinical samples collected	

[a] Race/ethnicity stratification based on the U.S. census.

☰ *Rapid Reference 5.3*

Reliability and Validity[a]

Strengths	Weaknesses
Internal consistency: very good to excellent, with the exception of the Validity scales.[b] Internal consistency for Conners EC Physical Symptoms scale (and Sleep Problems subscale) varies with age, reaching the "good" range by 3 years old for girls and by 4 years old for boys.	Conners CBRS Hyperactivity/ Impulsivity scale not reported for most of the analyses; unclear if this was omitted from the analyses or just from the tables.
Test-retest reliability: solid for all Conners assessments and forms, particularly parent and teacher report. Conners 3 Peer/Family Relations has lower reliability than other scales, but still acceptable.	Test-retest reliability for Conners CBRS self-report data is low for some scales (e.g., Separation Fears).
Inter-rater reliability: moderate correlations, consistent with expectations.[c]	On the Conners 3 and Conners CBRS, some teacher inter-rater reliability correlations fall below .60. The Conners EC manual does not report inter-rater reliability for teacher data.[d]
Factorial validity: CFA confirmed EFA, adequate fit of model to data. Nice balance of empirical structure from CFA/EFA with theoretical concepts as needed (i.e., some scales retained due to clinical relevance, even if not supported by factor analyses, such as the DSM-IV-TR symptom scales).	Factorial validity: High intercorrelations between some scale pairings.
Across-informant correlations: Moderate, supporting the need to collect data from different types of informants particularly for assessment of school-aged children. Mean across-informant correlations: • Conners 3: P&T = .60, P & SR = .56, T & SR = .48 • Conners CBRS: P&T = .53, P & SR = .51, T & SR = .39. • Conners EC: P&T = .75	

(continued)

Strengths	Weaknesses
Convergent and divergent validity: Manuals include many correlation studies with a variety of relevant rating scales (see below). In general, results support convergent and divergent validity. • Conners 3: CRS–R, BASC-2, ASEBA, BRIEF • Conners CBRS: CRS–R, BASC-2, ASEBA, BRIEF, CDI, MASC • Conners EC: BASC-2, ASEBA, BRIEF-P, Vineland-II	
Discriminative validity: Multiple clinical studies are presented in the manuals (clinical groups listed below). The mean overall correct classification rate for each Conners assessment, averaged across all scales and across all rater types, is in the good to very good range. Results indicate that, in general, the Conners assessments help differentiate each clinical sample from the general population sample, as well as each clinical sample from other clinical samples. • Conners 3: Disruptive Behavior Disorders, Learning Disorders, ADHD (all subtypes) • Conners CBRS: Disruptive Behavior Disorders, Learning Disorders, Learning and Language Disorders, ADHD (all subtypes), Anxiety Disorders, Major Depressive Disorder, Bipolar Disorder, Pervasive Developmental Disorders • Conners EC: Delayed Cognitive Development, Delayed Communication Development, Delayed Social/Emotional Development, Delayed Adaptive Development, Disruptive Behavior Disorders, ADHD	

[a] See Rapid Reference 1.27 for explanation of these terms.

[b] Validity scales for the Conners assessments were not developed around a central theme, only as a group of indicators regarding possible response bias. Therefore, it is not concerning that internal consistency for Conners 3 and Conners CBRS Validity scales is low. Internal consistency not reported for Conners EC Validity scales.

[c] If inter-rater reliability is high, there is little justification for collecting data from multiple raters. As expected, there is more variability for Teacher data than Parent data, since teachers observe students in different settings (e.g., different subject matter, various peer groups).

[d] Conners EC manual indicates that most 2- to 6-year-old children are cared for by a single teacher or daycare provider; this is not necessarily true, particularly in commercial daycare settings.

≡ *Rapid Reference 5.4*

Administration and Scoring

Strengths	Weaknesses
Manuals clearly explain administration and scoring.	C3 and CBRS scoring and guideline changes from interpretive updates not reflected on QuikScore forms yet—could cause confusion for those who have not downloaded these updates (particularly for the Validity scales).
Objective scoring procedures are simple and help reduce risk of examiner bias. Statistically based procedure for handling missing data; indicates when it is unreliable to proceed with scoring.	Hand-scoring requires careful attention to avoid clerical errors.
Straightforward software program on USB drive available for computerized scoring of an unlimited number of Conners assessments. Data stored on your computer; program can be used on any computer with the USB drive attached. Computerized report can be exported for use in your written report.	Software program is for scoring only; no administration option. Must use the same computer to access stored data. Only one username and password can be created per USB drive. Software program is a Windows program that is not compatible with Macintosh computers.
Simple online administration/scoring available for any computer with Internet access (including both Windows-based and Macintosh computers). Can create multiple usernames and passwords per online account. Can print paper form, generate e-mail link, or ask rater to complete on your office computer or laptop. Data stored online; can be reviewed and scored from any computer with internet access. Computerized report can be exported for use in your written report.	

(continued)

Strengths	Weaknesses
Paper-pencil and electronic administration and scoring options give great flexibility. E-mail administration option is particularly useful for obtaining results; computerized scoring (software or online) is straightforward and reduces risk of clerical errors.	
T-scores reflect age- and gender-based expectations; combined gender norms available if needed in a specific setting. Percentiles available for use when explaining results to parents and teachers who are unfamiliar with T-scores.	
Record forms are color-coded for ease of selection and scoring.	
Can be administered and scored by supervised staff member (as long as interpretation and feedback provided by qualified professional).	
One-time cost of software program (unlimited uses) is attractive to groups with high patient volume. Pay-per-use of online scoring is attractive to clinics using fewer Conners assessments.[a]	
Feedback report available for many forms; can be given to layperson as part of feedback session (after obtaining appropriate consent from parent/guardian).	

[a] At the time this chapter was prepared, the Conners 3 scoring software was $263 USD versus $1.50 USD per form online scoring; thus, the break-even point is 175 scored Conners 3 forms. The Conners CBRS scoring software was $367 USD versus $1.50 USD per form online scoring; thus, the break-even point is 245 scored Conners CBRS forms. The Conners 3 and Conners CBRS combination scoring software was $600 USD versus $1.50 USD per form online scoring; thus, the break-even point is 400 scored forms. If you anticipate using the Conners assessments more times than the "break-even point" before 2018, buy the software; less than that number of uses, choose the online version. See also note in Rapid Reference 3.1 regarding availability of online subscription model; pricing is customized for this model.

≡ Rapid Reference 5.5

Interpretation

Strengths	Weaknesses
Manual urges examiners to use Conners assessments responsibly, in the context of a multimodal evaluation by a qualified professional.	Risk for misuse of DSM-IV-TR Symptom scale scores by those who do not follow cautions about additional criteria that are required for diagnosis.
Scales and subscales can both be interpreted due to good psychometrics. Subscales, subclusters, and item-level analysis help explain elevated scale scores.	
Step-by-step interpretation sequence helps systematic and accurate understanding of results, without overlooking any elements.	
Results yield information directly relevant to diagnostic discussions and intervention planning.	
Computerized reports include narrative text and cautions; correspond to interpretation sequence in manuals. Critical items help you recognize issues that must be addressed even when scales are not elevated. Progress and Comparative reports indicate when differences between assessments are statistically significant.	C3 and CBRS interpretive updates overly cautious in treatment of validity scales; changed calculation of validity scales and interpretation guidelines. Possible response bias is not indicated when rater bias is subtle.
Mathematical formula used to determine whether change between two administrations is statistically significant (Reliable Change Index, or RCI). Integrated with computerized Progress report; can also be used with hand-scoring the Conners C3, Conners ECGI, Conners CI, Conners 3AI, or Conners 3GI.	
Quick reference card provided to summarize interpretation sequence and intervention planning.	

🐿 TEST YOURSELF 🐿

1. **Which of the following factors were considered in developing and selecting items for the Conners assessments?** *Mark all that apply.*

   (a) Clinical wisdom

   (b) Relevant research

   (c) Multiple theoretical frameworks

   (d) Statistical procedures

   (e) Multicultural issues

2. **The Conners 3 and Conners CBRS can be used to assess children who are:**

   (a) 2 to 6 years old

   (b) 5 to 12 years old

   (c) 3 to 16 years old

   (d) 6 to 18 years old

3. **It is difficult to compare results from the parent, teacher, and self-report forms of the Conners 3 because there are so many differences in the scales.** *True or false?*

4. **The standardization samples for the Conners assessments were stratified by which of the following?** *Mark all that apply.*

   (a) Age

   (b) Gender

   (c) Race/Ethnicity

5. **Across-informant correlations for the Conners assessments support gathering data from more than one type of informant.** *True or false?*

Answers: 1. a, b, c, d, e; 2. d; 3. False; 4. a, b, c; 5. True

Six

CLINICAL APPLICATIONS OF THE CONNERS ASSESSMENTS

Elizabeth P. Sparrow

This chapter discusses ways the Conners assessments can be used in clinical and educational settings. It begins with a brief overview of the structural elements of these settings, including DSM-IV-TR and IDEA 2004. Various applications of the Conners assessments are then discussed, ranging from individual evaluations to research and programmatic uses. The chapter ends with a summary of clinical studies involving the Conners assessments, which may be helpful as you consider the relevance of individual results for identification and treatment of a child.

STRUCTURAL ELEMENTS

Most professionals who use the Conners assessments are guided by the DSM, the ICD, IDEA 2004, or a combination of these classification systems. Each of these describes rules that must be followed when diagnosing a disorder or identifying student needs, which precedes providing intervention or treatment. Even in research settings, most studies involve a set of criteria that must be met by all study participants. While comprehensive coverage of these systems is beyond the scope of this book, this section provides a brief orientation to the main structural components and how they relate to the Conners assessments.

DSM

The Diagnostic and Statistical Manual, Fourth Edition, Text Revision (DSM-IV-TR; APA, 2000)[1] is the set of rules used by most mental health professionals when diagnosing mental health disorders. A diagnosis is simply a label for a cluster of symptoms that tend to overlap and co-occur. Diagnoses are a necessary part of obtaining services and funding and can also help connect a child's symptoms to relevant bodies of literature (e.g., effective treatment options, potential risks). Each of the DSM-IV-TR diagnoses has a list of rules, or "criteria," for diagnosis. These diagnostic guidelines typically have a general description followed by a list of specific symptoms. Most diagnoses specify an absolute number of symptoms that must be present and how frequent/severe each symptom must be. Additional criteria often include age of onset, persistence of symptoms, pervasiveness of symptoms, level of impairment, frequency/severity of symptoms, and differential diagnosis (see Caution below; see also DSM-IV-TR).

CAUTION
....
DSM-IV-TR Diagnosis

No structured interview, rating scale, or other instrument can substitute for appropriate training and experience in application of the DSM-IV-TR. It is particularly important to remember that a diagnosis cannot be assigned just because a certain number of symptoms are present. The DSM-IV-TR has a number of criteria that must be met before a diagnosis can be assigned, including:

- Symptom count: the number of symptoms that are present. Some diagnoses require certain levels of symptoms in more than one category.
- Age of onset: when symptoms of the disorder first began causing impairment.
- Course of symptoms: whether the symptoms are constantly present or have periods of remission. Also referred to as "persistence."
- Pervasiveness of symptoms: if the symptoms are present in more than one setting.
- Level of impairment: if the symptoms are associated with impaired functioning and how much impairment. Required for most DSM-IV-TR diagnoses. Some diagnoses specify there must be impairment in multiple settings (e.g., social, academic, occupational).

---

1. Some assessors may be more familiar with the DSM-IV (APA, 1994). The DSM-IV-TR contains the same key diagnostic criteria and diagnoses but reflects text revisions about these diagnoses.

- Frequency/severity of symptoms: how often the symptoms occur and how severe/intense they are. Some behaviors are present in the general population and only become "symptoms" when they reach a certain level of frequency/severity.
- Differential diagnosis considerations: other conditions/diagnoses that could lead to the child's presentation must be considered as alternate explanations or co-existing (i.e., comorbid). Some rules prohibit the simultaneous use of two diagnoses; other rules urge specific caution about combinations of diagnoses.

Note that, with few exceptions, the DSM-IV-TR does not have age- or gender-specific criteria for diagnosis. This is in contrast to research findings (including results from analyses of the Conners assessment data; see Rapid Reference 1.24) that indicate for some diagnoses there are significant age- and gender-based differences in expression. As discussed elsewhere in this book (including Rapid Reference 4.6), the DSM-IV-TR symptom scales on the Conners assessments provide ways to assess these age- and gender-neutral, absolute standards from the DSM-IV-TR via the symptom counts, while also allowing a developmentally sensitive way to capture atypicality for boys and girls.

Specific DSM-IV-TR diagnoses are discussed later in this chapter, but this summarizes the main structural elements of this system.

ICD

Another classification system that is used internationally is the "International Statistical Classification of Diseases and Health Related Problems" (ICD), which tends to be used in medical settings. The ICD-9-CM and ICD-10 were in use at the time this book was prepared (9th edition, Clinical Modification; 10th edition, WHO, 2004). For the most part, a child diagnosed by DSM-IV-TR criteria is likely to meet ICD criteria for the matching diagnosis. There are minor differences in the criteria and hierarchies between these two systems. DSM-IV-TR information from the Conners assessments translates easily for use by professionals who operate under an ICD-based system.

IDEA

Within the U.S. educational system, another classification system is used. The Individuals with Disabilities Education Improvement Act of 2004 (IDEA 2004) is a federal law that is enacted by states, local educational agencies (LEAs), and educational service agencies to ensure access to free, appropriate public education (a.k.a., FAPE) for children with disabilities and their families. IDEA 2004 also exists to improve educational outcomes for these children through a combination of identification and intervention. As part of the identification component, IDEA 2004 specifies 13 categories for children with disabilities, and indicates that children ages 3 to 9 years may be eligible to receive services under the label "developmental delays." The Conners assessments help you comply with IDEA 2004 requirements for identification and intervention, including "response to intervention" or RTI (see Rapid Reference 6.1). Conners results can be linked to relevant categories of student need from IDEA 2004 (see Rapid Reference 6.1).

The federal law does not require diagnosis for a child to receive services; in fact, this most recent revision of the law emphasizes the use of RTI rather than formal assessment for some children. "Procedural safeguards" are outlined in IDEA 2004 to help support appropriate evaluation and placement decisions. Most aspects of IDEA 2004 require evidence of impaired functioning in the school setting in order for a student to receive special education and related services (this is not required for young children).

≡ Rapid Reference 6.1

Conners Assessments and IDEA 2004

IDEA 2004 specifies a number of important standards for identification and intervention in the U.S. educational system. The Conners 3, Conners CBRS, and Conners EC address these standards in the following ways:

Identification

- Evaluation procedures:
  - Use assessment tools that are not racially or culturally discriminatory: *Representative normative samples of the Conners assessments and cultural considerations during development reduce racial and cultural bias.*
  - Select assessment materials in the child's native language: *Conners assessments are available in English and Spanish versions.*[a]
  - Assess specific areas of educational need: *Conners 3, Conners CBRS, and Conners EC provide scores for specific concerns that directly impact education.*
  - Do not determine an appropriate educational program based on a single procedure: *These rating scales are designed to be used with multiple informants across multiple settings within the context of a multimodal evaluation.*
- Overidentification and disproportionality: The federal government has mandated that we must work together to reduce disproportionate representation of racial and ethnic groups in special education and related

services, to the extent the representation is the result of inappropriate identification. *These norm-referenced rating scales provide an objective way to identify students with educational needs, thus reducing possible overidentification due to examiner bias based on race/ethnicity. The representative normative samples (see above) also help reduce disproportionate representation based on racial/ethnic bias rather than actual student needs.*

- Educational needs: Determine the nature and extent of Special Education and Related Services needed, including academic and behavioral. Social-Emotional learning is also listed as a potential need. *The Conners 3, Conners CBRS, and Conners EC address these important areas of potential need for a student, and results can suggest targets for intervention.*
- Eligibility: Determine a student's eligibility for special education and related services, based not just on identifying area of need but also on evidence of impairment in the school setting.
  - IDEA 2004 specifies 13 categories of disability. *The Conners 3 and Conners CBRS include information about 5 of these categories, including: Autism, Emotional Disturbance, Other Health Impaired, Specific Learning Disability, and Speech/Language Impairment. Tables link Conners scores with possible areas of IDEA 2004 eligibility to facilitate this consideration.*
  - IDEA 2004 also specifies that a student (3 to 9 years old) may receive services for Developmental Delays in Physical, Cognitive, Communicative, Social/Emotional, and/or Adaptive development. *The Conners EC provides information about possible delays in all five of these areas. The Conners CBRS includes relevant information when considering delays in Communication and Social/Emotional Development.*

Intervention

- IEP development, review, and revision:
  - Develop goals for initial IEP. *Results from the Conners 3, Conners CBRS, or Conners EC can help identify and prioritize student needs, leading to specific goals for an IEP.*
  - Measure progress toward goals during regular review of the IEP. Suggest new or updated goals for IEP revisions. *Repeat administration of the Conners assessments can document progress in identified areas, suggest areas of treatment to modify, and suggest new goals that may need to be added.*
- Assist in developing positive behavioral interventions. *Conners tools can help you identify the need for positive behavioral assessments, establish baselines for the behaviors, suggest targets for positive behavioral intervention, monitor progress, and support decisions to discontinue, maintain, or increase positive behavioral supports.*

Identification and Intervention: Response to Instruction/Intervention (RTI)

- Identify students in grades K through 12 who require academic and/or behavioral supports in order to succeed in the general education setting (a.k.a., "early intervening services"). *The Conners assessments can assist in screening behavioral needs and aspects of academics, suggesting areas that might need to be targeted for a group of students and identifying subsets of students who may benefit from targeted group intervention.*

(continued)

- Monitor student response to intervention in an objective way. *Repeat administrations of the Conners 3, Conners CBRS, and Conners EC can help document a student's baseline in a given area and then monitor her response to intervention. The use of norm-referenced results increases objectivity during interpretation.*
- If a student does not show positive response to proactive or group interventions, refer for comprehensive evaluation (particularly with regard to specific learning disability). *Results from the Conners assessments can help suggest a referral for comprehensive, multidisciplinary evaluation to determine if the student is eligible for more intensive services such as offered through special education and related services.*

[a] Additional translations may be available; check with the publisher if another language is needed. At the time this book was prepared, some forms were also available in French.

Section 504

Section 504 of the Rehabilitation Act is another federal mandate that a student qualifies for accommodations in the regular education setting when he has physical/mental impairment (e.g., issues with alertness) that substantially limits at least one major life activity. These accommodations are described in a "Section 504 plan" and usually include physical and structural accommodations (e.g., reduced distraction setting for standardized testing, use of a laptop for written assignments, access to notes from a classmate). Results from the Conners assessments can be used to identify specific accommodations that may be appropriate for a student under a 504 plan.

APPLICATIONS

The Conners assessments can be used in a number of ways for an individual child, group of children, or even a program. This section will cover these various applications in more detail.

Diagnostic Applications

The most typical way the Conners assessments are used is diagnostic assessment of an individual child. The Conners 3, Conners CBRS, and Conners EC provide information that contributes significantly to evaluation of a student's needs and assessment of diagnostic criteria. All three of these assessment tools offer coverage of key concepts for evaluation of a child, including behavioral, emotional, social, and other aspects of functioning. The Conners 3 and Conners CBRS include information that can be used to suggest DSM-IV-TR diagnoses for further consideration. When used in the context of a responsible evaluation, the Conners assessment tools are very informative about an individual.

Treatment Applications

It is not sufficient to identify a label or diagnosis for a child; the main goal of most referrals and assessments is to identify ways to help the child. All of the Conners assessments can help plan, monitor, and adjust treatment. The relative elevations of scales may suggest priorities for treatment, as it is more effective to target a few things at a time (rather than attempting to fix everything simultaneously). Elevated item scores on the Conners assessments can indicate specific targets within the treatment plan. When one of the rating scales is administered repeatedly, results can easily be compared to determine whether there has been any progress and, if so, in which areas (see Rapid Reference 6.2).

☰ Rapid Reference 6.2

Significant Change

All of the Conners assessments include "reliable change index" (RCI) values, by which you can determine if the change in a rater's ratings over time is statistically significant. Statistical significance is automatically indicated on the computerized Progress reports and can also be determined when hand-scoring.

Statistical significance is not necessarily the same as clinical significance. For example, it would be clinically meaningful if a child who struggled to overcome school refusal agreed to attend school one day a week without an hour-long tantrum, even if the associated change in ratings was not statistically significant. Likewise, the amount of change between two administrations may be statistically significant, but if both T-scores are in the "Very Elevated" range, the improvement may not be perceptible in a regular education classroom.

When a Conners assessment is used to measure change over time, you may need to review change in raw scores as well as change in T-scores. This is particularly recommended when a child has changed age groups between two assessments; that is, if he falls in a different 1-year age band for the Conners 3 and Conners CBRS, or if he falls in a different 6-month age band for the Conners EC. When a child moves across age groups, the T-score can change just because the comparison group changed (even if the raw score and ratings stay the same). It is helpful to compare the total raw scores for each scale to assess any change in symptom frequency/intensity. Raw score review is especially important for the Conners EC Developmental Milestone scales, including individual items. Interval progress on a few critical skills may not be reflected in the overall T-score but could be very important in knowing that a child is making progress.

At times, re-administration of a Conners assessment may identify failure to improve with treatment. Repeated administrations are also important for identifying new concerns that may emerge or become more apparent as others are remediated. As such, results from the Conners assessments can help determine when treatment goals require modification, including increased intensity, decreased intensity, maintenance-level services, or even discontinuation; these results can also suggest addition of new goals or different treatment approaches to help reach old goals.

In educational settings, there is increased emphasis on RTI. The Conners assessments can identify areas that require intervention for a student; repeat administrations can help determine if the student is showing a positive response to the intervention. This includes behavioral and some academic issues—the two main places RTI is mentioned in IDEA 2004—and also emotional/social issues—equally relevant for a student's functioning in the school setting.

When using the Conners assessments to monitor treatment, it is best to administer them at least twice before beginning the intervention. These first two administrations together help determine the baseline for behaviors as a single set of scores can be misleading (e.g., a child is typically referred when things are at the worst and "can not get any worse"). This may not always be realistic, however, and the use of normative data references helps reduce your reliance on qualitative data for assessing treatment response.

If assessing response to a time-dependent treatment, such as medication, it is important to rate the child over a period when he was being prescribed the medication and it was in effect. For example, if a child takes a short-acting stimulant medication each morning, it would make sense to collect data from his morning teachers to help establish whether it was effective. Data from the afternoon teachers, after the medication effects had decreased, might be a useful set of comparison data. Similarly, a medication that requires several weeks to build up to therapeutic levels should be assessed after the child has reached and maintained those levels for a full month. These principles apply even for nonpharmaceutical treatments; for example, if cognitive therapy is recommended for a child with depression, allow time for the child to establish rapport with her therapist, plus a full month of treatment before repeating the Conners assessment.

Also be sure to collect data from raters who can describe relevant aspects of a child's functioning. For example, if a treatment is intended to improve a child's reading skills, ask his reading teacher to complete the chosen Conners assessment. If a treatment targets his concentration, gather data from raters who observe the child in settings that demand concentration (e.g., school, sports events, homework).

DON'T FORGET

....

Treatment Issues

- Ideally, you should administer the Conners assessment at least twice before beginning treatment.
- Complete at least 1 month of treatment before repeating the Conners assessment.
- Include times of day that are relevant to when the treatment is effective.
- Gather data from raters who can describe the child in relevant settings.
- Consider raw scores as well as standardized scores, particularly when the child had a birthday between administrations of the Conners assessments (or even a half-birthday, in the case of the Conners EC).

Group Applications

The Conners assessments can also be used to assess or describe a group of children. Part the RTI theory describes proactively identifying students who might benefit from intervention without necessarily completing a full evaluation or being placed in a special education setting. The Conners assessments can help quickly identify students who have weaknesses in a certain area, whether it be anger management, learning, social functioning, or another topic included on that form. For large numbers of students, the Conners scores could be used to match students for preliminary RTI efforts (e.g., a group of students with the highest Conners scores might receive more intensive intervention, a group with borderline scores might receive less frequent intervention in a larger group setting). Results from the Conners assessments might also help identify which students should be referred for further evaluation rather than RTI. For example, if one of the students in a group screened with the Conners CBRS had elevated scores on the Hyperactivity/Impulsivity scale, the DSM-IV-TR ADHD Hyperactive-Impulsive scale, the Conners CI, and the ADHD Indicator, this could support further evaluation of possible ADHD. Use of the Conners assessments to screen a group of students is not ideal for collection of teacher data unless one of the 10-item forms was used, as the teacher would have a large number of forms to complete. Screening applications are more reasonable for parent and self-report forms. When Conners data are collected for screening purposes, extreme caution must be used in interpreting and reporting results, as the data are not being reviewed in the same context as an individual evaluation and the clinician does not have the same personal knowledge of the student.

Research Applications

Use of the Conners assessments in research is really an extension of group applications. Results from the Conners tools can be used to describe character-istics of a group of children—either those entering a particular study or those responding to a particular intervention. For example, it would be reasonable to use scores from the Conners assessments as part of inclusion/exclusion criteria for a study, then report that "all participants had T-scores greater than 85 on the Conners 3-P Executive Functioning scale." In a study of a medication or other treatment, Conners scores might help characterize the children who responded or who did not respond (e.g., children whose initial Conners 3-SR Hyperactivity/Impulsivity T-score was greater than 70 showed a statistically significant decrease; those with initial T-scores in the 55 to 70 range did not reach statistical significance after treatment with the active compound).

Regardless of how the Conners assessments are used in a research setting, it is critical that participants and their guardians are aware of the limits on information they will receive at the individual level. In some studies, the participants receive no individual results; when individual results are provided, the context must be described. As mentioned in "Group Applications" above, gathering Conners results in a research setting is generally different from an individual assessment (except in cases such as research clinics where individual patients agree to share their data for research purposes). Responsible distribution of individual results will include a referral to a qualified clinician in case the parent or child has questions about the results.

CAUTION

Interpreting Individual Results from Group or Research Administrations

When data are collected about a group of students, use great caution in interpreting and reporting the results for individuals. This same caution applies when individual results are provided from data collected for research purposes.

Program Applications

For those of you involved with developing, maintaining, and funding educational and/or treatment programs, it is relevant to consider the Conners assessments for evaluating the effectiveness of these programs. By selecting the relevant

Conners tool to describe areas you are targeting in the program, you could collect data about students at entry into the program and then at regular intervals during their participation. This information could enhance the program in many ways. You could capture data that help predict which students respond best to which interventions, which could reduce time spent on trial-and-error determination of placement. You could use Conners data to illustrate the effectiveness of the program for a group of students; these data could then be used to support funding requests to enlarge the program or extend your outreach. Repeated administrations might identify certain areas that are not being addressed in your program so that you might find ways to meet these student needs. Regardless of your exact application, it is important to recognize the value of these statistically sound, clinically founded tools for assessing and describing a program. Depending on the analytic approach used and the number of students you can describe, you may want to consider using T-scores in the statistical analyses as these will adjust for age and gender.

CLINICAL GROUPS

Conners assessment scores for a number of clinical groups are included in the test manuals (Validity chapters), including information about significant score differences between different groups and classification accuracy of the scores. This information helps support the clinical utility of these assessments as part of a diagnostic evaluation. The special groups studied are listed in Rapid Reference 6.3.[2] The General Population sample was randomly selected from the normative sample.

Clinical Samples

Children included in the clinical groups for Conners 3 and Conners CBRS studies were identified by each clinical data collection site as having one primary diagnosis, based on a multimodal assessment by a qualified professional using DSM-IV-TR or ICD-10 criteria. Clinical groups for Conners EC studies reflect broader categories, as it can be difficult to be accurate and specific when diagnosing young children; regardless, each child included in the Conners EC clinical samples had a formal diagnosis.

---

2. Sample size varies for these analyses due to omitted items on some scales; see Rapid References 1.25 and 1.26 for the total number of clinical cases gathered.

Different clinicians may have used different interpretations of the diagnostic criteria. Within each group, there may be different levels of severity and different symptom presentations. The clinical samples were not stratified by gender or age (see tables in Standardization chapters for Conners 3 and Conners CBRS test manuals; see Appendix in Conners EC manual). The Conners 3 and Conners CBRS test manuals do not report age distribution of these clinical samples (see Appendix for this information in Conners EC manual. Diagnoses included in each clinical group are diverse in some instances (e.g., Anxiety Disorders sample includes Generalized Anxiety Disorder, Separation Anxiety Disorder, Social Phobia, and Obsessive-Compulsive Disorder).

≡ Rapid Reference 6.3

Sample Sizes for Clinical Studies

Conners 3 Full-Length[a]	Parent	Teacher	Self-Report
ADHD-Inattentive	105–110	67–80	72–77
ADHD-Hyperactive/Impulsive	41–44	30–38	37–39
ADHD-Combined	121–125	84–107	121–126
Disruptive Behavior Disorders	53–55	40–50	56–60
Learning Disorders	105–110	104–108	102–104
General Population	188–193	182–194	167–172

Conners CBRS Full-Length[a]	Parent	Teacher	Self-Report
Disruptive Behavior Disorders	44–46	44–45	46–50
Learning Disorders[b]	104–125	103–127	97–104
ADHD-Inattentive	76–83	70–75	68–78
ADHD-Hyperactive/Impulsive	35–38	33–35	33–36
ADHD-Combined	119–130	97–105	116–130
Anxiety Disorders	56–61	47–51	55–59
Major Depressive Disorder	37–40	36–40	39–41

Bipolar Disorder	25–28	25–26	26–28
Pervasive Developmental Disorders	27–28	34–40	24–26
General Population	183–194	181–191	154–168

Source: Information in this table was provided by the MHS Research and Development department.

Conners EC Full-Length[a]	Parent	Teacher
Delayed Cognitive Development (includes Mental Retardation)	45–48	53–55
Delayed Communication Development (includes Expressive, Receptive, and Mixed Receptive-Expressive Language Disorders)	41–43	44–47
Delayed Social or Emotional Development (includes disorders related to Anxiety and Depression)	39–42	36–40
Delayed Adaptive Development (includes PDD spectrum diagnoses)	72–73	68–73
Disruptive Behavior Disorders (includes CD and ODD)	28–30	35–36
ADHD (all subtypes)	53–57	66–70
General Population	71–75	72–75

Source: Information in this table was provided by the MHS Research and Development department.

[a] Sample sizes used in these analyses vary depending on omitted items for each scale in each sample. See Rapid Reference 1.25 and 1.26 for the total group size.

[b] Children with language disorders (e.g., Expressive Language Disorder, Receptive Language Disorder, Mixed Receptive-Expressive Language Disorder) were included with the Learning Disorder group for analyses including the Language subscale of Academic Difficulties. The test manual does not specify whether the sample sizes reported here include children with Language Disorders.

Cautions Regarding Use of Group Data

Keep in mind that the following statistics are based on group data. The samples may not be representative of the entire diagnostic group. Although this information about score differences between groups is informative when interpreting results for a child, none of these scores can justify accepting or rejecting a diagnosis. Diagnosis must be assigned following DSM criteria. Even when a score is statistically strong for predicting group membership, there will be individuals who are misclassified by that score (i.e., no scale has 100 percent classification accuracy). It is important to avoid the trap of becoming focused on identifying the "right" diagnosis to the point that you lose sight of the ultimate goal of most assessments—helping an individual child. Remember to use the Conners assessment results as tools to help as you consider various diagnostic possibilities as well as to guide treatment recommendations.

DON'T FORGET
Discriminative Validity

Remember, a statement about discriminative validity of a scale is based on group data, meaning it uses a composite of the data from each group rather than comparing individual data for each child in each group. It is possible for an individual with the target diagnosis to score lower on a given scale, but, on average, most children with that diagnosis will have higher scores on the relevant scale than will children from the general population or children from other clinical groups. See also Rapid References 1.27 and 1.28.

ANCOVAs and DFAs

One or more target groups were identified for each scale on the Conners assessments, based on clinical predictions. Analyses of Covariance (ANCOVAs) were conducted to identify significant differences between groups (controlling for age and gender). Discriminant Function Analyses (DFAs) were conducted to assess the ability of scores to predict group membership (controlling for age and gender). These analyses considered the target clinical group versus the General Population sample, as well as the target clinical group versus other clinical groups. (See Rapid Reference 6.4 for an illustration of these clinical study questions).

Results from clinical studies with the full-length forms are summarized below in terms of relative elevations of the various samples (Rapid References 6.5 through 6.7). Please see the relevant test manual for specific statistical findings.[3] Also provided below are classification statistics for the Conners 3 ADHD Index and the Conners Clinical Index from the Conners CBRS (Rapid Reference 6.8).

3. Each test manual reports results from ANCOVAs and DFAs in the "Validity" chapter for the full-length form. See also chapters in each manual that describe similar findings for short forms and index forms. Data are not presented in the test manuals for clinical groups that were not targets for these assessments.

≡ Rapid Reference 6.4

Illustration of some clinical study questions for Conners 3.

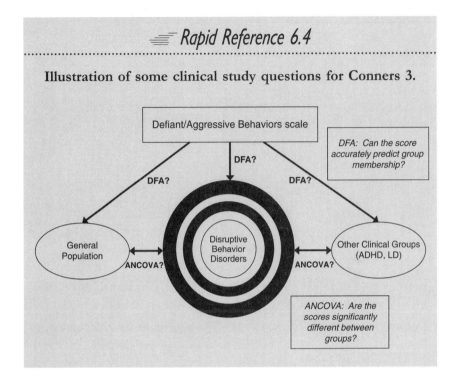

For the Conners 3 and Conners CBRS, the ADHD groups were not always statistically different from each other. This is not surprising given that one subtype diagnosis does not indicate there are no symptoms of the other subtype; in fact, these often co-occur at some level. For simplicity, this summary describes the three ADHD groups as a whole; see the relevant test manual for specific examples of when a score difference was statistically significant among these groups.

Attention-Deficit/Hyperactivity Disorder (ADHD)

ADHD is one of the most common referral reasons for school-aged children, and it is one of the most prevalent disorders in youth. There are three subtypes of ADHD: Predominantly Inattentive type, Predominantly Hyperactive/Impulsive type, and Combined type. The Inattentive type is characterized by persistent problems with inattention that begin in early childhood and cause impairment in at least two aspects of functioning. Some of these are primary inattention (e.g., poor attention to details) and others are secondary (e.g., seeming not to listen,

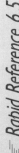

Rapid Reference 6.5

Performance of Clinical Samples on the Conners 3 Scales

Scale	Target Group(s)	Relatively Low Scores	Moderate Scores	Relatively High Scores
Inattention (P & T)	ADHD-Inattentive AND ADHD-Combined	General Population	Learning Disorders Disruptive Behavior Disorders	ADHD (all subtypes)
Inattention (SR)	ADHD-Inattentive AND ADHD-Combined	General Population Learning Disorders	Disruptive Behavior Disorders	ADHD (all subtypes)
Hyperactivity/Impulsivity (P & T)	ADHD-Hyperactive/ Impulsive AND ADHD-Combined	General Population Learning Disorders	ADHD-Inattentive	ADHD-Hyperactive/ Impulsive ADHD-Combined Disruptive Behavior Disorders
Hyperactivity/Impulsivity (SR)	ADHD-Hyperactive/ Impulsive AND ADHD-Combined	General Population Learning Disorders	ADHD-Inattentive Disruptive Behavior Disorders	ADHD-Hyperactive/ Impulsive ADHD-Combined
Learning Problems/ Executive Functioning (T only)	Learning Disorders; ADHD (all subtypes)	General Population	Disruptive Behavior Disorders	ADHD (all subtypes) Learning Disorders

Learning Problems (T subscale)	Learning Disorders	General Population Disruptive Behavior Disorders		Learning Disorders ADHD (all subtypes)
Executive Functioning (P)	ADHD (all subtypes) AND Learning Disorders	General Population Learning Disorders	Disruptive Behavior Disorders	ADHD (all subtypes)
Executive Functioning (T subscale)	ADHD (all subtypes) AND Learning Disorders	General Population Learning Disorders		ADHD (all subtypes) Disruptive Behavior Disorders
Defiance/Aggression	Disruptive Behavior Disorders	General Population Learning Disorders ADHD-Inattentive	ADHD-Hyperactive/Impulsive ADHD-Combined	Disruptive Behavior Disorders
Peer Relations (P & T)	Disruptive Behavior Disorders AND ADHD (all subtypes)	General Population Learning Disorders		ADHD (all subtypes) Disruptive Behavior Disorders
Family Relations (SR)	Disruptive Behavior Disorders AND ADHD (all subtypes)	General Population Learning Disorders	ADHD (all subtypes)	Disruptive Behavior Disorders

(continued)

Scale	Target Group(s)	Relatively Low Scores	Moderate Scores	Relatively High Scores
DSM-IV-TR ADHD Inattentive	ADHD-Inattentive AND ADHD-Combined	General Population Learning Disorders	Disruptive Behavior Disorders	ADHD (all subtypes)
DSM-IV-TR ADHD Hyperactive/Impulsive (P & T)	ADHD-Hyperactive/Impulsive AND ADHD-Combined	General Population Learning Disorders	Disruptive Behavior Disorders ADHD-Inattentive	ADHD-Hyperactive/Impulsive ADHD-Combined
DSM-IV-TR ADHD Hyperactive/Impulsive (SR)	ADHD-Hyperactive/Impulsive AND ADHD-Combined	General Population Learning Disorders	ADHD-Inattentive	ADHD-Hyperactive/Impulsive ADHD-Combined Disruptive Behavior Disorders
DSM-IV-TR CD	Disruptive Behavior Disorders	General Population Learning Disorders ADHD-Inattentive	ADHD-Hyperactive/Impulsive ADHD-Combined	Disruptive Behavior Disorders
DSM-IV-TR ODD	Disruptive Behavior Disorders	General Population Learning Disorders ADHD-Inattentive	ADHD-Hyperactive/Impulsive ADHD-Combined	Disruptive Behavior Disorders

Source: General patterns described in this table are based on data from tables describing univariate effect of group membership on Conners 3 scores and differences between targeted clinical groups and the general population for the Conners 3 in the *Conners 3rd edition manual* (Multi-Health Systems, 2008).

Note: P = Parent, T = Teacher, SR = Self-Report

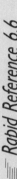

Rapid Reference 6.6

Performance of Clinical Samples on the Conners CBRS Scales

Scale	Target Group(s)	Relatively Low Scores	Moderate Scores	Relatively High Scores
Emotional Distress (P & T)	Anxiety Disorders AND Major Depressive Disorder	General Population Learning Disorders	ADHD (all subtypes) Disruptive Behavior Disorders	Anxiety Disorders Major Depressive Disorder Bipolar Disorder Pervasive Developmental Disorders
Emotional Distress (SR)	Anxiety Disorders AND Major Depressive Disorder	General Population Learning Disorders Pervasive Developmental Disorders	ADHD (all subtypes) Disruptive Behavior Disorders	Anxiety Disorders Major Depressive Disorder Bipolar Disorder
Upsetting Thoughts (P only)	Anxiety Disorders AND Major Depressive Disorder	The qualitative differences among groups on this subscale shift gradually, with average raw scores ranging from 0.51 (LD) to 4.21 (Bipolar)		

(continued)

Scale	Target Group(s)	Relatively Low Scores	Moderate Scores	Relatively High Scores
Upsetting Thoughts/ Physical Symptoms (T only)	Anxiety Disorders AND Major Depressive Disorder	General Population Learning Disorders ADHD (all subtypes) Disruptive Behavior Disorders	Bipolar Disorder Pervasive Developmental Disorders	Anxiety Disorders Major Depressive Disorder
Worrying (P only)	Anxiety Disorders	General Population Learning Disorders ADHD (all subtypes) Disruptive Behavior Disorders	Pervasive Developmental Disorders	Anxiety Disorders Major Depressive Disorder Bipolar Disorder
Social Anxiety (T only)	Anxiety Disorders	General Population Learning Disorders ADHD (all subtypes) Disruptive Behavior Disorders	Bipolar Disorder Pervasive Developmental Disorders Major Depressive Disorder	Anxiety Disorders
Defiant/ Aggressive Behaviors	Disruptive Behavior Disorders	General Population Learning Disorders Anxiety Disorders ADHD-Inattentive	ADHD-Hyperactive/ Impulsive ADHD-Combined Bipolar Disorder	Disruptive Behavior Disorders

		Major Depressive Disorder Pervasive Developmental Disorders (P & SR)	Pervasive Developmental Disorders (T)	Learning Disorders ADHD (P; all subtypes)
Academic Difficulties (P & T)	Learning Disorders	General Population Anxiety Disorders Major Depressive Disorder Disruptive Behavior Disorders	Bipolar Disorder Pervasive Developmental Disorders ADHD (all subtypes)	
Academic Difficulties (SR)	Learning Disorders	The qualitative differences among groups on this subscale shift gradually, with average raw scores ranging from 8.55 (General Population) to 15.05 (LD)		
Language (P & T subscale)	Learning and Language Disorders	General Population Anxiety Disorders Major Depressive Disorder Disruptive Behavior Disorders	Bipolar Disorder Pervasive Developmental Disorders ADHD (all subtypes)	Learning and Language Disorders

(continued)

Scale	Target Group(s)	Relatively Low Scores	Moderate Scores	Relatively High Scores
Math (P & T subscale)	Learning Disorders	The qualitative differences among groups on this subscale shift gradually, with average raw scores ranging from: Parent: 2.29 (General Population) to 5.15 (ADHD-Combined) Teacher: 1.95 (Anxiety) to 6.08 (LD)		
Hyperactivity (Teacher only)	ADHD-Hyperactive/ Impulsive AND ADHD-Combined	General Population Anxiety Disorders Learning Disorders ADHD-Inattentive Major Depressive Disorder Pervasive Developmental Disorders	Disruptive Behavior Disorders Bipolar Disorder	ADHD-Hyperactive/ Impulsive ADHD-Combined
Hyperactivity/ Impulsivity (P & SR)	Data for this scale were not reported in the test manuals			

				Pervasive Developmental Disorders
Social Problems (P subscale, T scale, not on SR)	Pervasive Developmental Disorders	General Population Learning Disorders ADHD (all subtypes) Disruptive Behavior Disorders Anxiety Disorders Major Depressive Disorder Bipolar Disorder		
Separation Fears (T subscale)	Anxiety Disorders	The qualitative differences among groups on this scale shift gradually, with average raw scores ranging from: Parent: 2.14 (LD) to 5.56 (Anxiety) Teacher: 0.40 (LD) to 3.84 (Anxiety) Self: 2.89 (General Population) to 5.69 (Bipolar)		

(continued)

Scale	Target Group(s)	Relatively Low Scores	Moderate Scores	Relatively High Scores
Perfectionistic and Compulsive Behaviors (P only)	Pervasive Developmental Disorders AND Anxiety Disorders	The qualitative differences among groups on this subscale shift gradually, with average raw scores ranging from 2.34 (Major Depressive Disorder) to 6.18 (PDD)		
Perfectionistic and Compulsive Behaviors (T only)	Pervasive Developmental Disorders AND Anxiety Disorders	General Population Learning Disorders ADHD (all subtypes) Disruptive Behavior Disorders Major Depressive Disorder Bipolar Disorder		Anxiety Disorders Pervasive Developmental Disorders
Violence Potential Indicator (P only)	Disruptive Behavior Disorders	General Population Learning Disorders Anxiety Disorders ADHD-Inattentive	ADHD-Hyperactive/ Impulsive ADHD-Combined	Disruptive Behavior Disorders Bipolar Disorder

			Major Depressive Disorder, Pervasive Developmental Disorders	Disruptive Behavior Disorders
Violence Potential Indicator (T & SR)	Disruptive Behavior Disorders	General Population, Learning Disorders, Anxiety Disorders, ADHD-Inattentive, Major Depressive Disorder, Pervasive Developmental Disorders (SR)	ADHD-Hyperactive/Impulsive, ADHD-Combined, Bipolar Disorder, Pervasive Developmental Disorders (T)	
Physical Symptoms	Anxiety Disorders AND Major Depressive Disorder	The qualitative differences among groups on this subscale shift gradually, with average raw scores ranging from: Parent: 3.80 (LD) to 8.94 (Bipolar) Teacher: 0.78 (LD) to 2.66 (Anxiety) Self: 5.81 (PDD) to 12.61 (Bipolar)		

(continued)

Scale	Target Group(s)	Relatively Low Scores	Moderate Scores	Relatively High Scores
DSM-IV-TR ADHD Inattentive (P)	ADHD-Inattentive AND ADHD-Combined	General Population Learning Disorders Anxiety Disorders	Major Depressive Disorder Pervasive Developmental Disorders Disruptive Behavior Disorders	ADHD (all subtypes) Bipolar Disorder
DSM-IV-TR ADHD Inattentive (T)	ADHD-Inattentive AND ADHD-Combined	General Population Learning Disorders Anxiety Disorders Major Depressive Disorder		ADHD (all subtypes) Bipolar Disorder Pervasive Developmental Disorders Disruptive Behavior Disorders
DSM-IV-TR ADHD Inattentive (SR)	ADHD-Inattentive AND ADHD-Combined	General Population Learning Disorders Anxiety Disorders Pervasive Developmental Disorders		ADHD (all subtypes) Major Depressive Disorder Bipolar Disorder Disruptive Behavior Disorders

DSM-IV-TR ADHD Hyperactive-Impulsive	ADHD-Hyperactive/Impulsive AND ADHD-Combined	General Population Learning Disorders Anxiety Disorders Major Depressive Disorder ADHD-Inattentive Pervasive Developmental Disorders (P & SR)	Disruptive Behavior Disorders (P & T) Bipolar Disorder (P & T) Pervasive Developmental Disorders (T)	ADHD-Hyperactive/Impulsive ADHD-Combined Bipolar Disorder (SR) Disruptive Behavior Disorders (SR)
DSM-IV-TR CD (P)	Disruptive Behavior Disorders	General Population Learning Disorders Anxiety Disorders Major Depressive Disorder ADHD-Inattentive Pervasive Developmental Disorders	ADHD-Hyperactive/Impulsive ADHD-Combined	Disruptive Behavior Disorders Bipolar Disorder
DSM-IV-TR CD (T & SR)	Disruptive Behavior Disorders	General Population Learning Disorders Anxiety Disorders Major Depressive Disorder Bipolar Disorder		Disruptive Behavior Disorders

(continued)

Scale	Target Group(s)	Relatively Low Scores	Moderate Scores	Relatively High Scores
DSM-IV-TR CD (T & SR) (continued)		ADHD (all subtypes) Pervasive Developmental Disorders		
DSM-IV-TR ODD	Disruptive Behavior Disorders	General Population Learning Disorders Anxiety Disorders Major Depressive Disorder ADHD-Inattentive Pervasive Developmental Disorders	ADHD-Hyperactive/ Impulsive ADHD-Combined Bipolar Disorder (T & SR)	Disruptive Behavior Disorders Bipolar Disorder (P)
DSM-IV-TR Major Depressive Episode (P & SR)	Major Depressive Disorder	General Population Learning Disorders Pervasive Developmental Disorders (SR)	Anxiety Disorders Disruptive Behavior Disorders ADHD (all subtypes) Pervasive Developmental Disorders (P)	Major Depressive Disorder Bipolar Disorder

DSM-IV-TR Major Depressive Episode (T)	Major Depressive Disorder	General Population Learning Disorders Anxiety Disorders Disruptive Behavior Disorders ADHD (all subtypes) Pervasive Developmental Disorders	Bipolar Disorder	Major Depressive Disorder
DSM-IV-TR Manic Episode (P)	Bipolar Disorder	General Population Learning Disorders ADHD-Inattentive Anxiety Disorders Major Depressive Disorder Pervasive Developmental Disorders	Disruptive Behavior Disorders ADHD-Hyperactive/Impulsive ADHD-Combined	Bipolar Disorder
DSM-IV-TR Manic Episode (T & SR)	Bipolar Disorder	The qualitative differences among groups on this subscale shift gradually, with average raw scores ranging from:		

(continued)

Scale	Target Group(s)	Relatively Low Scores	Moderate Scores	Relatively High Scores
		Teacher: 1.75 (General Population) to 6.02 (Disruptive Behavior Disorders) Self: 4.39 (Anxiety) to 9.59 (Bipolar)		
DSM-IV-TR GAD	Anxiety Disorders	General Population Learning Disorders ADHD-Inattentive Pervasive Developmental Disorders (SR)	Disruptive Behavior Disorders ADHD-Hyperactive/ Impulsive ADHD-Combined Anxiety Disorders (P) Major Depressive Disorder (P & T) Pervasive Developmental Disorders (P & T)	Bipolar Disorder Anxiety Disorders (T & SR) Major Depressive Disorder (SR)
DSM-IV-TR SAD	Anxiety Disorders	The qualitative differences among groups on this subscale shift gradually,		

		with average raw scores ranging from: Parent: 2.52 (LD) to 6.91 (Anxiety Disorders) Teacher: 0.31 (LD) to 3.92 (Anxiety Disorders) Self: 2.52 (PDD) to 7.80 (Anxiety)		
DSM-IV-TR Social Phobia (P & SR)	Anxiety Disorders	The qualitative differences among groups on this subscale shift gradually, with average raw scores ranging from: Parent: 2.88 (General Population) to 6.34 (PDD) Self: 2.43 (PDD) to 7.18 (Anxiety)		Anxiety Disorders
DSM-IV-TR Social Phobia (T)	Anxiety Disorders	General Population Learning Disorders Major Depressive Disorder		

(continued)

Scale	Target Group(s)	Relatively Low Scores	Moderate Scores	Relatively High Scores
DSM-IV-TR Social Phobia (T) (continued)		Bipolar Disorder ADHD (all subtypes) Pervasive Developmental Disorders Disruptive Behavior Disorders		
DSM-IV-TR OCD (P & SR)	Anxiety Disorders	The qualitative differences among groups on this subscale shift gradually, with average raw scores ranging from: Parent: 0.89 (LD) to 4.60 (Bipolar Disorder) Self: 3.29 (LD) to 7.31 (Bipolar)		
DSM-IV-TR OCD (T)	Anxiety Disorders	General Population Learning Disorders ADHD (all subtypes) Disruptive Behavior Disorders	Major Depressive Disorder Bipolar Disorder	Anxiety Disorders Pervasive Developmental Disorders

DSM-IV-TR Autistic Disorder (P & T)	Pervasive Developmental Disorders	General Population Learning Disorders Anxiety Disorders ADHD (all subtypes) Major Depressive Disorder Bipolar Disorder (T) Disruptive Behavior Disorders	Bipolar Disorder (P)	Pervasive Developmental Disorders
DSM-IV-TR Asperger's Disorder (P & T)	Pervasive Developmental Disorders	General Population Learning Disorders Anxiety Disorders ADHD (all subtypes) Major Depressive Disorder Bipolar Disorder (T) Disruptive Behavior Disorders	Bipolar Disorder (P)	Pervasive Developmental Disorders

Source: General patterns described in this table are based on data from tables describing univariate effect of group membership on Conners CBRS scores and differences between targeted clinical groups and the general population for the Conners CBRS in the *Conners Comprehensive Behavior Rating Scales manual* (Multi-Health Systems, 2008).

Note: P = Parent, T = Teacher, SR = Self-Report

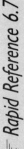
Rapid Reference 6.7

Performance of Clinical Samples on the Conners EC Scales

Scale	Target Group(s)	Relatively Low Scores	Moderate Scores	Relatively High Scores
Inattention/ Hyperactivity	ADHD	General Population Communication Social/Emotional	Cognitive Adaptive	Behavior ADHD
Defiant/Aggressive Behaviors	Behavior	General Population Cognitive Communication Social/Emotional Adaptive	ADHD	Behavior
- Defiance/Temper	Behavior	General Population Cognitive Communication Social/Emotional Adaptive ADHD		Behavior
- Aggression	Behavior	General Population Cognitive Communication Social/Emotional Adaptive ADHD		Behavior

Social Functioning/ Atypical Behaviors	Adaptive	General Population ADHD	Cognitive Communication Social/Emotional Behavior	Adaptive
- Social Functioning	Adaptive	General Population ADHD	Cognitive Communication Social/Emotional Behavior	Adaptive
- Atypical Behaviors	Adaptive	General Population Cognitive Communication Social/Emotional Behavior ADHD		Adaptive
Anxiety	Social/Emotional	General Population Cognitive Communication Adaptive (T) ADHD	Adaptive (P) Behavior	Social/Emotional
Mood and Affect (P)	Social/Emotional[a]	General Population Cognitive Communication	Social/Emotional ADHD	Adaptive Behavior
Mood and Affect (T)	Social/Emotional[a]	General Population Cognitive Communication ADHD	Social/Emotional Adaptive	Behavior

(continued)

Scale	Target Group(s)	Relatively Low Scores	Moderate Scores	Relatively High Scores
Physical Symptoms (P)	Social/Emotional	General Population Cognitive Communication Adaptive Behavior ADHD		Social/Emotional
Physical Symptoms (T)	Social/Emotional	The qualitative differences among groups on this subscale shift gradually, with average raw scores ranging from 1.17 (General Population) to 4.51 (Social/Emotional)		
Sleep Problems (P only)	Social/Emotional	The qualitative differences among groups on this subscale shift gradually, with average raw scores ranging from: 1.30 (General Population) to 4.18 (Social/Emotional)		
Adaptive Skills	Adaptive AND Cognitive	General Population Communication Social/Emotional Behavior ADHD		Cognitive Adaptive
Communication	Adaptive AND Communication AND Cognitive	General Population Social/Emotional Behavior ADHD	Communication	Cognitive Adaptive

Motor Skills (P)	Adaptive AND Cognitive	General Population Social/Emotional Behavior ADHD	Communication	Cognitive Adaptive
Motor Skills (T)	Adaptive AND Cognitive	General Population Social/Emotional	Communication Behavior ADHD	Cognitive Adaptive
Play	Adaptive AND Cognitive	The qualitative differences among groups on this subscale shift gradually, with average raw scores ranging from: Parent: 1.20 (ADHD) to 6.88 (Adaptive) Teacher: 1.42 (General Population) to 7.05 (Adaptive)		
Pre-Academic/ Cognitive	Cognitive	General Population Social/Emotional Behavior ADHD	Communication	Cognitive Adaptive

Source: General patterns described in this table are based on data from tables describing univariate effect of group membership on Conners EC scores in the *Conners Early Childhood manual* (Multi-Health Systems, 2008).

Note: P = Parent, T = Teacher

[a] For this ANCOVA, the "Behavior" sample was excluded from the Other Clinical Groups comparison due to overlap in symptoms for temper/irritability between Social/Emotional and Behavior groups.

≡ *Rapid Reference 6.8*

Performance of Conners 3 ADHD Index and Conners Clinical Index

Scale	Target Group	Rater	Overall Correct Classification Rate (%)	Sensitivity (%)	Specificity (%)
Conners 3 ADHD Index	ADHD	Parent	83	80	87
		Teacher	79	75	83
		Self-Report	77	69	84
Conners CI Disruptive Behavior Disorder Indicator	Disruptive Behavior Disorder	Parent	88	80	96
		Teacher	91	89	93
		Self-Report	82	76	88
Conners CI Learning and Language Disorder Indicator	Learning and Language Disorder	Parent	85	85	85
		Teacher	82	85	80
		Self-Report	83	80	85

Conners CI Mood Disorder Indicator	Major Depressive Disorder	Parent	89	83	95
		Teacher	85	81	89
		Self-Report	77	67	88
Conners CI Anxiety Disorder Indicator	Anxiety Disorder	Parent	70	53	88
		Teacher	76	69	83
		Self-Report	82	77	87
Conners CI ADHD Indicator	ADHD	Parent	84	77	90
		Teacher	74	64	84
		Self-Report	78	74	81

Source: Information in this table was provided by the MHS Research and Development department.

which can be the consequence of not attending to conversation). The Hyperactive/Impulsive type is characterized by persistent problems with hyperactivity and/or impulsivity that begin in early childhood and cause impairment in at least two aspects of functioning. These symptoms are motoric (e.g., fidgeting and squirming), verbal (e.g., blurting out the answer before a question is finished), and social (e.g., intruding on others' activities). The Combined type includes significant features of both Inattention and Hyperactivity/Impulsivity. Many children with ADHD show deficits in executive functioning (particularly those with Inattentive features; see Rapid Reference 1.12). There are high levels of comorbidity with the Disruptive Behavior Disorders and Learning Disorders. Children with ADHD are at risk for developing anxiety and mood disorders. The most effective treatment for ADHD is generally a combination of medication and behavioral therapy (Conners et al., 2001).

The Conners 3 and Conners CBRS clinical studies described above had three samples representing each subtype of ADHD. For some analyses, these subtypes were combined. Statistically significant differences (p < .001) occurred between the ADHD group and the General Population sample for all scales that had ADHD samples as the target clinical group(s).[4] Overall correct classification rate was 70 percent or higher ("good") for the majority of scales with ADHD as the target; a number of these scales had classification rates that were 80 percent or higher ("very good"). An exception was Conners 3 Peer/Family Relations, which had low classification accuracy for ADHD (Parent form = 61 percent, Teacher = 64 percent, Self = 65 percent; note that this scale performed better for Disruptive Behavior Disorders). The Conners 3-T Executive Functioning subscale had subpar classification rates for ADHD (68 percent). Finally, self-reported inattention scales were less accurate for overall correct classification rates (Conners 3-SR Inattention scale = 65 percent, Conners 3-SR DSM-IV-TR ADHD Inattentive scale = 67 percent, Conners CBRS-SR DSM-IV-TR ADHD Inattentive scale = 68 percent). The Conners 3 ADHD Index showed good to very good overall correct classification rates. The Conners CI ADHD Indicator performed similarly.

For the Conners EC, the ADHD sample had statistically different scores from the General Population sample (p < .001) on the Inattention/Hyperactivity scale. This scale had overall correct classification rates in the "excellent" range (Parent = 96 percent, Teacher = 90 percent).

---

4. The Conners CBRS Hyperactivity/Impulsivity scale was not reported in Conners 3 manual's ANCOVA or DFA tables for the Parent or Self-Report forms; summary statements in this section do not include this scale.

Qualitatively, the ADHD samples for all Conners assessments had high scores on relevant scales (i.e., scales for which these samples were the target). These scales all represent either primary deficits of ADHD (i.e., inattention, hyperactivity, and impulsivity) or key associated concepts (e.g., executive functioning, learning problems, peer relations). The one exception was Conners 3-SR Family Relations, on which the ADHD samples scored lower than the Disruptive Behavior Disorders sample. The ADHD sample had a relatively high average raw score for the Conners 3 Learning Problems scale/subscale and for the Conners CBRS-P Academic Difficulties scale[5] (neither of these targeted the ADHD sample); this may be due to the high level of comorbidity between ADHD and LD. Because the ADHD subtypes were grouped in different combinations for different Conners 3 and Conners CBRS analyses, it is difficult to make general statements about how they are different. For many of the scales, the average raw scores for each ADHD subtype sample appear similar; exceptions are noted in Rapid References 6.5 through 6.6.

Disruptive Behavior Disorders (DBDs)

The Disruptive Behavior Disorders, including Oppositional Defiant Disorder (ODD) and Conduct Disorder (CD) are also fairly prevalent in youth. Typical features of ODD include oppositional and defiant behaviors, including disobedience and hostility toward authority figures. Psychosocial and behavioral treatments are recommended for ODD. CD is characterized by behaviors that violate the basic rights of others or break significant societal rules (e.g., run away, truancy). Symptoms include aggression to people and animals, destruction of property, deceitfulness, theft, and serious rule violations. Effective treatments for CD tend to be multimodal, involving psychosocial treatments and medications.

In the clinical studies described above, children with ODD and children with CD were combined into a single DBD group. Statistically significant differences ($p < .001$) occurred between the DBD group and the General Population sample for all scales that had DBD as the clinical target. Overall correct classification rates were "excellent" (90 percent or higher) for relevant Conners EC scales; they were 80 percent or higher ("very good") for the majority of relevant Conners 3 and Conners CBRS scales. One exception was Conners 3 Peer Relations, which had "good" classification accuracy for DBD (Parent = 79 percent, Teacher = 78 percent). For self-reported data, overall correct classification rates were "very good" (80 percent or higher), with the exception of the Conners 3-SR DSM-IV-TR

---

5. This same pattern was not apparent for Teacher or Self-Report data on the Conners CBRS.

ODD scale, which was "good" (79 percent). The Conners CI Disruptive Behavior Disorder Indicator had very good overall correct classification rates.

Qualitatively, the DBD sample had high scores on relevant scales (i.e., scales for which these samples were the target). These scales all represent either primary symptoms of DBD (i.e., defiance/aggression) or key associated concepts (e.g., peer relations). The DBD sample also had relatively high scores on scales reflecting inattention, hyperactivity, and impulsivity for all three Conners assessments; this may represent the high rates of comorbidity between DBD and ADHD. An unexpected finding was high scores on the Conners 3-T Executive Functioning subscale; this pattern was not found for parent data. The average scores for the DBD sample were also high for the Conners EC Mood and Affect scale, which was not predicted.

Learning Disorders (LDs)[6]

Learning Disorders in the DSM-IV-TR are diagnosed based on a discrepancy model that requires test scores in a given area to be lower than expectations based on age, intelligence, and appropriate education. Specific learning disorder diagnoses include Reading Disorder (discrepancies in reading accuracy and/or comprehension), Mathematics Disorder, and Disorder of Written Expression. As is required for all DSM-IV-TR diagnoses, these deficits must cause significant impairment. Reading Disorder accounts for most of the LD diagnoses; it is rare to see the other forms of LD without comorbid reading difficulties.

Children with any combination of the three LD diagnoses described above represented the LD sample for most of the Conners 3 and Conners CBRS clinical studies described above. The exception was the Conners CBRS Academic Difficulties: Language subscale, for which the clinical group also included children with language disorders. Statistically significant differences ($p < .001$) occurred between the LD group and the General Population sample for all scales that included LD as the clinical target, with the exception of the Conners 3-P Executive Functioning scale ($p = .025$). Overall correct classification rate was "good" for the Conners 3 Learning Problems scale/subscale (Parent = 75 percent, Teacher = 74 percent, Self = 72 percent), but low for the Conners 3 Executive Functioning scale/subscale (Parent = 57 percent, Teacher = 63 percent, Self = n/a). For the Conners CBRS, overall correct classification rates were 70 percent or higher ("good") for all scales targeting LD, except Conners CBRS-P Academic Difficulties: Math (Parent = 68 percent, Teacher =

---

6. This diagnostic group was not referenced in the Conners EC manual.

72 percent). The Conners CI Learning and Language Disorder Indicator had very good overall correct classification rates.

Qualitatively, the LD sample had high scores on scales assessing learning problems. This sample did not show high levels of associated executive functioning deficits on the Conners 3. Overall, primary learning scales on the Conners 3 and Conners CBRS performed well for identifying and describing children with LD.

Language Disorders[7]

The DSM-IV-TR includes a category of Communication Disorders, which contains Expressive Language Disorder and Mixed Receptive-Expressive Language Disorder[8] as well as an articulation disorder and stuttering. The DSM-IV-TR diagnostic criteria for Expressive Language Disorder and Mixed Receptive-Expressive Language Disorder are discrepancy based, like the Learning Disorders, and require evidence of impairment. The Conners EC Delayed Communication Development sample included children with Expressive, Receptive, and Mixed Receptive-Expressive Language Disorders.

This clinical sample was combined with the Cognitive and Adaptive samples to be the target for analyses involving the Conners EC Communication scale. The differences in average raw scores between this combined clinical group and the General Population sample were statistically different (p < .001). Differences between each targeted clinical group and the general population were not reported for the Conners EC scales, so more specific information is not available. Overall correct classification rates were good to very good (Parent = 81 percent, Teacher = 76 percent). Qualitatively the average raw score for the Communication sample was noticeably lower than those for the Cognitive and Adaptive samples, but it was still higher than the other samples.

Mental Retardation (MR)[9,10]

In the DSM-IV-TR, a diagnosis of Mental Retardation requires three key features. First, intellectual functioning must be significantly below average on individual

---

7. This diagnostic group was not described in the Conners 3 or Conners CBRS manuals, although children with Language Disorders were included in one analysis for the Conners CBRS.

8. Interestingly, the diagnosis Receptive Language Disorder is not listed in the DSM-IV-TR.

9. This diagnostic group was not referenced in the Conners 3 or Conners CBRS manuals.

10. The term "Intellectual Disability" (ID) is preferred by some, but the DSM-IV-TR uses "MR." See Schalock et al. (2007) for further discussion.

testing (i.e., 70 or below). Second, the person must show significant impairment in at least two areas of adaptive functioning (e.g., functional communication, self-care). Third, these deficits must begin before 18 years old (this is primarily to differentiate MR as a developmental disorder as opposed to an acquired condition, e.g., secondary to brain injury).

Children with a diagnosis of MR were included in the Delayed Cognitive Development sample for the Conners EC clinical studies described above. This clinical sample was combined with other clinical samples for analyses involving the Developmental Milestone scales, with the exception of Pre-Academic/Cognitive. The combination of Cognitive and Adaptive samples was statistically different from the General Population sample (p < .001) for these comparisons (with Communication included for the Communication scale); the Cognitive sample was statistically different from the General Population sample (p < .001) for the Pre-Academic/Cognitive sample. Differences between each targeted clinical group and the general population were not reported for the Conners EC scales, so more specific information is not available. Overall correct classification rates were "very good" (80 percent and higher) for these scales, with the exception of Play (Parent = 75 percent, Teacher = 76 percent). Qualitatively, the average raw score for the Cognitive sample was high on relevant Conners EC scales.

Mood Disorders

This DSM-IV-TR category describes diagnoses for which disturbance in mood is the primary feature, including Major Depressive Disorder and Bipolar Disorder.[11] As mentioned in Rapid Reference 1.20, the DSM-IV-TR uses four "building blocks" to describe the Mood Disorders: Major Depressive Episode, Manic Episode, Mixed Episode,[12] and Hypomanic Episode.[13] The presence and absence of these four mood episodes help identify which Mood Disorders are possible. See Rapid Reference 6.9 for a brief summary of various diagnostic combinations (keeping in mind that additional criteria are required, as is true for all DSM-IV-TR diagnoses).

---

11. Other diagnoses in this category include Dysthymic Disorder (a mild form of Major Depressive Disorder) and Cyclothymic Disorder (a mild form of Bipolar Disorder). See the DSM-IV-TR for more information.

12. When a Major Depressive Episode and a Manic Episode occur in the same one-week period.

13. Literally "below manic" (i.e., "hypo" means below); a Hypomanic Episode is a milder version of the Manic Episode requiring shorter duration (symptoms persisting over a four-day period rather than a week) and less severity (i.e., observable by others but not severe enough to include psychotic features, require hospitalization, or cause marked impairment).

≡ *Rapid Reference 6.9*

Mood Disorder Building Blocks

DSM-IV-TR Diagnosis	Major Depressive Episode	Manic Episode	Mixed Episode	Hypomanic Episode
Major Depressive Disorder	At least one	Never	Never	Never
Bipolar I Disorder (*2 possible combinations*)	Not required	At least one	Not required	Not required
	Not required	Not required	At least one	Not required
Bipolar II Disorder	At least one	Never	Never	At least one

Major Depressive Disorder (MDD)[14] in youth can be characterized by irritable mood, physical symptoms, and social withdrawal rather than frank sadness. One survey found that 14 percent of adolescents reported a history of experiencing one or more Major Depressive Episodes; very few of these youth had a history of treatment (SAMHSA, 2006). Bipolar Disorder may include depressive periods, but it requires the presence of Manic, Mixed, or Hypomanic episodes. Researchers in the area of pediatric Bipolar Disorder disagree as to whether the DSM-IV-TR criteria are appropriate for children; some publications describe a "rapid cycling" form of pediatric Bipolar Disorder. Prevalence of DSM-IV-TR Bipolar Disorder is very low across the lifespan—less than 2 percent of the general population. Recommended treatments for depression are often multimodal, combining medication and cognitive-behavioral therapy.

In clinical studies with the Conners CBRS, statistically significant differences (p < .001) occurred between the MDD group and the general population sample for all scales that targeted MDD. Overall correct classification rates for parent and teacher data were mostly in the "very good" range (exceeding 80 percent),

---

14. In the past, this condition was called "unipolar depression" as it referred to one end of the mood spectrum (i.e., "uni" = one, "polar" = end), in contrast to "bipolar depression," which referred to two extremes (i.e., "bi" = two).

with the exception of the Physical Symptoms scale (Parent = 73 percent, Teacher = 77 percent). Self-report data for scales targeting MDD had "good" overall correct classification rates.

The MDD sample was combined with the Anxiety Disorders sample for ANCOVA contrasts involving the Conners CBRS Content scales (see Rapid Reference 6.6). These two clinical groups did not differ statistically for average raw score on the Emotional Distress scale/subscales or Physical Symptoms scale, with the exception of self-report data on the Physical Symptoms scale (higher average raw score for MDD sample than Anxiety sample). The MDD sample had high scores on all expected scales. There were unexpected findings of high scores on the Emotional Distress: Worrying subscale for the parent data, the DSM-IV-TR ADHD Inattentive scale for the self-report data, and the DSM-IV-TR GAD scale for the self-report data. These elevations were not observed for the other rater types. For the most part, scales on the Conners CBRS reflecting primary issues of emotional distress and depression, as well as associated issues of physical symptoms, performed well in describing the sample of children with MDD.

Conners CBRS assessments completed by and about children with Bipolar Disorder were grouped into one sample (i.e., no distinction between Bipolar I and Bipolar II). This sample was the target for the DSM-IV-TR Manic Episode scale and was statistically different (p < .001) from the General Population in all contrasts for this scale. Overall correct classification rates were good to very good across raters (Parent = 88 percent, Teacher = 84 percent, Self = 78 percent). The Bipolar sample had high scores on the appropriate scale. Surprisingly, the Bipolar sample also had high scores on many other scales, including Emotional Distress, Violence Potential Indicator (Parent only), and the DSM-IV-TR symptom scales for ADHD Inattentive, ADHD Hyperactive/Impulsive, CD (Parent only), ODD (Parent only), Major Depressive Episode (Parent and Self), and GAD. In fact, this sample had the highest or second highest average raw score for almost every Conners CBRS-P scale described in the ANCOVA tables. Assuming that the diagnoses were correctly assigned for children in this clinical sample, this suggests that parents of children with Bipolar Disorder may have a tendency to report high levels of many types of symptoms.[15] In sum, the DSM-IV-TR Manic Episode scale performed as expected for the sample of children with Bipolar Disorder.

The Conners CI Mood Disorder Indicator, which was based on a sample of children with diagnoses including Major Depressive Disorder, Dysthymic

---

15. It would be interesting to know if the Negative Impression index tends to be elevated for ratings of children with Bipolar Disorder.

Disorder, and Bipolar Disorder, had very good overall correct classification rates for Parent and Teacher data and good classification rates for self-report data. The relevant Conners EC clinical sample, Social/Emotional, included mood and anxiety disorders. The average raw score for this combined clinical sample was statistically different from the General Population (p < .001) for the Mood and Affect scale and the Physical Symptoms scale (including the Conners EC-P Sleep Problems subscale). Overall rates of correct classification were 80 percent or higher ("very good"), with the exception of Physical Symptoms (Parent = 81 percent, Teacher = 79 percent) and Sleep Problems (Parent = 78 percent, Teacher = n/a). This clinical sample had the highest scores on the Physical Symptoms and Sleep Problems scale/subscale. As mentioned previously, there were other clinical samples with higher scores than the Social/Emotional group for the Mood and Affect scale.

Anxiety Disorders

Anxiety disorders are fairly prevalent in youth, with a recent survey showing higher rates in girls than boys (U.S. Department of Health and Human Services, 1999). This diagnostic category has high comorbidity; about half of the children with an Anxiety Disorder have at least one other diagnosis. The Anxiety Disorder sample for the Conners CBRS included children with Generalized Anxiety Disorder (GAD), Separation Anxiety Disorder (SAD), Social Phobia, and Obsessive-Compulsive Disorder (OCD). Most anxiety disorders respond to cognitive-behavioral approaches, with adjunct medication in some cases.

GAD (which includes "Overanxious Disorder of Childhood") is a pattern of overwhelming anxiety and worry that is hard to control. Children with GAD often worry about issues like competence and performance in academic, social, and athletic domains. They may require frequent reassurance and may be perfectionistic. These children often try very hard to be pleasers, although sometimes they are described as difficult because they refuse to do a task if not guaranteed success.

Symptoms of SAD match the diagnosis name—excessive anxiety about being separated from family or home. These symptoms often include physical complaints, angriness, and physical acting out. School refusal is a common situation in which symptoms of SAD are seen. It is important to remember that SAD symptoms can be triggered by the act of separation and also by the fear of separation.

Social Phobia is usually observed in response to performance situations, which may involve social interactions. This disorder involves excessive anxiety about situations in which the child could be embarrassed. Symptoms include avoiding such situations, panic attacks, or extreme dread. In children, this diagnosis requires the capacity for social interaction (as opposed to social issues seen in the Pervasive Developmental Disorders), and the symptoms must occur not only with adults but also with peers. Social Phobia in children often includes tantrums, crying, clinginess, and/or mutism. Children with this diagnosis may refuse to attend school, do poorly in school, and/or be socially isolated.

The diagnosis of OCD requires either obsessions or compulsions.[16] Obsessions are thoughts that a person finds distressing and tries to remove from his mind, sometimes through compulsions. Compulsions are repetitive behaviors that the person feels he must do to remove obsessions, reduce distress from obsessions, or prevent a feared event.[17] For a repetitive behavior to be considered a compulsion, it must be either excessive (e.g., washing hands for 10 minutes after touching trash) or not realistically connected to the event (e.g., counting to 12 to prevent a bad grade). In addition to excessive washing and counting, common compulsions in children include checking/re-checking and repetitively putting things into a certain order. Compulsions may be more apparent at home, with secondary effects such as academic deterioration noted at school.

Clinical studies with the Conners CBRS included a clinical sample of children with GAD, SAD, Social Phobia, or OCD, referred to as the Anxiety Disorders sample. This sample was the clinical target for a number of scales. The Anxiety Disorders sample had a statistically different score than the General Population for all of these scales—most at the $p < .001$ level; the Conners CBRS-P Perfectionistic and Compulsive Behaviors scale differed at $p = .004$, and the Physical Symptoms scale at .002 (Parent) and .03 (Self). Overall correct classification rates were "good" (70 percent or higher) for most of these scales, with the exception of Separation Fears (Parent = 71 percent, Teacher = 72 percent, Self = 68 percent), Perfectionistic and Compulsive Behaviors (Parent = 66 percent, Teacher = 77 percent, Self = n/a), Physical Symptoms (Parent = 67 percent, Teacher = 75 percent, Self = 66 percent), and DSM-IV-TR SAD (Parent = 71 percent, Teacher = 74 percent, Self = 67 percent); rates were in the "very good" (80 percent or higher) range for a number of CBRS-T scales/subscales (Emotional Distress, 83 percent; Upsetting Thoughts/Physical Symptoms, 83 percent;

16. The diagnosis of OCD is different from the diagnosis of Obsessive Compulsive *Personality* Disorder (OCPD), which is a rigid personality style involving perfectionism and control. Although many laypeople use the term "OCD" to refer to a focus on details, it would be more accurate to use the term "OCPD" in such instances.

17. Note the reasons why behaviors are repeated for OCD; this is different from repetitive behaviors observed with Tic Disorders such as Tourette's.

DSM-IV-TR GAD 82 percent, Social Phobia 81 percent, OCD 86 percent). The Conners CI Anxiety Disorder Indicator had good to very good overall correct classification rates.

As noted previously, the Conners CBRS Anxiety Disorders sample was grouped with the MDD sample for some ANCOVA contrasts (see "Mood Disorders" section above for these results). The Anxiety Disorders sample had high scores on the expected scales, with the exception of Physical Symptoms (all raters) and DSM-IV-TR GAD (Parent report). In general, the Conners CBRS scales involving symptoms and correlates of various anxiety disorders were elevated for the Anxiety Disorders sample, although the performance for this group was not as strong as for other clinical samples. This may be related to the heterogeneous nature of this sample, which included children with four different types of diagnoses. Teacher-reported data were stronger than results from parents or youth in terms of classification rates.

As mentioned above, the relevant Conners EC clinical sample, Social/Emotional, combined mood and anxiety disorders. For the Conners EC Anxiety scale, the average raw score for this clinical sample was statistically different from the General Population sample (p < .001). Overall correct classification rates were very good (Parent = 90 percent, Teacher = 87 percent). This clinical group had the highest average raw score of all the samples reported for the Conners EC Anxiety scale.

Pervasive Developmental Disorders

Finally, a sample of children with Pervasive Developmental Disorders (PDDs; including Autistic Disorder, Asperger's Disorder, and PDD, Not Otherwise Specified, or PDD-NOS) was included in the clinical studies described above. This DSM-IV-TR diagnostic category requires severe, pervasive impairment in reciprocal social interaction, communication, and stereotyped behavior/interests/activities.

A diagnosis of Autistic Disorder may be considered when there is severe impairment in all three of these areas. So-called "classic" autism involves a lack of verbal and nonverbal communication skills; children with this degree of severity are typically diagnosed in early childhood. The term "high-functioning autism" is often used to describe children with this diagnosis who have intact cognitive and communicative skills; it is possible for children at this end of the autistic spectrum to be misdiagnosed until middle school or even high school.

The primary difference between Asperger's Disorder and Autistic Disorder lies in the communication domain; a diagnosis of Asperger's Disorder requires intact cognitive and early language development. Although early language *development* is intact, aspects of language such as reading body language and understanding figures of speech, sarcasm, inference, and humor can be problematic for people with this diagnosis.

The third diagnosis included in this study group, PDD-NOS, describes children with significant features of autism but who do not meet full criteria for an actual diagnosis of Autistic Disorder, Asperger's Disorder, or another PDD diagnosis. For all of the diagnoses in the PDD category it is common to see associated anxiety, inattention, and executive dysfunction. Most treatment programs focus on behavioral issues, and modality of treatment varies with severity of symptoms and impairment.

The Conners CBRS PDD sample was statistically different from the General Population sample for relevant scales.[18] Overall correct classification rates were 80 percent or higher ("very good"), with some approaching 90 percent (i.e., DSM-IV-TR Autistic Disorder, Parent = 89 percent, Teacher = 89 percent). Qualitatively, the PDD sample had high scores on scales assessing the symptoms of these disorders, including social problems and perfectionistic/compulsive behaviors. Although not named as the primary target for other scales, the average raw score for the PDD sample was relatively high for Emotional Distress (Parent and Teacher), DSM-IV-TR ADHD Inattentive (Teacher), and DSM-IV-TR OCD (Teacher). Although not quite as extreme, the DSM-IV-TR Social Phobia scale showed the same pattern (average score for the PDD sample was the highest of all samples for Parent report, and the lowest for Self-Report). It is tempting to draw the conclusion that these scales represent associated features, as anxiety and inattention are often described in children diagnosed with PDD; however, it is interesting to note that, in all three of these cases, self-reports from children in the PDD sample were in the lowest group of average raw scores. Without further investigation it is difficult to say whether this contrast represents parent/teacher assumptions (e.g., they assume the child must be in distress, whereas the child is actually comfortable with his situation), limited self-awareness (e.g., the child does not realize that she is not attending well), or a host of other explanations. With the exception of the high scores mentioned above, average scores for the PDD sample were often the lowest for each rater and scale and the standard error (SE) was *always* the largest for each scale (indicating high variability within the PDD sample).

---

18. Note that the relevant scales only occur on Parent and Teacher reports; no scales on the Conners CBRS-SR had PDD as the target group.

In sum, Conners CBRS scales targeting the PDD clinical sample did very well in terms of classification, despite greater statistical variation for this sample. For the most part, raters describing these children did not report high levels of other symptoms. An interesting exception to note is the high levels of emotional distress and inattention described by observers but not reported by children about themselves.

The Delayed Adaptive Functioning sample for the Conners EC included young children with diagnoses in the PDD category. For the Social Functioning/Atypical Behaviors scale/subscales there were statistically significant differences ($p < .001$) between this clinical group and the General Population sample. Overall correct classification rates were excellent (90 percent or higher) in most cases, with the Social Functioning subscale in the very good range (Parent = 90 percent, Teacher = 87 percent). This clinical sample had the highest of all average raw scores for these targeted scale/subscales. This clinical sample also had a high score on the Conners EC-P Mood and Affect scale; this was unexpected.

As mentioned in the "Mental Retardation" section previously, the Adaptive sample was combined with the Cognitive sample for analyses involving most of the Developmental Milestone scales (see Rapid Reference 6.7). The average raw score for these combined clinical samples was statistically different from the General Population sample ($p < .001$) for each of these comparisons. Differences between each targeted clinical group and the general population were not reported for the Conners EC scales, so more specific information is not available. Overall correct classification rates were "very good" (80 percent and higher) for these scales, with some rates higher than 90 percent. Qualitatively, the average raw score for the Adaptive sample was high on relevant Conners EC Developmental Milestone scales.

🐾 TEST YOURSELF 🐾

1. **The Conners assessments can help you comply with IDEA 2004 in what ways?** *Mark all that apply.*

   (a) Reducing racial and cultural bias

   (b) Specifying which disability category is the best for a student

   (c) Developing goals for initial IEP and revisions for subsequent IEPs

   (d) Identifying students who require supports to succeed in the general education setting

   (e) Monitoring student response to intervention (RTI)

2. What is the "RCI," and why is it helpful?

(a) The "rating correlation indicator" indicates how closely parent and teacher data correlate with each other.

(b) The "reading correspondence inconsistencies" describes when inconsistencies in self-report data could be due to reading difficulties.

(c) The "reliable change index" helps determine if the change in ratings over time is statistically significant.

(d) The "rating correspondence indicator" marks when the difference between a T-score and a percentile is statistically significant.

3. A diagnosis of Bipolar Disorder requires a history of at least one Major Depressive Episode and at least one Manic Episode.
True or false?

4. Which of the following types of information must be examined to determine a DSM-IV-TR diagnosis? *Mark all that apply.*

(a) Age of onset

(b) Course of symptoms

(c) Pervasiveness of symptoms

(d) Frequency, severity, and number of symptoms

(e) Level of impairment

5. Which of the following are appropriate ways to use the Conners assessments? *Mark all that apply.*

(a) In a diagnostic assessment for an individual child

(b) To monitor progress (or lack of progress) with interventions

(c) To screen a group of children

(d) To describe characteristics of a group of children

(e) To evaluate effectiveness of an educational or treatment program

Answers: 1. a, c, d, e; 2. c; 3. False; 4. a, b, c, d, e; 5. a, b, c, d, e

Seven

ILLUSTRATIVE CASE REPORTS

Elizabeth P. Sparrow

his chapter presents case studies of three children who were referred for neuropsychological evaluations. Each child was administered relevant tests, including the Conners assessments.

The first case report is of Brian Jones, a 9-year-old boy who was referred due to academic underachievement in the context of ADHD. His test battery includes the Conners 3, as well as tests of attention, executive functioning, memory, and other domains. The second case report is of Darby Reed, an 11-year-old girl whose initial referral sounded very similar to that of Brian Jones. Additional information gained from Darby's parents indicated that ADHD might not be the only area of concern, so the Conners CBRS was used to gather a broader range of information about her functioning at home and school. Darby's test battery includes IQ, achievement, and other assessment tools. The final case report is of Josh Kane, a 5-year-old boy whose parents were concerned about possible Asperger's Disorder. His test battery includes the Conners EC, a test of cognitive ability, and other measures.

The goal of this chapter is to illustrate application of key principles described in this book, including the responsible use of the Conners assessments within a comprehensive battery. Written reports have many stylistic differences depending on the setting and the professional's personal preferences, among other factors. The reports provided in this chapter are not representative of all report types (see Rapid Reference 7.1). Test data are presented in tables embedded within each report. The identifying information for each child has been changed to maintain confidentiality.

Rapid Reference 7.1

Written Reports

There are many ways to write reports, and the best solution varies by situation. Some of the things you see in these three case studies are stylistic. For example, I choose to write the history section in bullets, as it is easier for me to find important information quickly this way than if the history was written in paragraphs.

Unless you can guarantee that only a qualified professional will receive the report, it is important to provide sufficient context with the test scores to help reduce misinterpretation. For this reason, I choose to give parents and teachers a small table at the beginning of the test results table that lists the average range of different types of scores.

I include tables with test names and scores to facilitate review of these results by other qualified professionals. Within the text of the results section, I describe the tasks involved in the different tests rather than referring to them by name. This helps readers understand what the child was asked to do (which is more important than which test it was). I usually avoid listing the test names in the text, unless it is necessary to prevent confusion. For purposes of this book, I have added the relevant Conners assessment and scale—this was not present in the original clinical documents.

I try to write the report in basic language, while including and explaining terms that parents may need to know in the future (e.g., "executive functioning").

I choose to embed the test results table within the report rather than append it at the end. This reduces the chances that the numbers will become separated from the interpretive context, as test scores must always be interpreted within the relevant context. Although not illustrated in this book, I put the text "CONFIDENTIAL INFORMATION—DO NOT RELEASE WITHOUT PERMISSION" at the bottom of each report page to remind readers that they must obtain written consent from the child's parent/guardian before giving the report to anyone else.

My recommendations tend to be specific and individualized for each child I see. Some recommendations are variations on a theme, adjusted for a child's developmental stage and unique needs. In my experience, labeling a child's struggles does not often lead to solving them. It is important for the assessor to take the next step to help parents and teachers translate the results into meaningful recommendations. Even though some of the recommendations may not be followed, they will help parents and teachers get started with ideas.

Finally, I try to include each child's relative strengths throughout the report, including background, test results, diagnostic summary, and recommendations. This includes positive prognostic indicators, when these can be identified. I believe that everyone makes more progress when given a balanced review that includes strengths; it is important for children to know that you appreciate their skills and for parents/teachers to remember that a child is not just a list of problems. Without awareness of strengths, you do not know which tools a child has available for fixing his difficulties, and it is difficult to recruit and keep the repair crew (i.e., treatment team, including parents and the child).

NEUROPSYCHOLOGICAL REPORT

Name: Brian Thomas Jones
Age: 9 years, 1 month
Grade: 3rd grade

Referral

Brian Jones, a 9-year-old boy, was referred for neuropsychological evaluation by his parents. This evaluation was recommended due to concerns about discrepancies between academic ability and academic performance. Specific concerns include:

- "Grades don't reflect ability"; Brian is currently in the second tier groups for reading and math, despite scoring well above average on recent assessment of academic achievement.
- Written language "is not that great"; he has lost his enthusiasm. He has difficulty with getting started on written language assignments and organizing his writing.

Background Information

Family Background

- Born in Los Angeles, California; moved to Maryland when he was 4.5 years old.
- One sibling, sister Avery (5 years younger).
- Mother completed bachelor's degree, worked as an office manager in the past, currently full-time mother.
- Father completed bachelor's degree, currently employed as a mortgage banker.
- Extended family history includes: ADHD, underachievement in the context of high IQ, extreme shyness, situational anxiety, depression, heavy drinking, Down's syndrome, clumsiness, moving too quickly.

Developmental and Medical History

- Pregnancy: Past-term (42 weeks), complicated by work-related stress. Drank 2 cups of coffee per day.
- Labor/Delivery: Induced with pitocin because past-term, 28-hour labor. Began preparing for C-section but he was delivered vaginally with vacuum extraction. Fetal monitor showed decrease in heart rate several times.

- Birthweight: 9 pounds, 8 ounces.
- Neonatal: Blue at birth, initial APGAR score was low but improved by second score. Discharged to home at 4 hours old with no concerns.
- Handedness: Right.
- Neurologic issues (brain injury, sustained fevers, loss of consciousness, seizures, etc.): None reported.
- Medications:
  - Current: Stimulant medication. Parents note side effects including: reduced appetite and weight loss and difficulty sleeping. Positive changes include improved alertness.
  - Past: None reported.
- Vision and Hearing: No concerns.
- Trauma, abuse, violence, or neglect: None reported beyond multiple changes at 4.5 years old (sister born, cross-country move).
- Infancy: Easy, quiet, contemplative, happy.
- First concerns: 4.5 years old, when moved to Maryland; Brian seemed withdrawn, had trouble making friends, and stopped making eye contact. Father notes some emotional changes predating the move.
- Development of skills and concerns:
  - Motor: On-time to early acquisition of milestones; no current concerns.
  - Cognitive: Early learning seemed appropriate. Current concerns include: attention, distractibility, learning, and math (addition and subtraction).
  - Language: On-time to early acquisition of milestones; no current concerns. "Hears what you're saying even if he seems to be ignoring you."
  - Social: On-time to early acquisition of milestones. Had a best friend in Los Angeles. Initial difficulty making friends after move to Maryland, but this has improved now that they are settled into the neighborhood.
  - Play: Early play was age-appropriate. Played with peers in Los Angeles. After moving to Maryland, Mrs. Jones arranged playdates, but they played with her because Brian was "nonresponsive to them." He now enjoys playing with neighborhood friends and schoolfriends.
  - Emotion: Very close relationship with father. Has always been shy and introverted, but became more so around move to Maryland. This emotional change was attributed to departure of several friends from his daycare setting. Currently shows a variable range of affect and can label his emotions. He usually recognizes emotions in others and responds appropriately. When he is nervous, he often becomes silly.
  - Behavior: No reported concerns.

- Sleeping: Difficulty sleeping since began medications; no concerns prior to that time.
- Activities of Daily Living: No concerns about eating and toileting. Independent for bathing, grooming, and dressing. Requires "a lot" of assistance to clean his room.
- Atypical Features: History of repetitive behaviors (e.g., repetitive throat-clearing, tapping chair with pencil/hand). Sensitive to loud sounds in crowded places, tags in shirts.

Past Evaluations, Diagnoses, and Treatments:

- 6 years old: Psychoeducational evaluation, referred by kindergarten teacher for suspected ADHD. IQ and achievement scores in average range. Below average scores on continuous performance test. No significant emotional or behavioral concerns. Diagnostic impression was ADHD. See Dr. Freet's report for full results.
- 8 years old: School-wide standardized achievement testing, scores ranged from average to superior.
- 8 years old: Psychiatric evaluation for possible medication trial; continuing to struggle academically. Diagnosed with ADHD and prescribed stimulant medication by Dr. Raoul; see his note for details.
- 9 years old: Psychoeducational evaluation, referred by 3rd grade teacher for possible Specific Learning Disorder (SLD). IQ testing supported average to superior ranges of functioning, with some variability among subtests and index scores. Achievement testing supported average to above average knowledge and application of academic skills. The examiner noted that Brian seemed to do better in the one-to-one setting than in the classroom setting. Please see Ms. Sieb's report for scores and additional details.

Academic History

- Early childhood (based on parent report): Daycare in Los Angeles; group of 6 children. Very nurturing; "spoiled him."
- White Memorial Preschool (based on parent report): Entered immediately after move to Maryland. Difficulty learning the routine; played alone.
- Root Elementary School (based on parent report and review of report cards/progress reports):
  - Kindergarten: Teacher had concerns about ADHD; referred for evaluation. Inattentive, poor focus, only followed 50 percent of commands, difficulty writing letters.

- 1st grade: Repetitive throat-clearing and tapping his chair. Other concerns included: hesitation about written work, difficulty focusing, difficulty learning math facts, fidgets, inattentive, short attention span.
- 2nd grade: Teacher had a master's degree in speech-language; Brian did well in her class, but concerns continued. Teacher notes indicate: fidgets, inattentive, incomplete classwork, short attention span, does not follow through, poor organization, daydreams, preoccupied with objects in desk, needs verbal reminders of task, limited class participation, needs preferential seating and physical cues, clumsy, makes disruptive noises, messy handwriting.
- Current: 3rd grade (last quarter)
  - Reading grades were C in 1st quarter and B in 2nd quarter.
  - Science grade dropped from an A in 1st quarter to a C in 2nd quarter.
  - Better spelling on spelling tests than in everyday writing.
  - Teacher notes indicate: rushes to finish, limited concentration, submits work below capabilities.
  - Recent progress report: "School work and habits have improved significantly over the course of this school year. Brian benefited from a goal chart (pay attention, slow down, take time with work) and has improved in his ability to receive corrections of written work."

Strengths (based on parent, teacher, and self-report): nice, quiet (per Brian, "I'm kind of quiet . . . that's my specialty"), fabulous imagination, good vocabulary, abstract thinking, figuring things out on the computer through trial and error, and "has a memory like an elephant."

Preferred Activities: computer games (fantasy games, spy games), hands-on activities (e.g., science projects, geometry), and reading.

Evaluation Procedures

- NEPSY: A Developmental Neuropsychological Evaluation (NEPSY): Selected subtests
- Conners' Continuous Performance Test, 2nd edition (CPT-II)
- Delis-Kaplan Executive Function System (D-KEFS): Selected subtests
- Children's Memory Scale (CMS): Stories, Sequences
- California Verbal Learning Test–Children's version (CVLT-C)
- Rey Complex Figure Test with Recognition Trial (RCFT)

- Clinical Interview
- Error analysis of recent work samples
- Conners 3rd Edition (Conners 3): Parent, teacher, and self-reports[1]

Validity

Instruments used are valid for Brian and for the referral question(s). The tests were administered by a qualified examiner (Elizabeth P. Sparrow, PhD, Licensed Psychologist). Observed behaviors during the evaluation were consistent with parent report of usual behaviors. Available validity indicators were all within acceptable limits, unless noted otherwise. Therefore, results of this evaluation are judged to be a valid representation of current neuropsychological functioning.

General Presentation

Brian was accompanied to the evaluation by his mother. He had no difficulty separating from her. He appeared small and thin for his chronologic age, with circles under both eyes. He was initially very interested in a puzzle ball on the shelf and appeared nonresponsive to the examiner. Once his attention was gained, he was very responsive to the examiner. Brian tended to look around the room rather than sustain eye contact, but he did demonstrate use of appropriate eye contact in conversation.

Brian seemed appropriately interested in test materials. He made frequent and repetitive noises, including throat-clearing, throat-clicks, swishing sounds, and other mouth noises. He hummed, grunted, sang, and spoke aloud while working. He drummed his fingers, rubbed the table, or scratched the tabletop when thinking about difficult items. Brian was very active during the evaluation. He changed his seating position multiple times (including standing and kneeling on the floor) and was generally fidgety and squirmy. Over the course of an independent 20-minute task, he took off one shoe, swung his feet back and forth, made tangential comments, stood, leaned on the table, and switched which hand he used to respond. Although Brian preferred knowing the endpoint of his work (e.g., how many more pages, what time is lunch), he persevered until the examiner told him to stop. He seemed aware of the relative difficulty of various

---

1. Parent reports were completed by Mrs. Jones. Teacher reports were completed by Ms. Keene, general education 3rd grade teacher, and Miss Brown, small reading group instructor; both described knowing Brian well.

items and self-adjusted his rate of work; however, on items that appeared easy he often picked an answer without considering all available options. He asked after initial items, "Are these the real things, or practice?" He responded well to reassurance.

These observations were made during testing, which was conducted in a quiet, reduced-distraction setting with one-to-one interaction. They are consistent with observations made in the previous evaluation. It is likely that Brian's presentation is somewhat different in a classroom setting, which has more distractions (visual and auditory) and less direct interaction.

At the time of this evaluation, Brian was being prescribed a stimulant medication. He took his regular dose of stimulant medication on the day of testing; this decision to conduct testing with medication was made by Brian's parents in consultation with Dr. Raoul.

TEST RESULTS AND INTERPRETATION

The results from Brian's performance during this neuropsychological evaluation are summarized in Table 7.1. Results from formal tests are reported as standardized scores, which compare Brian's performance with other students who are the same age. Standardized scores take a variety of forms, including those summarized in the following table. Higher scores generally represent better performance, unless noted otherwise (e.g., Conners 3).

Intellectual Ability: Results from intellectual assessment at 6 years old (*WPPSI-R*) were in the average range. At that time, Brian had not participated in any treatment for symptoms of inattention.

Table 7.1. Standardized Score Results

Standardized Score	Average Range of Scores
Scaled Score (ScS)	7 to 13
Standard Score (SS)	85 to 115
T-score (T)	40 to 60
z-score (z)	-1.00 to $+1.00$

Because intellectual ability was assessed within the past 6 months, it was not necessary to repeat this testing. Results from the recent administration of the *WISC-IV* indicate above average functioning overall, with some significant variations within Brian's profile. Please see Ms. Sieb's report for scores. Aspects of her findings will be described as needed in relevant sections of this report.

CAUTION

Repeated Testing

When a child has been tested repeatedly and/or recently, it may not be necessary or helpful to test that area again. Repeated testing can reduce a child's energy and motivation levels. Check test manuals to determine how often it is appropriate to repeat a test. Consider whether you will gain enough additional information to make it worthwhile. Determine if you can get adequate information by repeating just a portion of the test. Above all, do not test unnecessarily.

Academic Achievement: Results from the evaluation at 6 years old (*YCAT*) indicated average academic skills in reading, mathematics, and writing at that time. Results from group testing at 8 years old indicated superior skills in reading, vocabulary, and language mechanics. Brian scored in the average range for other academic skills at that time (including language, math, and math computation).

Academic achievement was assessed in the past 6 months with the *WIAT-II* (see Ms. Sieb's report for details); there was no need to repeat this testing at this time. All composite scores were in the above average range for Brian's age. He had average range scores for Reading Comprehension, Listening Comprehension, and Written Expression. The examiner commented that variable attention and poor organization of ideas seemed to impact his performance on these subtests.

Mrs. Jones, Ms. Keene, and Brian all reported more difficulties with learning than would be expected for 9-year-old boys (*Conners 3: Learning Problems*). Review of the items from this rating scale suggested that these difficulties include spelling, reading, understanding instructions, and getting the big picture. Miss Brown, Brian's reading group instructor, commented that she does not observe actual decoding, reading comprehension, or spelling problems, but that Brian seems to need more structure than other students to consistently demonstrate his skills in these areas. She notices a difference in the assignments he completes in her small group compared to those completed in the classroom. Her ratings for the Learning Problems subscale were in the Average range.

Neuropsychological Functioning

Scores from neuropsychological evaluation are provided in Tables   7.2 through 7.6 and will be discussed further in subsequent sections of this report.

Speed: Overall, Brian earned scores in the average to high-average range on timed tasks, including those from recent evaluation (*WISC-IV*). Speed of

Table 7.2. D-KEFS Results

D-KEFS	Measure	ScS
Trail Making Test	Visual Scanning	7
	Number Sequencing	14
	Letter Sequencing	14
	Number-Letter Switching	13
	Motor Speed	13
Verbal Fluency Test	Letter Fluency	16
	Category Fluency	13
	Category Switching: Total Correct	11
	Category Switching: Switching Accuracy	11
Twenty Questions Test	Initial Abstraction	13
	Total Questions Asked	10
	Total Weighted Achievement	9
Tower Test	Total Achievement Score	15

Table 7.3. NEPSY Subtest Results

NEPSY Subtest	Scaled Score or Percentile
Auditory Attention and Response Set	ScS = 11
- Attention Task	ScS = 13
- Attention Omissions	>75th Percentile
- Attention Commissions	>75th Percentile
- Response Set Task	ScS = 10
- Response Set Omissions	>75th Percentile
- Response Set Commissions	26th − 75th Percentile
Visual Attention	ScS = 12
- Cats Time	26th − 75th Percentile
- Cats Omissions	26th − 75th Percentile
- Cats Commissions	26th − 75th Percentile
- Faces Time	>75th Percentile
- Faces Omissions	26th − 75th Percentile
- Faces Commissions	26th − 75th Percentile
Visuomotor Precision	ScS = 9
- Car Time	>75th Percentile
- Car Errors	26th − 75th Percentile
- Motorcycle Time	26th − 75th Percentile
- Motorcycle Errors	11th − 25th Percentile

Table 7.4. Other Test Results

Other Tests	Standardized Score
CMS: Stories	
- Immediate Free Recall	ScS = 13
- Immediate Thematic Recall	ScS = 14
- Delayed Free Recall	ScS = 11
- Delayed Thematic Recall	ScS = 10
- Delayed Recognition	ScS = 11
CMS: Sequences	ScS = 11
RCFT:	
- Copy	> 16th Percentile
- Time to Copy	> 16th Percentile
- Immediate Recall	T = 47
- Delayed Recall	T = 50
- Recognition Total Correct	T = 60

Table 7.5. CVLT-C Results

CVLT-C	Raw Score	Standardized Score (z-score unless indicated otherwise)
List A Total Trials 1–5	47 (6 + 8 + 10 + 11 + 12)	$T = 53$
List A Trial 1 Free Recall	6	0.0
List A Trial 5 Free Recall	12	0.5
List B Free Recall	5	–0.5
List A Short-Delay Free Recall	13	1.5
List A Short-Delay Cued Recall	11	0.5
List A Long-Delay Free Recall	10	0.5
List A Long-Delay Cued Recall	10	0.0
Semantic Cluster Ratio	1.4	0.0
Serial Cluster Ratio	3.0	0.5
Learning Slope	1.5	0.5
Perseverations (Total)	5	–0.5
Intrusions (Total)	3	–0.5
Correct Recognition Hits	15/15	1.0
False Positives (Total)	1/30	–0.5

information processing and responding does not appear to be a primary concern at this time.

Attention/Executive Functions: Results from the evaluation at 6 years old (*IVA-CPT*) indicated adequate impulse control but deficient regulation of attention.

During this evaluation, Brian exerted significant effort to focus, direct, and sustain his attention. When he was asked to stand still with his eyes closed for just over 1 minute, he began making noises and moving within the first 5

Table 7.6. Conners 3 Results

Conners 3		Parent Mrs. Jones	Teacher Ms. Keene General Ed.	Teacher Miss Brown Reading	Self-Report
Response Style	Positive Impression	OK	OK	OK	OK
	Negative Impression	OK	OK	OK	OK
	Inconsistency Index	OK	OK	OK	OK
	Inattention	90	71	71	75
	Hyperactivity/Impulsivity	67	58	51	52
	Learning Problems/Executive Functioning	n/a	67	64	n/a
Content	Learning Problems	73	62	57	65
	Executive Functioning	82	72	68	n/a
	Defiance/Aggression	47	46	44	46
	Peer Relations	63	46	46	n/a
	Family Relations	n/a	n/a	n/a	48

(continued)

Conners 3		Parent Mrs. Jones	Teacher Ms. Keene General Ed.	Teacher Miss Brown Reading	Self-Report
DSM-IV-TR	ADHD, Inattentive	86 Probably Met	73 Probably Met	71 Probably Met	73 Probably Met
	ADHD, Hyperactive-Impulsive	59	58	50	51
	Conduct Disorder	44	45	45	49
	Oppositional Defiant Disorder	47	44	44	40
Impairment	Academic	Severe	Severe	Severe	Severe
	Social	Moderate	Mild	Absent	Absent
	Home	Moderate	n/a	n/a	Mild
Index Scores	Conners 3 ADHD Index	98%	92%	87%	83%
	Conners 3 Global Index	70	63	61	n/a
	- Restless-Impulsive	78	68	66	
	- Emotional Lability	48	44	44	
Screener Items	Anxiety	✓	—	—	✓
	Depression	✓	—	—	✓
Critical Items	Severe Conduct	—	—	—	—

Note: High scores on the Conners 3 indicate high levels of concern. All scores are *T*-scores unless otherwise indicated.

seconds despite his best efforts. His difficulties sustaining attention and body posture during this simple task resulted in a borderline range score. When he was given a 14-minute computerized test of vigilance, he scored within the average range overall. This vigilance test did not penalize him for changing body position.

He showed some use of strategy in problem solving, but limited planning skills. He often began novel problem-solving tasks quickly and in a disorganized fashion, then revised his approach as his first attempt failed. His second attempt typically reflected better strategy use. Visual problem-solving deficits were noted on simple tasks as well, such as reflected in his haphazard scanning pattern on several worksheets where he was required to find and mark certain shapes. These deficits in problem solving were also apparent on items requiring social problem solving or other verbal skills. When presented with a familiar problem-solving task (*20 Questions*), Brian showed successful application of a formulaic approach (e.g., begin by asking if it is an animal), but he had difficulty sustaining the approach over his following questions (e.g., switching strategies by asking about a few colors, then asking about function, then colors again). Brian very much enjoyed a hands-on novel problem-solving task and persevered even on the most difficult items; however, his approach was generally not strategy-driven nor did he plan well.

When items appeared easy, he responded impulsively without considering all possibilities. He had difficulty inhibiting urges, as noticed in his difficulty staying quiet and remaining seated. When he was explicitly instructed to not touch the manipulatives placed on the table, he had great difficulty leaving them alone.

Brian showed evidence of perseveration (i.e., becoming "stuck" on an idea or item). This difficulty with cognitive flexibility was reflected in his tendency to return to the same topics in answering items. This affected his performance on a verbal fluency task. He was asked to say as many words as he could think of that began with a certain letter; his response was, "I don't want to say any bad words." Although his overall score for first-letter fluency was exceptional, he produced fewer words that began with "F" than any other letter. When he was asked why he appeared distressed during this task, he responded, "I knew a bad word but I didn't want to say it." He made significantly more errors than expected for his age on a mental flexibility task (*D-KEFS TMT Number-Letter Sequencing, Set-Loss Errors* at 14th cumulative percentile rank).

Difficulty with regulation of self-monitoring was also observed. Brian repeated words during verbal fluency tasks, scoring in the impaired range due to the high number of repetition errors for his age (*D-KEFS VFlu Set-Loss Errors* ScS = 5). He also had difficulty maintaining set (e.g., keeping instructions in mind without reminders), as seen by the inclusion of words that did not belong in that category (e.g., "carrot" when listing fruits, "Ann" when listing boys' names, "pit" when listing words beginning with the letter A; *D-KEFS VFlu Repetition Errors* ScS = 3).

Thus, overall, Brian had difficulty with aspects of attention and executive functioning. These deficits are pervasive and impact his functioning in many settings. Brian, his mother, and his teachers all reported high levels of concern about problems with inattention and executive functioning (*Conners 3: Inattention, Executive Functioning*). Mrs. Jones reported additional concerns about Brian's self-control (*Conners 3: Hyperactivity/Impulsivity, Conners 3GI Restless-Impulsive*) that were not reflected on the teacher ratings. This may be due to the time frame during which Brian's medications are most effective (i.e., in effect during the school day, wearing off by the time he gets home). Functionally, Brian is earning average grades in lower academic instruction groups; this reflects his compensatory efforts to overcome attentional and executive deficits. As executive demands continue to increase (e.g., more long-term projects, scheduling demands, decreased teacher involvement, increased organizational demands), it is likely that Brian will have difficulty continuing to compensate unless he learns better strategies. The current pattern of underachievement relative to intellectual ability is highly consistent with executive deficits.

Language: Comprehension of spoken language appeared intact when Brian was attending to the examiner. He did not initiate or sustain conversation, although he did respond to the examiner's questions. Brian's spoken language was poorly formulated and disorganized. He typically made several efforts to begin a sentence before completing it and often repeated portions of the sentence while thinking about how to finish what he was saying. At times, he trailed off into a whisper before completing a response. Brian mixed the order of syllables in words (e.g., said "Samilla" and "Salimma" for "Melissa" during a memory test) and inserted space in the middle of words. He had difficulty producing specific words, using gestures and nonspecific language (a.k.a., "word-finding" errors). He even commented on these difficulties at one point, saying, "How do I say this . . . this is hard . . . I know what it is, I just can't find the word." At times he substituted a word from the same semantic category (e.g., saying "shingle" while pointing to a door hinge, or "eyebrow" while pointing to eyelashes).

In contrast to these concerns, Brian exhibited a high average knowledge of words (*WISC-IV Vocabulary*). He is able to follow simple commands. His language deficits likely are secondary to executive deficits (e.g., organization, retrieval of specific words, problem solving) rather than a primary language deficit.

Visual Processing: Basic visual perception was intact. Brian completed visual reasoning tasks at an average to high average level, although he had more difficulty with abstract geometric reasoning. On a visual-spatial problem-solving task, Brian's disorganized first approach resulted in completion of several items after time ran out. Despite loss of points for those items, he earned an overall score in the above average range. Although his approach to copying a complex figure was disorganized and fragmented, Brian's good visual skills allowed him to compensate for these executive deficits and earn a score in the average range. Overall, Brian's visual processing skills appear to be intact at this time.

Memory and Learning: Brian is able to remember up to 7 numbers in sequence on a brief, immediate, rote memory task; this performance was above age-based expectations (*WISC-IV Digit Span Forward*). When he was required to manipulate information while remembering it ("working memory"), he showed similar skills; however, it must be noted that these tasks involved very simple information (e.g., reversing a series of numbers, alphabetizing letters).

Brian showed average levels of performance on a list-learning task, including immediate free recall, delayed free recall, and recognition memory. Similarly, Brian did well on a story memory task. He scored in the above-average range for immediate recall of two short stories that he heard read aloud only once. He recalled an average amount of the stories after a 30-minute delay and was able to correctly answer 26/30 yes-no questions about the stories. Although his scores were in the average to above-average ranges for this story memory test, it is interesting to note that the information he forgot was primarily names of people, names of places, days, and dates. This may indicate that he approached the story memory task with a visual strategy; if so, he could learn to picture name-tags on people, location signs, and marked calendar pages as part of his visual strategy for remembering auditory information. Brian also scored in the average range when unexpectedly asked to reproduce a complex design after copying it once. Overall, these results support age-appropriate encoding, storage, and retrieval of rote verbal and visual information.

Sensorimotor Functions: Brian's visual and auditory responses were within normal limits. He ambulated independently, with no notable abnormalities in gait. Brian gripped the pencil in his right hand, using a modified tripod grip with the index knuckle concave. He exerted a great deal of pressure on the pencil, resulting in a dark, heavy line and high levels of hand fatigue. Brian seemed aware of his hand fatigue, as he commented before beginning a 3-minute worksheet, "I bet I'm gonna get tired." He scored in the average range when asked to trace a curved path that was ¼-inch wide, but his accuracy dropped into the borderline range when the curved path was ⅛-inch wide.

Adaptive Functioning

Mr. and Mrs. Jones reported that Brian demonstrates age-appropriate skills in most aspects of adaptive functioning, including functional communication, functional academics, options for leisure time, home/school living, health and safety, and self-care. He has difficulty with self-direction and social skills. His exploration of the community has been restricted given concerns about safety, which limits interpretation of skills in this area.

Although Brian's parents describe intact skills for most aspects of adaptive functioning, he does not consistently initiate their appropriate use. Executive deficits can often impact independent use of these skills. Brian will likely benefit from developing habits, as the use of routine reduces the impact of poor initiation skills.

Social, Emotional, and Behavioral Functioning

Brian's parents report good early development of social awareness, social motivation, and social skills. They describe that, although Brian was shy as a young child, he formed close friendships with peers who attended the same daycare. When they relocated to Maryland from California, he had initial difficulty forming new attachments in the neighborhood and at school. He has since formed a close friendship with a neighborhood peer. He also plays with other boys in the neighborhood, as well as playdates with school friends. Mrs. Jones described Brian's friendships as, "Once he makes a friend, they tend to stay loyal." She indicated that she wished he had more close friends, like she does. Although Brian's mother reports concerns about his friendships, his teachers do not describe the same concerns in the school setting (*Conners 3: Peer Relations*).

Mr. Jones reported that he noticed a change in Brian's emotional status prior to their move to Maryland. Brian reportedly became more withdrawn than usual when several of his daycare friends graduated to preschool. Brian did not switch placements because of the impending move. He began showing symptoms of anxiety with the family's relocation, but these seem to have improved as he has settled into his new neighborhood and school. Parent- and self-report rating scales indicate mild concerns about symptoms of anxiety and depression, but these were not noted in the school setting (*Conners 3: Screener items*). It is possible that Brian hides these feelings from his teachers.

Brian's parents and teachers do not report significant concerns about his behavior in the past month (*Conners 3*).

When Brian was asked if he would change anything in his life, he said no, that he likes being different. When offered three wishes, he wished for "a trillion dollars, a tank, and my very own very very modern computer with all the games I like." He reported, "I used to stress out about math, but I don't now." When asked about life goals, Brian said, "I want to be an engineer . . . I like designing things, creating things. I used to make lots of things from my building blocks."

SUMMARY OF RESULTS

Results from recent intellectual assessment (*WISC-IV*) are higher than findings from the evaluation when Brian was 6 years old (*WPPSI-R*). This change likely represents better demonstration of abilities following treatment for symptoms of inattention. It is possible that the change in scores is not clinically meaningful but is due to use of two different measures. Regardless, Brian recently scored in the above-average range on a standardized administration of a measure of intellectual functioning. This suggests that Brian's intellectual abilities are at least in the above-average range and possibly higher given limitations imposed by his attention and executive functioning.

Results from the current evaluation indicate that the following skills are generally intact:

- Knowledge of words
- Visual processing
- Hands-on problem solving
- Memory for visual and auditory information
- Vigilance during a structured task (while taking stimulant medication)
- Comprehension of spoken language
- Visual perception
- Visual-spatial problem solving
- Memory, including:
  - Immediate rote memory
  - Verbal learning
  - Visual memory

Brian had more difficulty with these areas:

- Attention (including focusing, directing, and sustaining attention)
- Executive functioning, including:
  - Organization
  - Initiation
  - Integration

- Planning
- Mental flexibility
- Self-monitoring
- Expressive language, especially formulation, organization, and word-finding
- Coordination of fine motor movements, including handwriting

DIAGNOSTIC IMPRESSIONS

In summary, Brian Jones is a 9-year-old boy who was referred for this neuro-psychological evaluation due to concerns about apparent discrepancies between academic ability and academic performance. Medical history includes some complications during labor and delivery. Brian has a history of difficulty adjusting to the family's move from California to Maryland. By parent report, he has an introverted personality but became more withdrawn just prior to their move. This has improved in the past few years. Brian has a history of repetitive behaviors first noted in 1st grade, ranging from repetitive throat-clearing to pencil-tapping. Academic concerns have included inattention, fidgeting, incomplete work, need for frequent redirection, avoidance of written work, difficulty learning math facts, and underachievement. Brian is currently being followed by Dr. Raoul for ADHD, for which he is prescribed a stimulant medication.

Report cards, teacher notes, and parent description all indicate a history of difficulty attending to academic tasks. During the past year, Brian's teacher noted improvement in checking his work and working more carefully; this may reflect effects of treatment, including a goal chart that his current teacher implemented. His teacher commented that he still needs improvement in paying attention. Results from this evaluation, in combination with Brian's history, support a DSM-IV diagnosis of *Attention-Deficit/Hyperactivity Disorder (ADHD), Inattentive type*. Parent-, teacher-, and self-report of attention problems indicate that Brian has more symptoms of ADHD-Inattentive type than typical for 9-year-old boys (*Conners 3: ADHD-Inattentive*). Many people associate the diagnosis of ADHD with the Hyperactive type, thinking of very active and impulsive children. Brian's presentation at this time involves less hyperactivity and more of the cognitive aspects (including inattention and impulsivity). Note that these impressions are based on Brian's functioning while taking medication prescribed for symptoms of ADHD; it is possible that symptoms would be more severe or that additional symptoms would be apparent if he was evaluated when not taking the medication.

The executive deficits described in this report are often found in children with ADHD and impact multiple aspects of their functioning. For example, even though Brian is very good at reading words (i.e., "decoding"), his executive deficits interfere with reading comprehension, as true comprehension requires him to make inferences and integrate multiple sources of information. As the complexity of reading assignments increases, he will require additional strategies and support to understand the meaning of passages. Another example of the impact of executive dysfunction is seen in Brian's expressive language. Even though he has good language knowledge, his executive deficits result in poor language formulation and reduced initiation of conversation, as well as word-finding errors. Also, with spelling, Brian shows good spelling skills when that is the focus of a task (e.g., a spelling test), but when he is forced to divide his cognitive resources among many demands, his spelling suffers (e.g., a written language assignment).

Bright children with ADHD can be at risk for symptoms of anxiety and depression, as they feel that they are constantly failing despite putting forth extra effort. Daily inconsistencies in performance are often perceived as "lazy," "being difficult," or "unmotivated." These types of perceptions feed into self-criticism and often result in truly not trying and giving up. This cycle of making mistakes (academically and socially) and criticism can result in lowered self-esteem and feelings of incompetence. Currently, Brian describes mild levels of emotional concerns (interview, rating scale), including mild irritability when anxious, mild worrying, and occasional feelings of worthlessness. His mother reported the same mild levels of concern and additional comments that Brian seems to enjoy certain activities less than before. These concerns were not noted in the school setting by either the classroom or small reading group teachers. It is important to provide Brian with proactive and preventative strategies for positive self-esteem so that he does not develop a secondary anxiety or mood disorder, particularly given the family history of anxiety, depression, and substance use disorders.

Children who are bright but have executive deficits are more likely to compensate for their deficits. This is a strength and can be maximized by teaching Brian specific strategies to use in compensation. This is also a liability, though, as bright children with executive deficits may "get by" in the early years of school, as their strengths and deficits average out into average-range grades. It is important to recognize the significant discrepancies between Brian's intellectual ability and his academic performances. If this discrepancy is not addressed with educational services, Brian will continue missing information and fall further behind his classmates, while struggling to understand why he is having difficulty. If he learns now how to work around his executive deficits, he is more likely to remain interested and engaged in his education.

By report, Brian has a history of making repetitive noises (e.g., throat-clearing). These behaviors are reportedly more apparent when Brian is feeling stressed. Without further information from Brian, it is difficult to determine whether he engages in these behaviors to relieve subjective distress or whether they are involuntary. If such repetitive sounds and/or behaviors persist, it will be important to consider possible diagnoses such as tic disorders or obsessive-compulsive features, as diagnosis of these specific disorders might guide aspects of treatment.

There are a number of positive prognostic factors for Brian. These include his level of intellectual functioning and his perseverance (a.k.a. "stubborn-ness"). Brian is highly invested in doing good work and is eager to please other people. When he is comfortable, he enjoys interacting with other people. He responds very well to specific praise about his efforts and achievements. He has an actively supportive family and is attending a school that is known for providing good resources and education (as demonstrated by the past two years of teachers who have gone above and beyond expectations to help him). With appropriate treatment and educational interventions, Brian will likely make good progress.

RECOMMENDATIONS

1. Educationally, Brian qualifies to receive special education services under federal handicapping condition Other Health Impaired (ADHD). As such, we recommend that an Individualized Education Plan (IEP) be developed to reflect appropriate service programming. An appropriate educational environment for Brian will consist of special education services including the following elements:
   a) Teachers who have experience with executive dysfunction,
   b) Small group instruction,
   c) Highly structured classroom setting,
   d) Occupational therapy consultation services:
      i. To evaluate benefit of using different writing utensils and writing surfaces to decrease pencil pressure, reduce hand fatigue, and improve handwriting,
      ii. To introduce and support use of computer for writing assignments (not necessarily touch typing method),
      iii. To support teachers in using visual, hands-on teaching techniques.

2. Although it can be a difficult balance programmatically, Brian requires an advanced academic curriculum within the context of these modifications and accommodations. Given his scores on standardized testing, he should be instructed above grade level for most subjects, while being provided with appropriate modifications and accommodations for his disability.

3. Whenever possible, use teaching methods that follow the guidelines of video games. The successful approach to teaching a child like Brian involves stimulating visual input, frequent and immediate feedback about skills, and concrete tracking of progress toward achievable goals.

4. It is important to use a multisensory approach to teaching Brian. Whenever possible, use hands-on and visual instruction. For example, touch-math is a good way to make math more visual. He will also benefit from using concrete manipulatives, such as used in certain math and phonics programs.[2]

5. Poor spontaneous direction of attention can affect academic and social performance. Results from this evaluation revealed that Brian can attend to specific aspects of a task when directed to do so. Therefore, he will benefit from explicit cues to improve his attention to relevant features of a situation. For example:

   a) When completing a math worksheet with mixed operations, help Brian highlight the operation signs before he starts each problem. Use a different color highlighter for each different type of operation (e.g., blue for subtraction, yellow for addition). This will draw his attention to this highly relevant feature of the task.

   b) When Brian is in the classroom, direct his attention to the most relevant aspect, typically the teacher, by using cues such as his name or a physical touch.

   c) Practice attending to different aspects of social communication. One way to try this is to interpret the moods of characters on a television show when the sound is muted. On another occasion, try interpreting the emotions using only the sound, without a picture. Help Brian practice attending to body language, tone of voice, and content of speech when he is engaged in conversation with family members.

---

2. In my actual reports, I usually give specific examples of the types of programs that may be helpful. These specifics have been removed for purposes of the book, so as to avoid the appearance of any endorsement for a specific product.

6. Brian will also benefit from external structure to organize materials and information.

a) Have "a place for everything, and everything in its place." Teach Brian to be very consistent with when and where he puts things. For example, when he comes in the door, his coat goes on the coat hook. This will need to be repeated several times with explicit instruction before Brian will learn the routine. If Brian forgets to put his coat on the hook, it is important to back-up to the step before hanging his coat up; thus, he will need to leave the house, re-enter, and hang the coat up. This helps the desired behavior become part of a routine and more likely to be completed independently.

b) When Brian is presented with a multistep task, help him break it into several smaller steps to prevent him from feeling overwhelmed by the organizational demands of the task. Write these steps in order on a note-card to create a "cue-card" for Brian to follow. As he completes each step, cue him to look back at the cue-card to see what is the next step. Eventually this will become more automatic and will increase Brian's ability to independently complete such tasks. Cue-cards can be used at school (e.g., long division, proof-reading), as well as at home (e.g., cleaning room, doing laundry, morning routines).

c) Teach Brian a system for note-taking while reading. This will increase his processing of the information, improve his overall comprehension by teaching him to integrate as he reads, and provide him with study materials for the test.

7. Encourage Brian to use a word processor to complete written assignments. This puts information in a format that allows Brian to approach the task as a multistep process, decreasing the impact of his executive deficits by allowing him to focus on one task at a time. For example, the first step might be to generate ideas, followed by the second step of selecting which to keep and which to delete. The third step might be sequencing the ideas, then the fourth step expanding each idea into a sentence or paragraph. A fifth step might be adding description words (e.g., adjectives, adverbs, stronger verbs), then a sixth step checking spelling (followed by grammar and punctuation). Dividing the complex task of writing into these smaller, more manageable steps will likely help re-engage Brian in the creative writing process.

8. Make sure Brian gets his full recess period. He needs time to move around during the school day, as well as opportunities to socialize.

It is critical that recess period is *not* used for Brian to complete assignments.

9. Given his limited initiation skills, Brian requires more prompts and cues. For example, he needs to be prompted to turn in his completed homework. He also requires prompts to initiate problem-solving skills. These do not need to be directive prompts; in most cases, he will require only a cue such as, "Brian, look at this math problem. What do you think is the first step?"

10. Other suggestions for appropriate academic modifications include:

   a) Increase external structure in Brian's school day. Give him a clear statement of expectations before he begins any task, and ask him to then show you what he is doing before he begins working independently.

   b) Structure his work into brief working periods separated by breaks. Be certain to give him clear end-points for each task.

   c) Alternate types of tasks that Brian is assigned; for example, a drawing task after completing a verbal task.

   d) Ensure that Brian is attending before beginning to learn new information. A gentle touch paired with his name can help orient his attention to the instructor.

   e) Help Brian organize information *before* he begins memorizing it. Help him to see how new information relates to previously learned knowledge or concepts. Make new facts meaningful for Brian.

   f) Use multiple-choice or yes/no questions to allow Brian to participate in class discussion and complete assignments. If fill-in-the-blank formats are used, provide a word list. Open-ended questions will penalize him for his language formulation difficulties rather than determine his knowledge.

   g) Structure Brian's time and tasks. Help him break long or complex projects into shorter, more manageable pieces. For example, rather than overwhelming him with an entire worksheet, fold it into quarters and alternate each portion of that worksheet with a different task. Show him how a large concept or project can be separated into smaller, more manageable pieces. This will decrease the complexity of information and increase Brian's likelihood of completing a task.

   h) Be aware of exactly what you say to Brian. He may take statements literally; if he does, this indicates a need to rephrase the instructions more explicitly rather than criticize him for misunderstanding.

Referrals

- Share results from this evaluation with prescribing psychiatrist, Dr. Raoul. Discuss with Dr. Raoul whether different medications or dosages might be appropriate to consider, given persistence of ADHD symptoms and physical issues that may be medication-related. He may wish to refer Brian and his parents to a local therapist who can teach them ways to support positive self-esteem. It is important to keep Brian's parents involved in ongoing treatment so that they may support and reinforce therapeutic goals in the home.

- The results from this evaluation were achieved while Brian was being prescribed a stimulant medication to reduce his symptoms of ADHD. If Dr. Raoul and the Jones are interested, a medication monitoring session may be scheduled to repeat a few tests when Brian is not taking his medication or when he is taking a different dosage. This would provide a comparison of performance in different conditions. Medication monitoring can only be conducted with the permission of the prescribing physician, as it involves changing a prescribed medication type/dose.

- Brian will also benefit from working with a specialist to learn explicit strategies to use in compensating for his executive deficits.

- The Jones family may wish to learn more about ADHD. One group that offers both support and education is CHADD (Children and Adults with ADHD). This organization provides support groups, information about legal rights, and resources. Contact information for the national office, as well as information about local support groups, is available on the Internet (www.chadd.org).

- Neuropsychological re-evaluation prior to Brian entering 6th grade. It is important to have updated recommendations for his school program at the time of transition to middle school, when most students are expected to have a greater degree of independent functioning in a less structured environment. This transition is often difficult for students with executive deficits.

The results of this assessment and these recommendations were shared and discussed with Mr. and Mrs. Jones in a feedback session. If there are further questions or concerns, please contact Dr. Sparrow.

Elizabeth P. Sparrow, PhD
Licensed Psychologist, Specializing in Clinical Neuropsychology

DON'T FORGET
....
Adding or Substituting Conners Assessments

Sometimes additional information becomes available after the referral is received. In the case of "Darby Reed" below, the initial test plan (based on referral) included the Conners 3. After conducting an interview with Darby's mother, it seemed that this was not a straightforward ADHD evaluation, but that other issues were complicating the picture. The Conners CBRS was substituted and provided very useful information in a number of relevant domains.

If the Conners 3 had been distributed before the interview, it would have been appropriate to ask raters to also complete the Conners CBRS once it became apparent that ADHD was less of an issue than previously believed.

NEUROPSYCHOLOGICAL REPORT

Name: Darby Reed
Age: 11 years, 5 months
Grade: 6th grade

Referral

Darby Reed is an 11-year-old girl who was referred for a neuropsychological evaluation by Dr. John Paul, Clinical Psychologist. This evaluation was recommended due to concerns about academic struggles in the context of Attention-Deficit/Hyperactivity Disorder (ADHD). Specific concerns include:

- In school, Darby works very hard and makes slow progress. Her performance is inconsistent and variable. Her teachers provide individualized instruction and help after school, and her mother spends a great deal of energy and time helping Darby with homework and test preparation.
- She does better on short-term testing than long-term testing (e.g., weekly quiz versus unit test); because of this pattern, some concern has been expressed about memory.
- Her academic difficulties are not limited to language but also include math. She still counts on her fingers for some calculations.
- Emotionally, Darby is "sensitive." She appears afraid of embarrassing herself and will not try new things until she is sure of success. She is more willing to attempt something new if she is in familiar surroundings.

Background Information

Family Background

- Lives with natural parents and her three siblings (Alexa 12 years old, Julie 8 years old, and Kenny 6 years old).
- Mother completed a B.S. in English and recalls school was "easy." She is currently a full-time mother and homemaker.
- Father completed high school degree and advanced trade certifications. He learns best by hands-on and visual activities. He is a steel worker.
- Family history includes: reading difficulties, attentional problems, severe anxiety, severe mood disorder (including depression and Bipolar Disorder), substance use, cigarette smoking (2 packs per day), and left-handedness.

Gestation, Birth, Neonatal History:

- Pregnancy: Full-term (42 weeks), complicated by history of possible miscarriage.
- Labor/Delivery: Induced, vaginal delivery, no complications.
- Birthweight: 8 pounds, 5 ounces.
- Neonatal: Discharged to home at 1 to 2 days old with no concerns.

Medical History:

- Handedness: Right.
- Medical conditions: Cold sores under nose during school year; flares with stress.
- Neurologic issues (brain injury, sustained fevers, loss of consciousness, seizures, etc.): None reported.
- Medications: Current: Daily vitamins, stimulant medication (since 8 years old). No other medication history.
- Vision: Wears prescription eye-glasses.
- Hearing: No concerns reported.
- Trauma, abuse, violence, or neglect: No concerns reported.

Developmental History:

- Infancy: Mother described as "easy," rarely cried, content to be left alone (although preferred to be with mother). Not cuddly initially but became cuddly as a toddler. Good eye contact; liked to watch what mother was doing.
- First concerns: 2 to 3 years old because she was not talking.
- Regressions: None reported.

- Development of skills and concerns:
  - Motor: Met gross and fine motor milestones early to on-time (e.g., tied shoes at 3 years old).
  - Language:
    - Expressive: Delayed spoken language.
    - Receptive: Seemed to develop skills within expected timeframe.
    - Nonverbal/gestural: Met early milestones within expected limits.
  - Social: Early milestones met within expected limits. Currently, will hesitate in unfamiliar group settings. Has close friends and enjoys social activities.
  - Play: Typical development. Creative and social imitative play developed appropriately. More reserved if older children present.
  - Cognitive/Academic: Early difficulties learning letters and numbers. Continued struggles with symbol-based learning (e.g., reading, math). Pattern of "learning" for a test but not remembering information/ skills later. For example, learned letters and numbers by end of preschool (with great effort at home and school) but forgot again by kindergarten. Continues to have difficulty with reading and written language. Struggles to find the right words to communicate in written and spoken language. Letter, number, and word reversals (e.g., on/no, b/d, 34/43).
  - Emotion: Appropriate development. Is capable of showing full range of emotions, but will not cry at school (waits until she is home). Has always been "sensitive." Responds appropriately to others' emotions; "very caring." Afraid of embarrassing herself in front of others; watches them and waits to try new things in private.
  - Behavior: No concerns reported.
  - Activities of Daily Living: No concerns reported about sleeping, eating, toileting, bathing, grooming, dressing, or domestic chores (e.g., cleaning her room).
  - Atypical Features: Some tactile sensitivities (sock seams, shirt labels, damp bathing suits), but can tolerate if necessary. No cognitive rigidity, stereotypical behaviors, unusual play/interests, stereotyped/idiosyn-cratic language, aggression/destruction, or self-injurious behaviors reported.

Previous Evaluations, Diagnoses, and Treatments:

- Evaluations: Please see original reports for data and additional information.

- 7 years old, City Public Schools: Achievement testing results were average to above average. Speech-language assessment showed average skills. No special education services recommended.
- 8 years old, Dr. John Paul, Clinical Psychologist: Psychoeducational evaluation; tested with stimulant medication (except for attention testing). Average intellectual abilities (with some significant strengths). Academic achievement skills generally average, with the exception of deficient reading comprehension. Ineffective and impulsive response style noted on vigilance test (off medications). Diagnosis: Attention Deficit Disorder.
- 10 years old, City Public Schools: Achievement testing, average overall (Reading fluency in borderline range). Examiner noted that Darby subvocalized during "silent" reading. Written work was off-topic, and Darby struggled with mathematics word problems. Math solutions seemed trial and error rather than systematic. Special education recommended for reading comprehension, applied math, and written language.
- Treatment:
  - 8 to 9 years old (2nd grade), Local Learning Center, reading and reading comprehension. Brought skills up to grade level, but lost these skills over summer.
  - 8 years old, pediatrician (Dr. Mary Freed) agreed to medication trial (stimulant medication).
  - 10 years old to present, Private math tutor, Kathy Matz. Helps Darby with hands-on and visual explanations of math. Has improved her math grade.

Academic/Daycare History:

- Birth to 4 years old: At home with mother.
- Pre-kindergarten to 4th grade: Friends Christian Academy, regular education. Some assistance from regular teacher in grammar and math during 2nd through 4th grades.
- 5th grade to present: Bowling Green Public School.
- No history of repeating or skipping a grade.
- Special education and related services:
  - 504 plan established prior to entering 5th grade to address symptoms of ADHD. Modifications/Accommodations include preferential seating, extended time on tests, and homework folder.

- Achievement testing (10 years old) reviewed after completion; educational team recommended use of general education interventions in 6th grade for reading, math, and written language then reassess (consistent with IDEA 2004 and response to intervention, or RTI). 504 plan continued for symptoms of ADHD.

Strengths: determined, diligent, kind, hard-working
Preferred Activities: soccer, running, family activities
Motivators: knowing that if she really tries, she can achieve something

Evaluation Procedures

- Wechsler Intelligence Scale for Children, 4th edition, Integrated (WISC-IV-Int): Core, selected supplemental subtests
- Wechsler Individual Achievement Test, 2nd edition (WIAT-II): Reading subtests
- Delis-Kaplan Executive Function System (D-KEFS): Selected subtests
- NEPSY: A Developmental Neuropsychological Evaluation (NEPSY): Selected subtests
- Conners' Continuous Performance Test, 2nd edition (CPT-II)
- Clinical Evaluation of Language Fundamentals, 4th edition (CELF-4): Selected subtests
- California Verbal Learning Test–Children's version (CVLT-C)
- Rey Complex Figure Test with Recognition Trial (RCFT)
- Purdue Pegboard
- Clinical Interview
- Conners Comprehensive Behavior Rating Scales (Conners CBRS): Parent and teacher reports
- Behavior Rating Inventory of Executive Function (BRIEF): Parent and teacher reports[3]

Validity

The instruments used are valid for Darby and for the referral question(s). The tests were administered by a qualified examiner (Elizabeth P. Sparrow, PhD, Licensed Psychologist). Standardized administration procedures were followed

---

3. Parent reports were completed by Judy Reed, Mother. Teacher reports were completed by Annie Mock, Math teacher, who has known Darby for 3 months, and Sammi Knott, Language Arts teacher, who has known Darby for 3 months.

for all measures, with one modification. The Conners CBRS-SR was read aloud to Darby given her struggles with reading comprehension, and she marked her responses on a separate sheet. Based on information in the test manual, it is unlikely that this impacts validity of these results. Observed behaviors during the evaluation were consistent with parent report of usual behaviors. Available validity indicators were all within acceptable limits, unless noted otherwise. Therefore, results of this evaluation are judged to be a valid representation of current neuropsychological functioning.

DON'T FORGET

Report Deviations from Standardized Administration

As discussed in Chapter 2, it is important to report when any variations from standardized administration occur, including why, what, and the expected impact. In this case, Darby had difficulty reading the rating scale (even with the 3rd grade reading level) due to her reading disorder.

TEST RESULTS AND OBSERVATIONS

The results from Darby's performance during this neuropsychological evaluation are summarized below. Results from formal tests are reported as standardized scores, which compare Darby's performance with other students who are the same age. Standardized scores take a variety of forms, including those summarized in the following table. Higher scores generally represent better performance, unless noted otherwise (e.g., *Conners CBRS, BRIEF*).

General Presentation: Darby was evaluated over three sessions (11/15, 11/17, and 11/23). After discussion with Darby's prescribing physician, it was decided that Darby would complete the majority of the evaluation without medication; she did not take her prescribed medication on 11/15 or 11/17. Darby did take her medication as prescribed on 11/23; on this date, she completed several short tests for comparison with off-medication performance (see Table 7.18). Darby's social, emotional, and behavioral presentation was similar across all three sessions.

Darby's mother brought her to each of the testing sessions. Darby had no difficulty separating from her mother to enter the testing room. She showed appropriate interest and awareness in the examiner and the clinic space. Darby appropriately asked for help and asked good questions when she required clarification. Self-care skills as observed were appropriate, and Darby demonstrated good manners.

Table 7.7. Standarized Score Results

Standardized Score	Average Range of Scores
Scaled Score (ScS)	7 to 13
Standard Score (SS)	85 to 115
T-score (T)	40 to 60
z-score (z)	−1.00 to +1.00

Darby demonstrated a positive attitude toward the evaluation. She tolerated frustration well, worked hard, and did not give up easily. She had no difficulty learning testing routines and was glad to help the examiner during the evaluation. She demonstrated appropriate emotional reactions and facial expressions. She repeatedly pinched the skin on her upper lip, leaving red marks on her face; this was observed during sessions with and without medication.

Darby showed some impulsivity. Sometimes she said she was finished with a task, then retracted that as she realized an error that needed to be corrected. At times, she asked her questions before instructions had been completed; if she had been patient, the information would have been provided. On the first testing date, Darby was slightly lethargic, with frequent yawns. On the date most of the language testing was completed (11/17), she appeared fidgety and restless.

Overall, Darby appeared interested in doing well and complying with the test requirements.

Intellectual Ability: Results from intellectual assessment at 8 years old (*WISC-IV*) were in the average range; Darby was tested on medication at that time. Results from the current administration of the *WISC-IV-Int* indicate average functioning overall, with some significant variations within Darby's profile. Darby's performance on a subtest of rote auditory memory and auditory working memory was in the impaired range; this score was significantly lower than expected given her other subtest scores. Because this subtest score reduced the *Working Memory Index (WMI)* to be significantly lower than the other index scores, it is not appropriate to use a *Full Scale IQ* score to summarize Darby's cognitive abilities. Her *Verbal Comprehension Index (VCI)* of 95 and her *Perceptual Reasoning Index (PRI)* of 94 support at least average cognitive abilities. Scores from the *WISC-IV-Int* are provided in the Table 7.8 and will be discussed further in subsequent sections of this report.

Table 7.8. WISC-IV-Int Subtest Results

WISC-IV-Int Subtest	Subtest Scaled Score (ScS)	Index Standard Score (SS)	Composite Standard Score (SS)
Similarities	7	Verbal Comprehension (VCI) SS = 95^	
Vocabulary	9		
Comprehension	11		
Information*	n/a		*The Full Scale IQ score is not a valid representation of Darby's abilities, given the significant discrepancies among the index scores.*
Word Reasoning*	n/a		
Block Design	8	Perceptual Reasoning (PRI) SS = 94^	
Picture Concepts	12 !!!		
Matrix Reasoning	7		
Picture Completion*	16		
Digit Span *Digit Span Forward* * *Digit Span Backward* *	4 !!! 4 6	Working Memory (WMI) SS = 77^	
Letter-Number Sequencing	8		
Arithmetic*	n/a		
Coding - *Cued Symbol Recall >25th Percentile* - *Free Symbol Recall >25th Percentile* - *Cued Digit Recall >25th Percentile* Coding Copy*	7 5	Processing Speed (PSI) SS = 88^	
Symbol Search	9		
Cancellation* *Cancellation Random* * *Cancellation Structured* *	9 10 7		

* = Supplemental subtest/score; not used in calculating Index or Composite scores unless noted otherwise in text.

n/a = not administered

!!! = score is statistically different from other subtest scores:

- Picture Concepts = significant strength (p < 0.05, Base Rate = 10%)
- Digit Span = significant weakness (p < 0.05, Base Rate = 5–10%)

^ = Discrepancies in Scores:
  - WMI < VCI (p < 0.05, Base Rate = 9.9%)
  - WMI < PRI (p < 0.05, Base Rate = 13.6%)
  - WMI < PSI (p < 0.15, Base Rate = 28.8%)
  - Digit Span < Letter-Number Sequencing (p < 0.05, Base Rate = 11.4%)
  - Similarities < Picture Concepts (p < 0.05, Base Rate = 7.6%)

Comparison of Darby's scores at 8 years old with her current results is important. "Scaled scores" are a way of comparing "raw scores" (the actual number of questions correct) with what is expected at that chronological age. Scaled scores that stay the same indicate age-appropriate gains over the time between the tests. Scaled scores that increase mean more gains have been made than most children make between those ages. Scaled scores that decrease can indicate slower progress or loss of skills.

- In general, Darby has continued to make age-appropriate gains, as most of her scaled scores have not changed significantly.
- Careful review of raw scores for Digit Span indicates that Darby's performance has stayed the same in this area; she has not *lost* any skills here, but she also has not made any gains. The Digit Span subtest score accounts for the lower Working Memory Index.
- Darby completed fewer items on the Coding subtest during the current evaluation. At 8 years old, her raw score was 59 (on medications), compared with 39 (off medications at 10 years old) and 48 (on medications at 10 years old). These scores are significantly different from each other, revealing two patterns. First, Darby's performance is better on this subtest when she is taking stimulant medication. Second, something has changed in the past 3 years that impacts her performance on this subtest. This will be discussed further in the Impressions section. The Coding subtest score accounts for the lower Processing Speed Index.

Academic Achievement: Given the recency of school evaluation (within the past 6 months), a full academic achievement battery was not administered. Specific reading subtests were completed to further investigate Darby's continued difficulties in this area. Qualitatively, oral reading was awkward, with limited prosody and fluency (consistent with "borderline" reading fluency results from school evaluation at 10 years old). Darby read aloud, even when she was asked to read silently. Reading seemed effortful for her, not automatic as it should for a

Table 7.9. WIAT-II Subtest Results

WIAT-II Subtest	Subtest SS (Age-based)	Composite SS (Age-based)
Word Reading	84	
Reading Comprehension	86	Reading SS = 83
Pseudoword Decoding	87	

Table 7.10. WIAT-II Supplemental Scores Results

WIAT-II Supplemental Scores	Quartile (Grade-based)
Reading Comprehension	1
Target Words	1
Reading Speed	1
Reading Rate	1

6th grader with average cognitive abilities. Quantitative results are listed in Tables 7.9 and 7.10. Darby's reading composite is significantly lower than expected, based on her cognitive abilities (*WISC-IV VCI*). She is performing in the lowest quartile of typical 6th grade students for reading comprehension, word pronunciation, speed of reading, and rate of reading.

Additional tests were administered to better understand Darby's reading deficits. Darby demonstrates weaknesses in phonological processing (*NEPSY Phonological Processing*). She also shows impairment in rapid retrieval of names for symbols, including letters. She has working memory deficits (see *WISC-IV-Int Working Memory Index, Digit Span*), which impact reading comprehension. As discussed further in the Impressions portion of this report, Darby has many features of a classic reading disorder and requires specialized instruction to address her deficits in this area.

Results from a rating scale completed by Darby's mother, teachers, and Darby herself indicated that she has more difficulties academically than expected for an 11-year-old girl (*Conners CBRS: Academic Difficulties, Total and subscales*), including math- and language-based. Mrs. Mock, Darby's Math teacher, commented that she had to guess about spelling, reading, and written language because she does not observe these on a regular basis. Mrs. Knott, Darby's L.A. teacher, skipped rating scale items that involved math performance.

DON'T FORGET
....
The Importance of "Multi's"

The discussion of *Conners CBRS* results for Darby's academic difficulties illustrates a point that has been reinforced throughout this book: It is important to obtain data from multiple sources about multiple settings. In Darby's case, different subject-matter teachers reported different observations.

Neuropsychological Functioning

Additional measures were administered to further examine Darby's performance on the *WISC-IV-Int* and *WIAT-II*, as well as to explore her functioning in other domains. These scores are provided in Tables 7.11 through 7.20, and will be discussed further in subsequent sections of this report.

CAUTION
....
Reporting Missing Data

If final scores for a test are based on incomplete data, it is important to indicate this in your report. Otherwise future evaluators may find different results and not understand why the difference occurred. The *Conners CBRS* data table for Darby shows one way of reporting results when some data are missing.

Speed: Darby's speed of information processing and responding is generally within the expected range for her age and cognitive abilities. She is slower than some of her peers when expected to use written symbols, such as letters and numbers. This type of information is not automatic for Darby. This impacts her rate of work for reading, writing, and math.

Attention: Behaviorally, Darby appeared internally distracted and "spaced out" at times; however, she was consistently responsive to the examiner when addressed directly. She earned average scores on all tests of attention, including visual and auditory attention as well as brief and sustained attention. All of these attention tests were completed *without* medication. Attention does not appear to be a primary concern at this time.

Executive Functions: "Executive functioning" is a term used to describe the so-called "higher order" skills of the human brain. It seems that certain parts of the human brain (including the frontal lobes and white matter tracts) help

Table 7.11. D-KEFS Results

D-KEFS	Measure	ScS
Trail Making Test	Visual Scanning	7
	Number Sequencing	10
	Letter Sequencing	9
	Number-Letter Switching	7
	Motor Speed	12
Verbal Fluency Test	Letter Fluency	10
	Category Fluency	10
	Category Switching: Total Correct	7
	Category Switching: Switching Accuracy	9
Color-Word Interference Test	Color Naming (4 errors, 5th Percentile)	11
	Word Reading (2 errors, 5th Percentile)	10
	Inhibition (6 errors, ScS = 8)	10
	Inhibition/Switching (10 errors, ScS = 3)	10
Twenty Questions Test	Initial Abstraction	7
	Total Questions Asked	10
	Total Weighted Achievement	10
Tower Test	Total Achievement Score	6

coordinate all of the brain's functions, just like a Chief Executive Officer (CEO) coordinates the activities of a large corporation. Skills that are thought of as executive functions include: organization (both physical and mental), prioritization, integration of information, forming and implementing a problem-solving strategy (with back-up plans if the first way does not work), efficiency, self-regulation (of thoughts, actions, and emotions), and mental flexibility.

The human brain continues developing after birth, and the last areas to reach maturity are the frontal lobes and white matter tracts. These areas continue

Table 7.12. NEPSY Subtest Results

NEPSY Subtest	Scaled Score or Percentile
Auditory Attention and Response Set	ScS = 11
- Attention Task	ScS = 12
- Attention, Omission Errors	11th – 25th Percentile
- Attention, Commission Errors	26th – 75th Percentile
- Response Set Task	ScS = 11
- Response Set, Omission Errors	26th – 75th Percentile
- Response Set, Commission Errors	>75th Percentile
Statue	>75th Percentile
Phonological Processing	ScS = 7
Speeded Naming	ScS = 9
- Time	26th – 75th Percentile
- Accuracy	26th – 75th Percentile
Comprehension of Instructions	ScS = 7
Imitating Hand Positions	ScS = 13
- Preferred Hand	>75th Percentile
- Nonpreferred Hand	>75th Percentile
Visuomotor Precision	ScS = 13
- Car Time	>75th Percentile
- Car Errors	26th – 75th Percentile
- Motorcycle Time	>75th Percentile
- Motorcycle Errors	26th – 75th Percentile
Narrative Memory	ScS = 9
- Free Recall	26th – 75th Percentile
- Cued Recall	26th – 75th Percentile
Sentence Repetition	ScS = 4

developing into early adulthood. Thus, as typically developing children grow older, we see increased ability to show self-control, be independent, and accept responsibility. This developmental path makes it difficult to recognize deficits in executive functioning at very young ages, because most young children have limited skills in this area (e.g., it is typical for a 2-year-old child to have a temper tantrum). These deficits in executive functioning become more apparent as

Table 7.13. CPT-II Measure Results

CPT-II* Measure	T-score
# Omissions	48
# Commissions	60
Hit Reaction Time (RT)	47
Hit RT Standard Error (SE)	44
Variability	45
Detectability (d')	64
Response Style (Beta)	48
Perseverations	46
Hit RT Block Change	48
Hit SE Block Change	48
Hit RT ISI Change	53
Hit SE ISI Change	58

* Note: Extreme scores on the CPT-II, whether high or low, indicate atypicality.

Table 7.14. CELF-4 Subtest Results

CELF-4 Subtest	ScS
Recalling Sentences	5
Understanding Spoken Paragraphs	8
Familiar Sequences	10
Number Repetition: - Forward - Backward	8 6 10

Table 7.15. CVLT-C Results

CVLT-C	Raw Score	Standardized Score (z-score unless indicated otherwise)
List A Total Trials 1-5	58 (7 + 11 + 12 + 13 + 15)	$T = 63$
List A Trial 1 Free Recall	7	+0.5
List A Trial 5 Free Recall	15	+1.5
List B Free Recall	6	0
List A Short-Delay Free Recall	15	+2.0
List A Short-Delay Cued Recall	13	+1.0
List A Long-Delay Free Recall	15	+2.0
List A Long-Delay Cued Recall	15	+1.5
Semantic Cluster Ratio	1.6	+0.5
Serial Cluster Ratio	3.3	+0.5
Learning Slope	1.8	+1.0
Perseverations (Total)	9	+0.5
Intrusions (Total)	3	−0.5
Correct Recognition Hits	14/15	0
False Positives (Total)	0/30	−1.0

children grow older (e.g., it is unusual for a 13-year-old child to have a temper tantrum).

It is important to consider information about everyday functioning when evaluating executive functioning. Parents and teachers are often aware of these deficits because they see children in unstructured situations where executive functioning is required. The very nature of most formal, standardized evaluations makes it difficult to detect executive deficits, as the child is evaluated in a highly structured, reduced-distraction setting with clearly stated rules and expectations.

Table 7.16. RCFT Results

RCFT	Score
Copy	≤1st Percentile
Immediate Recall	$T = 43$
Delayed Recall	$T = 41$
Recognition Total Correct - True Positives - False Positives - True Negatives - False Negatives	$T = 46$ >16th Percentile >16th Percentile >16th Percentile >16th Percentile

Table 7.17. Purdue Pegboard Results

Purdue Pegboard	Z-Score
Dominant Hand	−1.12
Nondominant Hand	0
Both hands, cooperatively	+0.20

Darby's performance suggests that aspects of her executive functioning are age appropriate, but she has significant deficits in other aspects of executive functioning. Darby was able to complete several dot-to-dot worksheets at an age-appropriate speed, for both letters and numbers. She scored in the average range when asked to rapidly name words that began with the same letter or that belonged in the same category. She demonstrated low average to average levels of mental flexibility on several tasks. Although Darby scored in the average range when asked to quickly name colors or read words aloud, she had more errors than expected for her age. This is consistent with aspects of reading disorder, in that Darby's access of this information is not automated. Darby used concrete levels of deductive reasoning to solve several puzzles, scoring in the average range for her age.

As discussed in the "Memory and Learning" section, Darby's rote auditory memory span is smaller than expected for her age. Within that limitation, she shows average ability to manipulate information ("working memory"). Darby scored lower than expected on tests involving abstract reasoning, primarily due to

Table 7.18. Medication Contrasts

Medication Contrasts	No Medication	With Medication	Significant Change?

Sentence Repetition:
  - NEPSY Sentence Repetition
  - CELF-4 Recalling Sentences
	ScS = 4	ScS = 5	NS

Number Repetition, Forward:
  - WISC-IV-Int Digit Span
  - CELF-4 Number Repetition
	ScS = 4	ScS = 6	NS

Number Repetition, Backward:
  - WISC-IV-Int Digit Span
  - CELF-4 Number Repetition
	ScS = 6	ScS = 10	Borderline

Number Repetition, Total:
  - WISC-IV-Int Digit Span
  - CELF-4 Number Repetition
	ScS = 4	ScS = 8	Borderline

WISC-IV-Int Coding	ScS = 7	ScS = 10	Borderline

NS = not statistically significant

her limited advance planning. This may be secondary to her small memory span (i.e., she could not remember more than a few steps at a time) rather than a true executive deficit. On several tasks, Darby demonstrated lack of organization. This was true for visual information as well as verbal information. Self-regulation was also subtly deficient, as exhibited by Darby's increased voice volume as cognitive demands were increased. Darby did show good sustained effort across multiple tasks.

Results from parent and teacher ratings of executive functioning indicate shared concerns about aspects of working memory. All three raters reported more concerns in this area than expected for an 11-year-old girl. Darby's math teacher reported additional concerns about Darby's ability to shift between tasks and self-initiate tasks. It is possible that Darby's memory deficits underlie her difficulties in self-initiation, as she struggles to make a plan for how or where to start a task.

Overall, many aspects of executive functioning are intact for Darby. She shows weak executive functioning skills in the following areas (see page 316):

Table 7.19. Conners CBRS Results

Conners CBRS		Parent Mrs. Reed	Teacher Mrs. Mock (Math)	Teacher Mrs. Knott (L.A.)	Self-Report
Response Style	Positive Impression	OK	OK	OK	OK
	Negative Impression	OK	OK	OK	OK
	Inconsistency Index	OK	OK	OK	OK
Content	Emotional Distress	Total = 70	Total = 90	Total = 73	66
		Upsetting Thoughts = 46	Upsetting Thoughts/Physical Symptoms = 88	Upsetting Thoughts/Physical Symptoms = 74	n/a
		Worrying = 70	Social Anxiety = 75	n/a	n/a
		n/a	n/a	Social Anxiety = 67	n/a
	Social Problems	59	38	38*	n/a
	Separation Fears	73	90	74	53
	Defiant/Aggressive Behaviors	44	47	47	45
	Academic Difficulties	Total = 84	Total = 71	Total = ?	90
		Language = 84	Language = 59	Language = 77	n/a
		Math = 80	Math = 84	Math = ?	n/a

Hyperactivity	n/a	44	44	n/a
Hyperactivity/Impulsivity	39	n/a	n/a	42
Perfectionistic and Compulsive Behaviors	70	77	46	n/a
Violence Potential Indicator	47	49	49	45
Physical Symptoms	71	90	90	57
ADHD, Inattentive	58	73	73	57
ADHD, Hyperactive-Impulsive	39	51	48	42
Conduct Disorder	43	47	47	51
Oppositional Defiant Disorder	42	47	47	38
Major Depressive Episode	54	53	53	53
Manic Episode	48	45	45	40
Generalized Anxiety Disorder	74 Met	90 Met	70	69
Separation Anxiety Disorder	70	89 Met	76	62 Met
Social Phobia	66 Met	76	59	62

DSM-IV-TR (category spanning Conduct Disorder through Social Phobia)

(continued)

Table 7.19. Conners CBRS Results (Continued)

Conners CBRS		Parent Mrs. Reed	Teacher Mrs. Mock (Math)	Teacher Mrs. Knott (L.A.)	Self-Report
DSM-IV-TR (continued)	Obsessive-Compulsive Disorder	52	66	66	47
	Autistic Disorder	46	38	38	n/a
	Asperger's Disorder	39	36	36	n/a
Impairment	Academic	Severe	Moderate	Severe	Severe
	Social	Mild	Absent	Mild	Mild
	Home	Moderate	n/a	n/a	Mild
Index	Conners Clinical Index	79%	68%	61%	87%
	- DBD Indicator	42	41	41	45
	- LLD Indicator	87	71	67	90
	- MD Indicator	61	65	65	49
	- Anx Indicator	73	90	71	57
	- ADHD Indicator	56	58	53	54
Other Clinical Indicators	Bullying Perpetration	—	—	—	—
	Bullying Victimization	—	—	—	—
	Enuresis/Encopresis	—	—	—	n/a
	Panic Attack	—	—	—	✓

		(see above)	(see above)	(see above)	(see above)	
	Pervasive Developmental Disorder	—	—	—	—	—
Other Clinical Indicators (continued)	Pica	—	n/a	n/a	n/a	—
	Posttraumatic Stress Disorder	—	—	—	—	—
	Specific Phobia	—	—	—	—	—
	Substance Use	—	—	—	—	—
	Tics	—	—	—	—	—
	Trichotillomania	—	—	—	—	—
Critical Items	Severe Conduct	—	—	—	—	—
	Self-Harm	—	—	—	—	—

NOTE: High scores on the Conners CBRS indicate high levels of concern. All scores are T-scores unless indicated otherwise.

* = Actual score may be higher due to one or more items with no responses.

? = Cannot be calculated due to too many items with no responses.

Table 7.20. BRIEF Scale Results

BRIEF Scale*	Parent	Teacher (Math)	Teacher (L.A.)	Index Parent, Math, L.A.	
Inhibit	42	49	45	Behavior Regulation $T =$ 37, 66, 45	Global Executive Composite $T =$ 49, 64, 51
Shift	38	85	45		
Emotional Control	37	57	46		
Initiate	50	69	50	Metacognition $T =$ 55, 62, 55	
Working Memory	62	75	65		
Plan/Organize	60	58	55		
Organization of Materials	46	46	52		
Monitor	52	49	49		

*Note: Higher scores on the BRIEF indicate higher levels of concern. All scores reported as T-scores.

- Rapid access of information that should be automatic by now (e.g., letters, numbers, colors)
- Abstract reasoning
- Planning and strategy formation/use
- Organization
- Self-initiation

It is important to support Darby with structure in her academic and domestic work so that she can demonstrate her knowledge without being penalized for these executive deficits. Suggestions for appropriate supports are provided in the Recommendations section of this report.

Language: Darby demonstrates functional expressive and receptive language, both verbal and nonverbal/gestural. Articulation is clear. She was softspoken for most of the evaluation, with the exception of becoming louder when she was concentrating harder on a difficult verbal task. Conversation was reciprocal and generally on topic.

Deficits in Darby's language include significant word-finding errors. Darby frequently used filler words (e.g., "oh, uh, you know") and nonspecific words (e.g., "the little ball thingy," "the squiggly line things"). At times, she substituted a related word that was not quite correct (e.g., said "bowtie" to describe a hair-ribbon, said "dots" for holes in a belt). She circumlocuted, or "talked around," words that she could not recall (e.g., when trying to think of the name of a bath-drain plug, she said, "oh, uh, the, the thing you push to make water stay in or go out"). Her spoken language was poorly organized (e.g., "Call your friend, or go get your friend, and tell them, that lives in the house"). As described earlier in this report, reading skills are deficient. Darby's language is not automated or rapid. She takes longer than expected to process information that is language-based but is generally able to understand when given adequate time. Darby struggles with abstract language and higher-order language such as involved in drawing inferences.

Overall, basic language appears fundamentally intact. Darby's deficits are in the executive aspects of language, including word-finding. She will benefit from working with a speech-language pathologist to learn compensatory strategies for the deficits described above. It is important to structure Darby's assignments and tests so that she is not penalized for these deficits.

Visual Processing: Overall, visual perception and visual reasoning are intact for Darby. She has difficulty with complex visual information, but this is due to her executive deficits (including organization and strategy) rather than a pure visual processing deficit. Given Darby's reading deficits and language impairment, the visual modality is a good modality of instruction, as long as visual materials are kept simple, uncluttered, and straightforward.

Memory and Learning: There are several different types of memory. "Memory span" refers to how many pieces of information you can hold in immediate memory for a very short time. "Working memory" refers to the ability to manipulate or change information while remembering it. "Short-term memory" refers to the ability to remember information for a short time, and "long-term memory" refers to the ability to remember information that has been stored for a longer time. "Encoding" refers to storing information in memory, and "retrieval" refers to finding and pulling that information back out of memory. Problems in "remembering" can occur if any part of this process is not functioning. Attentional deficits also impact memory, because you must attend to information before you can encode it. Information can enter memory through different sensory modalities (e.g., seeing versus hearing). Memory can be language-based or visual (e.g., remembering the word "fish" versus picturing an actual fish). Memory tests can be "explicit" (i.e., when you are directly told to remember something), "implicit" (i.e., when you are not directly told to remember something, but most people would understand it was important), or "incidental" (i.e., when you do not expect to need to remember something).

For example, if a teacher says, "Remember this, it will be on the test," this is explicit memory. An example of implicit memory is any material taught in the class (i.e., the teacher does not say it will be on the test, but it is reasonable to expect it could be on the test). An example of incidental memory testing is being asked, "What did your teacher wear yesterday?" (i.e., something that you did not expect to need to know).

As previously mentioned, Darby's *memory span* is smaller than expected at her age. Across many types of memory tests, she demonstrated an immediate auditory span of four pieces of information when the information was not meaningful (e.g., random numbers). Her memory span improved into the average range when the information was meaningful to Darby (e.g., items on a shopping list). A small memory span impacts many aspects of Darby's functioning. A small memory span impacts her reading comprehension. Because she struggles to remember more than four items, she has difficulty decoding each word and retaining its meaning as she reads the rest of the sentence and paragraph. A small memory span limits Darby's listening comprehension, particularly as language becomes more complex and requires multiple steps to be remembered. A small memory span can impact planning, as it is difficult for Darby to remember all the aspects of an assignment as well as her plan for completing the assignment. It is important for Darby to learn ways of compensating for her small memory span.

Darby's performance on tests of sentence repetition was characterized by nonsensical errors. These errors suggest that she attempted to use rote memory on this task rather than treating the sentences as meaningful information. By using rote memory, she limited herself to her small memory span of four items and lost the intended meaning of most sentences. For example, when Darby heard a sentence like, "The man sitting by the bird statue is my father," her repetition distorted the meaning to become, "The bird sitting next to the man is my father." Given other testing results, it is likely that if Darby practiced visualizing the meaning of sentences she would more accurately repeat them.

Working memory is limited by Darby's small memory span. Within her memory span, she appears to have adequate ability to manipulate information. Testing results suggest that *short-term* and *long-term memory* are both age-appropriate, including *encoding* and *retrieval* of *explicit* and *incidental* information in both the *visual* and *auditory* modalities.

The primary concerns with regard to memory and learning are:

- small memory span (four items), which impacts working memory, reading comprehension, listening comprehension, and planning

- tendency to rely on rote memory (when memory is better for information that Darby understands)

It is important to help Darby learn strategies for dealing with her small memory span, as well as ways to make information more meaningful (and therefore easier to remember).

Sensorimotor Functions: Darby wore her prescription eyeglasses for the evaluation; corrected vision was functional. Eye contact was appropriate. Hearing and walking both appeared functional. Darby used her right hand for handwriting, grasping the pencil close to the point in a modified tripod grip (thumb wrapped over index finger). She pressed hard on the pencil tip, causing the first joint of her index finger to collapse. This type of pencil use suggests that Darby may not be receiving adequate sensory feedback from her fingers to her brain; as she presses harder, it increases the amount of sensory information that is sent to the brain. This type of pencil grip is problematic, in that it limits Darby's use of her fingers to manipulate the pencil, forcing her to use larger muscle groups (e.g., elbow, shoulder) to complete fine motor tasks such as handwriting. This results in more rapid physical fatigue.

Consistent with the hypothesis of limited sensory feedback, Darby required visual guidance to complete a hand movement task. Despite this subtle deficit, Darby earned a high average score on the sensorimotor task and average to high average scores on dexterity and pencil manipulation tasks. No significant overflow movements were noted.

Overall, Darby may have reduced sensory feedback from her fingers to her brain. She benefits from supplemental visual guidance. Her pencil grip likely results in rapid physical fatigue. Darby will likely benefit from using a computer for written assignments.

Adaptive Functioning: This area was not directly assessed. Based on Mrs. Reed's report, Darby shows appropriate levels of functional communication, self-care, health/safety awareness, social functioning, community use, and domestic skills (e.g., household chores). This does not appear to be an area of concern at the present time.

Social, Emotional, and Behavioral Functioning: Darby demonstrated appropriate social awareness and interaction during the evaluation. According to parent-, teacher-, and self-report, she is not experiencing difficulties in social functioning in the home, school, or community settings (*Conners CBRS: Social Problems*). Darby's teachers do describe some anxiety in the social setting (*Conners CBRS: Social Anxiety*). This is consistent with interview data from Mrs. Reed, as she reported that Darby seems afraid of being embarrassed in front of peers. She stated that Darby has always been "sensitive," but that she waits until she gets home before crying about any difficult events during the school day. During the evaluation and interview, it appeared that Darby is highly motivated by making efforts to please others. This places her at risk, as it is difficult to please everyone all the time.

Mrs. Reed reported that Darby feels and recognizes the full range of emotions. She responds appropriately to the emotions of other people. Darby, her mother, and her teachers all report concerns about emotional distress, including worrying, social anxiety, and separation fears; these worries also appear to be expressed physically at times (e.g., headaches and stomach-aches; *Conners CBRS: Emotional Distress and related scales*). During the evaluation, Darby was noted to pull the skin above her upper lip, resulting in red marks. This may be related to increased stress and anxiety.

Related to this, Darby seems to seek perfection at times, placing very high expectations on herself. Her mother and math teacher both described perfectionistic tendencies on a rating scale (*Conners CBRS: Perfectionistic and Compulsive Tendencies*). In interview, Darby described worries including getting a bad grade and something bad happening to her family. These worries suggest that, in addition to perfectionism, Darby may have separation anxiety issues. Darby's mother and teachers all reported significantly more signs of separation anxiety than typical for an 11-year-old girl (*Conners CBRS: Separation Fears*); however, Darby did not report high levels of separation anxiety. It is possible that she is less aware of the roots of her anxiety; conversely, it may be that she has more generalized anxiety that her parents and teachers are assuming is separation related.

Overall, Darby presents with features of anxiety, including perfectionism, social anxiety, and separation anxiety. She exhibits physical signs of her anxiety, including aches/pains and skin-related problems. When people are anxious, they can appear inattentive, as they may be concentrating on their worries instead of the task.

Behaviorally, there are no significant concerns. Darby tends to fidget when she is thinking, particularly during language-based tasks. This fidgeting is not pervasive across settings or content areas, though. She has some verbal impulsivity, which may be related to feelings of anxiety. Parent-, teacher-, and self-report did not indicate significant concerns about compliance, activity levels, or impulsivity (*Conners CBRS: Defiant/Aggressive Behaviors, Hyperactivity, Hyperactivity/Impulsivity*).

Other Results: Although medication monitoring was not the purpose of this evaluation, some data were collected that might be useful in approaching a medication monitoring plan. Please see Table 7.18 for relevant data discussed here.

In general, Darby scored in the average range on tests of brief and sustained attention even when she was not taking her medication. While there is no definitive test result that indicates whether medication should be used, most people who need stimulant medications show significant deficits on these types of tests, particularly the computerized continuous performance test (CPT, e.g., *Conners CPT-II*). Darby's scores on the *CPT-II* were in the average range. Darby's score on tests requiring her to repeat sentences or random numbers did not change significantly with medication.

Two tests showed a pattern of change over the past evaluations.

- Darby's raw score for repeating numbers in the reverse order (*WISC-IV Digit Span, CELF-4 Number Repetition*) changed from 6 at 8 years old (on medications) to 4 (on medications) and 3 (off medications) at 11 years old.
- The raw score for translating a code (numbers and symbols; *WISC-IV Coding*) changed from 59 at 8 years old (on medications) to 48 (on medications) and 39 (off medications) at 11 years old.

This trend suggests that Darby's performance on these types of tasks does benefit from stimulant medication. This does not necessarily indicate that she *should* be on medication, as most people show improvement on these types of tasks when they are given stimulants (e.g., improved functioning with moderate amounts of caffeine). In fact, certain professions use small amounts of stimulants to improve their performance (e.g., military personnel in battle).

Comparison of the raw data from 2004 and 2007 indicates that the trend is not entirely due to presence or absence of medication. Darby's performance dropped over these 3 years. It is possible that she was less comfortable with the current examiner, although this did not seem to be the case during conversation between tests. No specific injuries were reported that might result in this change in functioning. Another possible explanation is that Darby's level of anxiety has increased over the past 3 years, which has interfered with her performance on these types of tests. As Darby's academic struggles have intensified, she may have become even more focused on achievement and success, resulting in increased anxiety. Finally, it is possible that these differences are spurious, meaning that they are not "real" differences, but coincidental (i.e., based on statistical probability: whenever administering multiple tests, some scores will go up, some will stay the same, and some will go down).

SUMMARY OF RESULTS

Results from this evaluation indicate that Darby has intact cognitive abilities. Her academic achievement is generally consistent with expectations based on age and ability, with the exception of reading, which is significantly lower than expectations.

Darby's skills in many areas are age-appropriate, including:

- Attention
- Basic language
- Aspects of executive functioning
- Visual perception and reasoning
- Memory and learning (for meaningful information)
- Speed of information processing and responding (for nonsymbol-based information)
- Social functioning
- Behavioral control

Specific areas of deficit include:

- Reading (decoding and comprehension)
- Memory span (only four items), which impacts working memory, comprehension, and planning
- Word-finding
- Higher-order language
- Aspects of executive functioning, including organization, automaticity, abstract reasoning, self-initiation, strategy formation/use, and planning
- Emotional functioning (features of anxiety)

OVERALL IMPRESSIONS

Darby Reed, an 11-year-old girl, was referred for this neuropsychological evaluation by Dr. John Paul due to concerns about academic struggles, including reading and word-finding difficulties. Family history is significant for reading difficulties, attention problems, anxiety, mood disorder, substance use, and a preference for hands-on learning. Darby has no significant neurologic history. Developmentally, she has always struggled with language and symbols (including letters and numbers). Despite significant effort, she makes slow progress academically. Her mother describes some concerns about Darby's emotional sensitivity.

Darby meets DSM-IV-TR criteria for a diagnosis of *Reading Disorder*. It is also appropriate to use the term "dyslexia" to describe Darby's reading deficits. Her test results include a statistically significant discrepancy between ability and achievement in this area. There is a family history of reading difficulties, and Darby has a personal history of struggling to read. From an early age, she had difficulty with skills such as learning her letters, numbers, and colors—all warning signs for later Reading Disorder. Darby has a history of delayed language development. Her deficits in phonological processing, reading comprehension, and word decoding are consistent with this diagnosis, particularly in conjunction with intact comprehension of spoken language. The presence of limited memory span (and therefore limited working memory) complicates this diagnostic picture by further impacting Darby's ability to compensate for her Reading Disorder. Her failure to demonstrate sustained progress despite adequate cognitive abilities and additional reading instruction suggests that Darby requires specialized instruction in this area rather than modified regular instruction.

Darby also meets DSM-IV-TR criteria for a diagnosis of *Expressive Language Disorder*, given her significant word-finding deficits that impact her communication of thoughts and ideas. For Darby, this includes spoken and written expression of language.

Information from interview, observations, and rating scales indicate many features of anxiety, including aspects of social anxiety, separation anxiety, and perfectionism as well as general anxiety. At this time, Darby does not meet full DSM-IV-TR criteria for any specific diagnosis of an anxiety disorder; therefore, these multiple symptoms are best described with the diagnosis *Anxiety Disorder, Not Otherwise Specified (NOS)*. Given the family history of anxiety, depression, and substance use, especially in combination with Darby's perfectionistic tendencies, it is important to provide Darby with enhanced coping skills. These coping skills will likely serve as protective factors for Darby in the future.

Parent and self-ratings on select items from the *Conners CBRS* are more consistent with ratings of children with a clinical diagnosis than those of children with no diagnosis. Within these items, Darby and her mother responded in a way that is consistent with children who have learning and/or language disorders. Darby's teachers both responded in a way that is consistent with children who have anxiety disorders. These number-based findings support clinical impressions and test data.

In the past, Darby was assigned a diagnosis of Attention-Deficit/Hyperactivity Disorder (ADHD), Predominantly Inattentive type. She has been prescribed stimulant medication for the past 3 years to address symptoms of this disorder. Dr. Paul's report from that evaluation (when Darby was 8 years old) indicated the difficulty of differentiating between primary inattention and primary anxiety. Often, the best way to determine this type of issue is to see what happens with treatment efforts and time. Darby's struggles have continued despite interventions to target symptoms of ADHD. It appears that her anxiety is more prominent now than it was in the past. Comparison of Darby's test performance on and off medication did not reveal striking benefit for the skills assessed. Mrs. Reed commented that she cannot tell when Darby is taking her prescribed medication; she has noticed that Darby requires refills every few months (rather than once per month, as should be the case if the medications were taken daily as prescribed). This suggests that part of the month being described by Darby's mother and teachers on rating scales included days without medication. Although all raters described more symptoms of ADHD than are typically seen in 11-year-old girls, Darby does not appear to meet full DSM-IV-TR criteria for this diagnosis at the present time. These results will be reviewed with Darby's prescribing physician. It is possible that Darby has ADHD that is currently in partial remission (perhaps due to intervention); it is also possible that symptoms of anxiety are masquerading as ADHD.

Darby's executive functioning deficits are consistent with a diagnosis of ADHD Inattentive type, but these deficits are nonspecific and can also be found with anxiety disorders or other diagnoses. Regardless of the diagnostic term, Darby has significant educational needs in relation to her executive deficits and requires services to address them.

These areas of concern are mitigated by a number of positive, protective factors. Darby is an interactive and engaging girl. She is likeable and pleasant. She has intact social skills and several close friends. She is diligent and highly motivated. She has intact cognitive abilities and functional communication skills. She is a member of a supportive and caring family. All of these factors positively impact long-term prognosis for Darby and support intensive treatment efforts to facilitate further progress and development.

RECOMMENDATIONS

1. Educationally, Darby qualifies to receive special education services under the primary federal handicapping condition Specific Learning Disability (SLD; reading/dyslexia). Consideration should also be given to her features of anxiety. As such, I recommend that an Individualized Education Plan (IEP) be created to replace the 504 plan. An appropriate educational environment for Darby will consist of special education and related services including the following elements:

- Teachers who have experience with reading disorders, executive dysfunction, and emotional needs
- Curriculum that is at or above grade level
- Modified instruction, including:
  - Visual and hands-on approaches to teaching
  - Decreased/modified verbal instruction
- Related services, including:
  - Intensive reading intervention services that have been shown to be effective for students with dyslexia (e.g., Orton-Gillingham, Visualize-Verbalize, Lindamood-Bell, Itchy's Alphabet www. itchysalphabet.com)
  - Speech and language services (SLT) to address word-finding errors, organization, and higher-order language needs
  - Occupational therapy (OT) consultation services, including access to a word processor or computer and keyboarding skills

2. Darby's educational team should consider providing Extended Year Services (EYS), given her history of regression in academic skills if not provided with constant maintenance activities by her mother. Furthermore, Darby should continue receiving special education and all specified related services during the summer (including reading, SLT, and OT).

3. Darby's language errors require specialized interventions with a speech-language pathologist. Outside of these therapy sessions, she requires modifications in instruction. Otherwise she will be unjustly penalized for her language impairment.

   - Demonstrate and show Darby what to do. Provide her with assistance to successfully complete a task. She will learn more through these techniques than by verbal instruction alone. Over repeated trials, the amount of support and assistance can be gradually decreased as Darby becomes more independent with successful task completion.
   - Use short, simple directions. Give Darby one or two steps at a time.
   - Teach Darby to take notes as she listens to instructions. Help her practice asking the speaker to wait while she gets her notepad and pencil so that she can jot down the key points for the task.
   - Ask Darby to explain a task or question before she begins working. This ensures that she understands the task before she makes a needless mistake.
   - Allow extra time for Darby to formulate her response and respond.

- Tell Darby what *to* do (rather than what *not* to do); for example, "Darby, circle your answers" (rather than, "Don't put big X-marks on the wrong ones").
- Use multiple-choice or yes/no question formats to allow Darby to participate in class discussion and complete assignments. Use similar formats for written tests also (e.g., multiple-choice, true-false, matching). Avoid open-ended questions that will tax her language formulation skills. Avoid fill-in-the-blank formats that will penalize her for word-finding deficits. If a test must be fill-in-the-blank format, provide a word bank that Darby can draw from in completing the test/assignment.
- If Darby's initial response does not completely answer the question, gently encourage her to tell you more. During this evaluation, Darby typically demonstrated full knowledge of the concept when given the opportunity to "talk her way around" to the answer.
- Reduce the amount of reading that is required of Darby. Help prioritize key sections with a highlighter or provide Darby with a bulleted list of key points from the reading.

4. Students with deficits in executive functioning often have difficulty with simultaneous processing. Darby should only be graded for one thing at a time. For example, if the point of an assignment is creativity, state this explicitly, and do not mark or grade down for neatness, spelling, or other types of errors. Similarly, help Darby learn to write in a step-wise fashion as described below.

5. As Darby learns to type, allow her to type written assignments. This reduces fine motor fatigue. Typing assignments on a computer also allows the writing process to be broken into multiple steps (e.g., idea development, organization, forming sentences, adding adjectives/adverbs, proofing for punctuation, grammar, and spelling).

6. Based on Darby's test results, the following suggestions are offered to make her learning process more effective and efficient.
   - Teach one new concept at a time, and build upon previously learned concepts. Help Darby see how new information relates to knowledge she already has, and help her integrate these pieces. Use associations to add new knowledge to previously mastered knowledge. Memorization of isolated facts via drill is *not* an appropriate teaching technique for Darby.
   - Make learning meaningful to Darby. She remembers information better when she understands. Try to connect new facts to

experiences from her life, or create experiences with her to reinforce new information.

- Help Darby organize information before she begins learning it. Group related concepts together during instruction, and be explicit about why these things belong together (e.g., The spelling words on today's list all have the /ow/ sound in them. Some use the letters "ow" like "wow," and some use the letters "ou" like "shout").
- Darby shows significant improvement in her learning each time she is exposed to the information. Use frequent review of concepts to help her master the information.

7. Use Darby's strengths in visual, hands-on learning when teaching her in the classroom or at home.

- Recognize that "visual and hands-on" does not necessarily mean "experiential" learning. In Darby's case, she might be overwhelmed by a teaching approach that expects her to independently extract a rule or information from a free-form experience. Darby is more likely to benefit from explicit instruction that presents information in the visual or hands-on modalities.
- Teach Darby to write or draw her thinking on paper, reducing the working memory load. She may benefit from learning visual organization techniques such as webbing and mapping to prepare for writing assignments.
- Touch-math is a good way to make math more visual.
- Darby will also benefit from using concrete manipulatives, such as used in certain math and reading programs.
- Regardless of which curricula are selected, it is important to show Darby rather than tell her.
- Provide visual anchors for Darby rather than presenting only auditory information.
- Structure visual materials so that there is not too much information on a page.
- Support Darby's athletic interests, such as soccer. Provide her with materials and opportunities to use these skills at home and school. These activities are important outlets for her, as well as a chance to reinforce Darby for doing something well.

8. Darby needs increased levels of support and structure. Regardless of diagnosis, people with executive deficits require more external structure than their peers because they have less self-generated structure.

- Structure can involve time elements.

- Help Darby set personal goals for what she will achieve in a 15-minute time period; then help her revise these goals at the end of 15 minutes.
- Alternate types of tasks on Darby's schedule—for example, a hands-on problem-solving task after completing a written task.
- Structure Darby's work time (at home or school) into brief working periods separated by breaks. Be certain to give her clear end-points for each task.
  - Structure can be cognitive.
    - Give Darby a short list of what needs to be accomplished so that she can learn to work more independently. As she develops good use of lists, work with her to learn how to make her own lists.
    - Help Darby structure complex information by showing her how to divide a big project into smaller, more manageable steps. Teach her to tackle one part of a task at a time, rather than being overwhelmed by the entire assignment. Given her limited memory span, help her learn to write down the steps as she plans.
    - Teach Darby a general problem-solving technique that she can apply to any situation. The general concept is to define the problem, decide if you need help in solving it, determine how to break the big problem into smaller pieces, and decide which order to address the smaller pieces.
    - Show Darby note-taking strategies and general study skills. Be certain that she focuses on how to make information meaningful, as this helps her remember it.

9. Recognize the role that fatigue plays across Darby's school day. Students with executive deficits and language impairment have to exert more effort than their peers. Therefore, they become more quickly fatigued. As Darby becomes fatigued, she is even less able to engage in problem solving and use language. Build flexibility into her schedule so that you can provide her with mental down-time if she seems to be having problems due to fatigue.

10. It is important for Darby's teachers, therapists, and parents to be aware of her perfectionistic tendencies and how much focus she places on pleasing others.
    - A negative comment will affect Darby longer than other children her age.
    - As Darby thinks about what she "did wrong," this will take her attention away from listening and learning.

- Place an emphasis on the positives—what Darby did correctly.
- For example, when grading Darby's work, mark only the correct answers and record the number correct at the top of the page.
  - If Darby missed only a few items but demonstrated knowledge of the concept, move on to the next concept.
  - If Darby missed many items, point out what she did well, followed by "time for teamwork" as you work through a few incorrect items together. When you feel Darby has a better grasp of the concept, ask her to do a few items while you comment on each correct step. Finally, ask her to finish the remaining items independently. This approach allows Darby to learn (which is the point of school) without being as focused on grades.
- Be conscious about responding to Darby in a warm, supportive manner.

11. Make sure Darby has time to be a child and to play. She enjoys physical, athletic activities; be certain to make time in her schedule for these things. If Darby is constantly focused on academics, she will miss out on other aspects of her development, including social and emotional. If her home and family time are spent entirely on homework, she will lose important relationships and leisure time.

Resources and Referrals

- Provide Darby with proactive therapy to address her symptoms of anxiety and improve her coping skills. Her tendency to deny "negative" emotions (like anger) and to seek perfectionism results in fragile defenses against stress. When people do not have adaptive ways to cope with stress, they can develop physical problems, anxiety disorders, or depression; some turn to substance use in an attempt to feel better. It is important to teach Darby effective ways to cope with stress so that she will have practiced good skills that are good habits when she needs them.
- If the Reeds are interested in pursuing the issue of whether medications are helpful for Darby, they should consider completing a blinded medication monitoring trial. Ideally, this involves cooperation between the prescribing physician and a pharmacist who can "blind" the medication by placing it in an opaque capsule and also create a blinded placebo (nonactive pill). Brief cognitive tests and rating scales should be completed in each of the conditions to facilitate objective and subjective comparisons of

Darby's functioning in each condition. If the Reeds or Darby's physician are interested in pursuing this option, I am available as a consultant.

- Darby's parents and teachers may wish to read the book, *Overcoming Dyslexia: A New and Complete Science-Based Program for Reading Problems at Any Level*, by Dr. Sally Shaywitz. Dr. Shaywitz explains reading difficulties such as dyslexia, including how to help struggling readers. This book also provides a chapter about questions to ask when considering various reading programs.

- The Reeds and Darby's school professionals may be interested in becoming involved with the International Dyslexia Association (IDA; www.interdys.org). This website includes educational facts as well as resources for intervention. The IDA also maintains a referral list of qualified reading specialists.

- Neuropsychological re-evaluation after 1 to 2 years of implementing these recommendations. It is possible that Darby's presentation and performance on neuropsychological measures will change as her anxiety is decreased. Follow-up evaluation will help clarify whether an additional diagnosis of ADHD is appropriate.

The results of this assessment and these recommendations were shared and discussed with Judy Reed in a feedback session. If there are further questions or concerns, please contact Dr. Sparrow.

Elizabeth P. Sparrow, PhD
Licensed Psychologist, Specializing in Clinical Neuropsychology

NEUROPSYCHOLOGICAL REPORT

Name: Josh F. Kane
Age: 5 years, 4 months
Grade: rising Kindergarten student

Referral

Josh Kane is a 5-year-old boy whose parents sought a neuropsychological evaluation due to concerns about atypical interests and behaviors. This is his first neuropsychological evaluation. Results will be used to determine diagnosis and inform treatment planning.

Specific concerns include the possibility of Asperger's Disorder. Josh has a history of flapping his hands when he is excited or upset. He is preoccupied with numbers and music and will spend hours writing "lists" of CD tracks, song titles, and song lengths from memory. (These lists consist of random letters for song titles, but the track and length numbers correspond to music CDs that Josh enjoys.) Josh also enjoys using refrigerator magnets to list CD tracks and song lengths on the refrigerator. He does not "draw pictures," but simply creates these repetitive lists. Play with peers is isolated or parallel rather than interactive; he prefers interacting with adults to interacting with peers. Less pressing concerns include his "clumsiness" and the length of time it takes him to complete any daily routine (e.g., takes a long time to get dressed in the morning because he is "singing, dancing, and in his own world").

Background Information

Family Background

- Lives in Local Town, Maryland with his natural parents and younger sister (Kate, 3 years old).
- Mother completed a B.S. and is currently a full-time mother.
- Father completed a B.S. and is currently an environmental engineer.
- Family history includes: Academic/career underachievement, reading disability/dyslexia, shyness, social awkwardness, tantrums, left-handedness, visual impairment, substance use (including alcohol and nicotine).

Gestation, Birth, Neonatal History:

- Pregnancy: Full-term (41 weeks), no reported complications.
- Labor/Delivery: Spontaneous, 8-hour labor, vaginal delivery.
- Birthweight: 10 pounds, 8.4 ounces.
- Neonatal: Discharged to home at 3 days old (monitored an extra day due to episodes of rapid breathing; resolved without treatment).

Medical History:

- Handedness: Right.
- Medical conditions/procedures: None noted.
- Neurologic issues (brain injury, sustained fevers, loss of consciousness, seizures, etc.): No known concerns
- Medications: No history of psychoactive medications. Took multivitamins while in preschool.
- Vision and Hearing: No known concerns.
- Trauma, abuse, violence, or neglect: No reported concerns.

Developmental History:

- Infancy: Happy, good disposition, cried appropriately. Content to be alone. Did not show anxiety about strangers. "An observer"; watched parents move around room.
- First concerns: Delayed speech; limited peer interactions; did not share peer interests.
- Regressions: None reported.
- Development of skills and concerns:
  - Motor:
    - Gross: Met early milestones within expected limits. Cannot ride tricycle. Poor awareness of body in space. Appears clumsy at times.
    - Fine: Met early milestones within expected limits. Difficulty with buttons, pencil grip, and scissoring.
  - Language:
    - Expressive: Atypical; first words did not emerge until 19 months old, phrases by 26 months old. Was using large words such as "automatically" by 3 years old.
    - Receptive: Met early milestones within expected limits.
    - Nonverbal/gestural: Met early milestones within expected limits.
  - Social: Smiled appropriately as infant. Was content to watch other children play in gymnastics/play class. Limited peer interaction, more isolated or parallel peer play. Overfriendly. Invades others' personal space. Interests do not match peer interests. Required explicit instruction for basic social skills (e.g., greeting teacher in the morning). Enjoys showing completed work to parents.
  - Play: Enjoyed cause-and-effect toys as young child. Now likes building very detailed construction projects. Some interactive play emerging with younger sister.
  - Cognitive/Academic: Concerns about attention, distractibility, and concentration began at 4 years old. Learned letters without difficulty; is already reading sight-words.
  - Emotion: Expresses full range of appropriate emotions, but more extreme than required for situation. Is aware of emotions in his family members and responds appropriately, but does not show the same awareness with peers. Feelings can be hurt easily (e.g., if classmate says, "I don't want to be your friend").
  - Behavior: Active, difficulty staying still. Rigidity/stubbornness sometimes results in task/activity refusal.

- Activities of Daily Living: No concerns about sleeping and eating. Delayed toileting (night-time control by 3.5 years old, daytime bowel control by 4.5 years old); waits to use bathroom (sometimes waits too long). Content to have parents take care of him (does not assert independence for dressing, bathing, grooming).
- Atypical Features:
  - Auditory, Tactile, Olfactory, Oral: No concerns reported.
  - Visual: Overfocus on details (e.g., notices a burned-out lightbulb on the Ferris wheel). History of light-gazing.
  - Rigidity: "Stubborn" insistence on routine.
  - Stereotypical behaviors: Hand-flapping when excited or frustrated. Medical records indicate history of toe-walking.
  - Play/Interests: Isolated/parallel play. No spontaneous imaginative/ representational play (will play with you if you start a theme, but will not continue when you leave). History of counting and memorizing the number of lamps in each person's house (at around 3 years old). History of fascination with lights (watching, turning on/off). Current overfocus on music CDs and numbers, as well as mechanical/electrical things. Memorizes CD track numbers/lengths, also who likes which songs on which CDs.
  - Language: Dysfluent at times, some repetition of initial word sounds, speaks too quickly at times, difficulty staying on topic. No reported history of echolalia, jargon, pronominal reversal.
  - Aggression/Destruction/Self-Injurious Behaviors: No concerns reported.
  - Other atypicalities:
    - Not as responsive to praise as others his age; more responsive to threat of losing preferred activities.
    - Limited initiation of activity.

Previous Evaluations, Diagnoses, and Treatments:

- 18 months old: Washington County Infants and Toddlers evaluation. Sought evaluation due to concerns about speech development. Evaluator noted no single words, but does point and gesture. Can follow simple commands.
- 3 years old: IEP Team meeting; determined "no educational disability." Discontinued Infants and Toddlers services.
- 4 years old: Preschool Speech-Language Screening. Passed audiologic examination. Concerns included poor speech intelligibility,

distractibility, and off-topic responses. Noted overbite and forward tongue movement.

- 4.5 years old: Local Institute, Dr. John Chou. Sought evaluation due to concerns about social reciprocity and cognitive function. Referred for further evaluation to rule-out possible PDD and/or ADHD.
- 4.5 years old: Child Find evaluation. Sought evaluation due to concerns about social skill development.
  - Psychological evaluation: Noted distractibility, off-topic comments, need for frequent redirection, hand-flapping, toe-bouncing. Concluded "moderate difficulties in the areas of social skills and pragmatic communication, most significantly in the group environment . . . somewhat restricted patterns of interest." Recommended ongoing assessment and monitoring as interventions are implemented. Referred to Project ACT for further resources.
  - Speech and Language Assessment: Noted need for structure, slight speech dysfluency. PLS-4 results were in the average range for expressive and receptive language.
- 4.5 years old: IEP Team meeting; determined "no educational disability."
- 5 years old: Project ACT (All Children Together) consultation. Referred by Child Find. Provided materials about transitioning to cooperative play, one classroom observation. Observations/treatment discontinued when ACT teacher resigned.
- 5 years old: Preschool Speech-Language Screening. Noted off-topic, fast speech rate, multiple dysfluencies, pragmatic issues (overfocus on specific topics), difficulty following directions. Recommended full evaluation for communication and social behavior.

Academic/Daycare History:

- No grades repeated or skipped.
- 3 years old to present: St. James Nursery School. General education placement.
  - 3-year-old class: No reported concerns.
  - 4-year-old and 5-year-old class: Taught by Mrs. White and assistant; approximately 9 to 12 children in class. Teacher concerns included:
    - Would rather watch or play alone than interact with peers
    - Prefers adults to peers
    - Atypical interests (music, CD player)

- o Easily distracted, loses focus
- o Off-topic answers to questions
- o Difficulty staying on task (unless preferred activity)
- o Repetitive hand movements
- o Needs assistance to make choices and decisions
- o Becomes silly, easily influenced by others
- o Very observant
- o Unresponsive when engaged in preferred activity
- Kindergarten: Plans to attend local public school kindergarten. Parents concerned about larger class size (approximately 20 to 25 children, one teacher, parent volunteer).

Strengths: (parent and teacher comments). Very happy, good with numbers, good sense of humor, intelligent, good observation skills, patient and caring, interested in how things work, self-confident, great memory for things he notices (e.g., CD track lengths).

Preferred Activities: playing with numbers (writing numbers, arranging magnetic numbers, watching numbers on electronic equipment), playing with cash register, construction activities (e.g., gears, blocks), dancing and listening to music.

Motivators: earning extra "music time" (with his CDs and numbers), being timed, candy.

Evaluation Procedures

- Differential Ability Scales (DAS): Upper Preschool level: Core, selected supplemental subtests
- NEPSY: A Developmental Neuropsychological Evaluation (NEPSY): Selected subtests
- Purdue Pegboard
- Projective Drawings
- Conners Early Childhood (Conners EC): Parent and teacher reports
- Behavior Rating Inventory of Executive Function (BRIEF): Parent and teacher reports[4]

---

4. Parent reports were completed by Grace Kane (mother); Teacher reports were completed by Ingrid White, who has taught Josh for almost 2 years.

Validity

Instruments used are valid for Josh and for the referral question(s). The tests were administered by a qualified examiner (Elizabeth P. Sparrow, PhD, Licensed Psychologist). Observed behaviors during the evaluation were consistent with parent report of usual behaviors. Available validity indicators were all within acceptable limits, unless noted otherwise. Therefore, results of this evaluation are judged to be a valid representation of current neuropsychological functioning.

TEST RESULTS AND OBSERVATIONS

The results from Josh's performance during this neuropsychological evaluation are summarized in the following tables. Results from formal tests are reported as standardized scores, which compare Josh's performance with other students who are the same age. Standardized scores take a variety of forms, including those summarized in Table 7.21. Higher scores generally represent better performance, unless noted otherwise.

General Presentation: Josh arrived for both testing sessions accompanied by his mother. He showed no difficulty separating from her when it was time to leave the waiting room and go into the testing room. He appeared curious about this new environment and investigated the toys and activities. He was aware of the examiner and generally responsive to her voice. He made appropriate eye contact and used eye gaze communicatively (e.g., looked at the examiner to see if his response was correct). It was difficult to obtain a response from Josh during free time when he was engaged in making lists of CD tracks. He was more interactive when the examiner initiated a construction task during play time. Josh readily initiated conversation. His responses were generally tangential. When conversation was not structured and directive, Josh returned to the topic of his music CDs

Table 7.21. Standardized Score Results

Standardized Score	Average Range of Scores
Scaled Score (ScS)	7 to 13
Standard Score (SS)	85 to 115
T-score (T)	40 to 60
z-score (z)	−1.00 to +1.00

(including certain track numbers, what year he acquired the CD, etc.). He spontaneously demonstrated good manners, including asking if the examiner was okay after she coughed. Other aspects of social interaction were less appropriate. Josh often reached for the examiner's nose or hair or put her finger on the tip of his nose.

Josh was quite active during the evaluation, although he remained seated and still for a longer period of time during free play when he was engaged in a preferred activity. He bounced in his seat, kicked a footrest under the table, even stood and danced at times during the evaluation. He was impulsive at times and had difficulty waiting for "go" on timed tasks. He was easily distracted and required frequent redirection to stay on task. He was very vocal, including nearly nonstop comments, singing, and sound effects. Josh had difficulty remaining quiet.

Atypical behaviors were noted at times, including hand-flapping when Josh was pressured to work quickly. He also inappropriately sniffed test materials during one task. Josh leaned very close to the worksheet during one task, in contrast with his appropriate examination of other visual stimuli. When he made a mistake, he became quite upset and required extreme intervention to continue working on the task. He also became upset when the examiner skipped a page in a book with numbered items (e.g., "Wait! You skipped #11! But we can't do #12 until we do #11!").

Josh appropriately asked for clarification or repetition of items. He also requested help on a difficult item by saying, "Can you help me, Dr. Sparrow? I need some help." He seemed generally happy during the evaluation, although he had variable tolerance for frustration.

In general, Josh appeared internally motivated to do a good job. As he became fatigued, his attention decreased and he became sillier. He benefited from increased structure and a modified environment at these times (i.e., the examiner made a point to speak calmly and quietly, limit her gestures, and lean in close to Josh). When confronted with difficult items, he tended to express physical complaints (e.g., neck ache, "I can't think, I'm too itchy"), complain of being "bored," or give up (e.g., "That's too tricky").

Intellectual Ability: During the present evaluation, Josh was administered the *Differential Ability Scales (DAS)* to assess his general cognitive abilities. The *DAS* is an individually administered battery of cognitive and achievement tests for children and adolescents aged 2 years 6 months through 17 years 11 months. The cognitive subtests were designed to measure specific, definable abilities in a manner that individual subtests can be interpreted. The *DAS* was developed from a developmental and educational perspective, making it very appropriate for use with children in this age range. Rather than providing an "intelligence quotient"

(IQ), the *DAS* provides a "General Conceptual Ability" (GCA) score that reflects the general ability of an individual to perform complex mental processing that involves conceptualization and the transformation of information. At Josh's age, the *DAS* also provides a "Verbal cluster" that is a composite of tasks involving more verbal abilities and a "Nonverbal cluster" that includes visual reasoning and visuospatial construction. Scores are provided in Table 7.22 and will be discussed further by domain in the following sections.

Results from the current administration of the *DAS* indicate average to high average ranges of functioning overall, with several skills in the above average range. Josh did particularly well on a visual reasoning task.

Academic Achievement: This was not a focus of the present evaluation. Josh scored in the above average range on a test that required early number concepts. He accurately demonstrated knowledge of the concepts same, more, and less. He showed ability to accurately count and to match numbers with corresponding groups of items. He had one letter reversal on a copying task, but this is still within normal limits for his age (although reversals should be

Table 7.22. DAS Subtest Results

DAS Subtest	T-score	Age Equivalent (years and months)	Index Scores	GCA
Verbal Comprehension	47	4y 10m	Verbal Cluster SS = 105	General Conceptual Ability (GCA)
Naming Vocabulary	59	6y 10m		
Picture Similarities	70	>7y 10m	Nonverbal Cluster SS = 110	
Pattern Construction	53	5y 10m		
Copying	43	4y 10m		
Early Number Concepts	64	6y 4m		SS = 112
Block Building	—	—		
Matching Letter-Like Forms	62	6y 7m		
Recall of Digits	—	—		
Recall of Objects: Immediate	49	5y 1m		
Recognition of Pictures	48	5y 1m		

monitored, given family history of dyslexia). Parent and teacher ratings indicate no concerns about Josh's pre-academic skills (*Conners EC: Pre-Academic/Cognitive*).

Neuropsychological Functioning

Additional measures were administered to further examine Josh's performance on the *DAS*, as well as to explore his functioning in other domains. These scores are provided in Tables 7.23 through 7.26 and will be discussed further in subsequent sections of this report.

Attention/Executive Functions: Parent and teacher descriptions of attention indicated variable attention span, ranging from very short for most activities to extremely long for preferred activities (e.g., watching the number display change on his CD player). Both Josh's mother and his teacher commented on a rating scale that this variability in performance made it very difficult to rate his attention, as both extremes describe him sometimes (*Conners 3: Inattention/Hyperactivity*). Parent ratings (*BRIEF*) revealed significant concerns about executive functioning, particularly Josh's ability to *initiate* problem solving or activity and his ability to sustain *working memory* (i.e., manipulate information while holding it in memory). Teacher responses on the *BRIEF* indicated these same concerns and an additional concern about Josh's ability to adjust to changes in routine or task demands (i.e. "shift"; a.k.a. *mental flexibility*). This is consistent with parent report in interview that Josh can be rigidly stubborn once he has decided something. It is likely that this stubbornness is not "difficult behavior," but truly a cognitive deficit that makes it difficult for Josh to consider other explanations or solutions to a situation.

Table 7.23. NEPSY Subtest

NEPSY Subtest	Scaled Score or Percentile
Tower	ScS = 8
Auditory Attention and Response Set	ScS = 13
- Attention Task	ScS = 12
- Attention, Omission Errors	>75th Percentile
- Attention, Commission Errors	>75th Percentile
- Response Set Task	ScS = 13
- Response Set, Omission Errors	>75th Percentile
- Response Set, Commission Errors	>75th Percentile

(continued)

Table 7.23. (Continued)

NEPSY Subtest	Scaled Score or Percentile
Visual Attention	ScS = 10
- Cats Time	26th – 75th Percentile
- Cats Omissions	26th – 75th Percentile
- Cats Commissions	26th – 75th Percentile
- Faces Time	11th – 25th Percentile
- Faces Omissions	26th – 75th Percentile
- Faces Commissions	>75th Percentile
Statue	11th – 25th Percentile
Speeded Naming	ScS = 10
- Time	26th – 75th Percentile
- Accuracy	>75th Percentile
Comprehension of Instructions	ScS = 11
Verbal Fluency	ScS = 13
- Animals	26th – 75th Percentile
- Foods/Drinks	>75th Percentile
Imitating Hand Positions	ScS = 7
- Preferred Hand	11th – 25th Percentile
- Nonpreferred Hand	3rd – 10th Percentile
Visuomotor Precision	ScS = 8
- Car Time	26th – 75th Percentile
- Car Errors	26th – 75th Percentile
- Motorcycle Time	26th – 75th Percentile
- Motorcycle Errors	26th – 75th Percentile
Narrative Memory	ScS = 11
- Free Recall	26th – 75th Percentile
- Cued Recall	>75th Percentile

Table 7.24. Purdue Pegboard Results

Purdue Pegboard	Z-Score
Dominant Hand	−2.35
Nondominant Hand	−2.07
Both hands, cooperatively	−2.16

Table 7.25. BRIEF Scale Results

BRIEF Scale	T-score: Parent	T-score: Teacher	Index Parent, Teacher	
Inhibit	56	56	Behavior Regulation $T = 54, 63$	Global Executive Composite $T = $ *, 65
Shift	57	73		
Emotional Control	49	60		
Initiate	65	66		
Working Memory	73	71	Metacognition $T = $ *, 64	
Plan/Organize	*	56		
Organization of Materials	43	61		
Monitor	57	59		

*These scores could not be calculated due to omitted items.
Note: High scores on the BRIEF indicate high levels of concern.

Table 7.26. Conners EC Results

Conners EC		Parent	Teacher
Response Style	Positive Impression	OK	OK
	Negative Impression	OK	OK
	Inconsistency Index	OK	OK
Behavior	Inattention/Hyperactivity	61	56
	Defiant/Aggressive Behaviors: Total	62	59
	-Defiance/Temper	61	62
	-Aggression	47	51
	Social Functioning/Atypical Behaviors: Total	90	88
	-Social Functioning	90	80
	-Atypical Behaviors	90	90
	Anxiety	46	60
	Mood and Affect	61	63
	Physical Symptoms: Total	64	83
	-Sleep (Parent only)	40	n/a

(*continued*)

Table 7.26. (Continued)

Conners EC		Parent	Teacher
Index	Conners EC Global Index: Total	65	62
	-Restless-Impulsive	65	60
	-Emotional Lability	64	67
Other Clinical Indicators	Cruelty to Animals	√	—
	Fire setting	—	—
	Perfectionism	√	√
	Pica	—	—
	Posttraumatic Stress Disorder	—	—
	Self Injury	—	—
	Specific Phobia	—	—
	Stealing	—	—
	Tics	√	—
	Trichotillomania	—	—
Developmental Milestones	Adaptive Skills	85	78
	Communication	58	58
	Motor Skills	76	76
	Play	90	90
	Pre-Academic/Cognitive	45	44
Impairment	Learning/Pre-Academic	Severe	Moderate
	Peer Interactions	Severe	Severe
	Home	Severe	n/a

Note: High scores on the Conners EC indicate high levels of concern. All scores are T-scores unless indicated otherwise.

During this evaluation, Josh showed qualitative signs of impaired attention and executive functioning. He was easily *distracted* by external stimuli (including sights and sounds) and internal stimuli (e.g., unrelated thoughts). He showed little use of *strategy* or planning in his approach to problem solving and tended to give up or break the rules if the solution was not obvious. Even on simple tasks, Josh showed a haphazard approach.

Another aspect of executive functioning that was problematic for Josh was *self-regulation*. This was evident in his actions, comments, and emotions. *Impulsivity* is part of poor self-regulation, as it represents difficulty regulating impulses. During this evaluation, Josh was unable to remain still and quiet for even a short period of time. For example, during a test that required him to "be a statue," Josh began talking and moving after only 30 seconds (resulting in a below average score). As previously noted, Josh had a running commentary throughout the evaluation, interrupted only by singing or sound effects. When Josh was told to work quickly, he showed higher activity levels and spoke more loudly. His speech also became more dysfluent when he was pressured to talk quickly. By parent report, when Josh shows emotions, they are usually bigger than called for by the situation. These are all examples of poor internal self-regulation. People who have difficulty with self-regulation tend to show extreme rather than moderate reactions. They seem to lack a "filter" to regulate how they react to their environments. As a result, they often show a magnification of whatever is occurring internally or externally (e.g., when in an unstructured situation, they may become even more silly than other children).

Related to self-regulation is *self-monitoring*, or the ability to self-observe, then use feedback from your environment to change your behaviors. Josh had difficulty with aspects of self-monitoring, including monitoring work he had already completed. For example, during one task, he marked some items ahead of where he was working. When he later arrived at that part of the worksheet, he commented, "Hey, did somebody do this already? Because I see some marks here" (seeming to have forgotten that he was the one who had marked the answers). In contrast, Josh showed appropriate self-awareness during other tasks. For example, he often noticed his own errors (although he became almost paralyzed by these mistakes, requiring encouragement to continue working). He commented during one task that required fast but accurate work, "But if I go too fast I might [make a mistake], so I'm gonna go slow." Josh requested prompts and aids during some tasks, such as asking the examiner to "write the words" or "give me the pictures" after an auditory learning task. Thus, aspects of self-monitoring are intact for Josh, while others are problematic.

As noted in teacher ratings and parent interview, Josh shows limited *mental flexibility*. During a problem-solving task, he tended to quickly attempt one solution; when this did not work, he did not come up with an alternate solution. Josh also tends to become "stuck" (a.k.a., to *perseverate*) on an idea or activity. This is evident in his current fascination with information about his music CDs, which excludes any other writing or drawing.

Josh also had difficulty with *sustaining* his efforts. For example, although his attention could be externally directed to a task, he required ongoing prompts to keep his attention on the task; he could not independently sustain his own attention unless the task was inherently interesting to him. This can be confusing to parents and teachers when a child shows good ability to direct and sustain attention to a preferred activity, but limited attention to other tasks. It helps to remember that everybody pays attention better when they are interested in a topic or they are highly motivated; this is typical. Difficulty directing and sustaining attention is related to executive deficits, as by this age most children are developing the ability to control their attention, thus being able to intentionally direct and sustain attention even for boring tasks. Thus, technically Josh does not have a true "attention" problem, but a "control of attention" problem; regardless, it causes functional impairment in the classroom, home, and community settings. Another example of difficulty sustaining was observed in Josh's difficulty sustaining a problem-solving approach (i.e., he gave up quickly). As will be discussed in the Sensorimotor section of this report, this deficit was also apparent in Josh's motor functioning.

Another aspect of executive functioning that was difficult for Josh was *integration and segregation*. Josh tends to only process one piece of information at a time; therefore, when he is presented with multiple pieces of information that he must integrate, he misses most of the information. This results in a response that is "off target" overall, because he is responding only to the part of the information that he processed. This is consistent with observations that his answers to questions can be "tangential." It is also consistent with aspects of his limited interactive play, as playing alone allows him to control how much information he receives at a given time. Children who have difficulty integrating information are more likely to interact with adults, because most adults intuitively adjust their expectations based on a child's response. Another way of saying this is that Josh is a "sequential" thinker more than a "simultaneous" thinker; he is more successful when asked to complete a task using a clearly defined step-by-step process. The opposite process from integration is segregation, or being able to break a large task into smaller steps. When Josh is presented with a problem or task, he often becomes quickly overwhelmed by the complexity of the task and does not know what to do. A good example of this is his reaction when asked to clean his room. He does not even know where to begin with this task. In contrast, when a parent structures the task (i.e., breaks it into smaller steps, given one at a time, such as "pick up your toys and put them here"), Josh can successfully complete the "room cleaning task." As Josh enters higher academic grades, this deficit will become more apparent (e.g., when he is asked to write a paragraph, he will be expected to simultaneously perform tasks such as idea generation, word finding, spelling, handwriting, punctuation, and capitalization). These deficits in integration and segregation are already impacting Josh's social interactions, as described above.

Overall, attention and executive functioning is a primary area of deficit for Josh. Specifically, he has difficulty with attentional control, as required to intentionally direct and sustain attention. He shows executive dysfunction in the areas of initiation, working memory, mental flexibility, self-regulation, self-monitoring, sustaining effort, integration, and segregation. The best approach to intervention for a person with deficits such as these is to provide increased levels of external support, structure, and supervision. The long-term goal is to teach Josh successful habits and skills that provide external prompts/cues without forcing him to rely on other people (e.g., using a dayplanner to track what must be accomplished, rather than needing his parents to nag him when he is 20 years old).

Language: Both Mrs. Kane and Mrs. White report communication skills that are age-appropriate (*Conners EC: Communication*). During the evaluation, some articulation errors were noted, including /r/, /sh/, and /sw/ (e.g., said /twicky/ for "tricky," said /sell/ for "shell," said /sitch/ for "switch"). Stuttering was noted, particularly when Josh was pressured to speak quickly. Expressive and receptive language were generally functional, although at times Josh's language was overly formal. Josh generally understood task directions after one explanation. Nonverbal/gestural language was vague. Although Josh did point to his responses when requested to do so, he did not always use his index finger. He often simply *looked* at his response without providing a gestural cue (until prompted to "touch it with your finger"). At other times, he pointed to the space between two options, again requiring a prompt to touch his answer.

When Josh was asked to quickly name pictures of colored shapes, he showed a number of interesting errors. (In contrast, he accurately demonstrated knowledge of shapes, colors, and sizes in a nonpressured naming task). When rushed, he showed increased rates of stuttering (e.g., "b-b-b-big"). He showed incorrect sequencing of words (e.g., "black little square," "blue circle big") and repetition of words (e.g., "blue square, blue, blue, small"). This reflects limited internalization of an implicit rule for word order (i.e., a rule that is usually not taught explicitly, but is absorbed and applied spontaneously by most children). Josh had difficulty correcting himself when he made mistakes and often had to interrupt the naming task to get back on track (e.g., "y-y-y-" followed by throat-clearing, "Let's see, where was I . . . b-b-big red circle."). Josh flapped his hands and jumped during this task, and he spoke more loudly as the task progressed. He evidenced some anxiety when informed of the time limit, saying, "I can't, I don't have enough breath to do it."

During a following directions task, Josh often repeated the command after the examiner before selecting his response. At times, he repeated the command incorrectly (and made the corresponding error in responding). He still scored in the average range for his age; however, it is likely that, as he becomes older, his scores on receptive language tasks will drop. This prediction is made because Josh's executive deficits make it difficult for him to process complexity; this will impact his ability to follow directions that are lengthy, have embedded sequence words (e.g., "Touch the circle but first touch the square"), or have embedded exception/exclusion/inclusion words (e.g., "Touch all the circles but not the red one").

Thus, overall, basic expressive and receptive language skills are intact. Josh continues to demonstrate speech errors and should be evaluated by a speech-language pathologist to determine successful treatment approaches to use in speech therapy. Josh also shows deficits in higher order language, including pragmatics, organization, and automaticity. These types of deficits are common in children who have executive deficits and should be addressed within speech-language therapy sessions.

Visual Processing: This is an area of relative strength for Josh. He scored in the average range for his age on tests of visual perception and tests of visual-spatial construction. He scored in the above average range on a test of visual reasoning. Josh's choice of play activities (when not allowed to write CD information) reflects this natural talent, as he enjoys building and construction activities—all visual and hands-on. Josh's lowest score in this domain was on a design-copying task. This task requires integration of visual input with motor output; in other words, it requires executive functioning.

In sum, visual and hands-on modalities are appropriate ways to work with Josh. It is important to be aware of the impact of his executive deficits even in this area of strength. For example, it will still be important to avoid complexity and to reduce integration requirements when working with him.

Memory and Learning: Overall, Josh scored in the average range on tests of immediate memory. Immediate memory is the skill required to describe information immediately after hearing or seeing it. Josh accurately recalled several facts from a short story after hearing it once. He remembered an additional 11 facts when asked questions about the story. This again shows his benefit from external structure and prompts/cues (as described in the Executive Functioning section). Josh was also able to remember an average number of items from a picture card that he saw for a short time.

At this time, there are no immediate concerns about memory and learning. As Josh becomes older, it will be relevant to evaluate additional aspects of memory and learning, such as retention of information over a delay and strategy use in organizing information in memory. Given his executive deficits, it is likely that Josh will require explicit instruction to learn how to organize information as he memorizes it.

Sensorimotor Functions: Josh showed functional vision and hearing during this evaluation. He seemed aware of visual and auditory stimuli and responded appropriately. He walked independently. He grasped the pencil with his right hand, using a tripod grip very close to the pencil tip. It is interesting that, when the pencil was placed on the table rather than being handed directly to Josh, he picked it up with his left hand, then placed it into his right hand; this suggests that he may not be fully right-dominant. Pressure on the pencil was heavy, resulting in a concave index finger and dark pencil marks. In fact, he pressed so hard on the pencil that it moved his paper. He spontaneously anchored worksheets with his left hand. Both Josh's mother and teacher reported more concerns about motor skills than typical for a boy his age, including both fine and gross motor skills (*Conners EC: Motor Skills*).

As alluded to in the Executive Functioning section of this report, Josh's deficits in sustaining were shown not only with cognitive tasks (e.g., attention, effort), but also with motor tasks. Josh showed "motor impersistence" at times. This literally means difficulty sustaining a motor plan/program or a body position. For example, when Josh was asked to stand still with his eyes closed, he made significant efforts to keep his eyes closed (including tightly squeezing his eyelids shut); however, he could not sustain this motor program. He was not able to effortlessly perform this simple motor task by simply closing his eyes and keeping them closed. This may be part of the reason that Josh is constantly in motion, as he may have difficulty sustaining body positions such as sitting upright in his seat.

Josh also demonstrated subtle signs of neuromotor immaturity during a dexterity task and a hand movement task. These errors were primarily "overflow movements" (literally meaning that a motor command to a specific body part "overflows" to other body parts). One type of overflow movement demonstrated was "orofacial overflow" (overflow from the hand to the mouth and face); for Josh this included lips stretching side-to-side, mouth opening and closing, and tongue thrusts. He also demonstrated "mirror movements" (overflow from one hand to the other hand so that they move as if mirroring each other). He had difficulty when both hands were required to do things simultaneously, trying to modify the task so that each hand could work sequentially (rather than at the same time). Furthermore, Josh often used his other hand to position his fingers, suggesting that he does not have adequate motor control to isolate and direct individual fingers.

It is important to note that these types of neuromotor immaturity are still within the normal range at Josh's age. However, it is likely that they will persist given other aspects of executive dysfunction. These errors are already impacting his functioning. He scored in the impaired range on the dexterity task and in the low average range on the hand position task.

The outcome of these deficits in motor control, persistence, and inhibition is that Josh has more difficulty (at a neurologic level) isolating, sustaining, and directing his motor plans. This results in greater levels of fatigue after a shorter time using his fingers or hands in a coordinated manner (e.g., after handwriting). It is fairly common to observe these subtle neurologic signs in people who have executive deficits, as both reflect poorly developed frontal systems (including the white matter tracts that connect all the areas in the brain). In a sense, these overflow movements provide a physical demonstration of the poor inhibitory skills in Josh's brain. Practically speaking, Josh will likely require reduced expectations for handwriting (amount of handwriting and quality of handwriting). Written assignments will need to be shortened, or Josh will need to dictate or type his responses. (Typing requires less coordination of fine motor plans, especially if Josh is allowed to be a two-finger typist.) Thus, if Josh continues to show these subtle signs of neuromotor dysfunction as he becomes older, he will require accommodations and modifications.

Adaptive Functioning: Josh's mother and teacher each rated items about skills involved in adaptive functioning (*Conners EC: Adaptive Skills*). Adaptive functioning is age-appropriate ability to independently demonstrate skills needed for survival in life. These skills include dressing, eating/drinking, toileting, hygiene, and helping. Both raters described very high levels of concern about Josh's adaptive functioning.

Adaptive functioning involves two components: having skills and independently initiating their appropriate use. Discussion of items on the parent and teacher forms revealed that Josh generally possesses age-appropriate skills for adaptive functioning; however, he does not independently apply these skills. For the most part, he is *capable* of performing age-appropriate skills, but he does not consistently *demonstrate* these skills. Executive deficits (including initiation) can impact independent use of these skills. Motivational issues can also impact independence in adaptive functioning.

At home, Josh prefers to let others take care of him. Even when he has a cold, he will allow his nose to drain into his mouth rather than use a tissue from the box placed right next to him. He does not mind his mother wiping his nose. He will not get dressed or bathe himself unless offered a very strong incentive (e.g., a full bag of small chocolate candies). He does feed himself dessert independently, but must be fed by his parents for nonsweet foods. Again, he does not mind the foods being offered and willingly complies, but he will not feed himself even when he is hungry. In terms of toileting, Josh knows when he needs to go, but he does not seem to mind wet pants and often continues playing rather than pausing to go to the bathroom. Josh sometimes helps with household chores, when given sufficient incentive to do so.

In the school setting, Josh also tends to be passive. He responds well to routine, so he is more successful with toileting as all children are required to go to the bathroom at set times throughout the day. Otherwise, he shows the same concerns as noted at home.

Overall, Josh is currently showing more dependence on others than is expected at his age. He does not appear to have a "skill deficit" per se. It is likely that his executive deficits (including initiation) and motivation levels limit his independent demonstration of skills. It is important to explicitly work with Josh to improve his adaptive functioning. Suggestions for how to do this are included in the recommendations below.

Social, Emotional, and Behavioral Functioning: Parent and teacher ratings both indicate highly significant concerns about social problems (*Conners EC: Social Functioning*). Josh is making progress, but he continues to prefer playing alone to playing interactively with peers. He tends to be an observer rather than a participator, unless explicitly required by an adult to join in the activity. As mentioned above, these social deficits may reflect Josh's core executive deficits. He also seems to find his own thoughts and activities so interesting that he may have reduced motivation to seek new input from others. It is important to continue actively intervening to increase social interaction in order to prevent further isolation. As Josh becomes older, his quirks may be more noticeable to peers, and he may become the target of bullying. It is important to help Josh develop more appropriate social survival skills.

Mrs. White (Josh's teacher) indicated mild concerns about features of anxiety, including perfectionism. Mrs. Kane also reported signs of perfectionism, although her ratings of anxious behaviors were not high (*Conners EC: Anxiety, Perfectionism*). It is possible that these symptoms are more evident in the classroom setting, where Josh is more aware of performance and achievement. Consistent with this hypothesis, Josh showed features of anxiety during this evaluation, including perfectionism, avoidance of items that he might fail, and physical complaints when he was missing items. Indeed, both parent and teacher reports indicated high concerns about physical complaints, which is how young children often show feelings of anxiety (*Conners EC: Physical Symptoms*). When Josh missed an item, he required intervention to continue working because he was so focused on his mistake. It is critical to proactively address Josh's perfectionism before it begins to show a greater impact on his functioning. If left untreated, these symptoms could develop into an anxiety disorder.

Results from parent and teacher ratings indicate concerns about extreme emotions that change quickly (*Conners EC: Emotional Lability*). This is consistent with descriptions of Josh as showing more extreme emotions than called for in a given situation. This can accompany executive dysfunction. Mild concerns were expressed about Josh's mood and affect (i.e., his expression of his feelings; *Conners EC: Mood and Affect*). Careful review of these concerns with Josh's mother and teacher suggests that these issues are due to low levels of emotional involvement rather than unhappiness (e.g., "Prefers to play alone" can be a symptom of depression or, as appears to be the case for Josh, related to low desire to interact with others).

Parent and teacher report both described concerns about restlessness and impulsivity (*Conners EC: Restless-Impulsive*). Behaviorally, Josh shows high activity levels, appearing restless much of the time. He acts impulsively and has difficulty controlling his body movements and verbal comments/sounds. As he becomes more fatigued, he shows even more silliness, to the point that it is likely disruptive in a group setting. These behavioral concerns are related to executive deficits.

Josh generally responded to increased levels of support and structure at these times. It is important to recognize that these behaviors are red flags that he requires more support and structure, rather than interpreting them as "problem behaviors" that are "intentional."

Mild levels of defiance and temper issues were reported at home and school (*Conners EC: Defiance/Temper*). In interview, Mrs. Kane clarified that Josh does not defy her in general, but that she observes these behaviors when she directs him to stop a preferred activity and switch to a different task. Aggression was not reported as a concern in either setting (*Conners EC: Aggression*).

Other: Results from rating scales indicate parent and teacher concerns about Josh's play skills (*Conners EC: Play*). He tends to play repetitively, with little demonstration of imagination or variation on his repeated themes and counting. Neither Mrs. Kane nor Mrs. White has observed Josh using objects to represent different things or action figures to represent people. Josh has not demonstrated imitative play (e.g., pretending to teach, cook, or clean like the adults in his world).

On the *Conners EC*, Mrs. Kane indicated that Josh is "occasionally" cruel to animals. This item was discussed, and she clarified that, when he gets overexcited, Josh chases the family cat around the house until he hides. She has not seen him be intentionally cruel to any animal or person. She also endorsed an item describing sudden twitches, which can sometimes describe motor tics. Her explanation of this item revealed that she meant Josh's hand-flapping, which seemed like a twitch to her. There were no other behaviors that she was considering when she replied to this item.

≡ Don't Forget

Investigate Item-Level Data

Item-level review of the Conners assessments is important, particularly for the Critical items and Other Clinical Indicators. In Josh's case, two of the Other Clinical Indicator items were flagged for further investigation. Rather than simply reporting these results, it is important to investigate. Discussion in this case revealed that the "cruelty to animals" item was not inappropriate for Josh's age, and that he does not seem to be showing atypical cruelty that warrants an immediate and intensive intervention. Investigation also clarified that Josh does not seem to be showing tic-like movements at this time; rather, his stereotyped behaviors (hand-flapping) were reported here.

OVERALL IMPRESSIONS

Josh Kane, a 5-year-old boy, presented with a history of concerns about delayed early speech-language development in the context of current atypical interests and behaviors. Results from testing support intact cognitive development in general. Specific deficits are noted in attention and executive functioning. These deficits impact aspects of his functioning, including higher order language, motor control, and initiation of adaptive functioning skills. Other areas assessed are globally intact, including basic language, memory/learning, and pre-academic knowledge. Josh shows a relative strength in the visual domain.

Diagnostically, Josh shows a number of atypical features in the context of otherwise intact development. He shows appropriate use of eye gaze and facial expression but has some deficits in other aspects of nonverbal communication. He does not show a specific point but is vague. He rarely uses gestures such as head-nodding. He shows poor awareness of personal space (but has benefited from explicit instruction with the stated rule, "Stay an arm's length away"). Despite intact cognitive development, Josh does not show age-appropriate peer relationships, preferring to play alone or be with adults. He is interested in sharing his accomplishments with his parents but does not show the same interest in sharing with peers. Early language development was delayed, but Josh subsequently acquired a good vocabulary. At times, he uses overly formal language. His play is generally limited to a few activities that are repetitive. He also shows an overfocus on restricted interests. In the past, these interests included counting lamps in people's homes; currently he is fascinated with information about certain music CDs. At times, Josh can be inflexible, preferring routine. It is difficult to interrupt him when he is engaged in a preferred activity. He has a history of stereotyped mannerisms, including toe-walking. He continues to show hand-flapping when he is excited or frustrated. He tends to become fixated on small parts of objects, having trouble seeing the big picture at times. These deficits in social interaction, social language, and symbolic/imaginative play were present from an early age and have persisted. These issues are significantly impairing for Josh in multiple settings, including learning, peer interactions, and home. Thus, Josh meets DSM-IV criteria for a diagnosis of *Pervasive Developmental Disorder, Not Otherwise Specified (PDD-NOS)*. This diagnosis is in the same category as the diagnoses "Autistic Disorder" and "Asperger's Disorder." Josh does not show a sufficient number of criteria to qualify for a diagnosis of Autistic Disorder. Although the media and public often use the term "Asperger's" loosely to describe children like Josh, he does not meet the DSM-IV requirements for Asperger's Disorder given his early developmental delays in language.

As is common among children with PDD-NOS, Josh shows deficits in aspects of attention and executive functioning. These deficits do not require a separate diagnosis, although they will respond well to treatments used for similar symptoms of Attention-Deficit/Hyperactivity Disorder (ADHD).

Josh also exhibits features of anxiety, including perfectionism, task avoidance, and physical complaints. It is common for children in the PDD spectrum to show symptoms of anxiety, and Josh does not meet full DSM-IV criteria for a specific diagnosis at this time. These features of anxiety should be proactively treated, though, to reduce the probability that Josh will develop an identifiable anxiety disorder in the future. Given the extended family history of limited coping techniques, it is critical to provide Josh with adaptive and functional ways to express and cope with his feelings. Otherwise he is at risk for developing a mood disorder or substance use disorder.

These areas of concern are mitigated by a number of positive, protective factors. Josh is an interactive and engaging young boy. He shows an emerging interest in peer relationships. He uses spoken communication, and he has intact cognitive skills. Although he is "stubborn" at times, he can tolerate change (especially when he is given advance notice). He is a member of a supportive and caring family. All of these factors positively impact long-term prognosis for Josh and support intensive treatment efforts to facilitate further progress and development.

RECOMMENDATIONS

1. Educationally, Josh qualifies to receive special education and related services under federal handicapping condition Autism ("PDD-NOS"). As such, we recommend that an Individualized Education Plan (IEP) be created to reflect appropriate service programming. It is likely that Josh's needs can be appropriately met at this time in a general education classroom, if he is provided with sufficient accommodations and modifications. An appropriate educational environment for Josh will consist of individualized education planning including the following elements:

   - Age-appropriate to advanced curriculum that is taught with an emphasis on visual and hands-on modalities
   - High levels of teacher interaction, including some one-to-one instruction
   - Highly structured classroom setting, with consistent expectations and routines

- Speech and language services to address articulation and higher order language needs (pragmatics, nonverbal communication, and formulation/organization of language)
- Social skills training, including both individual instruction and classroom integration of skills
- Occupational therapy services to address written communication (handwriting, typing), fine motor skills (e.g., buttoning), and other activities of daily living

2. Josh needs increased levels of support and structure. Regardless of diagnosis, people with executive deficits require more external structure than their peers because they have less self-generated structure.

- Structure for Josh can be physical.
  - Create a study carrel for him at home that has all materials that he needs and physical barriers on the sides to help him keep his visual attention on the task.
  - Create a homework folder that Josh uses to place assignments in throughout the schoolday then uses to return completed homework from home. Josh will require assistance and reminders to use this folder until it becomes routine.
  - We also recommend using a communication book for Josh's teachers and parents to stay in touch about academics as well as emotional functioning at school. This can be a simple spiral-bound notebook that is kept in his homework folder and reviewed by parents and teachers each day.
  - Ensure that Josh is attending before beginning to teach new information. A gentle touch paired with his name can help orient his attention to the instructor.
- Structure can also involve time elements.
  - Establish a schedule with Josh so that he can predict what activity will be coming next. As Josh gains better coping skills, he will work toward tolerating the unexpected, but for the present time, he needs predictability and consistency.
  - Alternate types of tasks on Josh's schedule; for example, a hands-on problem-solving task after completing a written task.
  - Structure Josh's work time (at home or school) into brief working periods separated by breaks. Be certain to give him clear endpoints for each task.
- Structure can be cognitive.

- Give Josh a clear statement of rules or expectations before he begins a task or enters a situation. If his actions suggest that he may have forgotten a rule, politely and discreetly ask him about the rule. He may just need help remembering to remember the rule.
- Give Josh a short list of what needs to be accomplished so that he can learn to work more independently. At his current prereading stage, this list may use pictures. As he develops good use of lists, work with him to learn how to make his own lists.
- Teach one new concept at a time and build upon previously learned concepts. Help Josh see how new information relates to knowledge he already has and help him integrate these pieces. Make new facts meaningful for Josh. Use visuals to illustrate new facts and hands-on learning to strengthen his memory traces.

3. Given the initiation deficits that Josh has, he will likely require prompting to begin a task at home or school (unless it is highly familiar). This prompt may be direction from a person or a visual prompt such as a cue-card that lists the steps needed to successfully complete a recurring task. For example, the "morning routine" cue-card might include pictures of using the bathroom, eating breakfast, brushing teeth, washing face, taking off pajamas, putting on clothes, and so on. A similar approach can be used for recurring routines at school. It may be helpful to laminate these cue-cards or cover them with clear contact paper so that Josh can mark off items as he completes them. This establishes the beginning of a good habit that can develop into using lists and day-planners to initiate and organize tasks later in life. This is an example of an externalized prompt that allows more independence than reminders given by another person.

4. At times, it can be difficult to determine why a student is not complying with a request. This is even more difficult in students with executive functioning. Possible factors to consider and suggestions are discussed below:
   - One of the hallmarks of executive deficits is variability in performance. It is important to recognize that this variability from day to day (or even within a given assignment) is probably not due to "laziness" or "failing to apply himself." Help Josh compensate for his executive deficits by providing the structure and support he needs. Be aware of other variables that affect his performance, such as fatigue, emotions, or illness. Students with executive deficits are

often more reactive to these factors and may require increased levels of support at times.

- It is important to monitor your own frustration with this variability and slow progress so that it is not transferred to Josh. Try inserting several similar but easier items to determine if his nonresponsiveness is related to difficulty or to noncompliance. Be certain to always obtain some compliance (even if it is just giving a command that Josh is certain to follow, such as, "Josh, eat this candy") before ending a task so that he does not learn that noncompliance results in escape from tasks.

- Always leave a task on a positive note. Although it is necessary to challenge Josh in order for him to make progress, always allow time to return to easier items before ending a task to ensure that Josh associates success with the task. Otherwise, he may avoid the task in the future.

- Allow Josh some limited choice in his school and home environments. For example, if two worksheets must be completed, allow him to choose the order in which he completes them. Another way to integrate choice while still ensuring everything is completed is to give him different pens to use for assignments or to offer him the choice of writing his answers or typing them on the computer.

5. Given Josh's focus on accuracy and perfectionism, it is critical to monitor how feedback is provided about his academic and behavioral performance.

- Recognize that a negative comment will affect Josh more severely and longer than other children his age, and it will disrupt further concentration, attention, and problem solving.

- Those who work with him need to be conscious of responding to him in a warm, supportive manner using positive comments—strive constantly to find something to compliment and reinforce (for academic performance as well as behavioral control). In other words, "catch him being good and comment on it."

- Grade Josh's papers by marking the items he gets correct (rather than marking his errors). This reinforces that he is learning the skills or concepts and decreases his focus on mistakes. If he does not demonstrate skill mastery, identify what he has mastered and build on this skill base. Present errors as opportunities to work together, rather than as things he has done wrong.

- Teach Josh how to make mistakes without becoming upset. Point out to him the times that you make mistakes, including the fact that it is only human to have errors.

6. Josh often becomes "stuck" on details, especially if he has made a mistake. He may need help to step back and look at the big picture. Check in with him frequently to ensure that he is making progress on his work, rather than losing time on one answer.

7. Use explicit instruction (visual, hands-on, demonstration) and behavioral techniques to address the deficits in adaptive functioning. It is likely that Josh will make significant gains when these skills are addressed explicitly. The initiation aspect of adaptive functioning will be aided by use of routines and good habits (as described above). Skills to teach might include household chores, such as setting the table, gathering dirty clothes, and simple meal preparation (e.g., making a sandwich).

8. Along the same lines, use habit and routine to address other concerns, such as daytime enuresis. Without a behavioral analysis, it is difficult to be certain about the exact reason Josh continues to have this problem. It may be helpful to insist on a rule that associates going to the bathroom with another part of his daily routine (e.g., "Always use the bathroom and wash your hands before a meal"). If these concerns persist, the Kanes may wish to consult with a behavioral specialist for a more thorough analysis of behaviors and specific treatment plan.

9. Consistency is important for Josh. Given his mental rigidity at times, it is very easy to enter a "power struggle" with him. One solution to avoiding power struggles is to use redirection rather than opposition. Another solution is a consistent behavior management approach. His parents have tried using time-out sessions in the past, but these were described as "ineffective, because he likes spending time alone." The Kanes may wish to try time-outs again, but using a system that helps clarify how to set up an effective time-out program and why it works. One system that many families find helpful is described in the book *1–2–3 Magic*, by Dr. Thomas Phelan. This book has the advantage of describing not only a "stop" system (to stop undesired behaviors), but also including a "start" system (to increase occurrence of desired behaviors).

10. Use a concrete, visual system to track Josh's accomplishments and progress. This system will be effective both at home and at school. During this evaluation, Josh enjoyed earning a sticker for each completed task. He placed each sticker on a "sticker trail" that showed how many things he had to complete before he earned a play break (or

a preferred activity). Rewards do not have to be monetary or material; they can include special activities such as taking a nature walk or making s'mores. Involve Josh in developing a list of things he would like to earn, using pictures to illustrate these choices. It may be useful to rotate activities that are available so that Josh does not lose motivation due to boredom. As this system is begun, use current motivators (e.g., earning 15 minutes of CD time, doing a fix-it project with Dad), then gradually begin introducing new activities that will be equally motivating.

11. Schedule regular structured playdates for Josh with neighborhood children and classmates. Create an activity that he can do with this playmate, rather than asking him to manage a completely unstructured situation. Discuss the plan with Josh before his playmate arrives so that any anxiety will be reduced. Review appropriate aspects of social functioning that are relevant to the situation before the playmate arrives. Activities that he might enjoy include duckpin bowling, going for a hike on a nature trail, or going to a rock-climbing gym that provides helmets and harness support.

12. It is also recommended that Josh participate in community activities that provide him with the chance to interact with other children in a social setting other than school. If appropriate opportunities are not available in the community, the Kanes may need to be creative in developing activities. Josh can be encouraged to practice skills that he is learning at home and school in these community settings.

13. Continue supporting Josh's visual and hands-on strengths. Provide him with materials and opportunities to use these skills at home and school. These activities are important outlets for him, as well as a chance to reinforce Josh for doing something well that he enjoys.

14. If the Kanes want to learn more about treatment options for Josh, they may wish to consult books about Asperger's. Even though Josh does not technically have "Asperger's," most of these treatment strategies will be effective for him. In particular, there is a good chapter in the book *Asperger Syndrome* (2000, edited by Klin, Volkmar, & Sparrow) that is entitled "Treatment and Intervention Guidelines for Individuals with Asperger Syndrome." This chapter provides a good orientation to critical elements of instruction and other treatment. The Kanes may wish to request this book through their public library system so that they can review the information and decide if they would like to purchase the book.

15. Many parents find it helpful to participate in an organization such as the Autism Society of America (ASA). Even though Josh does not have "Autistic Disorder," his diagnosis of PDD-NOS is on the autism spectrum. Such organizations provide educational sessions as well as grassroots support for the issues that parents of children with autism-related symptoms face. The Kanes will likely find that they benefit from participating in their local chapter of the ASA, and they can help other families at the same time. Local chapters have resident knowledge of available community resources and strategies. The Kanes can find more information about PDD-NOS, as well as identify their local chapter of the ASA, on the Internet at www.autism-society.org. If the first local chapter meeting they attend focuses on the needs of students with more severe impairment, they may wish to visit another chapter to identify families who have similar issues to those they face with Josh.

Referrals

- The Kanes may wish to consult with a therapist who uses a combination of cognitive and behavioral techniques, as well as play therapy. This therapist should be a licensed professional who specializes in working with young children and their families, and who regularly sees children with anxiety. The primary goal of treatment is addressing features of anxiety through increasing coping skills, learning self-soothing techniques, and letting go of mistakes rather than fixating on them. The potential interaction of anxiety with social situations might also be addressed. Other goals for these sessions (depending on the therapist's areas of expertise) might include the daytime enuresis mentioned previously, or expanding age-appropriate play skills (to facilitate increased social interaction). It is important that Josh's parents are included in some sessions so that they can learn how to reinforce therapeutic techniques at home and support Josh's use of new coping skills. The Kanes should contact their insurance company to identify providers who can provide these services within their insurance network.
- Re-evaluation with a qualified pediatric neuropsychologist who has experience working with students in the autism spectrum. This re-evaluation is recommended in approximately two years to measure progress made and to ensure that treatment programs are providing appropriate services for Josh. It will be important to have an appropriate

treatment plan before he enters the 3rd grade as this is often an educational transition point (when students with executive deficits can have more difficulty).

The results of this assessment and these recommendations were shared and discussed with Josh's parents (Grace and Joshua Kane) in a feedback session. If there are further questions or concerns, please contact Dr. Sparrow.

Elizabeth P. Sparrow, PhD
Licensed Psychologist, Specializing in Clinical Neuropsychology

🐊 TEST YOURSELF 🐊

1. **Which of the following statements are *true* about written reports? *Mark all that apply.***
   (a) Only qualified professionals may read written reports.
   (b) Test names and scores should not be included in written reports.
   (c) Recommendations should be specific and individualized for each child.
   (d) A child's strengths and intact skills should be discussed.

2. **Once the Conners 3 has been given, you cannot also ask the rater to complete a Conners CBRS.**
   True or false?

3. **If you deviate from standardized administration of the Conners assessments, what should you do in the written report? *Mark all that apply.***
   (a) Report the scores as usual; only indicate variations from standardized administration if it is a legal case.
   (b) Describe any variations from standardized administration.
   (c) Do not report scores, as the results are not valid if you deviate from standardized administration.
   (d) Re-administer the Conners assessments in a standardized format before writing the report; ignore the first set of results.

4. **What should you do if results on the Conners assessments are different for two raters describing the same child? *Mark all that apply.***
   (a) Use the validity scales to decide which rater's results are more valid, and discard the other rater's results.
   (b) If the difference is between two parents, base your report on results from the parent who spends more time with the child.
   (c) If the difference is between two teachers, gather additional information to see which teacher knows the child better.

(d) Consider factors that could help you understand why these raters have different observations of the same child.

(e) Do not report results from the Conners assessments as they are inconclusive.

5. **It is inappropriate to review the rater's responses to individual items; only composite scores should be considered when interpreting results from the Conners assessments.**

   True or false?

6. **Even when you follow standard procedures for handling missing data, you still need to indicate that the scores were prorated in the written report.**

   True or false?

   Answers: 1. c, d; 2. False; 3. b; 4. d; 5. False; 6. True

Appendix A

ACRONYMS AND ABBREVIATIONS USED IN CONNERS ASSESSMENTS

Acronym/Abbreviation	Name/Meaning
ADHD	Attention-Deficit/Hyperactivity Disorder
AG	Defiance/Aggression (C3 Scale)
AH	*DSM-IV-TR* ADHD Hyperactive-Impulsive (C3 Scale)
AN	*DSM-IV-TR* ADHD Inattentive (C3 Scale)
AQ	Additional Questions
BPD	Bipolar Disorder
C3	Conners 3rd Edition™
C 3AI	Conners 3 ADHD Index
C 3GI	Conners 3 Global Index
CBRS	Conners Comprehensive Behavior Rating Scales™
CD	*DSM-IV-TR* Conduct Disorder (C3/CBRS Scale)
CI	Clinical Index
Conners EC	Conners Early Childhood™
CRS–R	Conners Rating Scale-Revised™
DD	Developmental Disability
DSM-IV-TR	*Diagnostic and Statistical Manual of Mental Disorders—Text Revision*
EBD	Emotional Behavioral Disability/Disorder
EC BEH	Conners Early Childhood Behavior
EC BEH(S)	Conners Early Childhood Behavior Short Form
EC DM	Conners Early Childhood Developmental Milestones
ECGI	Conners Early Childhood Global Index
ED	Emotional Disability
EF	Executive Functioning (C3 Scale/Subscale)
FR	Family Relations (C3–SR Subscale)
GAD	Generalized Anxiety Disorder

362

Acronym/Abbreviation	Name/Meaning
GI	Conners 3 Global Index Total (C3 Scale)
HY	Hyperactivity/Impulsivity (C3 Scale)
ID	Intellectual Disability
IDEA	Individuals with Disabilities Education Act
IDEA 2004	Individuals with Disabilities Improvement Act of 2004
IM	Impairment
Imp	Impulsivity
IN	Inattention (C3 Scale)
IncX	Inconsistency Scale (Validity Scale)
LD	Learning Disability
LE	Learning Problems/Executive Functioning (C3 Scale)
LP	Learning Problems (C3 Scale/Subscale)
MDE	Major Depressive Episode
ME	Manic Episode
MHS	Multi-Health Systems
NI	Negative Impression Scale (Validity Scale)
NOS	Not Otherwise Specified
OCD	Obsessive-Compulsive Disorder
OD	*DSM-IV-TR* Oppositional Defiant Disorder (C3 Scale)
ODD	Oppositional Defiant Disorder
OHI	Other Health Impairment
P	Parent Report
PI	Positive Impression Scale (C3/CBRS/EC Validity Scale Indicators)
PR	Peer Relations (C3 Scale)
PTSD	Posttraumatic Stress Disorder
RCI	Reliable Change Index
RTI	Response to Intervention
SAD	Separation Anxiety Disorder
SEM	Standard Error of Measurement
SR	Self Report
T	Teacher Report
USB	Universal Serial Bus
VPI	Violence Potential Indicator (CBRS)

Source: This list of abbreviations was compiled and provided by Dr. Penny Koepsel (personal communication, November 4, 2009).

Appendix B

CALCULATING A CONFIDENCE INTERVAL (CI) FOR CONNERS ASSESSMENTS

$$68\% \text{ CI} = T\text{-score} \pm SEM_1$$
$$95\% \text{ CI} = T\text{-score} \pm (2 \times SEM_1)$$

I t is not difficult to calculate a CI by hand. Standard Error of Measurement (SEM_1) can be printed on the computerized report (option to include). SEM_1 can also be looked up in the relevant test manual Reliability chapters. When looking up SEM_1 be certain to use the correct table for:

- Assessment type (which manual)
- Form (which chapter)
- Rater (which table)
- T-score (*not* raw score; which table)
- SEM_1 (*not* SEM_2; which section of the table)
- Gender (which column)
- Age group (which subcolumn)

For example, consider Brian Jones, a 9-year-old boy described in the first case study of Chapter 7. Ratings from his reading teacher, Miss Brown, produced a T-score of 71 for Conners 3-T Inattention. The Conners 3 manual, Chapter 11 Reliability, has tables for the full-length Conners 3 SEM_1 values. In my copy of the manual (first printing), Table 11.8 lists T-score *SEMs* for the Teacher form. Looking under SEM_1 in the "Male" column, I see the subcolumn for Brian's age group, "6-9." The SEM_1 for Inattention is 2.24, so this is the value I use to calculate a CI for the Conners 3-T Inattention scale.

$$T\text{-score} = 71$$
$$SEM_1 = 2.24$$
$$95\% \text{ CI} = 71 \pm (2 \times 2.24)$$
$$= 71 \pm (4.48)$$
$$= 66.52 \text{ to } 75.48 \text{ (which I would report as "95\% CI} = 67 - 75")$$

Appendix C

SAMPLE TABLES FOR REPORTS

Conners 3		Parent	Teacher	Self-Report
Response Style	Positive Impression			
	Negative Impression			
	Inconsistency Index			
Content	Inattention			
	Hyperactivity/Impulsivity			
	Learning Problems/ Executive Functioning	n/a		n/a
	Learning Problems			
	Executive Functioning			n/a
	Defiance/Aggression			
	Peer Relations			n/a
	Family Relations	n/a	n/a	

(continued)

Conners 3		Parent	Teacher	Self-Report
DSM-IV-TR	ADHD, Inattentive			
	ADHD, Hyperactive-Impulsive			
	Conduct Disorder			
	Oppositional Defiant Disorder			
Impairment	Academic			
	Social			
	Home		n/a	
Index Scores	Conners 3 ADHD Index	%	%	%
	Conners 3 Global Index - Restless-Impulsive - Emotional Lability			n/a
Screener Items	Anxiety			
	Depression			
Critical Items	Severe Conduct			

Note: High scores on the Conners 3 indicate high levels of concern. All scores are T-scores unless indicated otherwise.

Conners CBRS		Parent	Teacher	Self-Report
Response Style	Positive Impression			
	Negative Impression			
	Inconsistency Index			
Content	Emotional Distress	Total	Total	
		Upsetting Thoughts	Upsetting Thoughts/ Physical Symptoms	n/a
		Worrying	n/a	n/a
		n/a	SocialAnxiety	n/a
	Social Problems			n/a
	Separation Fears			
	Defiant/Aggressive Behaviors			
	Academic Difficulties	Total	Total	
		Language	Language	n/a
		Math	Math	n/a
	Hyperactivity	n/a		n/a
	Hyperactivity/ Impulsivity		n/a	
	Perfectionistic and Compulsive Behaviors			n/a
	Violence Potential Indicator			
	Physical Symptoms			
DSM-IV-TR	ADHD, Inattentive			
	ADHD, Hyperactive-Impulsive			

(*continued*)

Conners CBRS		Parent	Teacher	Self-Report
DSM-IV-TR	Conduct Disorder			
	Oppositional Defiant Disorder			
	Major Depressive Episode			
	Manic Episode			
	Generalized Anxiety Disorder			
	Separation Anxiety Disorder			
	Social Phobia			
	Obsessive-Compulsive Disorder			
	Autistic Disorder			n/a
	Asperger's Disorder			n/a
Impairment	Academic			
	Social			
	Home		n/a	
Index	Conners Clinical Index - Disruptive Behavior Disorder Indicator - Learning and Language Disorder Indicator - Mood Disorder Indicator - Anxiety Disorder Indicator - ADHD Indicator	%	%	%

Other Clinical Indicators	Bullying Perpetration			
	Bullying Victimization			
	Enuresis/Encopresis			n/a
	Panic Attack			
	Pervasive Developmental Disorder	(see above)	(see above)	
	Pica		n/a	
	Posttraumatic Stress Disorder			
	Specific Phobia			
	Substance Use			
	Tics			
	Trichotillomania			
Critical Items	Severe Conduct			
	Self-Harm			

Note: High scores on the Conners CBRS indicate high levels of concern. All scores are T-scores unless indicated otherwise.

Conners EC		Parent	Teacher
Response Style	Positive Impression		
	Negative Impression		
	Inconsistency Index		
Behavior	Inattention/Hyperactivity		
	Defiant/Aggressive Behaviors: Total - Defiance/Temper - Aggression		
	Social Functioning/Atypical Behaviors: Total - Social Functioning - Atypical Behaviors		
	Anxiety		
	Mood and Affect		
	Physical Symptoms: Total - Sleep (Parent only)		n/a
Index	Conners EC Global Index: Total - Restless-Impulsive - Emotional Lability		
Other Clinical Indicators	Cruelty to Animals		
	Fire setting		
	Perfectionism		
	Pica		
	Posttraumatic Stress Disorder		
	Self Injury		
	Specific Phobia		
	Stealing		
	Tics		
	Trichotillomania		

Developmental Milestones	Adaptive Skills		
	Communication		
	Motor Skills		
	Play		
	Pre-Academic/Cognitive		
Impairment	Learning/Pre-Academic		
	Peer Interactions		
	Home		n/a

Note: High scores on the Conners EC indicate high levels of concern. All scores are T-scores unless indicated otherwise.

Appendix D

CALCULATING CONNERS CI INDICATOR SCORES FROM FULL-LENGTH CONNERS CBRS FORM

O wners of this book may photocopy the following worksheets for use when calculating the Conners CI Indicators from the full-length Conners CBRS form.

Instructions for Worksheet Use:

1. Identify the rater type (parent, teacher, self).
2. Decide which method you will use to calculate the Conners CI:
   a. *Computer:* You have access to the Conners CBRS scoring software program and will enter the 24 items as a Conners CI form.
   OR
   You have access to the Conners online scoring program and do not mind paying to score the 24 items as a Conners CI form.
   b. *Hand-calculation:* You do not have access to the Conners CBRS scoring software program (or you do not wish to pay additional online scoring fees), but you do have access to the Conners CI QuikScore forms with embedded normative data tables.
3. Select the correct worksheet for the rater type and calculation method.
4. Use the Conners CBRS full-length form that was completed by the rater to record his ratings for the items listed on the worksheet.
5. Calculate the Conners CI Indicator scores.
   a. *Computer:* Simply enter the 24 ratings as a Conners CI form, using the same demographics and dates as recorded on the original full-length Conners CBRS. The Conners CI report will provide the five Indicator scores.
   b. *Hand-calculation:* There are two steps:
      i. Add the five ratings together for each Indicator and record this raw sum. Note the exception for one reverse-scored item on the Teacher form.

ii. Look up the *T*-score for each Indicator's raw sum using the *T*-score tables embedded within each Conners CI QuikScore form. Record this *T*-score.

1. Be sure you are using the correct QuikScore form for the rater type (parent, teacher, self).

2. Be sure you are using the correct page and column within the QuikScore form (boy/girl, age).

	Obtaining Conners CI Indicators from the Conners CBRS-P (Software Worksheet)		**Parent Software**

Indicator*	Full-Length Item #	Parent Rating	Conners CI Item
ADHD, ANX	4		1. Has trouble concentrating.
DBD	5		2. Has trouble controlling his/her anger.
ANX	7		3. Muscles get tense when worried about something.
DBD	13		4. Doesn't care about the feelings or rights of others.
MD	21		5. Feels rejected.
ADHD	23		6. Has trouble organizing tasks or activities.
LLD	26		7. Has trouble reading.
ADHD	28		8. Leaves seat when he/she should stay seated.
LLD	40		9. Has trouble sequencing the steps in math (for example, carrying or borrowing).
MD	53		10. Has lost interest or pleasure in activities.
MD	65		11. Does not follow through on instructions (even when he/she understands and is trying to cooperate).
LLD	66		12. Can pronounce words but has difficulty understanding what they mean.
ANX	68		13. Worries about many things.
DBD	75		14. Threatens others.
ADHD	86		15. Does not seem to listen to what is being said to him/her.

MD	94		16. Is sad, gloomy, or irritable for many days at a time.
DBD	127		17. Actively refuses to do what adults tell him/her to do.
LLD	128		18. Spelling is poor.
ANX	135		19. Worries about things before they happen.
LLD	158		20. Has trouble finding the right words.
MD	162		21. Takes a long time to complete classwork or homework.
DBD	163		22. Annoys other people on purpose.
ADHD	169		23. Interrupts others (for example, butts into conversations or games).
ANX	176		24. Avoids social situations or becomes distressed when required to participate.

*DBD = Disruptive Behavior Indicator, LLD = Learning and Language Disorder Indicator, MD = Mood Disorder Indicator, ANX = Anxiety Disorder Indicator, ADHD = ADHD Indicator

DBD Indicator T-score =
LLD Indicator T-score =
MD Indicator T-score =
ANX Indicator T-score =
ADHD Indicator T-score =

Obtaining Conners CI Indicators from the Conners CBRS-P (Hand-Calculation Worksheet)			Parent Hand-Calculation
Conners CI Item	**Full-Length Item #**	**Parent Rating**	**Indicator***
2. Has trouble controlling his/her anger.	5		DBD Sum = $T =$
4. Doesn't care about the feelings or rights of others.	13		
14. Threatens others.	75		
17. Actively refuses to do what adults tell him/her to do.	127		
22. Annoys other people on purpose.	163		
7. Has trouble reading.	26		LLD Sum = $T =$
9. Has trouble sequencing the steps in math (for example, carrying or borrowing).	40		
12. Can pronounce words but has difficulty understanding what they mean.	66		
18. Spelling is poor.	128		
20. Has trouble finding the right words.	158		
5. Feels rejected.	21		MD Sum = $T =$
10. Has lost interest or pleasure in activities.	53		
11. Does not follow through on instructions (even when he/she understands and is trying to cooperate).	65		
16. Is sad, gloomy, or irritable for many days at a time.	94		
21. Takes a long time to complete classwork or homework.	162		

1. Has trouble concentrating.	4		ANX
3. Muscles get tense when worried about something.	7		
13. Worries about many things.	68		
19. Worries about things before they happen.	135		Sum =
24. Avoids social situations or becomes distressed when required to participate.	176		$T =$
1. Has trouble concentrating.	4		
6. Has trouble organizing tasks or activities.	23		
8. Leaves seat when he/she should stay seated.	28		ADHD
15. Does not seem to listen to what is being said to him/her.	86		Sum =
23. Interrupts others (for example, butts into conversations or games).	169		$T =$

*DBD = Disruptive Behavior Indicator, LLD = Learning and Language Disorder Indicator, MD = Mood Disorder Indicator, ANX = Anxiety Disorder Indicator, ADHD = ADHD Indicator

			Teacher Software
Obtaining Conners CI Indicators from the Conners CBRS-T (Software Worksheet)			

Indicator*	Full-Length Item #	Teacher Rating	Conners CI Item
ADHD	5		1. Doesn't pay attention to details; makes careless mistakes.
ADHD	6		2. Acts as if driven by a motor.
MD	20		3. Fails to complete schoolwork or tasks (even when he/she understands and is trying to cooperate).
ANX	35		4. Becomes irritable when anxious.
LLD, ADHD	42		5. Avoids or dislikes things that take a lot of effort and are not fun.
DBD	54		6. Says mean things to others.
DBD	57		7. Doesn't care about the feelings or rights of others.
LLD	67		8. Does not give enough detail when answering questions.
LLD	78		9. Has trouble sequencing the steps in math (e.g., carrying or borrowing).
MD	89		10. Has periods of irritability lasting for at least one week.
DBD	105 (R)		11. Offers help or sympathy if someone is upset or hurt. (R)
LLD	110		12. Confuses math signs (e.g., $+$, $-$, x, $\div$).
ADHD	112		13. Leaves seat when he/she should stay seated.
MD	122		14. Seems tired; has low energy.
LLD	125		15. Has trouble understanding what he/she reads.

DBD	126		16. Actively refuses to do what adults tell him/her to do.
DBD	135		17. Is angry and resentful.
ANX	140		18. Complains about aches and pains.
MD	169		19. Feels inappropriately guilty.
ANX	186		20. Has trouble controlling his/her worries.
ANX	194		21. Appears "on edge," nervous, or jumpy.
MD	198		22. Feels rejected.
ADHD	199		23. Has trouble concentrating.
ANX	200		24. Panics about social situations or when doing things in front of people.

*DBD = Disruptive Behavior Indicator, LLD = Learning and Language Disorder Indicator, MD = Mood Disorder Indicator, ANX = Anxiety Disorder Indicator, ADHD = ADHD Indicator

(R) = reverse scored; enter teacher *rating* and the computer software will adjust.

DBD Indicator *T*-score =
LLD Indicator *T*-score =
MD Indicator *T*-score =
ANX Indicator *T*-score =
ADHD Indicator *T*-score =

Obtaining Conners CI Indicators from the Conners CBRS-T (Hand-Calculation Worksheet)			Teacher Hand-Calculation	
Conners CI Item	**Full-Length Item #**	**Teacher Rating**		**Indicator***
6. Says mean things to others.	54			DBD Sum = *T* =
7. Doesn't care about the feelings or rights of others.	57			
11. Offers help or sympathy if someone is upset or hurt. (R)	105 (R)	0 1 2 3	3 2 1 0	
16. Actively refuses to do what adults tell him/her to do.	126			
17. Is angry and resentful.	135			
5. Avoids or dislikes things that take a lot of effort and are not fun.	42			LLD Sum = *T* =
8. Does not give enough detail when answering questions.	67			
9. Has trouble sequencing the steps in math (e.g., carrying or borrowing).	78			
12. Confuses math signs (e.g., $+, -, x, \div$).	110			
15. Has trouble understanding what he/she reads.	125			
3. Fails to complete schoolwork or tasks (even when he/she understands and is trying to cooperate).	20			MD Sum = *T* =
10. Has periods of irritability lasting for at least one week.	89			
14. Seems tired; has low energy.	122			
19. Feels inappropriately guilty.	169			
22. Feels rejected.	198			

4. Becomes irritable when anxious.	35		
18. Complains about aches and pains.	140		
20. Has trouble controlling his/her worries.	186		ANX Sum = $T =$
21. Appears "on edge," nervous, or jumpy.	194		
24. Panics about social situations or when doing things in front of people.	200		
1. Doesn't pay attention to details; makes careless mistakes.	5		
2. Acts as if driven by a motor.	6		
5. Avoids or dislikes things that take a lot of effort and are not fun.	42		ADHD Sum = $T =$
13. Leaves seat when he/she should stay seated.	112		
23. Has trouble concentrating.	199		

*DBD = Disruptive Behavior Indicator, LLD = Learning and Language Disorder Indicator, MD = Mood Disorder Indicator, ANX = Anxiety Disorder Indicator, ADHD = ADHD Indicator

(R) This item is reverse-scored. Circle the rating in the first column, then circle the score in the second column. Use the *score* when calculating the sum for the DBD Indicator.

| Obtaining Conners CI Indicators from the Conners CBRS-SR (Software Worksheet) | | | **Self-Report Software** |

Indicator*	Full-Length Item #	Self Rating	Conners CI Item
DBD	6		1. I bully or threaten other people.
MD	16		2. The future seems hopeless to me.
ADHD	17		3. I interrupt other people.
LLD	18		4. I am behind in my schoolwork.
ADHD	29		5. I feel like I am driven by a motor.
ADHD	32		6. I have trouble keeping myself organized.
DBD	36		7. I know where to get a gun or another serious weapon when I need one.
LLD	57		8. It is hard for me to think of ideas for stories or papers.
MD	72		9. I feel like things are not going well in my life, and I can't do anything about it.
DBD	75		10. I do dangerous things.
MD	97		11. I feel like nobody cares about me.
LLD	102		12. Reading is hard for me.
ANX, ADHD	113		13. I have trouble keeping my mind on things.
ADHD	114		14. I run or climb even when I am not supposed to.
ANX	128		15. I have trouble stopping myself from worrying.
LLD	129		16. I have trouble following instructions.
ANX	137		17. I feel tired, like I don't have enough energy.
DBD	144		18. I do things to hurt people.

MD	146		19. I think about hurting myself.
ANX	150		20. When I'm worried, I suddenly have trouble breathing, or my heart pounds really fast.
DBD	157		21. People make me so mad that I lose control.
ANX	164		22. I have a lot of fears.
MD	167		23. I am discouraged.
LLD	169		24. I am a slow reader.

*DBD = Disruptive Behavior Indicator, LLD = Learning and Language Disorder Indicator, MD = Mood Disorder Indicator, ANX = Anxiety Disorder Indicator, ADHD = ADHD Indicator

DBD Indicator *T*-score =
LLD Indicator *T*-score =
MD Indicator *T*-score =
ANX Indicator *T*-score =
ADHD Indicator *T*-score =

Obtaining Conners CI Indicators from the Conners CBRS-SR (Hand-Calculation Worksheet)			Self-Report Hand-Calculation
Conners CI Item	**Full-Length Item #**	**Self Rating**	**Indicator***
1. I bully or threaten other people.	6		DBD Sum = T =
7. I know where to get a gun or another serious weapon when I need one.	36		
10. I do dangerous things.	75		
18. I do things to hurt people.	144		
21. People make me so mad that I lose control.	157		
4. I am behind in my schoolwork.	18		LLD Sum = T =
8. It is hard for me to think of ideas for stories or papers.	57		
12. Reading is hard for me.	102		
16. I have trouble following instructions.	129		
24. I am a slow reader.	169		
2. The future seems hopeless to me.	16		MD Sum = T =
9. I feel like things are not going well in my life, and I can't do anything about it.	72		
11. I feel like nobody cares about me.	97		
19. I think about hurting myself.	146		
23. I am discouraged.	167		
13. I have trouble keeping my mind on things.	113		ANX Sum = T =
15. I have trouble stopping myself from worrying.	128		
17. I feel tired, like I don't have enough energy.	137		
20. When I'm worried, I suddenly have trouble breathing, or my heart pounds really fast.	150		
22. I have a lot of fears.	164		

3. I interrupt other people.	17		
5. I feel like I am driven by a motor.	29		ADHD Sum = $T =$
6. I have trouble keeping myself organized.	32		
13. I have trouble keeping my mind on things.	113		
14. I run or climb even when I am not supposed to.	114		

*DBD = Disruptive Behavior Indicator, LLD = Learning and Language Disorder Indicator, MD = Mood Disorder Indicator, ANX = Anxiety Disorder Indicator, ADHD = ADHD Indicator

References

Achenbach, T. M., & Rescorla, L. A. (2001). *Manual for the ASEBA School-Age Forms & Profiles.* Burlington: University of Vermont, Research Center for Children, Youth and Families.

American Psychiatric Association (APA; 2000). *Diagnostic and statistical manual of mental disorders, 4th Edition, Text Revision.* Washington, DC: American Psychiatric Association.

Conners, C. K. (1969). A teacher rating scale for use in drug studies with children. *American Journal of Psychiatry, 126*: 884–88.

Conners, C. K. (1989, 1990). *Conners' Rating Scales manual.* Toronto, Ontario, Canada: Multi-Health Systems.

Conners, C. K. (1997). *Conners' Rating Scales—Revised Technical manual.* Toronto, Ontario, Canada: Multi-Health Systems.

Conners, C. K. (2008a). *Conners 3rd edition manual.* Toronto, Ontario, Canada: Multi-Health Systems.

Conners, C. K. (2008b). *Conners Comprehensive Behavior Rating Scales manual.* Toronto, Ontario, Canada: Multi-Health Systems.

Conners, C. K. (2009). *Conners Early Childhood manual.* Toronto, Ontario, Canada: Multi-Health Systems.

Conners, C. K., Epstein, J. N., March, J. S., Angold, A., Wells, K. C., et al. (2001). Multimodal treatment of ADHD in the MTA: An alternative outcome analysis. *Journal of the American Academy of Child and Adolescent Psychiatry, 40*: 159.

Conners, C. K., Erhardt, D., & Sparrow, E. P. (1999). *Conners' Adult ADHD Rating Scales (CAARS)—Technical Manual.* Toronto, Ontario, Canada: Multi-Health Systems.

Conners, C. K. & Research & Development Department, MHS (2009a). *Interpretive update to Conners 3.* Downloaded from http://downloads.mhs.com/conners/C3-Supplement.pdf on April 30, 2009.

Conners, C. K. & Research & Development Department, MHS (2009b). *Interpretive update to Conners CBRS.* Downloaded from http://downloads.mhs.com/conners/CBRS-Supplement.pdf on April 30, 2009.

Individuals with Disabilities Education Improvement Act of 2004 (IDEA 2004). Pub L. No. 108–446, 118 Stat 2647 (2004). [Amending 20 U.S.C. 1400 et seq.].

Gioia, G.A., Espy, K.A., & Isquith, P.K. (2003). *Behavior Rating Inventory of Executive Function—Preschool Version* (BRIEF-P). Odessa, FL: Psychological Assessment Resources, Inc.

Gioia, G. A., Isquith, P. K., Guy, S. C., & Kenworthy, L. (2000). *Behavior Rating Inventory of Executive Function* (BRIEF). Lutz, FL: Psychological Assessment Resources.

Gould, M. S., Marrocco, F. A., Kleinman, M., Thomas, J. G., Mostkoff, K., et al. (2005). Evaluating iatrogenic risk of youth suicide screening programs: A randomized controlled trial. *JAMA, 293*: 1635–1643.

Kovacs, M. (2003). *Children's Depression Inventory Technical Manual Update.* Toronto, Ontario, Canada: Multi-Health Systems, Inc.

March, J. S. (1997). *The Multidimensional Anxiety Scale for Children (MASC).* Toronto, Ontario, Canada: Multi-Health Systems, Inc.

Parker, J. D., Bond, B. J., Reker, D. L., & Wood, L. M. (2005). Use of the Conners-Wells Adolescent Self-Report Scale (short form) with children. *Journal of Attention Disorders, 8*(4): 188–94.

Reynolds, C. R., & Kamphaus, R. W. (2004). *Behavior Assessment System for Children, Second Edition* (BASC-2). Circle Pines, MN: AGS Publishing.

Schalock, R. L., Luckasson, R. A., Shogren, K. A., et al. (2007). The renaming of Mental Retardation: Understanding the change to the term Intellectual Disability. *Intellectual and Developmental Disabilities, 45*: 116–124.

Sparrow, S. S., Cicchetti, D. V., & Balla, D. A. (2005). *Vineland Adaptive Behavior Scales: Second Edition (Vineland II), Survey Interview Form/Caregiver Rating Form.* Livonia, MN: Pearson Assessments.

Substance Abuse and Mental Health Services Administration (SAMHSA). (2006). *Results from the 2005 national survey on drug use and health: National findings.* (Office of Applied Studies, NSDUH Series H-30, DHHS Publication No. SMA 06-4194). Rockville, MD. Retrieved August 10, 2007, from http://oas.samhsa.gov/nsduh/2k5nsduh/2k5results.pdf.

U.S. Department of Health and Human Services. (1999). *Mental health: A report of the surgeon general.* Rockville, MD: U.S. Department of Health and Human Services.

U.S. Department of Health and Human Services. (1999). *Mental Health: A Report of the Surgeon General.* Rockville, MD: U.S. Department of Health and Human Services, Substance Abuse and Mental Health Services Administration, Center for Mental Health Services, National Institutes of Health, National Institute of Mental Health. Retrieved August 10, 2007, from http://www.surgeongeneral.gov/library/mentalhealth/pdfs/front.pdf.

World Health Organization (WHO; 2004). ICD-10: *The international statistical classification of diseases and related health problems, Volumes 1-3,* Tenth revision, 2nd edition. Geneva: World Health Organization.

Annotated Bibliography

American Academy of Pediatrics (AAP; 2004). *Caring for your baby and young child: Birth to age 5, 4th edition.* New York, NY: Bantam Books.
  Can be recommended to parents; easy to read. Provides discussion of normal development, including relevant milestones, as well as tips regarding developmentally appropriate toys and activities. Includes discussion of concerns that may arise at various ages. At the time this manuscript was prepared, a 5th edition of this book was scheduled to be released.

American Psychiatric Association (APA; 2000). *Diagnostic and statistical manual of mental disorders, 4th Edition, Text Revision.* Washington, DC: American Psychiatric Association.
  Explains the structure and use of the DSM-IV-TR. Includes full diagnostic criteria for all diagnoses included on the Conners assessments, with additional text regarding differential diagnosis considerations.

Conners, C. K. (2008a). *Conners 3rd edition manual.* Toronto, Ontario, Canada: Multi-Health Systems.
  Includes the administration and scoring procedures for the Conners 3 as well as norms. Coverage of interpretation and intervention planning. Includes information about the reliability and validity of the Conners 3 as well as other psychometric characteristics of the measure.

Conners, C. K. (2008b). *Conners Comprehensive Behavior Rating Scales manual.* Toronto, Ontario, Canada: Multi-Health Systems.
  Includes the administration and scoring procedures for the Conners CBRS as well as norms. Coverage of interpretation and intervention planning. Includes information about the reliability and validity of the Conners CBRS as well as other psychometric characteristics of the measure.

Conners, C. K. (2009). *Conners Early Childhood manual.* Toronto, Ontario, Canada: Multi-Health Systems.
  Includes the administration and scoring procedures for the Conners EC as well as norms. Coverage of interpretation and intervention planning. Includes information about the reliability and validity of the Conners EC as well as other psychometric characteristics of the measure.

Hallowell, E. M. & Ratey, J. J. (1994). *Driven to distraction: Recognizing and coping with Attention Deficit Disorder from childhood through adulthood.* New York, NY: Simon & Schuster.
  Can be recommended to parents; easy to read. This book presents information about diagnosis and treatment through a series of vignettes and reflections. See also the companion volume by the same authors (Answers to Distraction, 1994), which is written in question-answer format and includes many practical tips about handling issues commonly associated with ADHD.

Klin, A., Volkmar, F. R., & Sparrow, S. S. (Eds). (2000). *Asperger Syndrome.* New York, NY: The Guilford Press.
  Written in a scholarly style, but contains worthwhile information. See particularly chapters on assessment issues, treatment/intervention guidelines, and adolescence/adulthood. The parent essays included toward the end of this book provide invaluable insight into the struggles and successes of people with Asperger's Disorder (as well as the survival tactics of their families).

Manassis, K. (2008). *Keys to parenting your anxious child,* 2nd edition. Hauppauge, NY: Barron's Educational Series.

Can be recommended to parents; easy to read. This book discusses the most typical anxieties that occur in childhood and adolescence, with a focus on how to help children cope with anxiety. Includes specific problem behaviors that can occur with anxiety.

Phelan, T. W. (2003). 1–2–3 Magic: Effective discipline for children 2-12. Glen Ellyn, IL: ParentMagic, Inc.

Can be recommended to parents; easy to read. This book helps establish an effective time-out program, including an explanation of why it works. Describes not only a "stop" system for undesired behaviors but also a "start" system for desired behaviors. Many examples help illustrate the points.

Siegel, B. (1996). *The world of the autistic child: Understanding and treating autistic spectrum disorders.* New York, NY: Oxford University Press.

Although written more than 10 years ago, this book remains one of my favorite books for those seeking to understand the Pervasive Developmental Disorders. Requires fairly sophisticated reading abilities, so may not be appropriate for all parents. Includes explanation of core deficits in autistic disorders and practical information about treatment resources. One of the few books to address parent reactions to this diagnosis, including the grieving process.

Shaywitz, S. (2003). *Overcoming dyslexia: A new and complete science-based program for reading problems at any level.* New York, NY: Knopf.

Can be recommended to parents; easy to read. Explains typical development of reading skills, and difficulties such as dyslexia. Includes practical treatment suggestions, including lists of resources and books on related topics. This book also provides a chapter about questions to ask when considering various reading programs. For those working with young children, see particularly section, "Clues to Dyslexia in Early Childhood" (in chapter entitled, "Should my child be evaluated for dyslexia?").

Sparrow, E. P. (2007). Empirical Bases for Assessment and Intervention. In S. Hunter & J. Donders (Eds), Pediatric neuropsychological intervention: A critical review of science and practice. Cambridge University Press.

Examines the purpose of assessment and explores the relationship between assessment and intervention. Includes discussion of how an assessment can guide intervention, and even serve as a form of intervention. Although written specifically about neuropsychological assessment and intervention, the general principles apply to any type of assessment and intervention.

About the Author

Elizabeth P. Sparrow, PhD, is a clinical neuropsychologist in Raleigh, North Carolina. She has collaborated with Dr. C. Keith Conners for over 15 years in clinical, research, and assessment development projects. She served as the primary clinical consultant for development and standardization of the Conners assessments, and continues to provide training on practical applications of these tools in schools, clinics, and research settings. Her publications reflect a strong commitment to improving psychological assessment and intervention for children and adults.

About the Contributors

Sara Rachel Rzepa, M.A., is the Manager of Data & Psychometrics at Multi-Health Systems, Inc. She has a strong background in statistics and psychometrics, and provided the statistical content for Chapter 1 of this book. Ms. Rzepa was an integral member of the development team for the Conners assessments. She has also been involved in development of numerous other MHS projects, including the Autism Spectrum Rating Scales (ASRS), the Multidimensional Perfectionism Scale (MPS), and the Social Adjustment Scale-Self Report (SAS-SR): Short and Screener. Ms. Rzepa continues to publish and present on statistical aspects of these many assessment tools.

Jenni Pitkanen, M.Sc., is the Manager of Product Development at Multi-Health Systems, Inc. Ms. Pitkanen played a pivotal role in the development of the Conners 3, Conners CBRS, and Conners EC. She co-authored Chapter 2 in this book, and also contributed to Chapter 1. Prior to her work on the Conners assessments, Ms. Pitkanen coordinated the Canadian standardization projects for the Wechsler Preschool and Primary Scale of Intelligence–Third Edition (WPPSI-III) and Wechsler Intelligence Scale for Children–Fourth Edition (WISC-IV). She is currently working to develop other assessment tools for clinical and educational use. Ms. Pitkanen often presents for local and national conferences on the Conners assessments as well as other measures published by MHS.

INDEX

Abbreviated Symptom Questionnaire (ASQ), 10, 13

Abbreviations used on Conners assessments, 362–363

Ability vs. opportunity, 166, 168

Absolute difference (Inconsistency Index), 122, 139–140

Absolute vs. relative (DSM-IV-TR Symptom scales), 162–163

Academic content of Conners assessments, 21, 185, 194, 198, 202

Acronyms used on Conners assessments, 362–363

Across-informant correlations, 56, 60, 62, 211

Adaptive Skills. *See* Conners EC Developmental Milestone scales: Clusters/subclusters

Additional questions, 22, 29, 31, 33, 37, 39, 43–44, 46-47, 49, 87, 92, 96, 98-99, 114, 117, 126, 131, 134, 149, 177, 186, 195, 199, 203, 362

ADHD. *See* Attention-Deficit/Hyperactivity Disorder

ADHD Index on Conners 3. *See* Conners 3 ADHD Index (Conners 3AI)

ADHD Index on CRS-R, 10, 18, 22

ADHD Indicator. *See* Conners Clinical Index (Conners CI, on Conners CBRS)

Administration:
  common rater errors, 98, 105, 151
  computerized (*See* Administration options)
  convenience, 79, 113
  cost, 78–79, 214
  environment, 80, 81
  limitations, 79, 213–214
  materials, 76–80, 137, 220
  online (*See* Administration options)
  options
    compared, 29–30, 37–38, 44–45, 78–79
    computerized, 28, 30, 38, 43, 45, 76–77, 78–79, 80, 81, 98–99, 103–104, 210, 213–214
    paper-and-pencil, 30, 38, 45, 76–77, 78–79, 103
  paper and pencil (*See* Administration options)
  preparation, 80
  procedures, 73–74, 80, 81, 84, 97–105, 213–214, 388
  software (*See* Administration options)

time requirement, 30, 38, 45, 80
tips, online, 98–99

Adoptive parent(s). *See* Who can rate Conners assessments

Age-based norms, 48–49

Age effects, 17, 48–49, 50–51, 211, 219

Age range, 2, 15, 16–17, 20, 83, 85, 88, 93, 151, 207, 209

Age references, 135, 136, 148, 165–168, 179

Ages of attainment, 135–136, 148, 165–168, 179

Analyses of Covariance (ANCOVAs), 63, 230–231

ANCOVA. *See* Analyses of Covariance

Annotated bibliography, 388–389

Answering rater questions, 73–74, 98, 99–100, 105

Anxiety Disorders. See also specific diagnoses in this category.
  Case studies, 271, 286, 289, 319–320, 321, 323–324, 329, 346, 350, 353, 358, 359
  General information, 28, 42, 193, 196–197, 201, 228–229, 255, 256, 262, 263–265, 266, 362–363, 389

Anxiety Disorder Indicator. *See* Conners Clinical Index (Conners CI, on Conners CBRS)

Anxiety items on the Conners 3. *See* Conners 3 Screener items

Applications of Conners assessments, 7–8, 81–84, 104, 221–227

Appropriate raters for Conners assessments, 3, 29, 37, 44, 74–76, 77, 224–225

Asperger's Disorder, 40, 42, 46, 90, 172, 199, 228–229, 265–267, 389. *See also* Case Studies: Asperger's Disorder

ASQ. *See* Abbreviated Symptom Questionnaire

Assessment Report. *See* Report options

Attention-Deficit/Hyperactivity Disorder (ADHD)
  Case studies, 288–289, 295, 323–324, 353. *See also* Case Studies: ADHD Predominantly Inattentive type
  General information, 18–19, 27–28, 31–32, 42, 81–82, 83, 87, 89, 92, 162, 170, 172–174, 183, 193–194, 196, 198, 200–202, 225, 228–229, 231, 254–255, 256–257, 258, 362, 388

Autism spectrum. *See* Pervasive Developmental Disorders (PDD)

Autistic Disorder
    Case studies, 314, 352–353, 359
    General information, 40, 42, 46, 90, 172, 194,
        198, 199, 202, 265–267, 389

Background information, recommended topics,
        190–191, 270. *See also* Case Studies:
        Background information
Base rates, 135, 136, 148, 165–168, 177, 179, 182
Behavior scales. *See main entry* Conners EC
        Behavior scales
Behavioral content of Conners assessments, 20,
        184, 192–193, 196, 200–201
Bipolar Disorder. *See* Mood Disorders
Book recommendations for parents, teachers, and
        professionals, 388–389
Building blocks for mood disorders. *See* Mood
        Disorders
Bullying, 90, 156, 157, 159, 193, 196, 350

CADS. *See* Conners' ADHD/DSM-IV Scales on
        CRS-R
Calculating confidence intervals (CI), 120, 364
Calculating Conners Clinical Index (Conners CI)
        Indicator scores, 43, 114, 130–131, 175,
        372–385
Case studies illustrating use of:
    Conners 3, 271–294
    Conners CBRS, 295–330
    Conners EC, 331–360
Case studies. *See also* Conners 3 case study;
        Conners CBRS case study; Conners EC
        case study; Test results and
        observations/interpretation (case
        studies)
    ADHD, Predominantly Inattentive type, 282,
        288–289, 313, 320, 323–324
    Anxiety Disorder NOS, 323
    Anxious features, 286, 289, 319–321, 323–324,
        329–330, 346, 350, 353, 358–359
    Asperger's Disorder, 314, 330, 352, 358
    background information, 271–274, 296–299,
        331–335
    diagnostic impressions, 288–290. *See also* Case
        studies: Overall impressions
    evaluation procedures, 274–275, 299, 335
    Expressive Language Disorder, 323
    general presentation, *See* Test results and
        observations/interpretation (case
        studies)
    medication monitoring, 294, 320–321, 329
    Obsessive-Compulsive features, 290
    overall impressions, 322–324, 352–353. *See also*
        Case studies: Diagnostic Impressions
    PDD-NOS, 352–353, 359
    Reading Disorder, 323, 330
    recommendations, 270, 290–294, 324–330,
        353–360
    referral question(s), 271, 295, 330–331

    referrals, 294, 359–360. *See also* Resources and
        referrals
    resources and referrals, 329–330. *See also*
        Referrals.
    summary of results, *See* Test results and
        observations/interpretation (case
        studies)
    tics, 290, 351
    validity statement, 275, 299–300, 336
CASS. *See* Conners'-Wells Adolescent Self-Report
        Scale on CRS-R
Categorical scoring, 117–119
CD. *See* Conduct Disorder
CGI. *See* Conners Global Index
Childcare Provider form. *See* Conners EC
        Teacher/Childcare Provider form
Choosing a Conners assessment, 81–83. *See also*
        Form selection
Classification rate. *See* Overall correct classification
        rate
Clinical Index. *See* Conners CBRS: Clinical Index
        (Conners CI)
Clinical judgment, 19, 26, 121–122, 143, 155–156,
        161–162, 165, 176, 181, 189
Clinical samples, 5, 17, 19, 26, 50–55, 63, 172, 175,
        195, 208, 210, 212, 227–229, 230–267
Clinical significance, 116, 189, 223
Clinical study questions, 230–231
Clinical training, 3, 73–74, 107–108, 115, 155–156,
        162, 192, 218,
Cognitive/academic content of Conners
        assessments, 21, 185, 194, 198, 202
Combined gender norms, 17, 48–49, 120, 135, 214
Common characteristics of high scorers, 112, 120,
        124, 125, 127, 132, 133, 155–160, 164,
        176, 191
Communication. *See* Conners EC Developmental
        Milestone scales: Clusters/subclusters
Comorbid, 6, 16, 18, 28, 219, 256–258, 263
Comparative report. *See* Report options
Computerized administration tips. *See*
        Administration tips
Computerized report. *See* Report options
Computerized scoring. *See* Scoring options
Computerized scoring tips. *See* Scoring tips
Computerized testing. *See* Administration options
Concerns. *See* Additional questions
Conduct Disorder (CD), 31, 39, 86, 89, 193, 196,
        201, 257–258, 362
Confidence intervals for T–scores (CI),
        120, 364
Conners 3
    additional questions, 31, 33, 87, 114, 126, 195,
        203. *See also main entry* Additional
        questions
    ADHD Index (Conners 3AI), *See* Conners 3
        ADHD Index
    Administration options, 29–30. *See also main
        entry* Administration

age range, 2, 20, 83, 85, 209. *See also main entry*
    Age range
case study, Brian Jones, 271–294. *See also* Case
    Studies; Test results and observations/
    interpretation (case studies)
    DSM-IV-TR Symptom scale: ADHD
        Inattentive, 282, 288
    Executive Functioning scale, 281, 284
    Hyperactivity/Impulsivity scale, 281, 284
    Inattention scale, 281, 284
    Learning Problems subscale, 277–278, 281
    Peer Relations scale, 281, 286
    Restless-Impulsive subscale, 282, 284
    Screener items, 282, 286
Content scales, 23, 31–32, 85, 114, 124, 148,
    154–156
Critical items, 182–184, 185, 194, 201. *See also main
    entry* Critical Items
vs. CRS–R, 15, 17–19, 20–22, 23, 33, 175, 203, 209
    development, 10, 14–15, 16, 17–19, 20–23,
        24–27
    DSM-IV-TR Symptom scale: ADHD
        Inattentive (case study), 282, 288
    DSM-IV-TR Symptom scales
        general information, 29, 31, 32, 86, 114, 118,
            121–122, 156, 158,161–163, 201, 211,
            215, 219
        symptom counts, 32, 111, 114, 119, 120,
            121–122, 125, 144–145,148, 158,
            161–162, 163, 182
        T-scores, 32, 114, 125, 144, 148, 156, 158,
            163
    examiner requirements, 3, 107–108, 115, 120,
        135, 143, 155, 214, 215
    Executive Functioning scale (case study), 281,
        284
    forms, 3, 28–30, 59, 74, 77, 83–84, 85–87, 110,
        187
    Global Index (Conners 3GI), *See* Conners 3
        Global Index
    Hyperactivity/Impulsivity scale (case study),
        281, 284
    Impairment Items, 22, 29, 31, 33, 87, 114, 125,
        148, 186, 195, 203. *See also main entry*
        Impairment Items
    Inattention scale (case study), 281, 284
    interpretation,
        with Conners CBRS, 148–149, 184–186,
            192–195
        with Conners EC, 148–149, 184–186,
            200–203
        with CRS–R, 175, 203
    interpretive text, 154, 155–156, 171, 173–174,
        176
    interpretive updates, 24, 32, 138, 139–141, 151,
        153, 154, 156, 206, 208, 213, 215, 386
    languages, *See* Translations
    Learning Problems subscale (case study),
        277–278, 281

length of forms, 29, 83–84
options, 29–30
overview tables, 2–3, 11, 20–22, 23, 29–30, 31
Peer Relations scale (case study), 281, 286
purpose, 2, 82–83
rater requirements, 3, 74–76, 77
rater types, 29, 32, 58, 59–60, 62–63, 74–75,
    187, 210, 212, 224–225
reading levels, 3, 18, 34, 76–77, 102, 209
report types, *See main entry* Report: Types
    (Assessment, Progress, Comparative)
Restless-Impulsive subscale (case study), 282,
    284
sample tables, 281–282, 365–366
scales/subscales listing, 31
scoring. *See main entry* Scoring
Screener items, 18, 20–21, 23, 29, 31, 32, 83, 86,
    114, 122–123, 126, 149, 177, 181, 184,
    193, 201
Screener items (case study), 282, 286
structure, 31
time required, 30
Validity scales, 24, 29, 32–33, 63, 64, 65, 87, 122,
    124, 138, 148, 195, 203, 388. *See also*
    Interpretation: Validity scales; Validity
    scales
Conners 3 ADHD Index (Conners 3AI)
    form, 3, 11, 18, 29–30, 59, 62, 77, 84, 85–87,
        107, 110, 114, 138, 215
    scale, 18, 22, 31, 33, 86, 114, 118–119, 125, 138,
        170–172, 173–174, 175, 186, 195, 203,
        230, 254, 256
Conners 3 Global Index (Conners 3GI)
    form, 3, 11–12, 29–30, 59, 62, 77, 84, 85–87,
        107, 110, 114, 125, 138, 215
    scale, 22, 33, 47, 86, 114, 125, 138, 148,
        175–176,186, 203
    subscales, 86, 114, 125, 138, 148, 153,
        175–176
Conners 3AI. *See* Conners 3 ADHD Index
Conners 3GI. *See* Conners 3 Global Index
Conners 3rd Edition. *See* Conners 3
Conners 3(S). *See* Conners 3 Short form
Conners 3 Short form (Conners 3(S)), 18, 29–30,
    59, 77, 84, 85–87, 110
Conners 3 vs. Conners CBRS, 185–187
Conners 10-item scale, 9, 10
Conners' ADHD/DSM-IV Scales on CRS-R
    (CADS), 13
Conners CBRS:
    Academic Difficulties scale (case study), 304,
        312
    additional questions, 39, 43, 92, 114, 131, 195,
        199. *See also main entry* Additional
        questions
    administration options, 37–38. *See also main entry*
        Administration
    age range, 2, 20, 83, 88, 209. *See also main entry*
        Age range

Conners CBRS (*continued*)
case study, Darby Reed, 295–330. *See also* Case
   Studies; Test results and observations/
   interpretation (case studies)
Clinical Index, 314, 323
Defiant/Aggressive Behaviors scale, 312, 320
Emotional Distress scale/subscales, 312, 320
Hyperactivity scale, 313, 320
Hyperactivity/Impulsivity scale, 313, 320
importance of multi's, 305
missing data, 305, 315
Perfectionistic and Compulsive Tendencies,
   313, 320, 323
reading aloud, 299–300
Separation Fears, 312, 320, 323
Social Anxiety scale, 312, 319, 320, 323
Social Problems scale, 312, 319
Clinical Index (case study), 314, 323
Clinical Index (Conners CI), *See* Conners
   Clinical Index (Conners CI)
common characteristics of high scorers,
   157–158. *See also main entry* Common
   characteristics
Content scales, 23, 39–40, 88–89, 114, 127–128,
   148, 154, 156–158
Critical items, 41, 90, 182–184, 185, 194,
   197–198. *See also main entry* Critical
   Items
vs. CRS–R, 15, 17–19, 20–22, 23, 203, 209
Defiant/Aggressive Behaviors scale (case
   study), 312, 320
development, 10, 14–15, 16, 17–19, 20–23,
   24–27
DSM-IV-TR Symptom Scales
   general information, 37, 39, 40, 89–90, 114,
      118, 121–122, 156, 158, 161–163,
      196–197, 211, 215, 219
   symptom counts, 40, 111, 114, 119, 120,
      121–122, 128–129, 144–145, 148, 158,
      161–162, 163, 182
   T-scores, 40, 114, 128–129, 144, 148, 156,
      158, 163, 183
Emotional Distress Scale/subscales (case
   study), 312, 320
examiner requirements, 3, 107–108, 115, 120,
   135, 143, 155, 214, 215
forms, 3, 37–38, 60, 74, 77, 83–84, 88–92, 175,
   187, 372–385
Hyperactivity scale (case study), 313, 320
Hyperactivity/Impulsivity scale, 313, 320
Impairment items, 22, 37, 39, 43, 91, 114, 129,
   148, 186, 195, 199. *See also main entry*
   Impairment Items
interpretation,
   with Conners 3, 148–149, 184–186, 192–195
   with Conners EC, 148–149, 184–186,
      195–199
   with CRS–R, 203
interpretive text, 154, 157–158, 171, 178

interpretive updates, 24, 39, 41, 119, 139–141,
   151, 153, 154, 157–158, 161, 177, 178,
   206, 208, 213, 215, 386
languages, *See* Translations
length of forms, 37, 83–84
modified administration (case study), 300
options, 37–38
Other Clinical Indicators, 20–22, 24, 39–41,
   90–91, 114, 123, 130–131, 141, 149,
   177, 181, 184–186, 193–194, 196–197,
   199. *See also main entry* Other Clinical
   Indicators
overview tables, 2–3, 11, 20–22, 23, 37–38, 39
Perfectionistic and Compulsive Tendencies
   (case study), 313, 320, 323
purpose, 2, 82–83
rater requirements, 3, 74–76, 77
rater types, 37, 40, 58, 60, 62–63, 74–75, 187,
   210, 212, 224–225
reading levels, 3, 18, 34, 76–77, 102, 209
report types, *See main entry* Report: Types
   (Assessment, Progress, Comparative)
sample tables, 312–315, 367–369
scales/subscales listing, 39
scoring, *See main entry* Scoring
Separation Fears (case study), 312, 320, 323
Social Anxiety scale (case study), 312, 319, 320,
   323
Social Problems scale (case study), 312, 319
structure, 39
time required, 38
Validity scales, 18, 22, 37–39, 41–42, 139, 186.
   See also Interpretation: Validity scales;
   Validity scales
Conners CBRS vs. Conners 3, 184–186, 192–199
Conners CI Indicator worksheets. *See* Conners
   Clinical Index
Conners CI Indicator scores, *See* Conners Clinical
   Index
Conners Clinical Index (Conners CI, on Conners
   CBRS)
case study illustrating use of, *See* Conners CBRS:
   Case study: Clinical Index
form, 3, 11, 18, 37–38, 60, 62, 77, 84,
   88–92, 107, 110, 114, 129–130, 138,
   175, 215
Indicators, 42–43, 90, 114, 129–131, 138, 175,
   183, 254–255, 372–385
   ADHD Indicator, 90, 130, 175, 183, 225,
      255, 256
   Anxiety Disorder Indicator, 90, 130, 175,
      255, 265
   Disruptive Behavior Disorder Indicator, 90,
      129, 175, 254, 258
   Learning and Language Disorder Indicator,
      90, 130, 175, 254, 259
   Mood Disorder Indicator, 90, 130, 175, 255,
      262–263
   Indicator worksheets, 372–385

scale, 22, 42–43, –90, 114, 129–130, 138, 170–172, 175, 186, 199, 195, 230, 254–255
Conners Comprehensive Behavior Rating Scales. *See* Conners CBRS
Conners Early Childhood. *See* Conners EC
Conners Early Childhood Behavior. *See* Conners EC Behavior
Conners Early Childhood Behavior Short form. *See* Conners EC Behavior Short form
Conners Early Childhood Developmental Milestones. *See* Conners EC Developmental Milestones
Conners Early Childhood Global Index. *See* Conners EC Global Index
Conners EC:
  Adaptive Skills cluster (case study), 342, 349
  Additional questions, 47, 49, 96, 114, 134, 199, 203. *See also main entry* Additional questions
  administration options, 44–45. *See also main entry* Administration
  age range, 2, 83, 93, 209. *See also main entry* Age range
  Aggression subscale (case study), 341, 351
  Anxiety scale,
    case study, 341, 350
    General information, 93, 132, 160, 180, 184, 197, 201, 265
    item-level analysis, 177, 180
  Behavior scales, *See main entry* Conners EC Behavior scales
  Case study, Josh Kane, 330–360. *See also* Case Studies; Test results and observations/ interpretation (case studies)
    Adaptive Skills cluster, 342, 349
    Aggression subscale, 341, 351
    Anxiety scale, 341, 350
    Communication cluster, 342, 345
    cruelty to animals, 342, 351
    Defiance/Temper subscale, 341, 351
    Emotional liability subscale, 342, 350
    Inattention/Hyperactivity subscale, 339, 341
    item-level data, 351
    Mood and Affect scale, 341, 350
    Motor Skills cluster, 342, 347
    Perfectionism, 342, 350, 353
    Physical Symptoms scale, 341, 350, 353
    Play cluster, 342, 351
    Pre-Academic/Cognitive cluster, 339, 342
    Restless-Impulsive subscale, 342, 350
    Social Functioning scale, 341, 349
    tics, 342, 351
  common characteristics of high scorers, 159–160, 164, 176. *See also main entry* Common characteristics
  Communication cluster (case study), 342, 345
  vs. CRS–R, 47, 175, 209
    case study, 339, 341

cruelty to animals, 342, 351
Defiance/Temper subscale (case study), 341, 351
development, 15–19, 24–27
Developmental Milestone scales, *See main entry* Conners EC Developmental Milestone scales
Emotional Lability subscale (case study), 342, 350
examiner requirements, 3, 107–108, 115, 120, 135, 136, 143, 155, 214, 215
forms, 3, 43–45, 61, 74–75, 77, 83–84, 93–96, 187
Global Index (Conners ECGI), *See* Conners EC Global Index
Impairment Items, 44, 47, 49, 95, 114, 134, 149, 186, 199, 203. *See also main entry* Impairment Items
Inattention/Hyperactivity scale
item-level analysis, 179
interpretation,
  with Conners 3, 148–149, 184–186, 200–203
  with Conners CBRS, 148–149, 184–186, 195–199
  with CRS–R, 175
interpretive text, 154, 159–160, 164, 167–168, 176, 179, 180
investigating item-level data (case study), 351
languages, *See* Translations
length of forms, 44, 83–84
Mood and Affect scale (case study), 341, 350
Motor Skills cluster (case study), 342, 347
Options, 44–45
Other Clinical Indicators, 34–36, 46–47, 95, 114, 123, 133–134, 148, 177, 181, 184–186, 196–197, 199–202. *See also main entry* Other Clinical Indicators
overview tables, 2–3, 12, 44–45, 47
Perfectionism (case study), 342, 350, 353
Physical Symptoms scale (case study), 341, 350, 353
Play cluster (case study), 342, 351
Pre-Academic/Cognitive cluster (case study), 339, 342
purpose, 2, 82–83
rater requirements, 3, 74–76, 77
rater types, 44, 58, 60, 61, 62–63, 74–75, 187, 210, 212, 224–225
reading levels, 3, 18, 76–77, 102, 209
report types, *See main entry* Report: Types (Assessment, Progress, Comparative)
Restless-Impulsive subscale (case study), 342, 350
sample tables, 341–342, 370–371
scales/subscales listing, 47
scoring, *See main entry* Scoring
Social Functioning scale (case study), 341, 349

Conners EC (*continued*)
  structure, 47
  subclusters. *See* Developmental Milestone
    scales
  tics (case study), 342, 351
  time required, 45
  Validity scales, 44, 47, 63, 64, 69–70, 95, 122,
    132, 148, 199, 203, 388. *See also*
    Interpretation: Validity scales; Validity
    scales
Conners EC BEH. *See* Conners EC Behavior form
Conners EC BEH(S). *See* Conners EC Behavior
    Short form
Conners EC Behavior form (Conners EC BEH),
    44–45, 61, 93–96
Conners EC Behavior scales, 43, 44, 46, 47, 93–94,
    114, 132, 147, 148, 154, 156, 159–160
Conners EC Behavior Short form (Conners EC
    BEH [S]), 44–45, 61, 84, 93–96
Conners EC Developmental Milestone(s)
  clusters/subclusters, 46, 47, 49, 94, 114, 133,
    135–136, 148, 164–165, 185
  form (Conners EC DM), 12, 44–45, 61, 62,
    93–96, 97
  scales, 43, 46, 47, 49, 70, 76, 94, 114, 117, 133,
    135–136, 147, 148, 153, 163–168, 179,
    182, 185, 195, 198, 200, 202, 208, 223,
    260, 267
Conners EC DM. *See* Conners EC Developmental
    Milestones form
Conners EC Global Index (Conners ECGI)
  form, 3, 12, 43, 44–45, 61, 62, 77, 84, 93–96,
    107, 110, 114, 133, 138, 215
  scale, 47, 94, 114, 133, 148, 175–176, 186, 199,
    203
  subscales, 94, 114, 133, 148, 153, 175–176
Conners ECGI. *See* Conners EC Global Index
Conners EC Global Index
  on Conners 3. *See* Conners 3 Global Index
  on Conners EC. *See* Conners EC Global Index
  on CRS–R (CGI), 10, 13, 22, 33, 47, 195, 203
Conners' Rating Scales (CRS), 9–10, 13, 47
Conners' Rating Scales–Revised (CRS–R), 12–13
  Compared with Conners 3, Conners CBRS, and
    Conners EC, 10–23
  interpreting with Conners 3, 15, 17–19, 20–22,
    23, 33, 175, 203, 209
  interpreting with Conners CBRS, 15, 17, 19,
    20–22, 23, 203, 209
Conners Third edition, *See* Conners 3
Conners'-Wells Adolescent Self-Report Scale on
    CRS–R (CASS), 10, 12–13, 15
Consent, 84, 108, 115–116, 214, 270
Content Scales. *See* Conners 3 Content Scales;
    Conners CBRS Content Scales
Convenience, 79, 110, 113
Convergent validity, 57, 60, 64, 65–70, 71, 212
Correct classification rate. *See* Overall correct
    classification rate

Cost
  administration, 78–79, 113
  scoring, 79, 113, 214
Critical Items
  General, 32, 35–36, 41, 87, 90, 115, 123, 126,
    131
  Self Harm, 41, 90, 182–183, 194, 198
  Severe Conduct
    on Conners 3, 182–184, 185, 194, 201
    on Conners CBRS, 41, 182–184, 185, 194,
      197
Cronbach's alpha. *See* Internal consistency
CRS. *See* Conners' Rating Scales
CRS–R. *See* Conners' Rating Scales–Revised
Cruelty, 34, 36, 156, 178, 181, 193, 196, 199, 200,
    351
Cultural relevance, 19, 25, 209, 220
Cut-off scores, 114, 122, 138, 151

Data storage, 28, 38, 43, 108–109, 112–113, 213
DBD. *See* Disruptive Behavior Disorders
Debriefing, 84, 101
Delayed Adaptive Development, 54, 212, 229, 267
Delayed Cognitive Development, 54, 212, 229, 260
Delayed Communication Development, 54, 212,
    229, 259
Delayed Social or Emotional Development, 54,
    212, 229
Depression items on the Conners 3. *See* Conners 3
    Screener items
Developing age, 135–136, 166, 167–168
Developmental Milestone scales. *See* Conners EC
    Developmental Milestone(s): Scales
Development of Conners assessments, 8–27
Developmental milestones on Conners
    assessments, *See* Conners EC
    Developmental Milestone(s)
DFA. *See* Discriminant Function Analyses
Diagnostic and Statistical Manual, Fourth Edition,
    Text Revision (DSM-IV-TR), 14, 16, 24,
    27, 40, 41, 51, 121, 162, 163, 170, 209,
    218–219, 223
Diagnostic cautions, 32, 40, 141, 161, 182, 215,
    218–219, 225, 226, 229–230
Diagnostic impressions (case studies). *See* Case
    Studies: Diagnostic impressions
Differential diagnosis, 6, 161, 218–219
Difficult scoring decisions. *See* Scoring: Difficult
    Decisions
Discriminant Function Analyses (DFAs), 63,
    230–231
Discriminative validity, 57, 58, 63, 212, 230–231.
    See also Overall correct classification
    rate; Sensitivity; Specificity
Disruptive Behavior Disorders (DBDs), 14, 28, 31,
    32, 42, 52, 54, 212, 228–229, 231, 254,
    256, 257–258. *See also* Conduct
    Disorder (CD); Oppositional Defiant
    Disorder (ODD).

Disruptive Behavior Disorder Indicator. *See* Conners Clinical Index (Conners CI, on Conners CBRS)
Distributing Conners results, 107, 108, 112, 115–116, 192, 214, 226
Divergent validity, 57, 64, 65–70, 71, 212
Double entry in computerized scoring, 137
Dressing. *See* Conners EC Developmental Milestone scales: Clusters/subclusters
DSM-IV-TR. *See* Diagnostic and Statistical Manual, Fourth Edition, Text Revision
DSM-IV-TR content on Conners assessments, 14–15, 16, 18, 31, 32, 39, 40–41
DSM-IV-TR diagnosis, cautions, *See* Diagnostic cautions
DSM-IV-TR Symptom Scales,
   interpretation of, 156, 158, 161–163
   missing data, 144, 145
   terms used, 121–122
   See also Conners 3; Conners CBRS
Dysthymic Disorder. *See* Mood Disorders

Eating/drinking. *See* Conners EC Developmental Milestone scales: Clusters/subclusters
E-mail administration. *See* Administration options: computerized; Modified administration: remote administration
Emotional content of Conners assessments, 20–21, 184, 193, 196–198, 201–202
Encopresis, 15, 349, 357, 359
Enuresis, 15
Evaluation procedures (case studies). *See* Case Studies: Evaluation procedures
Examiner qualifications/requirements, 3, 107–108, 115, 120, 135, 136, 143, 155, 214, 215
Executive functioning, explained, 27–28
Executive functioning, in case studies, 280, 283–284, 285, 286, 287, 288–289, 305–307, 309–311, 316. 317, 322, 324, 339, 343–345, 346–350, 352–353
Expert review, 25
Exporting data, 112, 213
Expressive language. *See* Case studies: Expressive Language Disorder; Conners EC Developmental Milestone scales: Clusters/subclusters

Feedback handout, 107, 108, 112, 115–116, 126, 131, 134, 214
Feedback session, important information to include, 189, 191
Fine motor. *See* Conners EC Developmental Milestone scales: Clusters/subclusters
Fire setting, 34, 36, 46, 181, 196, 200
Flags on Conners assessments. *See* Critical Items; Other Clinical Indicators; Screener Items
Follow-up evaluation, 82, 83, 84, 192, 198, 330
Forms. *See main entries under headings listed below.*

Conners 3: forms
Conners 3 ADHD Index (Conners 3AI): form
Conners 3 Global Index (Conners 3GI): form
Conners 3 Short form (Conners 3(S))
Conners CBRS: forms
Conners Clinical Index (Conners CI, on Conners CBRS): form
Conners EC: forms
Conners EC Behavior form (Conners EC BEH)
Conners EC Behavior Short form (Conners EC BEH [S])
Conners EC Developmental Milestones: form (Conners EC DM)
Conners EC Global Index (Conners ECGI): form
Form selection, 81–84, 295
Foster parent(s). *See* Who can rate Conners assessments

GAD. See Generalized Anxiety Disorder
Gender effects, 17, 50–51, 48–49, 211, 219
Gender-based norms, 17, 48–49, 120
General population sample, 26, 63, 121, 212, 227, 230, 256–261, 265–267
General presentation (case studies). *See* Case Studies: General presentation
Generalized Anxiety Disorder (GAD), 89, 197, 228–229, 263, 362
Global Index. *See* Conners Global Index; Conners 3 Global Index; Conners EC Global Index
Grandparent(s). *See* Who can rate Conners assessments
Gross motor. *See* Conners EC Developmental Milestone scales: Clusters/subclusters
Group administration, 81, 104–105
Group applications of Conners assessments, 8, 81, 104, 225–226
Group data, cautions, 175, 182, 229–230
Guidelines for administration. *See* Administration procedures
Guidelines for interpretation. *See* Interpretation strategy

Hand-scoring tips. *See* Scoring tips
Helping. *See* Conners EC Developmental Milestone scales: Clusters/subclusters
High scores, 57, 110, 118, 120, 148, 155–156, 157–158, 159–161, 177, 192, 366, 369, 371
History information, recommended topics, *See* Background information, recommended topics
History of Conners assessments, 8–10
Hygiene. *See* Conners EC Developmental Milestone scales: Clusters/subclusters
Hyperactivity Index, 8, 9, 10, 13
Hypomanic Episode. *See* Mood Disorders

ICD. *See* International Statistical Classification of Diseases and Health Related Problems

ID. *See* Intellectual Disability

IDEA 2004 (Individuals with Disabilities Education Improvement Act of 2004), 16, 24–25, 110, 115, 123, 135, 209, 217, 219–222, 224

IEP. *See* Individualized Education Plan

Impairment Items, 14, 19, 33, 43, 49, 114, 148, 169–170, 186, 191. *See also* Impairment Items *under* Conners 3, Conners CBRS, and Conners EC

Inconsistency Index (IncX). *See* Validity scales

IncX (Inconsistency Index). *See* Validity scales

Index forms:
    Conners 3AI (*See* Conners 3 ADHD Index)
    Conners 3GI (*See* Conners 3 Global Index)
    Conners CI (*See* Conners Clinical Index)
    Conners ECGI (*See* Conners EC Global Index)

Index scores on Conners assessments, 171–177

Indicated (DSM-IV-TR Symptom scales), 118, 120, 121–122, 160–161, 163, 182,

Indicated (Validity scales), 139, 151–152, 215

Indicators on the Conners CI. *See* Conners Clinical Index

Individual applications of Conners assessments, 7, 82, 222–223

Individualized Education Plan/Program (IEP), 221–222, 290, 324–325, 353–354

Individuals with Disabilities Education Improvement Act of 2004. *See* IDEA 2004

Informed consent, *See* Consent

Initial evaluation, 82, 84, 153, 192, 195, 200, 202

Instructions for administration. *See* Administration procedures

Intellectual disability (ID), 259, 387

Internal consistency, 55–56, 59–61, 211–212

International Statistical Classification of Diseases and Health Related Problems (ICD), 24, 51, 217, 219, 227

Internet administration. *See* Administration options: computerized; Modified administration: remote administration

Internet scoring. *See* Scoring options

Interpretable scores, 118, 120–126, 150–168

Interpretation:
    Additional questions, 149, 177, 186, 195, 199, 203
    Behavior scales, 147, 148, 154, 156, 159–160, 196–199, 200–202
    Conners 3, 148–149, 155–156, 171, 173–174, 175, 176, 182–183, 184–186,
    Conners 3 and Conners CBRS, 148–149, 184–186, 192–195
    Conners 3 and Conners EC, 148–149, 184–186, 200–203
    Conners 3AI, 148, 170–175, 182, 186, 195, 203
    Conners 3GI, 148, 175–176, 186, 195, 203

Conners CBRS, 148–149, 157–158, 161, 171, 172, 175, 178, 182–183, 184–186,

Conners CBRS and Conners 3, *See* Interpretation: Conners 3 and Conners CBRS

Conners CBRS and Conners EC, 148–149, 184–186, 195–199

Conners CI, 42, 148, 170–172, 175, 183, 186, 199

Conners EC, 148–149, 159–160, 164, 165, 166, 167–168, 179, 180, 182–183, 184–186,

Conners EC and Conners 3, *See* Interpretation: Conners 3 and Conners EC

Conners EC and Conners CBRS, *See* Interpretation: Conners CBRS and Conners EC

Conners ECGI, 148, 175–176, 186, 199, 203

Content scales, 148, 154–156, 157–158, 178, 192–194, 196–199, 200–202

Critical items, 35–36, 149, 177, 181–183, 184, 193, 196, 197, 200

CRS–R and Conners 3, 175, 203

CRS–R and Conners CBRS, 203

CRS–R and Conners EC, 175

Developmental Milestone(s)
    Clusters/subclusters, 148, 164, 185
    items, 148, 165–168, 179–181, 182
    scales, 147, 148, 163–168, 185, 195, 198, 200, 202

Discrepancies
    Between raters, 187–188
    Conners 3AI *T*-scores and Probability scores, 172,
    Conners CBRS DSM-IV-TR Symptom scale *T*-scores and Conners CI Indicator *T*-scores, 183
    Conners DSM-IV-TR Symptom scale *T*-scores and Symptom counts, 162
    DSM-IV-TR Symptom scales, 148, 156, 158, 161–163, 182, 183, 185, 193–199, 201–202
    Impairment items, 148–149, 169–170, 186, 195, 199, 203
    Index scores, *See* Interpretation *entries for each Index score*

integrating:
    Conners results with other data, 188–189
    results from a single rater, 183–186
    results from multiple dates, 189, 223
    results from multiple raters, 183, 187–188

item-level, 147, 149, 150, 155, 165–168, 176–183, 187

Other Clinical Indicators, 24, 114, 123, 130–131, 133–134, 141, 148–149, 177, 181, 183–186, 193–194, 196–197, 199–202

percentiles, 153–154, 191

probability scores, 148, 170–174

profile of *T*-scores, 148–149, 169, 187–188

response style (*See* Interpretation, Validity scales)
Screener items, 149, 177, 181, 184, 193, 201
Subscales if main scale not elevated, 153
threats to validity, 148, 150–151
T-scores, 148–149, 159–154, 156, 162–164, 166, 169, 172, 173–176, 183, 187, 191, 203
Validity scales, 24, 32, 41, 56–57, 118, 122, 124, 127, 132, 138–140, 143, 144–145, 148, 150–153, 182, 187, 195, 207, 212, 215. *See also main entry* Validity scales.
Interpretation steps. *See* interpretation strategy
Interpretation strategy, summarized, 148–149
Interpretive text, 154, 155–160, 164, 167–168, 171, 173–174, 176, 178–180
Interpretive updates to the Conners 3 and Conners CBRS, 24, 32, 39, 41, 119, 138–141, 151, 153–158, 161, 177, 178, 206, 208, 213, 215, 386
Inter-rater reliability, 55–56, 58, 59–61, 211–212
Intervention. *See* Treatment issues
Interview, recommended background information, *See* Background information, recommended topics

Languages, *See* Translations
Language Disorders, 42, 54, 172, 212, 229, 254, 258–259, 323
LD. *See* Learning Disorders
Learning and Language Disorder Indicator. *See* Conners Clinical Index (Conners CI, on Conners CBRS)
Learning Disorders (LD), 15, 42, 52, 63, 172, 194, 198, 212, 228–229, 254, 256–257, 258–259, 324
Legal guardian(s). *See* Who can rate Conners assessments
Length of acquaintance, 76
Length of forms, 29, 37, 44, 83–84
Limitations, 41, 79, 113, 206
Links with IDEA 2004. 16, 110, 112, 123, 126, 131, 134, 220–221

Mailing Conners assessments, 81, 103, 104
Major Depressive Disorder (MDD). *See* Mood Disorders
Major Depressive Episode, 41, 89, 198, 260–263, 363
Manic Episode, 41, 89, 198, 260–263, 363
Mastery age, 135–136, 166, 167–168
MDD (Major Depressive Disorder). *See* Mood Disorders
Medication monitoring (case studies). *See* Case Studies: Medication monitoring
Mental Retardation (MR), 54, 229, 259–260, 267, 387
Met (DSM-IV-TR Symptom scales), 121–122, 145, 158, 161–162, 163
MHS. *See* Multi–Health Systems, Inc.

Missing data, 113, 142, 143–145, 213, 305
Mixed Episode, 92, 162, 260–261
Modified administration:
    group administration, 81, 104–105
    off-site administration, *See* Modified administration: Remote administration
    reading aloud, 77, 99–100, 102, 103, 300
    remote administration, 81, 102–104
Mood Disorders, 14, 28, 41, 42, 156, 172, 181, 228, 229, 255, 256, 260–263, 265, 289, 353
See also Major Depressive Episode; Manic Episode; Mixed Episode
Mood Disorder Indicator. *See* Conners Clinical Index (Conners CI, on Conners CBRS)
Motivation
Motor skills. *See* Conners EC Developmental Milestone scales: Clusters/subclusters
Motor tics. *See* Tics
MR. *See* Mental Retardation
Multi-Health Systems, Inc. (MHS), contact information, 10
Multiple informants/raters, 5–6, 7, 8, 16, 19, 25, 63, 74–75, 116, 149, 183, 187–188, 212, 220, 305. *See also* Inter-rater reliability; Across-informant correlations
Multiple modalities, 5–6, 8, 51, 220, 227
Multiple responses, 100, 105
Multiple settings, 5–6, 7, 8, 16, 74–75, 169, 218, 220, 305

Negative Impression Index (NI). *See* Validity scales
Negatively worded items, 19, 23–24. *See also* Positively worded items
NI (Negative Impression Index). *See* Validity scales
Normative data, 16, 19, 25, 48–49, 75, 100, 104, 120, 151, 176, 224, 372

Observations and comments, 101
Obsessive-Compulsive Disorder (OCD), 14, 52, 228, 263–265
Obsessive-Compulsive features (case study). *See* Case Studies: Obsessive-Compulsive features
OCD. *See* Obsessive-Compulsive Disorder
ODD. *See* Oppositional Defiant Disorder
Omitted items, 101. *See also* Missing data
Online administration tips. *See* Administration tips
Online scoring. *See* Scoring options
Online subscription model, 79, 113, 214
Opportunity vs. ability, 166–167, 168
Oppositional Defiant Disorder (ODD), 14, 18, 28, 32, 52, 54, 82, 172, 229, 257–258
Other Clinical Indicators, 18, 20–22, 24, 34–36, 39–41, 46–47, 90–91, 95, 114, 123, 130–131, 133–134, 141, 148–149, 177, 181, 183–186, 193–194, 196–197, 199–202
Output. *See* Scoring output
Overall correct classification rate, 57, 58, 63, 212, 227, 230, 254, 256–267

Overall impressions (case studies).
    See Case Studies:
        Overall impressions.
Overview tables, 2–3, 11, 12, 20–22, 23, 29–30, 31, 37–38, 39, 44–45, 47

Panic attack, 14, 91, 264
Password, 113, 213
PDD. *See* Pervasive Developmental Disorders
PDD-NOS. *See* Case Studies: PDD-NOS;
    Pervasive Developmental Disorders
Pearson's r. *See* Psychometric terms
Percentiles, 114, 120, 153–154, 191, 214
Perfectionism, 10, 14, 18, 123, 158, 197, 263, 264, 266, 320, 323, 328–329, 350, 353, 356–357
Pervasive Developmental Disorder Not Otherwise
    Specified (PDD-NOS). *See* Pervasive
    Developmental Disorders
Pervasive Developmental Disorders (PDD), 14, 28, 40, 42, 51, 53, 54, 172, 199, 212, 229, 264, 265–267, 352–353, 359, 389
    See also Asperger's Disorder; Autistic Disorder
Phobia. *See* Social Phobia; Specific Phobia
PI (Positive Impression Index). *See* Validity scales
Pica, 15, 160, 187, 200, 203
Pilot data, 15, 25–26, 34, 40, 48
Play. *See* Conners EC Developmental Milestone
    scales: Clusters/subclusters
Positive Impression Index (PI). *See* Validity scales
Positive interactions with the rater, 97, 101
Positively worded items, 19, 23–24, 117, 119, 150, 182
Posttraumatic Stress Disorder (PTSD), 14
Pre-Academic/Cognitive. *See* Conners EC
    Developmental Milestone scales:
    Clusters/subclusters
Preparing to administer Conners assessments, 76–77, 78, 80
Probability scores, 114, 122, 170–171, 172
Programmatic use of Conners assessments, 8, 226–227
Progress report. *See* Report options
Prorating a scale score, 143–144, 145
    See also Prorating DSM-IV-TR Symptom Count
Prorating DSM-IV-TR Symptom Count, 144, 145
Prospective research, 161–162
Psychometric terms, 56–57
Psychometrics, 26, 49–50, 55–71, 143, 150, 211–212, 227, 388
PTSD. *See* Posttraumatic Stress Disorder
Purpose of assessment, 2, 82–83

Qualified professional, 73, 107, 108, 120, 135, 155, 214, 215
Qualitative scores, 114, 122–123, 181
    See also Interpretation, item–level

QuikScore forms
    availability, 74
    cautions, 98, 105

Race/ethnicity effects, 5, 26, 50, 51, 210, 221
Rater requirements, 3, 74–76, 77
Rater types, 29, 32, 37, 40, 44, 55, 58–63, 74–75, 187, 210, 212, 224–225
Rating scale:
    applications, 4–8
    selection, 81–84
    use in responsible assessment, 6–7
Raw scores, 110, 117–118, 119, 120, 122, 135, 138, 144–145, 148–149, 151–152, 153, 158, 165, 223, 225
RCI. *See* Reliable Change Index
Reading Disorder. *See* Case Studies: Reading
    Disorder; Learning Disorders
Reading levels, 3, 18, 34, 76–77, 102, 209
Reading Conners assessments aloud, 77, 99–100, 102, 103, 300
Receptive language. *See* Conners EC
    Developmental Milestone scales:
    Clusters/subclusters
Recommendations (case studies). *See* Case Studies:
    Recommendations
Recommended reading, 386–387
Record review, recommended background
    information, *See* Background
    information, recommended topics
Red flags on Conners assessments. *See* Critical
    Items; Other Clinical Indicators;
    Screener Items
Re-evaluation, *See* Follow–up evaluation
Reference scores, 123, 135–136. *See also* Age
    references; Base rates; Links with IDEA
    2004
Referral question(s) (case studies). *See* Case
    Studies: Referral question
Referrals (case studies). *See* Case Studies:
    Referrals
Relative vs. absolute (DSM-IV-TR Symptom
    scales), 162–163
Reliability, 26, 55, 56, 59, 61, 143, 211–212
Reliable Change Index (RCI), 9, 19, 110, 116, 189, 215, 223, 363
Remote administration, 81, 102–104
Repeated testing, caution, 277
Report
    important information to include, 190–191, 270
    options, 111–112, 113–116, 114, 115–116
    samples, *See* Case studies
    sample tables, *See* Sample tables for reports
    sample text. *See* Common characteristics of high
        scorers
    Types (Assessment, Progress, Comparative), 19, 30, 38, 45, 111, 112, 115–116, 215
Required reading level, *See* Reading levels
Research use of Conners assessments, 8, 226

Resources and referrals (case studies). *See* Case Studies: Resources and referrals
Responding to rater questions, 73–74, 99–100, 101–102
Response bias indicators. *See* Validity scales
Response options for raters, 99, 142
Response style. *See* Interpretation, Validity scales
Response to Intervention (RTI), 7, 116, 220–222, 224–225, 299
Responsible assessment, 6, 144, 155, 223, 226
Retrospective research, 161–162
Reverse scoring, 110, 117, 119, 135, 150, 177, 182
RTI. *See* Response to Intervention

SAD. *See* Separation Anxiety Disorder (SAD)
Sample messages for remote administration (online, mailing), 103–104
Sample tables for reports,
  Conners 3, 281–282, 365–366
  Conners CBRS, 312–315, 367–369
  Conners EC, 341–342, 370–371
Score ranges, 138, 153–154, 170, 172, 183
Score types on Conners assessments, 114, 118, 120–136, 153–154
Scoring:
  Convenience, 79, 110, 113
  Cost, 113, 214
  Conners 3GI subscales, *See* Conners 3 Global Index subscales
  Conners CI Indicators, *See* Conners Clinical Index
  Conners ECGI subscales, *See* Conners EC Global Index subscales
  difficult decisions (missing or questionable responses), 141–145
  errors, ways to reduce, 136–138
  limitations, 113, 213–214
  materials, 111, 137
  online (*See* Scoring options, computerized)
  options,
    compared, 111–113
    computerized (online, software, USB), 108–109
    hand-scoring (QuikScore form), 110–113, 137–138
  output, 111–112, 113–116
  software (*See* Scoring options, computerized)
  time required, 30, 38, 45, 113, 207
  tips
    computerized, 136–137
    hand-scoring, 137–141
Scoring by hand. *See* Scoring options
Screener Items. *See* Conners 3 Screener items
Screening with Conners assessments, 8, 81, 82–83, 84, 104, 221, 225
Section 504 of the Rehabilitation Act, 222, 298–299
Selecting a form, *See* Form selection
Self- Harm Critical items. *See* Critical Items, Self-Harm

Self-injury, 34, 35, 181–182
  See also Critical Items, Self-Harm
SEM. *See* Standard Error of Measurement
Sensitive topics, 33–34, 35–36
Sensitive to treatment effects, 33, 47, 175, 206
Sensitivity. 5, 33, 47, 57, 58, 63, 254
Separation Anxiety Disorder (SAD), 89, 197, 228–229, 263, 363
Severe Conduct Critical Items. *See* Critical Items, Severe Conduct
Short forms:
  Conners 3(S). *See* Conners 3 Short form
  Conners EC BEH. *See* Conners EC Behavior form
  Conners EC BEH(S). *See* Conners EC Behavior Short form
  Conners EC DM. *See* Conners EC Developmental Milestones form
  See also Index forms
Significant change, 7, 19, 110, 112, 116, 189, 215, 223
  See also Reliable Change Index
Social content of Conners assessments, 21, 184, 194, 198, 202
Social, emotional, and behavioral functioning (case studies), 286–287, 320–321, 349–351
Social Phobia, 14, 52, 228, 263–265, 266, 323
Software package. *See* Scoring options
Spanish translations, *See* Translations
Specific Phobia, 14
Specificity, 5, 57, 58, 63, 254
Speed of information processing (case studies), 278–280, 305
Standard Error of Measurement (SEM), 110, 111, 124–130, 132–133, 363, 364
Standardization, 5, 15, 26, 48, 49–71, 100, 102, 206, 207, 210, 228
Standardized administration, 74, 84, 100, 102, 104, 142, 300
Standardized scores, 153–154, 187, 191
Statistical significance, 7, 19, 110, 112, 116, 189, 215, 223
  See also Reliable Change Index
Stealing, 34, 36, 193, 196, 200
Strengths. *See* Additional questions
Strengths and weaknesses of scales:
  administration and scoring, 213–214
  interpretation, 215
  overview, 206–208
  reliability and validity, 211–212
  standardization, 210
  test development and content, 208–210
Structure of Conners assessments, 31, 39, 47
Substance abuse. *See* Substance Use Disorders
Substance dependence. *See* Substance Use Disorders
Substance Use Disorders, 15, 289, 296, 322, 323, 329, 353

Summary of results (case studies). *See* Test results and observations/interpretation (case studies)
Symptom counts. *See* DSM-IV-TR Symptom Scales

Technical support. *See* Multi-Health Systems, Inc.
Technician, acceptable use of, 73, 107–108, 120, 135, 155, 214, 215
Test development and content, 208–210. *See also* Development of Conners assessments
Test environment, 81
Test materials, 76–77, 78, 80, 111, 137, 210
Test results and observations/interpretation (case studies), 295–330, 336–351
  academic achievement, 271, 277, 298, 303, 322, 338
  adaptive functioning, 286, 319, 349
  attention, 280–284, 305, 339
  executive functions, 280, 305–306, 309–311, 316–317, 339
  general presentation, 275–276, 300–301, 336–337
  intellectual ability, 276–277, 284, 289, 301, 337–338
  language, 284, 316–317, 345–346
  medication monitoring, 294, 320–321, 329–330
  memory and learning, 285, 317–318, 347
  neuropsychological functioning, 278–285, 300–305, 336–339
  other results, 320–321, 351
  summary, 287–290, 322
  sensorimotor functions, 285, 319, 347–348
  social, emotional, and behavioral functioning, 286–287, 319–320, 349–351
  speed, 278–280, 305
  visual processing, 285, 317, 346–347
Test-retest reliability, 55–56, 59, 61, 211
Test Yourself, 105–106, 204–205, 216, 267–268, 359–360
Testing, intelligent, xi
Tics, 15, 46, 160, 264, 290, 351. *See also* Case Studies: Tics
Time limits for Conners assessments, 80
Time of day, 75, 190, 225, 328
Toileting. *See* Conners EC Developmental Milestone scales: Clusters/subclusters
Translations (Spanish, French, other), 19, 25, 27, 28, 29, 30, 37, 38, 43, 44, 45, 83, 209, 220–222
Treatment applications, 223–225
Treatment issues, 225
Treatment monitoring, 7, 82–83, 84, 223–225. *See also* Reliable Change Index
Treatment planning, 7, 223

Trichotillomania, 15, 20, 39, 47, 91, 95, 131, 134, 184, 197, 201, 315, 342, 369–370
Trigger scores, 114, 122, 123
T-score limits, 120, 144, 153, 154
T-scores, 114, 120, 153–154, 191, 214

Updates, *See* Interpretive updates to the Conners 3 and Conners CBRS
USB scoring. *See* Scoring options
Username, 113, 213

Validity, *See also* Interpretation: Validity
  in case studies. *See* Case Studies: Validity statement
  instruments used for comparison, 56–57, 63–71
  and reliability of scales, 26, 55–71, 143, 150, 211–212, 227, 388
  scales on Conners assessments, 18–19, 151–153, 152–153, 207, 209, 212
    Inconsistency Index (IncX), 19, 24, 87, 91, 95, 114, 122, 139–140, 144–145, 152–153, 195, 199, 203
    Negative Impression scale (NI), 19, 24, 87, 91, 95, 114, 118, 119, 139, 152, 182, 195, 199, 203, 262
    Positive Impression scale (PI), 18–19, 24, 87, 91, 95, 114, 118–119, 139, 151–152, 182, 195, 199, 203
  threats to, 148–151
Violence potential, 22, 24, 37, 39, 89, 118, 128, 141, 158, 161, 177, 178, 183, 186, 194, 199, 240, 262, 313, 363, 367
Violence Potential Indicator
  cautions, 24, 141, 161
  item-level analysis, 118, 161, 178, 183, 194, 199
  scale, 22, 24, 39, 89, 118, 128, 141, 158, 161, 177, 178, 183, 186, 194, 199, 262
Visual processing (case studies), 285, 287, 317, 346–347
Vocal tics. *See* Tics

Weighted scoring, 117–118, 119, 141, 178, 183,
Who can administer Conners assessments, 73–74
Who can interpret Conners assessments, 155
Who can rate Conners assessments, 74–75
Who can score Conners assessments, 107
Wording in rating scales, 9, 23–25, 34, 195
Working memory, 318–319
  in case study, Brian Jones, 285
  in case study, Darby Reed, 301–304, 310, 311, 316–318, 322–323, 327
  in case study, Josh Kane, 339, 341, 345
Write-in items. *See* Additional questions
Written reports, 109, 111–112, 191, 213, 269, 270